Theory and Practice of
FEMINIST LITERARY
CRITICISM

Bilingual Press/Editorial Bilingüe

Studies in Literary Analysis

Under the General Editorship
of Gary D. Keller

Address
Bilingual Press
Dept. of Foreign Languages
and Bilingual Studies
106 Ford Hall
EASTERN MICHIGAN UNIVERSITY
Ypsilanti, Michigan 48197
313-487-0042

Theory and Practice of
FEMINIST LITERARY CRITICISM

edited by

Gabriela Mora

and

Karen S. Van Hooft

Bilingual Press/Editorial Bilingüe
YPSILANTI, MICHIGAN

ISBN: 0-916950-23-9
Printed simultaneously in a softcover edition. ISBN: 0-916950-22-0

Library of Congress Catalog Card Number: 81-67051

PRINTED IN THE UNITED STATES OF AMERICA

Cover design by Christopher J. Bidlack

Acknowledgment

"Ideology and *The Mysteries of Udolpho*" by Mary Poovey, reprinted from article of the same title in *Criticism*, Vol. 20, No. 4 (1979), pp. 307-330, by permission of the Wayne State University Press. Copyright 1979 by the Wayne State University Press.

TABLE OF CONTENTS

Foreword

As a review of the Table of Contents of this volume reveals, the editors have attempted to bring together a representative selection of the work that is being done in the field of feminist literary criticism. When we began the task of selecting the papers to be included, two problems immediately arose: How would we define or delimit the field of "feminist literary criticism," given the diverse nature of the studies that fall under this designation, and how would we organize the contents of this particular volume in order to both reflect this diversity and present a coherent idea of the interests and concerns of feminist critics.

With respect to the first problem, it became apparent that the crucial factor was whether or not, in employing the phrase "feminist criticism," we were speaking of a critical methodology, in the sense that one speaks of a structuralist, formalist, semiotic, or any other literary methodology. The need to explore this issue gave impulse to the introductory study by Gabriela Mora, "Crítica feminista: Apuntes sobre definiciones y problemas." Written especially for this volume, this paper summarizes the different positions with respect to the definition of feminist criticism, and the notes provide a useful guide to further reading on the subject.

We next proceeded to the organization of the papers selected for this collection. This was complicated by the fact that we had decided to include papers on Spanish, Spanish American, English, American, French, and Italian literatures. We felt that the inclusion of authors writing in different languages and different periods harmonized well with the trend toward interdisciplinary studies promoted by feminist scholars. At the same time this selection cut across the limited national categories into which academic studies have been divided for so long. One option we considered was to group the papers by language or national literature. However, as the reader will have noted in the Contents, this would have resulted in a rather lopsided grouping in favor of the Spanish-language literatures; in addition, some papers crossed national boundaries. (The editors were gratified at the opportunity to include so many fine papers on Spanish and Spanish American authors since feminist scholars working in the Hispanic literatures have had considerably less exposure than those in other fields.) The other possible organizations we considered—chronological order by author studied or some sort of thematic grouping—did not lend themselves to the selection at hand.

The groupings that did emerge seemed to reflect three of the primary areas of interest to feminist critics: (1) the exploration of theoretical questions such as the definition of feminist criticism; the ideological premises underlying both the feminist and masculinist readings of literature; the woman writer's struggle to create her own language, thus freeing herself from phallocentric discourse; and the formulation of new directions for future scholarship; (2) the study of works by women, including the re-examination of well-known writers and the rediscovery and study of the many more whose contributions have been lost to us for too long; (3) the rereading of works by men in order to re-evaluate the authors' depiction of women as an important part of their total world view.

Thus our format emerged: Section I is comprised of articles that discuss theoretical questions in feminist criticism, lay the groundwork for future theoretical formulations, or suggest new critical directions. The concluding article in this section by the writer Luisa Valenzuela is intended as a bridge between the theoretical articles and the studies in Section II, which are applications of the feminist critical perspective to works written by women. These are ordered chronologically by author studied in the hope that a sequential reading might reveal some possible changes that have taken place over time in women's literary endeavors. The final section (III), which is also ordered chronologically, is comprised of studies dealing with topics of interest to feminist critics but this time focusing on works by men.

The original inspiration for this volume was the "Fifth Annual Colloquium on Contemporary Methods of Literary Analysis: An Interdisciplinary Approach to Feminism," sponsored by York College of the City University of New York and held at the Graduate Center (CUNY) on May 11, 1979. From the nearly three dozen papers read at the colloquium and later submitted for possible publication, fourteen were chosen for this volume. Three other papers were selected from a number of submissions by scholars who were contacted about this projected collection.

We would like to express our appreciation to the numerous colleagues who assisted us in the preparation of this volume. A special word of thanks is owed to the contributors for their positive response to our suggestions for revisions and their cooperation during the editing process.

GABRIELA MORA
RUTGERS UNIVERSITY

KAREN S. VAN HOOFT
EASTERN MICHIGAN UNIVERSITY

I. Theoretical Approaches

CRITICA FEMINISTA:
APUNTES SOBRE
DEFINICIONES Y PROBLEMAS

Gabriela Mora

Aun los que juzgan con socarrón escepticismo la cuantía de actividades desplegadas bajo la rúbrica del feminismo, no pueden negar que el impulso del movimiento ha llegado hasta la bien guardada fortaleza académica. La creciente cantidad de estudios, antologías, reuniones y cursos, prueba la existencia de la lectura feminista en la enseñanza de la literatura, aunque todavía hay problemas relacionados a definiciones y métodos. Estas páginas se proponen revisar someramente algunas posiciones en torno a la teoría y a la práctica de este tipo de lectura, resumir las tareas llevadas a cabo y proporcionar una bibliografía básica a través de las notas al final del cuerpo del trabajo.

Crítica feminista

La diversidad de puntos de vista sobre el significado tanto de la palabra *crítica*, como del vocablo *feminista*, ha contribuido a obstaculizar el hallazgo de una definición aceptable para todas las posiciones. Sobre el primer concepto—en el cual no nos vamos a detener—basta examinar la nutrida bibliografía existente.[1] Sobre el segundo, ciertas bases de común acuerdo entre las practicantes feministas permiten un acercamiento al asunto.

Simone de Beauvoir llama *feministas* a los hombres y mujeres que pugnan por cambiar la condición social de la mujer como parte de la lucha de clases, pero sin subordinarse totalmente a ella.[2] Para Beauvoir es muy claro que el feminismo es una manera de luchar contra la sociedad tal como existe hoy, y para ella el movimiento debe ser necesariamente de izquierda.[3]

En una variada gama de posiciones políticas, la mayoría de las estudiosas norteamericanas reconoce que el *status* social inferior de la mujer ha sido el resorte generador de su práctica de lectura feminista. Annette Barnes asegura que si el crítico, además de ser partidario de los derechos iguales para los sexos, piensa que las mujeres no son inferiores a los hombres, y cree que todavía se ignora lo que específicamente es "masculino" y "femenino", es feminista.[4] Annis Pratt, más cerca de lo estrictamente literario, comparte la opinión de que la injusta condición social de la mujer impulsa el feminismo, y preconiza explorar cómo esa condición ha sido reflejada en la literatura. Según Pratt, la preocupación feminista admitiría diversos tipos de críticas (ella habla de "Feminist Criticisms"), en los que el uso de métodos ya establecidos (arquetípico, marxista, estructuralista, etc.) se subordinaría a dicha preocupación.[5]

La poeta Adrienne Rich es la autora de una de las más divulgadas definiciones de lo que ella llama "crítica feminista radical" en una práctica que una de sus exégetas ha denominado "el feminismo orgánico de Rich".[6] La base ética de esta definición es compartida por la mayoría de las estudiosas que ven su labor profesional ligada activamente a la transformación de la sociedad. Para Rich,

> una crítica radical de la literatura de impulso feminista deberá tomar la obra, ante todo, como una clave para vivir, para saber cómo hemos vivido hasta ahora, cómo se nos ha guiado a imaginar nuestro ser, cómo nuestra lengua nos ha atrapado a la vez que nos ha liberado, y cómo podemos empezar a ver, y por lo tanto a vivir de manera nueva.[7]

La íntima relación de este tipo de lectura con los problemas sociales llevó a Cheri Register a identificar "crítica feminista" con "crítica cultural", a Elaine Showalter a mantener que "el feminismo toma seriamente la literatura como una crítica de la vida", y a Marcia Holly a propugnar una activa militancia a través de dicha práctica.[8]

Como se transparenta en las palabras de las autoras citadas, la lectura feminista considera fundamental la revisión de los códigos culturales en que se inserta la obra literaria.[9] Insatisfechas con los valores definidores que se han inscrito en el concepto *mujer*, las feministas buscan desenmascarar este signo, cuestionando el consenso de ciertas nociones, explorando la relación entre apariencia y realidad del objeto signado y su uso literario.[10] Dejando de lado la obvia diferenciación biológica de los sexos, las feministas estudian el significado de lo "masculino" y lo "femenino" como mitos culturales cambiantes, sometidos a presiones económicas, políticas, de la moda, etc.[11] Como entidades abstractas, dichos conceptos se ven como producto de la relación observada entre los objetos reales, que en el caso hombre/mujer ha sido una relación de oposición absoluta y jerárquica.[12] Conscientes de los desvíos a que llevaron tantos principios "científicos", hoy día en descrédito, las feministas luchan por construir un sistema que reconozca "el estatus diferencial, pero no jerarquizante" de la oposición que presentan los sexos.[13]

Es obvio que el debilitamiento de la fe en las ciencias (al que el feminismo ha contribuido) se ha agregado a la dificultad de los términos en el camino de la definición estricta, que por lo demás algunas piensan es imposible obtener.[14] El rechazo natural a la autoridad emanada de teorías que sirvieron para justificar la opresión de la mujer (Freud, Jung, Erickson, et al.) ha llevado al enjuiciamiento de ellas y a preguntarse si la búsqueda de definiciones y métodos "de rigurosidad científica" no llevaba a la trampa de las falsas idolatrías dicotómicas que el femenismo rechaza.[15]

El convencimiento de que la ausencia de una definición aceptable para todas las posiciones no ha disminuido la efectividad de la labor, impulsó a las editoras de *Female Studies VI* a recomendar el uso de la frase *perspectiva feminista* como denominación para el tipo de crítica que ellas promueven.[16] Subscribiéndonos a tal denominación, y siguiendo en parte la descripción que dan para su tarea, proponemos la siguiente fórmula tentativa como herramienta inicial de trabajo: Una lectura de perspectiva feminista se preocupa de examinar la representación literaria de la mujer, poniendo de relieve los prejuicios sexistas evidenciados a través de los aspectos discursivos y narrativos de la obra, con cuidada atención a la función del signo "mujer" en las estructuras generales y específicas, especialmente los motivos y conductas que se le atribuyen, y las imágenes y símbolos que se asocian a él.[17]

Aceptando el hecho de que la obra literaria es fundamentalmente una creación de lenguaje, la feminista tiene presente que ella es además, al decir de Segre, "una trasmisión de estados mentales, de ideales y de juicios acerca del mundo".[18] Por esto la estudiosa exige relacionar el texto con acciones y preocupaciones humanas, en el afán de descubrir las semejanzas, las discrepancias, lo alterado y lo borrado entre el objeto empírico mujer y los rasgos que los códigos le han impuesto en la literatura. Esta naturalización requerida por la perspectiva feminista está impulsada tanto por la creencia de que este proceso está siempre en el sustrato del fenómeno literario, como cree Jonathan Culler,[19] y porque éste es un medio—entre otros—de anudar la exégesis a las inquietudes existenciales. En otras palabras, la feminista considera la literatura como fuente de conocimiento y, por lo tanto, como instrumento para influir en el mundo, como Rich lo expresara tan elocuentemente en páginas anteriores.

La práctica

En la realización de su tarea, las feministas se han concentrado en ciertas áreas que ya cuentan con apreciable cantidad de estudios. El intento más constante ha sido redescubrir y revalorar los escritos de mujeres que en el pasado no recibieron adecuada atención. El examen de las obras rescatadas del anonimato, más aquellas que gozaron de algún renombre, va permitiendo poco a poco una aproximación a cuestiones generales y otras más específicas, algunas de las cuales presentan dificultades que llevará tiempo resolver.[20]

La colección de material permite, por ejemplo, estudiar los momentos históricos de mayor desarrollo de los trabajos literarios femeninos, e inquirir el por qué y el cómo de tales momentos. Así, para ilustrar con un caso, el expresivo formato de la introducción de *New French Feminisms*, una antología editada por Elaine Marks e Isabelle de Courtivron, deja entrever parte de la compleja red de motivos detrás del hecho de que el escribir no se concibiera como actividad femenina. La decapitación de la francesa que pedía derechos para la mujer a manos de sus colegas revolucionarios, es uno entre múltiples sucesos de una aplastante cadena de acontecimientos, mostrados en ese libro, que ayuda a explicar el paupérrimo número de escritoras, o el generalizado fenómeno de la creadora que no se tomaba en serio como tal.[21]

Relacionado con el tabú social se examina, entre otros asuntos, cómo la escritora se autocensuró (y sigue haciéndolo) a sabiendas de que su labor rompía reglas sociales establecidas. El trabajo interdisciplinario y colectivo—uno de los rasgos propugnados por el feminismo—trata de determinar hasta qué punto la autocensura en temas, lengua, personajes, etc. se manifestó en esfuerzos deliberados para crear mundos inventados que se acercaran al patrón cultural que definía lo femenino y lo masculino.

Por ejemplo, la autocensura originada en la represión sexual, padecida ciertamente por los dos sexos, sin duda presenta formas especiales en relación a la escritura de la mujer. Si, como afirma Foucault, el hombre reaccionó a la represión sexual hablando de sexo,[22] ¿qué pasó con la mujer, a quien se le prohibía el conocimiento no sólo de las palabras relacionadas con el asunto, sino del fenómeno en su totalidad? y ¿cómo se tradujo este hecho en la escritura femenina?[23]

En las indagaciones feministas no se olvida, naturalmente, que en el problema de censuras y restricciones hay que tomar en cuenta el peso enorme de las convenciones literarias que, a través de escuelas, movimientos o plumas renombradas, juegan un papel decisivo en la factura poética del creador de cualquier sexo. Porque parece claro, en muchos casos, que ciertos arquetipos—la Dama, la pícara, la heroína romántica, . . . —deben más a la imitación de modas literarias que a reflexiones autoriales fruto de vivencias existenciales. No obstante, se trata de traer a la luz no sólo taxonomías, sino de aproximarse a las explicaciones de sus orígenes. Ejemplares en esta dirección son las reflexiones de Julia Kristeva en *El texto de la novela*, que abren incitantes posibilidades para estudios de relación entre cambios semióticos e histórico-sociales de importantes repercusiones.[24] O, la meditación de la misma estudiosa en torno al mito de la Virgen María, su uso por "una nueva sociedad basada en el intercambio y la producción acelerada", y los imperativos psicológicos del sistema patriarcal.[25]

Fuera de estas cuestiones generales, hay otras más específicas cuya realización va dando frutos valiosos. Todas estas tareas son cauces agregados al conducto central que trata de resolver el espinudo problema de si existe o no una manera de escribir femenina y, en caso afirmativo, cuáles serían sus rasgos distintivos. La más estudiada de estas áreas concierne al tipo de imagen de la mujer que la literatura ha proyectado a través del tiempo. Estas imágenes se buscan tanto en las obras de escritores[26] como de escritoras, aunque el énfasis se pone sobre estas últimas.[27] La repetición de ciertos estereotipos—la pasiva, el ángel de la casa o la devoradora de hombres, la madre abnegada, la soltera amargada, etc.—se puede relacionar, obviamente, con las influencias sociales y literarias mencionadas antes.[28] Clave en este asunto es el rastreo de los escritos que rompen los estereotipos tradicionales, y el análisis de las circunstancias que los originaron. Porque no bastará conocer los valores que la literatura exaltó en las figuras femeninas. Habrá que averiguar el por qué de la exaltación de unos valores sobre otros, lo que llevará directamente al examen de las ideologías imperantes y, por ende, al inevitable carácter político de la lectura feminista.[29]

Otra labor favorecida por muchas estudiosas se ha detenido en la observación de los asuntos y motivos que aparecen con mayor frecuencia entre las autoras. Hay evidencia, por ejemplo, de una abundante cantidad de obras centradas alrededor del problema del matrimonio desgraciado. Así, Annis Pratt, que estudia la novela, subcategoriza grupos tales como "de la rebelión marital", "de los efectos fatales del matrimonio", entre otros que se repiten en el período que ella estudia.[30] Jean E. Kennard, partiendo del motivo literario de los "dos cortejantes", estudió las elaboraciones que escritores de ambos sexos hicieron de tal motivo y de la convención del matrimonio como feliz final para las heroínas, materia que le permitió ahondar en las mutuas influencias entre literatura y sociedad.[31]

La atención dada a la obra de las escritoras de diversas épocas ha puesto de relieve la frecuencia del motivo del suicidio en sus trabajos. El hecho real de la autodestrucción de tantas creadoras, eco expresivo de la circunstancia desmedrada del sexo en la sociedad, se ha añadido al fenómeno literario, impidiendo que el asunto se trate como simple moda artística.[32]

El examen de la escritura de las autoras ha llevado, como es de suponer, al descubrimiento del uso reiterado de ciertas figuras que encapsulan poéticamente las ideas centrales de un texto. Así, por ejemplo, se ha encontrado una copiosa repetición de imágenes expresivas de los conceptos de encierro y escape. Las metáforas sugeridoras de espacios constrictivos y estáticos reiteradas en las obras de las escritoras tendría, según Gilbert y Gubar, una función estética diferente a las figuras de "prisión" usadas por los varones.[33]

El hallazgo repetido de construcciones metafóricas del concepto *volar* pareciera confirmar el juicio de Hélène Cixous de que "Flying is woman's gesture".[34] Estas construcciones que en los niveles más aparentes se asocian, casi siempre, a la prisión doméstica que sufren heroínas y narradoras, en niveles más profundos pueden ser, a veces, índices de fenómenos que contradicen directamente las caracteríticas asociadas con lo "femenino" tradicional.[35]

Dando por sentado que ni uno ni otro sexo puede reclamar exclusividad en la invención de recursos retóricos que forman parte del acervo cultural general, las feministas se interesan por averiguar si el acondicionamiento social diferente de la mujer ha dado lugar a expresiones *sui generis* en su obra literaria. Para esto se analiza el habla vertida por la creadora en sus personajes femeninos a la luz de los más recientes descubrimientos de la lingüística, con resultados tentativos hacia la formación de una teoría.[36] En estudios específicos sobre la narrativa se ha comprobado la frecuencia del tipo confesional entre las escritoras de diversas regiones y épocas.este fenómeno origina, por supuesto, muchas especulaciones. Si, como afirman Gilbert Y Gubar, la autodefinición precede necesariamente a la autoaserción,[37] ¿es la frecuencia de la forma confesional indicación de una necesidad imperativa de autoexploración originada en la ignorancia en que la sociedad mantuvo a la mujer sobre ella misma? ¿Y tiene esta autoexploración formas características reveladoras de vacilaciones, dudas, alienación del Yo, como cree Annette Kolodny, entre otras?[38] Las respuestas a estas y a otras preguntas, que abarcan áreas de especialización diferentes, se van obteniendo poco a poco a través del trabajo aunado de las estudiosas de la literatura en conjunción con psicólogas, sociólogas e historiadoras, práctica que el femenismo ha impulsado desde sus comienzos.[39]

Siempre dentro de la narrativa, los estudios feministas observan si la autora examinada elige protagonistas masculinos o femeninos, se analizan sus características, así como las de los narradores y otros personajes de ambos sexos cuyos comentarios —importante apoyo para conocer la visión de mundo que crea la obra— se revisan bajo las premisas que preconiza esta perspectiva. Del mismo modo, las descripciones de cosas, lugares, naturaleza —indicios que pueden llegar a tener la importancia de un personaje— se estudian como expresiva glosa de la posición ante el mundo y ante la mujer ofrecida por la obra.[40]

Naturalmente, como en otros tipos de análisis, el final de las narraciones ha generado particular atención. La prevalencia del "final feliz" traducido en matrimonio para los personajes femeninos (y de desgracia cuando no se efectúa) se enfoca hoy desde nuevas perspectivas abiertas por el progresivo cambio que va experimentando la situación de la mujer en la sociedad.[41]

En cooperación con las practicantes de otras disciplinas, se comienzan a releer con nuevos ojos algunos textos que han sido verdaderos manuales prescriptivos de la cultura femenina. A la revisión de novelas y cuentos, la búsqueda en revistas y periódicos de diversas épocas, comienza a formar un arsenal de testimonios que a través de ensayos, comentarios, proverbios, avisos, etc., funcionaron como modelos de conducta para la mujer.[42] Si se arguye que este fenómeno existe también en relación al sexo masculino, lo que es cierto, se trata ahora de poner de relieve los rasgos otorgados a cada sexo y su significado frente a las "estrategias de conocimiento y de poder", en lenguaje de Foucault,[43] que han permitido el dominio de un grupo sobre el otro.

Dado el breve tiempo del resurgimiento feminista que generó el tipo de lectura del cual venimos escribiendo, la resistencia que todavía encuentra en el mundo académico, y la heterogeneidad de las posiciones políticas de sus practicantes, el balance del trabajo efectuado hasta ahora es positivo. Naturalmente que hay áreas necesitadas de mayores exploraciones. Las más importantes en el terreno teórico, creemos, inciden en problemas que atañen al fenómeno artístico general, que las diferentes corrientes críticas han intentado resolver, pero que todavía están lejos de respuestas definitivas: Las cuestiones, por ejemplo, del referente y su transformación en objeto literario;[44] o las del estilo, indagación esta última que, espoleada por las conjeturas de Richardson y Woolf, siguen en resultados tentativos.[45] Por otro lado, la carencia de un "sistema coherente" que defina la crítica literaria feminista que, según Annette Kolodny, resulta de la diversidad de las áreas cuestionadas,[46] se explica también—como se evidenció en páginas anteriores—por el rechazo a seguir las sendas epistemológicas que han fracasado como herramientas para influir en el mejoramiento social.

En cuanto a la práctica, el escollo mayor reside tal vez en la decisión que la estudiosa debe hacer en relación a la calidad del texto que desea analizar, y los cartabones tradicionales de valoración. En este terreno la labor feminista, dice Kolodny, ha servido para demostrar que las escuelas críticas han sido incapaces de abordar la obra de las escritoras de manera justa y apropiada. Según esta autora, la lectura feminista está dilucidando, entonces, no sólo problemas estéticos, sino además está cuestionando los cánones establecedores de jerarquías de calidad, obligando al reexamen de los principios y los métodos que han contribuido a formar nuestros juicios.[47]

Sea labor transitoria de compensación, sea tarea establecida con más largo porvenir, no se puede negar que la lectura feminista añade hoy nuevas posibilidades interpretativas de la obra literaria. En esta época en que ciertos estudiosos se esfuerzan por devolver a la crítica una dirección hermenéutica, y otros insisten en otorgar al lector una posición fundamental en la "concretización" de la obra,[48] parece natural que la perspectiva feminista sea también considerada. Porque ella se acomoda bien con algunos de los principios de las dos corrientes citadas. Si la interpretación hermenéutica tiene que ver con la vida representada literariamente, y maneja la literatura como una forma de conocimiento,[49] esto calza con las metas feministas. Por otro lado, este tipo de lectura es también una "reacción" al sistema de pensamiento elegido e incorporado en el repertorio de la obra.[50] Llámese "repertorio" o "código", la lectora feminista está reaccionando en contra de la divulgación de falsos conceptos sobre la mujer perpetuados a través de la literatura. Discutiendo ideas que arraigadas por siglos tomaban como natural lo que era producto cultural, el feminismo impulsa nuevas lecturas de viejos textos, desafía antiguas percepciones, ayuda a "desfamiliarizar" lo que de pura costumbre se había dejado de ver. El peligro de caer en una posición ciega de antagonismo frente a lo masculino lo previene la raíz ética del movimiento que, bien entendido, se opone a nociones que puedan servir de apoyo a cualquier tipo de abuso represivo.

RUTGERS UNIVERSITY

Notas

[1]Se puede comenzar, por ejemplo, con la discusión y bibliografía de René Wellek en *Concepts of Criticism* (New Haven: Yale University Press, 1973), pp. 31-36.

[2]Dorothy Kaufmann McCall, "Simone de Beauvoir, *The Second Sex*, and Jean-Paul Sartre", *Signs*, V, 2 (Winter 1979), p. 222.

[3]Alice Jardine, "Interview with Simone de Beauvoir", *Signs*, citado en nota 2, p. 227.

[4]Annette Barnes, "Female Criticism: A Prologue", *The Authority of Experience: Essays in Feminist Criticism*, eds. Arlyn Diamond y Lee R. Edwards (Amherst: The University of Massachusetts Press, 1977), p. 9.

[5]Annis Pratt, "The New Feminist Criticisms: Exploring the History of the New Space", *Beyond Intellectual Sexism: A New Woman, A New Reality*, ed. Joan I. Roberts (New York: David McKay Co., 1976), pp. 176-177.

[6]Marilyn R. Farwell, "Adrienne Rich and an Organic Feminist Criticism", *College English*, 39, 2 (October 1977), pp. 191-203.

[7]Ibid., p. 193. Nuestra traducción.

[8]Cheri Register, "American Feminist Literary Criticism. A Bibliographical Introduction", *Feminist Literary Criticism: Explorations in Theory*, ed. Josephine

Donovan (University Press of Kentucky, 1975), p. 10. Elaine Showalter, "Literary Criticism", *Signs*, I, 2 (Winter 1975), p. 437. Marcia Holly, "Consciousness and Authenticity Toward a Feminist Aesthetic", Donovan, *Feminist Literary Criticism*, p. 67.

[9]Usamos la noción de código cultural en el sentido explicado por Roland Barthes en su *S/Z* trad. Richard Miller. (New York: Hill and Wang, 1974), p. 20.

[10]Lynn Surenick revisa fases del desarrollo del concepto de lo femenino en "On Women and Fiction", *The Authority of Experience*, eds. Diamond y Edwards, pp. 32-43. También lo hace Sydney Janet Kaplan en *Feminine Consciousness in the Modern British Novel* (Urbana and Chicago: University of Illinois Press, 1975), pp. 3-5. Agate Nesaule Krouse discute diferentes posiciones feministas y define lo que ella entiende por feminismo literario en "Toward a Definition of Literary Feminism", *Feminist Criticism: Essays on Theory, Poetry and Prose*, eds. Cheryl L. Brown y Karen Olson (Metuchen, New Jersey: The Scarecrow Press, 1978), pp. 279-90.

[11]Una excelente revisión histórica del mito de la femineidad hace Lisa Appignanesi en *Feminity and the Creative Imagination: A Study of Henry James, Robert Musil and Marcel Proust* (London: Vision Press, 1973), pp. 1-19.

[12]Como introducción al problema de la diferencia sexual y su relación con el concepto de género, véase el estudio de Nancy Chodorow, "Feminism and Difference: Gender, Relation and Difference in Psychoanalytic Perspective", *Socialist Review*, 46, 9, 4 (July-August 1979), pp. 51-69.

[13]La frase es de Julia Kristeva en *El texto de la novela*. (trad. Jordi Llovet. Barcelona: Lumen, 1974), p. 84; forma parte de sus especulaciones sobre la institucionalización de las diferencias jerárquicas entre los sexos a propósito del culto de la Dama.

[14]Gayatri Spivak sostiene que "no rigorous definition of anything is ultimately possible" en "Feminism and Critical Theory", *Women's Studies International Quarterly*, I, 3 (1978), p. 241.

[15]Mary Daly, en *Beyond God the Father: Toward a Philosophy of Women's Liberation* (Boston: Beacon Press, 1973), habla de "Metodolotría" (p. 11) y la necesidad del "Metocidio" (p. 12).

[16]*Female Studies VI. Closer to the Ground Women's Classes, Criticism, Programs—1972*, eds. Nancy Hoffman, Cynthia Secor, Adrian Tinsley (Old Westbury: The Feminist Press, 1972), p. 101.

[17]En *Female Studies VI,* p. 99, se lee: "Feminist criticism, then, is concerned to examine the representation of women in literature, the motives and behaviors assigned to them, their function in the plot, the images and symbols associated with them, and the descriptive and judgmental biases of the narrative point of view." Al hablar de aspectos discursivos y narrativos, seguimos la distinción, basada en los estudios de Benveniste, entre *discurso* (caracterizado por la presencia de la subjetividad de un *yo*), y *relato* (el escrito que tiende a la objetividad y desaparición del narrador). Esta división, muy general (puesto que las dos categorías casi nunca aparecen en su estado puro), permitiría separar en dos cualquier espécimen literario. Ver Gerard Genette, "Fronteras del relato", *Análisis estructural del relato*, trad. Beatriz Dorriots de *Communications* 8 (Buenos Aires: Tiempo Contemporáneo, 2a ed., 1972), pp. 203 y 205.

[18]"The literary message is not only a linguistic communication but also a transmission of states of mind, of ideals, and of judgements about the world". Cesare

12   DEFINICIONES Y PROBLEMAS

Segre, "Narrative Structures and Literary History", *Critical Inquiry*, III, 2 (Winter 1976), p. 273.

[19] Jonathan Culler, *Structuralist Poetics*. *Structuralism, Linguistics and the Study of Literature* (Ithaca, New York: Cornell University Press, 1975), p. 144.

[20] Entre los generales, el arduo problema de la relación entre naturaleza y cultura, crucial para el feminismo, y que se viene discutiendo por tan largo tiempo.

[21] *New French Feminisms. An Anthology*, eds. Elaine Marks e Isabelle de Courtivron (Amherst: The University of Massachusetts Press, 1980), pp. 10-27.

[22] Michel Foucault, *The History of Sexuality. Volume I: An Introduction* (New York: Vintage Books, 1980), p. 94.

[23] A esto se refiere Elaine Showalter en "Literary Criticism", *Signs*, I, 2 (Winter 1975), p. 451.

[24] *El texto de la novela*, pp. 82-84.

[25] Julia Kristeva, "Hérétique de L'Amour", *Tel Quel* 74 (Hiver, 1977), p. 46.

[26] Kate Millet y su *Sexual Politics* (Garden City: Doubleday, 1970), reactivó la investigación del sexismo entre los escritores. Un destacado estudio en esta área es el de Susan Fox, "The Female as Metaphor in William Blake's Poetry", *Critical Inquiry*, III, 3 (Spring 1977), pp. 507-19.

[27] Elaine Showalter en el artículo citado en nota 23 menciona los estudios más significativos de la abundante bibliografía existente sobre imágenes literarias de la mujer.

[28] Véase el trabajo de B. Aldaraca en este volumen.

[29] Lillian S. Robinson comienza su *Sex, Class, and Culture* (Bloomington: Indiana University Press, 1978) afirmando el carácter ideológico, moral y revolucionario de la crítica feminista (p. 3) y mantiene que ciertos estereotipos femeninos han estado siempre al servicio de las clases dirigentes (p. 10).

[30] Annis Pratt, en *Beyond Intellectual Sexism*, p. 180.

[31] Jean E. Kennard, *Victims of Convention* (Hamden, Conn.: Archon Books, 1978).

[32] Por supuesto el suicidio es tanto motivo literario como hecho existencial entre los dos sexos. Sin embargo, dada la desproporción en el número de escritoras, la cantidad de suicidas entre ellas es muy grande: Virginia Woolf, Anne Sexton, Sylvia Plath, en lengua inglesa; Alfonsina Storni, Alejandra Pizarnik, entre las hispanoamericanas, para mencionar sólo algunas.

[33] Sandra M. Gilbert y Susan Gubar, *The Madwoman in the Attic. The Woman Writer and the Nineteenth-Century Literary Imagination* (New Haven: Yale University Press, 1979), pp. 86-87.

[34] Hélène Cixous, "The Laugh of the Medusa", trad. Keith Cohen y Paula Cohen, *Signs*, I, 4 (Summer 1976), p. 887. Recuérdense a este propósito los significativos títulos de las obras de Kate Millet: *Flying*, y E. Jong: *Fear of Flying*.

[35] La creencia de que la mujer era incapaz de especulaciones abstractas o razonamientos políticos la han roto las obras ensayísticas y de ficción de Beauvoir, Doris Lessing o Nadine Godimer, para nombrar sólo las muy conocidas. La preocupación política de las narradoras hispanoamericanas se señala en mi estudio "Narradoras hispanoamericanas: Vieja y nueva problemática en renovadas elaboraciones" incluido en este volumen.

[36] Siguiendo a Natalie Sarraute, Donovan habla de "tropismic awareness" como rasgo caracterizador de la escritura femenina en *Female Studies VI*, p. 147. Para una extensa bibliografía sobre esta materia consúltese "Perspectives on Language

and Communication" de Cheris Kramer, Barrie Thorne y Nancy Henley, *Signs*, III, 3 (Spring 1978), pp. 638-51.

[37]Gilbert Y Gubar, *The Madwoman* p. 17.

[38]Annette Kolodny, "Feminist Literary Criticism", *Critical Inquiry*, II, 1 (Autumn 1975), pp. 79-80. El lenguaje no asertivo de las mujeres en la narrativa de las hispanoamericanas se señala en el estudio citado en nota 35.

[39]La labor colectiva e interdisciplinaria que las feministas promueven se ha visto confirmado por innumerables trabajos firmados por dos o más autoras. Para una discusión sobre este asunto, véase "In Defiance of the Evidence: Notes on Feminist Scholarship" de Elaine Reuben, *Women's Studies International Quarterly*, I, 3 (1978), p. 217.

[40]Buen ejemplo de este tipo de análisis son las notas que hace Annette Kolodny sobre "The Yellow Paper" de Charlotte Perkins Gilman y "A Jury of her Peers" de Susan Keating Glaspells, en "A Map for Rereading: Or, Gender and the Interpretation of Literary Texts", *New Literary History*, XI, 3 (Spring 1980), pp. 455-64.

[41]Consúltese el libro de Kennard, nota 31.

[42]Véase de Gaye Tuchman, Arlene Kaplan y James Benet, *Hearth and Home*: *Images of Women in the Mass Media* (New York: Oxford Press, 1978). Para Hispanoamérica: Cornelia Butler Flora, "Women in Latin American Fotonovelas: From Cinderella to Mata Hari", *Women's Studies International Quarterly*, II, 1, (1980), pp. 95-104.

[43]*The History of Sexuality*, p. 105.

[44]Esta es una cuestión fundamental para la posición de la crítica feminista. Una apertura al problema se halla en "Notes Toward a Theory of the Referent" de Thomas E. Lewis, *PMLA*, 94, 3 (May 1979), pp. 459-75.

[45]Josephine Donovan comenta las observaciones de Dorothy Richardson y Virginia Woolf en "Feminist Style Criticism", *Female Studies VI*, pp. 139-49.

[46]Annette Kolodny, "Dancing Through the Minefield: Some Observations on the Theory, Practice and Politics of a Feminist Literary Criticism", *Feminist Studies*, VI, 1 (Spring 1980), p. 2.

[47]Ibid., p. 7.

[48] Estamos traduciendo el inglés *realization* que usa Wolfgang Iser en su *The Implied Reader Patterns of Communication in Prose Fiction from Bunyan to Beckett* (Baltimore: The Johns Hopkins University Press, 1974), p. 274.

[49]Félix Martínez Bonati, "Hermeneutic Criticism and the Description of Form", *Interpretation of Narrative*, eds. Mario J. Valdés y Owen J. Miller (Toronto: University of Toronto Press, 1978), p. 79.

[50]Wolfgang Iser define lo que entiende por repertorio del texto en "The Reality of Fiction: A Functionalist Approach to Literature", *New Literary History*, VII, 1 (Autumn 1975), pp. 21 y siguientes. Este trabajo y el del profesor Martínez Bonati mencionado en la nota 49 pueden ser utilizados con provecho en la exploración del problema del referente, aludido antes.

THE "I" IN ADRIENNE RICH: INDIVIDUATION AND THE ANDROGYNE ARCHETYPE

Betty S. Flowers

I. The Necessity of the Androgyne

It seems to be the case that wherever there is difference, there is hierarchy. Whenever opposites occur, one pole of the pair assumes value over the other. If there is white and black, reason and emotion, day and night, up and down, male and female, one role takes precedence in value, dignity, power:

+ *pole*	- *pole*
white	black
reason	emotion
day	night
up	down
universal	particular
objective	subjective
God	Satan
male	female

A corollary to this axiom seems to be that in general like poles are associated with each other. Thus, the positively charged "reason" of the reason-emotion duality is likely to be associated with the positively charged "male" of the male-female duality, and so on.

I think much of what is criticized as being defensive or hostile or shrill in the voices of contemporary women poets has its roots in this apparently irresistible logic:

> If: male (God, objective, etc.) is the opposite of female (Satan, subjective, etc.),
> and: good is the opposite of bad,

then: if male (etc.) is good, female (etc.) must be bad.

On some level, then, whenever we assert that "female" or any other negatively charged pole is "good," we find ourselves under the necessity to assert that all other negative poles are good. For example, if female is declared good, then "emotion," which belongs by association with female, must also be good. In keeping with this associational logic, an argument that something usually considered negative is positive tends to imply that its opposite, what was formerly valued as positive, is actually negative. To put this more directly:

If: female (Satan, emotion, etc.) is not – but +,
then: male (God, reason, etc.) must be not + but –.

So an argument *for* women, because of this seemingly irresistible pull of language, often implies an argument *against* men. The women making this argument, who battle the negative charges in an attempt to transform them into positive, find themselves fighting a hydra-headed monster—where one negative is transformed, two more grow in its place. If, for example, emotion is argued to be positive rather than negative, then emotion itself becomes redefined into "positive emotion" and "negative emotion":

Re-definition

+ *pole*	– *pole*
"masculine" emotion	"feminine" emotion
(Achilles weeps for Patroclus)	(Matilda shrieks at a mouse)

Even the critics' words such as "defensive," "hostile," and "shrill" must be fought since by value charge they belong to the female. The critic does not accuse; he merely uncovers what is "objectively" there:

+ *pole*	– *pole*
male	female
offensive	defensive
generous	hostile
mellow	shrill

To make the language ours by changing all the negative charges to positive seems to me an impossible task. Women can declare a beginning; we can birth ourselves anew into the world in spite of the destiny implied by our history. But language *is* its history and does not exist apart from it. The weight of connotation and etymology, which, for example, pulls "hysterical" to the realm of women, cannot be fought directly. We cannot declare the word inoperative because it is unfair or because its connotations are untrue. What we can do, however, is to explore an alternative way of responding to pairs of opposites. Eastern thinkers have explored the "either/and," the paradoxical union of opposites in which, seen as a whole, the positive and negative poles become interdependent. In the *I Ching*, for example, too much of a positively charged virtue becomes negative in value. Seen in this way, pairs of opposites are as void of hierarchical value as negative and positive charges in an electric current, or the upness and downess of quarks, or the mutually exclusive but paradoxically necessary models of light as waves, light as photons.

In the West, except for the generally paradoxical nature of much of modern physics, we have very few models for the union of positive-negative poles. God is in Heaven and Satan is in Hell, and while it has sometimes been hinted that the existence of one is necessary to the existence of the other, this mutual interdependence has not carried over to our thinking about the necessity of incorporating into our value systems the qualities of Satan as we do those of God or the necessity, in the growth of the self, of incorporating the female as we incorporate the male. For the most part, our images are of overcoming, not of uniting: God over Satan, St. George over the dragon, St. Augustine over the prostitute.

We do, however, have one richly endowed image for the transforming of opposites to unity and wholeness, and that is the image of the androgyne. Jung's theories and those of others have done much to reveal just how rich our resources in this image are. The alchemical marriage of the male and female aspects of the psyche, the union of conscious and unconscious, of the positive we attribute to ourselves and the negative we project onto others, implies a transvaluation of values so radical that for centuries the idea implicit in the image was protected as a secret doctrine. It is not surprising, then, that with the re-valuing of the negative pole of opposites that accompanies the re-valuing of the female, the image of the androgyne should become more and more important.

"I am the androgyne!" the voice of "The Stranger" asserts. For the many readers who have taken this to be Rich's own voice, there is evidence in her criticism, in her comments about her own writing, in the story her life makes, and in the stories her poems tell to elaborate upon and support this assertion, at least for the middle stages of her writing career. Much of the criticism of Rich's poetry, and indeed much of all feminist criticism of women's writing, has used biographical facts and thematic concerns as a major basis upon which to assign value. Although this approach is certainly supportable, it offends those who see such strategies of criticism as a special pleading, or mere theme hunting, or banner waving. "Too bad for them," one might say, with some justice; such objections tend to ignore a central aim of feminist criticism:

> A radical critique of literature, feminist in its impulse, would take the work first of all as a clue to how we live, how we have been living, how we have been led to imagine ourselves, how our language has trapped as well as liberated us; and how we can begin to see—and therefore live—afresh.[1]

But in literary studies, we have come further in understanding "how we have been led to imagine ourselves" than in understanding "how our language has trapped as well as liberated us." This is partly because it is easier to see images than to think about the means we use for thinking. In fact, it might be questioned whether we can ever hope to understand language by using language itself. The problem is similar to the one Jung posed in relation to the self: the self cannot view itself without positing an Other. Just as we can see our eyes only by projecting an image of ourselves onto a mirror and observing its reflections, so we can see the unknown in ourselves only by looking at the images we have projected, whether in dreams, fantasy or literature.

The images of women in our predominantly male-authored literature are now being explored not as images of woman as she is, but as projections of the female aspect of the male psyche. The growth in awareness of how these images have functioned as projections is clearly documented in Rich's poetry. Numerous readers—and Rich herself—have commented on the transformation from the tightly formal poems of *A Change of World* (1951) to the less restricted style and more overtly feminist subject matter of the later poetry.[2] Wendy Martin titles her study of this development "From Patriarchy to the Female Principle,"[3] a characterization which seems even more fitting since Rich's *Of Woman Born*[4] appeared.

The re-evaluation of the negatively charged pole and the movement toward a new vision of the opposites is a transformative process undergone in the structure of Rich's language as well as in its imagery. Now that we are learning to recognize "how we have been led to imagine ourselves," we must begin to look more closely at how we have been led to use the language as a means of imagining.

As a way of beginning this exploration, I have narrowed my focus to one aspect of the language of Rich's poetry: the position of the narrative voice in relation to its subject matter and its audience. Here it is not the static image of the androgyne I will be using as a model, but the process of transformation that leads to androgyny.

Of necessity I can discuss only a few representative poems, chronologically arranged to highlight the development. I use the term "development" with the understanding that, as in all psychic growth, the old remains with the new, the child still lives in the adult, and the voice of the Fathers can still be heard even in the most recent of Rich's female-centered poems—but with a difference.

II. In Bondage to the Father

The dominant voice in Rich's first volume of poetry, *A Change of World*, is what might be called the "universal I." It is the most common voice in English lyric poetry, the voice of Shakespeare and Shelley, of Tennyson and Eliot, and of W. H. Auden, who himself praised *A Change of World* for exactly what it had not changed or challenged, saying "the poems a reader will encounter in this book are neatly and modestly dressed, speak quietly but do not mumble, respect their elders but are not cowed by them, and do not tell fibs. . . ."[5]

The authority of such a voice lies in the implicit assumptions to which we assent when we enter the world of the poem:

1. Poetry, like philosophy and unlike politics, involves that which we humans have in common.
2. But unlike philosophy, poetry exists in the realm of the subjective, of the individual.
3. That which is the most personal is also the most universal.

Thus, in *A Change of World*, as in most lyric poetry, it is not surprising to find frequent shifts of voice within the same poem from the singular I to the plural we. The transition is smooth, does not call attention to itself, because the universal I *is* the "we," *is* the human in general.

But there is another assumption to which we must assent in order to acknowledge the authority of this voice and that is that the universal I is sexless, an assumption that the history of philosophy as well as poetry has supported. We have learned to read most poems with this assumption, and most poems do nothing to disturb it:

> Now that your hopes are shamed, you stand
> At last believing and resigned,
> And none of us who touch your hand
> Know how to give you back in kind
> The words you flung when hopes were proud:
> *Being born to happiness*
> *Above the asking of the crowd,*
> *You would not take a finger less.*

> We who know limits now give room
> To one who grows to fit his doom ("Afterward").

As printed in *A Change of World*, this poem seems to speak of
a universal human situation, the disappointment of hopes leading
to the resignation of the wise ("We who know") and the final irony
of the "growth" to fit a "doom." In general, it fits a universal motif:
men are born to die, we are all heirs of Adam's Fall, and so forth.

Twenty-four years later, in *Poems: Selected and New* (1975),
the poem appeared with one minor change—the pronoun "his" in
"his doom" had become "her." Rich explained this change in a note
to "The Tourist and the Town":

> The pronouns in the third part of the poem were originally mas-
> culine. But the tourist was a woman, myself, and I never saw her as
> anything else. In 1953, when the poem was written, some notion of
> "universality" prevailed which made the feminine pronoun suspect,
> "personal." In this poem, and in "Afterward" in *A Change of World*,
> I have altered the pronouns not simply as a matter of fact but be-
> cause they alter, for me, the dimensions of the poem.[6]

With this one change in pronoun, the dimensions of the poem are
no longer felt as universally human but as the situation of woman.
In addition, the new pronoun exerts a tremendous influence on the
voice of the poem—"We who know" comes to be read as "We [wom-
en] who know."

Now, too, the implied relation to the reader changes. If the voice
of the poem is that of a woman talking about the condition of wom-
en, the poem is not philosophical but political, not an image of the
universal human condition, but a statement of protest for women
and an implicit criticism against men. Even the conventions within
which the poem stands seem to shift ground, from those of lyric form
to those of rhetoric, argumentation. Thus, if poems are like persons,
as Auden says, we see that with one change of pronoun, a philosophical poet becomes a political feminist.

A summary of how the reading of the poem changes with the
change in pronoun might look like the following:

original "his" version	*later "her" version*
subject: universal (applies to all humans)	subject: particular (of interest primarily to women)
impact: philosophical	impact: political
tone: resigned, wise	tone: critical, rebellious

The poem in all other ways remains the same; but, as we have
seen, to change the sex of the speaker is to change the poem, even in

terms of its traditional lasting value: What is universal is what lasts; what is merely political will die when the cause dies. In terms of the traditional value structure, when the voice becomes feminine, the poem itself seems to move from eternal time to mere historical time; to put it another way, if literature is institutionalized subjectivity, as Roland Barthes says, the voice of the universal I is the voice of the Fathers.

It is in order to join the voices of the Fathers that a hero such as Tamino in Mozart's *The Magic Flute* battles the forces of the Mother, the Queen of the Night. In this mythological symbolism, the first step in the process of uniting the male and female within the (male) self involves the separation of oneself from the female, as imaged by the Mother, and all she represents—chaos, the tyranny of the unconscious, the formlessness of subjective emotions.

The danger for the (male) poet or hero who undertakes this night journey is that he may be overwhelmed by the contents of his unconscious and go mad, speaking in a language so personal that no one can understand. But better madness, so the myth goes, than never to undertake the journey at all. And at the end of the fearful night is the bright pantheon of poets, the voices of those who have learned their own speech—Chaucer, Shakespeare, Milton, Eliot. . . .

But what of the female poet? If, in the process of individuation, she must separate herself from the tyranny of the Father within her, will she not be separating herself from that very voice to which she aspires, the universal I? How is she to master the animus within and learn to use him as a guide to the riches of the unconscious, as the male poet does his anima/Muse, if to call upon the masculine is to call upon the weight of centuries of (male) poetic tradition? How is she to learn her own voice?

The poems in *A Change of World* offer three main responses: (1) She can refuse to take the journey.

> She who has power to call her man
> From that estranged intensity
> Where his mind forages alone,
> Yet keeps her peace and leaves him free,
> And when his thoughts to her return
> Stands where he left her, still his own,
> Knows this the hardest thing to learn ("An Unsaid Word").

Here the omniscient voice posits a "she," an Other whose emotions can be conveyed, even with some sympathy, but who does not speak for herself. "An Unsaid Word" is itself an image of non-speaking.

(2) She can take the persona of a man, as in "The Uncle Speaks in the Drawing Room."

(3) She can image the struggle without participating in it. The voice of "Aunt Jennifer's Tigers" describes the dead creator, still with her "terrified hands," while the tigers in the picture she has created "do not fear the men beneath the tree." Rich later spoke about this third strategy:

> Looking back at poems I wrote before I was 21, I'm startled because beneath the conscious craft are glimpses of the split I even then experienced between the girl who wrote poems, who defined herself in writing poems, and the girl who was to define herself by her relationships with men. "Aunt Jennifer's Tigers," written while I was a student, looks with deliberate detachment at this split. . . . In writing this poem, composed and apparently cool as it is, I thought I was creating a portrait of an imaginary woman. But this woman suffers from the opposition of her imagination, worked out in tapestry, and her life-style, "ringed with ordeals she was mastered by." It was important to me that Aunt Jennifer was a person as distinct from myself as possible—distanced by the formalism of the poem, by its objective, observant tone—even by putting the woman in a different generation.[7]

In these early poems the poet's voice is still in bondage to the Father.

III. Polarization

The first step in the creation of the consciousness of self seems to involve the division of that which was one into two. In the foreword to *A Change of World*, Auden says, "In a young poet, as T. S. Eliot has observed, the most promising sign is craftsmanship for it is evidence of a capacity for detachment from the self and its emotions without which no art is possible."[8] But this statement, authoritatively universal in its form, approaches that primal division from one side only.

Detaching oneself from the realm of the Mothers (emotions) makes symbolic sense for the individuation of the male poet. The female poet must detach herself from the realm of the Fathers if she is not to remain bound to a derivative, even if well-crafted, form. The statement rephrased from a female perspective might go something like this: "In a young poet, the most promising sign is an honesty and intensity of feeling, for it is evidence of a capacity for the transcendence of inherited forms and voices without which no art is possible."

When the (male) hero has successfully overcome the realm of the Mothers, he is greeted with a hero's welcome. But after the (female) poet has separated herself from the Fathers within, she still has to face the Fathers without. As Rich put it:

> If a man is writing, he's gone through all the nonsense and said, "Okay, I am a poet and I'm still a man. They don't cancel each other out or, if they do, then I'll opt to be a poet." He's not writing for a hostile sex, a breed of critics who by virtue of their sex are going to look at his language and pass judgment on it. That does happen to a woman.[9]

Initially, the division of the one into two, the polarization, is imaged not as a Father-daughter conflict, but as a Mother-daughter opposition, for it is through the Mother that the voice of the Father is first heard. So it is with the voices of "Snapshots of a Daughter-in-Law," the title poem of the 1963 volume which Rich and others have seen as a turning point in her poetry:

> Until then I had tried very much *not* to identify myself as a female poet. Over two years I wrote a 10-part poem called "Snapshots of a Daughter-in-Law," in a longer, looser mode than I'd ever trusted myself with before. It was an extraordinary relief to write that poem. It strikes me now as too literary, too dependent on allusions; I hadn't found the courage yet to do without authorities, or even to use the pronoun "I"—the woman in the poem is always "she."[10]

While the female in the poem is "she," the "she" is often addressed as "you"; in fact, Part 1 begins, "You, once a belle in Shreveport" and ends, "your daughter / wipes the teaspoons, grows another way." The speaker in Part 1 is personally addressing the descriptions of the daughter to the mother, so that it is not only the reader who must take notice of mother and daughter but the mother within the poem who must notice as well. Put succinctly: The direct "you" is aimed at the Mother.

In addition to this new relationship between narrator and audience, there is also the third-person omniscient voice so familiar from Rich's earlier poems. In "Snapshots," this voice appears through quotation, as in Part 1:

> and play a Chopin prelude
> called by Cortot: "*Delicious recollections*
> *float like perfume through the memory.*"

Again, in Part 2, there is a quoted voice, this time that of the "angels chiding" the daughter. They speak directly to her just as the voice of Part 1 has spoken to the Mother and in tone seem like an extension of that earlier narrative voice. But the voice of the entire section within which the angels speak is a third-person voice, one much nearer the quoted voice of Cortot than its own direct "you" predecessor in Part 1.

By the time we reach Part 3 we are listening to the voice of the universal I, which we recognize immediately by the generalized authoritative statement of the first line: "A thinking woman sleeps with monsters." Characteristic of this voice is the tendency toward allusion to the classics, literature, personified Nature; in this section, there are no fewer than seven allusions in fourteen lines.

Although the voice of the universal I dominates Part 3, a close look at its second stanza reveals an interesting crack in the narrative mask:

> Two handsome women, gripped in argument,
> each proud, acute, subtle, I hear scream
> across the cut glass and majolica
> like Furies cornered from their prey:
> The argument *ad feminam*, all the old knives
> that have rusted in my back, I drive in yours,
> *ma semblable, ma soeur!*

In these last three lines, we do not know for certain who is talking to whom: one arguing woman to another; the speaker to the women; or, because of the allusion to Eliot's allusion to Baudelaire's "*Hypocrite lecteur! —mon semblable—mon frère!*" we may conclude that the speaker is talking primarily to her readers. The transformation from *frère* to *soeur*, which prefigures the later his to her switch of "Afterward," occurs here embedded in a quotation.

The location of the voice becomes even more problematic in Part 4, which is structured on a series of participles ("Knowing," "Reading," "writing," "dusting") with no identifiable subject. Mother, daughter, all thinking women, the speaker, the reader—all are implicated:

> Reading while waiting
> for the iron to heat,
> writing, *My Life had stood—A Loaded Gun—*
> In that Amherst pantry while the jellies boil and scum, . . .

With the allusion to Emily Dickinson ("*My Life had stood—a Loaded Gun—*"), a female literary ancestor becomes another possible *ma soeur.*

Part 5 consists of three lines:

> *Dulce ridens, dulce loquens,*
> she shaves her legs until they gleam
> like petrified mammoth-tusk.

Each of these lines is of a different voice: line one, the voice of a male writer speaking of woman; line two, the voice of an objective female observer, one who informs, who paints pictures of reality that have no place in the ideal images of the Father; and line three, the voice of the image-maker, namer of that which is lost, frozen, unseen, or existing only in potential.

Each of the next four sections is constructed as a polarity between a quotation (often the voice of a Father) and one or a combination of several of the voices that have been previously introduced. For example, Section 8 begins: " 'You all die at fifteen,' said Diderot, / and turn part legend, part convention." The voice which answers this Father is the voice of "we women":

> Deliciously, all that we might have been,
> all that we were—fire, tears,
> wit, taste, martyred ambition—
> stirs like the memory of refused adultery
> the drained and flagging bosom of our middle years.

The last section (Part 10) is entirely the voice of the visionary "I," which, in describing the future, ends by shifting from "I" to the (female) communal "ours."

> but her cargo
> no promise then:
> delivered
> palpable
> ours.

In "Snapshots," the universal lyric voice has become a medley of polarized voices, talking not so much with each other as *at* each other. On one level, the poem has the unity of a family photograph album in that all the pictures are connected with each other through related images. Seen in terms of voices rather than pictures, the poem is not a collage, like the voices of *The Waste Land*, but a kind of poetic trial drama in which the accused in the form of great writers (the Fathers) speak directly, followed by a host of voices speaking against them.

Thus the poetic persona of "Snapshots" is not so much fragmented as polarized, with each pole aware of the other's existence. There is direct confrontation, a struggle for the supremacy of one voice over the others, with the voice of the female communal "ours" apparently triumphant in the end.

There is a development, too. Whereas in the beginning of the poem the polarization is between the objective observer and the direct you, by the end of the poem the polarization is clearly that between male and female—the male voice of authority (*"Not that it is done well, but / that it is done at all?*...") versus the female voices, each responding from a different angle to the voice of the Father.

IV. The False Androgyne

In the individuation process, after polarization comes the attempt to unite the two, male and female, in the symbolic "sacred marriage" of mythology. An interesting marriage situation—although not itself a marriage—occurs in "Antinoüs: The Diaries" (in the collection *Snapshots of a Daughter-in-Law*, 1963).

Antinoüs, to quote *Webster's Biographical Dictionary*, was "page and favorite of Emperor Hadrian at Rome; noted for his beauty; drowned himself in Nile; subject of many works of art." Such beautiful young boys, beloved of powerful men, often provide the model for the image of the androgyne, not because they are objects of homosexual desire, but because as men they exhibit the qualities traditionally assigned to women. Mercury, favorite companion of Jupiter, is frequently depicted as the androgynous being who presides over the alchemical marriage. Angels, the messengers of God, are often painted as androgynous beings, slender, beautiful, gentle, with long curls but boys' names, who neither "give nor receive in marriage."

In "Antinoüs: The Diaries," the speaker is ostensibly androgynous because although the embodiment (Antinoüs) is male, the voice (diaries) speaks as a woman ("What is it I so miscarry?"). Moreover, Antinoüs is to the Emperor as female is to male: Valued for youth and beauty as a sexual object, s/he is the subject, not the creator, of art. What remains of the historical Antinoüs are not diaries or records of his voice, his thoughts, his being, but statues, the image of his body in a hundred temples and towns. To his deified image was attributed a power that his living person never enjoyed.

As the object or end of the individuation process, this common image of the androgyne is false because it fails to give birth to itself as subject. Whether in male or female guise, the eternally beautiful companion of Jupiter, or of the Roman Emperor, or of the male lyric poets, is still an object, still the imaged Other of the Fathers.

The voice which speaks from this image is a familiar voice, telling "The old, needless story" of the victim:

> What is it I so miscarry?
> If what I spew on the tiles at last,
> helpless, disgraced, alone,
> is in part what I've swallowed from glasses, eyes,

> motions of hands, opening and closing mouths,
> isn't it also dead gobbets of myself,
> abortive, murdered, or never willed?

V. Birth of the Multiple Voice

In the process of transformation, in the birthing of a new self, the old self never really dies:

> Things look at you doubly
> and you must look back
> ("Prospective Immigrants Please Note," *Snapshots)*

Thus, where there were two elements of the psyche (male-female), now there are four (old male-female, new male-female).

"The Afterwake" (in *Snapshots*) mirrors this alchemical birthing process of the one couple becoming the two. The title begins the process of splitting by suggesting a multiplicity of associational directions: afterbirth, that membrane of union and separation within the womb which is "born after"; after wake, in the sense of a funeral; after wake, as in water, the track of something gone before; after wake, implying sleep.

The poem begins with the old male-female couple, the male as "you," the female "I": "Nursing your nerves / to rest, I've roused my own . . . ." Soon after the initial sleeper-waker couple is introduced, a new male character appears, the personified "Sleep" who "sees you behind closed doors," while "I slump in his front parlor." Then a new female is introduced ("But I'm / like a midwife . . .") and the alchemical quaternity is complete:

| *old couple* | "you," sleeper | — | "I," waker |
| *new couple* | Sleep | — | midwife |

For the remainder of the poem, the drama is played out on the allegorical level of the new couple, Sleep and midwife. The relationship of "I" to "you" is perceived now as the relationship of "midwife" to "Sleep." The voice, the I of the poem is "with her," the midwife ("the birthyell still / exploding in her head") and not with the male Sleep "behind closed doors":

> Yes, I'm with her now: here's
> the streaked, livid road
> edged with shut houses
> breathing night out and in.

The I here has not lost the character of waker but has added to its former persona that of midwife, the one who helps to birth against the closed doors and fatigue of the night.

In "Planetarium," from *The Will to Change* (1971), the "I" becomes not double but multiple, a kaleidoscope of voices that includes the stars, the constellations, the woman looking at them, and the instrument she uses. The multiple voice of the poem is particularly interesting in light of the single-couple polarity of an earlier companion poem, "Orion,"[11] in which the I talks to the masculine constellation as a "fierce half brother, staring / down from that simplified west."[12]

Unlike the quotations in "Snapshots," the embedded voices of the Fathers of astronomy in "Planetarium" do not form a pole against which the female voices struggle but are themselves subsumed within the world of the planetarium where the sister and brother astronomers, Caroline and William Herschel, work together. At the end of the poem, the explosion of voices and images is brought together in the first person "my body," which becomes, in a way, both the voice of the poem and the image the voice is speaking about:

> I have been standing all my life in the
> direct path of a battery of signals
> the most accurately transmitted most
> untranslateable language in the universe
> I am a galactic cloud so deep   so invo-
> luted that a light wave could take 15
> years to travel through me   And has
> taken   I am an instrument in the shape
> of a woman trying to translate pulsations
> into images   for the relief of the body
> and the reconstruction of the mind.

VI. Toward the Androgyne

The explosion of voices, the multiple location of the mask of the speaker, is explored further in *Diving Into the Wreck* (1973), where the making of a new voice, a point of view adequate to carry the female half of experience, is one of the primary concerns. Perhaps more than any other of Rich's poems, the title poem "Diving into the Wreck" can be called a product of the androgynous voice. Here there is not merely an image of the androgyne presented, but an experience of the process of making the androgyne.

At first, the speaker of the poem resists male/female identification, partly because the environment is a symbolic ship of the self, rather than any of the male or female spaces into which the land is

usually divided, and partly because the speaker images itself in a
diving costume, that curious asexual body necessary for survival
in both the world of the sea and the world of space. "I," the diver explores "the wreck and not the story of the wreck / the thing itself and
not the myth," until suddenly, reaching "the place," the voice splits,
polarizing into male-female:

> This is the place.
> And I am here, the mermaid whose dark hair
> streams black, the merman in his armored body
> We circle silently
> about the wreck
> we dive into the hold
> I am she: I am he

And then, immediately, the "he/she" becomes the wreck itself; all
things become the polarized couple whose voice is a singular subject
with a plural verb—"the one who find our way":

> I am she: I am he
>
> whose drowned face sleeps with open eyes
> whose breasts still bear the stress
> whose silver, copper, vermeil cargo lies
> obscurely inside barrels
> half-wedged and left to rot
> we are the half-destroyed instruments
> that once held to a course
> the water-eaten log
> the fouled compass
>
> We are, I am, you are
> by cowardice or courage
> the one who find our way
> back to this scene
> carrying a knife, a camera
> a book of myths
> in which
> our names do not appear.

Underwater, the diver's voice becomes polarized, then fused.
But we are made to hear the identity of this voice with the original
land voice and so to feel that on some deep level, the voice is always
androgynous.

In contrast, the speaker of "The Stranger" (*Diving into the
Wreck*, 1973) *asserts* its identity as the androgyne:

> if I come into a room out of the sharp misty light
> and hear them talking a dead language
> if they ask me my identity
> what can I say but

I am the androgyne
I am the living mind you fail to describe
in your dead language.

While the speaker is characterized as androgynous, the voice itself is not androgynous in the sense that the voice of "Diving" is. "The Stranger," rather than combining opposites in one unified voice, simply sets up a new pair of opposites: "I" against "they."

VII. The Communal "I"

As "The Stranger" shows, without the process of making the androgynous voice anew in each poem—without, in effect, an infinite series of "Diving into the Wreck" poems—the androgynous voice cannot exist. It can only be made or asserted, it cannot simply be.

It cannot simply be because the voice involves not only what is spoken, but what is heard; it involves not only the poet, but the reader. The "voice of the androgyne" must be read as such; but we are so practiced in reading the universal I that unless the voice were tagged "androgyne," we would, as a matter of habit, read "I" as the purportedly sexless universal I.

Where does that leave those who wish to help us liberate ourselves from the shackles of our own language? I think the only answer at this stage lies not in the assertion of the androgyne, but in a further exploration of the polarization process which leads to the androgyne.

This Rich does in her more recent poetry, in which she brings to our consciousness the neglected female pole of the poet's voice. In these later books, the assumption that the I is female is so pervasive that when the speakers are male, they are identified as such. For many readers this has been experienced as a step backwards, an indulgence of the personal or political concerns of the moment at the expense of the universal:

> The effect of all this on Adrienne Rich's writing has not been good, for though the poet need not manifest the organic wholeness of the traditional novelistic vision, obviously, she is responsible for more than a series of intensely noted fragments. There is some pleasure in watching her manage her combination of intimate detail and abstract rumination, in pondering her attempt to forge an authentic language deserving of the name dialogue, but we are impressed by the absence of that steady largeness of vision, those marked traits of character formed and expanding, that we marveled at in her earlier writing. The will to change has turned the poet from wholeness to analytic lucidity.[13]

What is striking about this and other critical reactions to Rich's recent work is that one can completely agree with the description of what has changed but not agree with the negative valuation put upon it. The dynamic movement of almost all the recent poems *is* a dialogue—between male and female, the old and the new, the universal I and the emerging communal I. Indeed, the vision has more to do with the clarity of analysis than with assertions of wholeness:

> If they call me man-hater, you
> would have known it for a lie
>
> but the *you* I want to speak to
> has become your death
>
> If I dream of you these days
> I know my dreams are mine and not of you
>
> yet something hangs between us
> older and stranger than ourselves
>
> like a translucent curtain, a sheet of water
> a dusty window
>
> the irreducible, incomplete connection
> between the dead and living
>
> or between man and woman in this
> savagely fathered and unmothered world
> ("From an Old House in America," Part 5).[14]

"From an Old House in America" explores a new quaternity, with the "I" of the present female speaking to the "you" of the past male.

Significantly, the place of the present male is empty. In the old male-female house, only the woman is present, alive, struggling to understand what could bring to birth a new (male) "you." In the past, man created woman in his own image. But this man is dead. For the new birth to occur, the present "I" must first understand "She," the past wife, and then re-create a new present.

And so the "I" of the first few sections speaks *of* the past wife but *to* the dead husband. In Part 7, the I moves out to become the Whitmanesque particular-in-the-universal ("I am an American woman . . ."), but with the particulars not of man but of woman. In Part 8, the voice is no "I" at all, but an "eye," a language carrying images. Among these, in Parts 9 and 10, appears the image of a woman, a she, and then multiples of she, the voices of the dead past.

In Part 11, we are back to the present I, but one whose past has been revealed so that the reader, male or female, is led to understand the radical polarization that follows:

> I cannot now lie down
>
> with a man who fears my power
> or reaches for me as for death
>
> or with a lover who imagines
> we are not in danger

The particular I becomes a communal I, one pole of a (female) "we"—(male) "they" opposition (Parts 12 and 13). Then the I disappears altogether. We are left with a scene, two voices speaking as in a drama (Part 14):

> *I try to understand*
> he said
>
> *what will you undertake*
> she said
>
> *will you punish me for history*
> he said
>
> *what will you undertake*
> she said

The dialogue is followed by a section in which the narrator seems to be identified with the female in her judgment of the male: "if you have not recognized / the Mother of reparations." By the end of these stanzas, however, the voice is clearly speaking to the female: "if you have not come to terms / with the women in the mirror." Thus, what has begun as the judgment of the male in Part 14 becomes in Part 15 the judgment of the female's progress toward self-revelation:

> if still you are on your way
> still She awaits your coming

In the last part (16) we come across the quotation-response pattern familiar to us from the earliest of Rich's poetry:

> "Such women are dangerous
> to the order of things"
>
> and yes, we will be dangerous
> to ourselves

But now the communal I answers the voice of the Fathers out of a weight of its own history, the history Rich has created for it in the poem. It is the particular voice of a woman speaking universally for all women— it is the communal I. Thus, when the speaker concludes the poem by saying "Any woman's death diminishes me," the statement is more than a mere assertion of personal feeling; it is a statement of fact about the "me" of the voice of "Everywoman."

The question arises: How will this polarization of the female voice in Rich and other poets affect the language?

To venture some predictions: First, as is already happening, female readers will become less inclined to offer their willing suspension of disbelief to the (male) universal I. The implicit instruction to the reader of the universal I is "See as I see; this is human." But now, when faced with something like the following, women and sensitive male readers will be less likely to empathize, to share the experience of the poet, than to analyze, to observe him doing what he is doing:

> I will have to accept women
>   if I want to continue the race,
>   kiss breasts, accept
>   strange hairy lips behind
>   buttocks. . .
> ("This Form of Life Needs Sex," Allen Ginsberg).[15]

A woman of the past might have experienced this as a "view of women"; now she is more likely to experience it as "a view of a man-viewing-women." In effect, women will begin to read the universal I as (male) I and to test any view of the world against their own experience. In doing this, they will be responding to the (male) I as men have responded to the (female) I for centuries—as particular, not universally human:

> Re-vision—the act of looking back, of seeing with fresh eyes, of entering an old text from a new critical direction—is for us more than a chapter in cultural history: it is an act of survival. Until we can understand the assumptions in which we are drenched we cannot know ourselves. And this drive to self-knowledge, for woman, is more than a search for identity: it is part of her refusal of the self-destructiveness of male-dominated society.[16]

Since language is its history, the (male) universal I will never be completely abolished, but it will be seen in a new light, as an assertion of universality from a necessarily limited (male), even if communal, viewpoint.

Given our culture and the history of our language, a truly androgynous voice is probably impossible to sustain. Yet, liberated from the tyranny of assumed (male) universality, perhaps we— female and male—can achieve true community, talking and listening

to one another and working toward the union of opposites within
each psyche that makes wholeness possible.
    But not yet. Now and for many years to come, Rich and other
poets will be exploring a new I—political, polarized, female:

> There are words I cannot choose again:
> 'humanism   androgyny
>
> Such words have no shame in them, no diffidence
> before the raging stoic grandmothers:
>
> their glint is too shallow, like a dye
> that does not permeate
>
> the fibres of actual life
> as we live it, now . . . ("Natural Resources").[17]

    Rich's recent, much publicized criticism of the term "androgyny"
calls for some comment, particularly in the context of this paper,
which sees the model of androgyny as a useful way of looking at the
development of her work. This is not the place for a political critique
of the term nor for an extended discussion of the topic, as was carried on in *Women's Studies* in 1974 (Vol. 2, no. 2). But I would like
to address, briefly, two of the much repeated criticisms of the term
because they have a direct bearing on the approach I have taken to
Rich's poetry.
    The first and most frequently heard objection is that the context
for the concept is itself sexist. Jung, the major explorer of the alchemical archetypes, is suspected—quite rightly, I think—of viewing women through a deeply masculine bias. Thus, when describing
the anima and animus or other aspects of the process of individuation, Jung sometimes seems to confuse females with female archetypes. The possibility of this confusion is, I believe, the greatest
danger in the feminist use of archetypal criticism. Whenever male/
female distinctions are made, stereotyping can result. But given our
long history of male/female distinctions, I think it is more helpful to
learn to think clearly about these distinctions than to avoid them.
An archetypally oriented criticism acknowledges male/female distinctions but locates them in the symbolism of the individuation
process, not in individual males or females.
    The second objection to "androgyny" is that, to quote Rich,
"the very structure of the word replicates the sexual dichotomy and
the priority of *andros* (male) over *gyne* (female)."[18] My response to
this is that syllabic position does not necessarily imply value priority.
If, for example, we looked at the word spatially rather than syllabi-

cally we would see the two sexes joined together in space, *andros* on the left, *gyne* on the right. Or if we see the word as historical, as I prefer to do, we have the *andros* (male) in the beginning giving way to the *gyne* (female) in the end—perhaps the prophetic analogue to a historical shift from male values to those of the female.

The most helpful way of using the term is to focus not so much on the image of the androgyne as on the process leading to wholeness that the image has usually symbolized. Looked at in this way, criticism of androgyny can be seen as an emphasis, even if overstated, on what is needed in order to achieve such wholeness. As Rich's poem asserts, the word androgyny "does not permeate / the fibres of actual life / as we live it, now." The individuation process requires us to experience the opposites before we can have conscious wholeness. We must know what the female is before we can presume to describe what a picture of the union of opposites—the androgyne— might look like.

UNIVERSITY OF TEXAS, AUSTIN

Notes

[1]Adrienne Rich, "When We Dead Awaken: Writing as Re-Vision," *College English*, 34 (October 1972), p. 18.

[2]See, for example, Albert Gelpi, "Adrienne Rich: The Poetics of Change" and Wendy Martin, "From Patriarchy to the Female Principle: A Chronological Reading of Adrienne Rich's Poems," both collected in Barbara C. Gelpi and Albert Gelpi, *Adrienne Rich's Poetry* (New York: Norton Critical Edition, 1975), pp. 130-48 and 175-89, respectively.

[3]Ibid.

[4]New York: Norton, 1976.

[5]*A Change of World* (New Haven: Yale Univ. Press, 1951), foreword, p. 11.

[6]*Poems Selected and New, 1950-1974* (New York: Norton, 1975), p. 247.

[7]"When We Dead Awaken," pp. 21-22.

[8]*A Change of World*, p. 10.

[9]David Kalstone, "Talking with Adrienne Rich," *The Saturday Review: The Arts* 4 (22 April 1972), p. 57.

[10]"When We Dead Awaken," p. 24

[11]In *Leaflets* (New York: Norton, 1969).

[12]Rich calls this "a poem of reconnection with a part of myself I had felt I was losing—the active principle, the energetic imagination, the 'half-brother' whom I had projected, as I had for many years, into the constellation Orion" ("When We Dead Awaken," p. 24).

[13]Robert Boyers, "On Adrienne Rich: Intelligence and Will," in Gelpi and Gelpi, p. 159; rpt. from *Salmagundi*, 22-23 (spring-summer 1973), pp. 132-48.

[14]In *Poems Selected and New, 1950-1974.*

[15]In *Planet News, 1961-67* (San Francisco: City Lights, 1968).

[16]"When We Dead Awaken," p. 18.

[17]*Ms.*, December 1977, p. 62.

[18]"The Kingdom of the Fathers," *Partisan Review*, 43, 1 (1976), fn. p. 30.

PRISONER IN UTOPIA

Giovanna Pezzuoli*

As a specific literary genre developed over the centuries, the utopian writings have usually taken the form of abstract dreams and intellectual constructions, all completely unrealizable. In this sense they immediately differentiate themselves from utopian experiments, which are essentially collective dreams or projects. These experiments represent, although in a contradictory way, an anticipation or a realization of behavior and needs that are in conflict with the existent society.[1]

Despite the particular purposes of various utopian visions—whether reformist, moralistic, eugenic, satirical, anarchic or communist—they are all characterized by paternalism, by the negation of individual self-determination. The mores are imposed uniformly; they may be more or less liberal, but in any case they do not allow transgressions.

According to Aldous Huxley, contemporary author of some utopias and anti-utopias, it is the passion for rules that destroys the good intentions of most utopian constructions. All activities, in work or in leisure time, seem to be organized in a rigid way, individuals are subjected to every kind of classification, and human complexity is simplified in the name of "nature," taken time and time again as law.

The result is that utopian states, whatever their specific form of government, seem to be definitely totalitarian. With few exceptions (probably Fourier or De Sade), utopias set themselves in oppo-

*This article presents an overview of the author's book *Prigioniera in Utopia* (Milan: Il Formichiere, 1978), to which the reader is referred for a fuller treatment of the subject.

sition to surrounding reality, inventing a logic of their own and a complex of rules for each aspect of human life and denying the individual the possibility of expressing him or herself outside an oppressive uniformity. This is particularly true, as we will see, with regard to the erotic dimension of these undesirable worlds. Individual space is extremely restricted in the name of the superior purposes of these tyrannic legislators: from Plato's *Republic* to Campanella's *Città del Sole*, from Cabet's *Icaria* to Wells's *A Modern Utopia*, the worlds of the imagination do not include the concepts of transformation, renewal and disorder.

The written utopias are essentially characterized by denial of practical action; it is not an accident that the epochs in which utopian writings are concentrated coincide with periods of regression following large social transformations, such as the Counter-Reformation or the epoch following the French Revolution.

Utopias, which cannot coexist with the reality around them, bind themselves necessarily to the idea of an "Elsewhere," a non-place where imaginary inhabitants can settle, challenging the laws of the known world. The geographical situation of utopias, born at the same time as the great voyages of discovery at the end of the fifteenth century, has continued to move toward the unknown: today it is beyond the moon, in the science-fiction reality of other universes.

If a persistent leitmotif of Utopia is the elimination of the autonomy of the individual, who is subjected to the immutable rules fixed by the uncontested will of the utopian writer, it is not accidental that the main target of the tyrannical attitudes of these solitary reformers is the female sex.

The anti-feminism of the utopian writers, which also exists in the ironic matriarchal utopias and in the communist utopias, reflects the patriarchal laws of the different historical periods. The women who populate the utopian worlds synthesize the various myths expressed by male culture, transposing to the imagination the distorted sexual ideas of the author.

In a hypothetical design of the feminine condition in Utopia, prostitutes are shut away in brothels in order not to corrupt the honest women, who are usually subjected to their husbands in very traditional monogamous marriages (see, for example, Restif de la Bretonne's *Le pornographe*, 1769, and *Les gymnographes*, 1777). The idealization of the mother and the corresponding contempt for sterile women are recurring themes in all the utopias based on eugenic purposes (Plato's *Republic*, 389-369 B.C.; Francesco Patrizi da

Cherso's *La città felice*, 1551; Tommaso Campanella's *La Città del Sole*, 1602; H. G. Wells's *A Modern Utopia*, 1905; Richard Walter Darré's *Neuadel aus Blut und Boden*, 1930). Sometimes there are emancipated women who are included in a productive context, but this kind of emancipation does not involve the refusal of the traditional role of housewife; on the contrary, that role is justified by the fact that it is chosen freely (see William Morris' *News from Nowhere*, 1890). The authors may also allow women to engage in free love in order to affirm them again as the easy prey of the male (as in Wilhelm Heinse's *Ardinghello und die Glückseligen Inseln*, 1785), or they may make them—along with commodities and children—common property, relegating them to a kind of ghetto (an example is Anton Francesco Doni's *Mondi celesti, terrestri ed infernali degli Academici Pellegrini*, 1552). The height of social elevation is reached by the matriarchal woman, who is free to exercise her tyranny on male subjects because of a complete reversal of roles (as in Simon Tyssot de Patot's *La Vie, les aventures et le voyage en Groënland du Rév. P. Cordelier Pierre de Mésange*, 1720, and Ludvig of Holberg's *Iter Subterraneum*, 1741). This reversal, in any case, often becomes grotesque and ironic.

It is doubtful whether any man could ever conceive a feminist utopia, for the male writer's progressive ideas cannot include the abolition of male power. Even the most coherent and comprehensive formulations of sexual egalitarianism[2] reproduce in their societies an image of woman as independent in her activities and free from moralistic bonds but nevertheless always devoted to male pleasure. She lacks real self-determination because of her unlimited sexual availability.

Because my focus is on Italian writers, I am choosing two significant periods—the Counter-Reformation and the early twentieth century, the beginning of fascism in Italy—in order to outline some examples of utopias. We can define these as eugenic or ambiguously emancipatory and examine their relationship to the historical situation of the two periods.

Generally, utopian writings developed only after the dissolution of the medieval world. The new rational order of the Renaissance confirmed and strengthened patriarchal authority. In the meantime, the restoration of Roman law, which replaced the feudal customs, excluded women more and more from inheritance rights by taking away from them the administration of the feif as well as the right to exercise justice. The female paid the highest price for the so-called Renaissance revolution: as the capitalistic system began to emerge, work in the guilds and in the corporations was organized for men's exclusive profit. Little by little men took over the most technical jobs, which had previously also been done by women, thereby pushing the latter into agricultural and domestic work. The decline of women's wages as compared to men's reflects the progressive deterioration of women's condition during the sixteenth and seventeenth centuries.

Luther relegated women to spindle and distaff, but the Council of Trent called for the excommunication of anyone who maintained that the matrimonial condition was superior to virginity and celibacy. Already by the end of the fifteenth century, when the repression of the Inquisition was reaching giant proportions and public denouncement was sufficient reason for condemning a woman to the stake, a papal bull of Innocenzo III had accused witches of having sexual relationships with the devil. In Sprenger's *Malleus Maleficarum* the male monopoly of the medical profession was legitimized by denouncing openly the activity of the popular healers: "If a woman dare to cure without having studied she is a witch and must die."[3] Thus in the epoch of the "triumph of rationality," the persecution of witches through trials, torture, and the stake began to take place; it was to continue for two hundred and fifty years.

The period following the Council of Trent was characterized by the involution and dispersion of the culture of opposition. It was during this period that Tomasso Campanella's utopian dream took place. The great rebels such as Campanella and Giordano Bruno, who were accused of heresy and persecuted because of their resistance to the established social and cultural order, developed their philosophical thought in the Kingdom of Naples, which was then under Spanish rule. The *Città del Sole* (1602), one of the numerous utopian cities of the sixteenth and seventeenth centuries, can be regarded as the idealization of the program of an unsuccessful Calabrian insurrection. This was basically a political-religious conspiracy, because of which Campanella was arrested in 1599.

Campanella resumes the strictly eugenic message that began in Plato's *Republic* many centuries before. Thus, as in Plato, the need to abolish the family in order to allow the best sexual matches coincides with an apparent democratism (education is similar for men and women while taking into account the relative weakness of the latter) and communist practices.

The "Solari" practice a rigorous communism with respect to women and commodities. Their houses, eating places, and recreation facilities are all common and clothing is all of the same color.

There are two basic principles guiding the morals and the religion of the inhabitants: procreation and education. Reproduction is controlled by prince Mor (Love), who together with Pon (Power) and Sin (Wisdom) cooperates with the Sun or "Metafisico," who is the leader of the town and has spiritual, temporal, religious and civic powers. Under the direction of Mor the "masters" decide the best sexual matches, having carefully examined the anatomy of inhabitants during wrestling matches in which men and women participate in the nude. The "Solari" mate every three nights at the time fixed by the Astrologer, after digesting their food and praying. Outside the place used for procreation there are statues of heroes (male) from which the women draw the necessary inspiration for a propitious conception. In spite of the rigid control of procreation, in which men and women are submissive instruments of the species, there is always a category of women who are "sterile" or "pregnant" or "without value," with whom the men can have sex for "delight" or "necessity" without submitting to the usual rituals.

We have already said that contempt for sterile women is an essential theme of all the eugenic utopias. Thus, woman's sexuality becomes a process completely channeled for reproductive purposes and her identity begins to coincide completely with that of the mother. And while motherhood may be honored and idealized, it is only in order to exercise more control over the progeny.

The "lively, strong and fine" women must instead compensate for the physical weakness of old priests and sages, who might otherwise generate a weak and ill progeny. The women who are forced to provide supplementary services for the sake of satisfying the "respectable" erotic needs of males seem to suffer the most from this eugenic super-exploitation. They are assigned to compensate for the men's defects and deficiencies, without in any way benefiting from a similar treatment: old and weak women do not receive the support of strong and handsome men. The laws are also stringent in other aspects of repression of the feminine sex. The only crimes that are punished with the death penalty, besides repeated sodomy, are the use of make-up and the wearing of high-heeled shoes by women.

In spite of the predominant religious-metaphysical aspect of Campanella's preaching, many elements of his vision of the future can be related to the specific historical situation. The rules limiting procreation to the strongest and healthiest people may be a reaction to the high birth rate among the poor of southern Italy; in addition, the communist ideas may arise as a rejection of the surviving feudal organization.

In utopian writings one is struck by the continuity of eugenic themes and by the corresponding persistence—under the guise of egalitarianism—of male privilege; it occurs from the Sparta of Lycurgus up to the Aryan selection promoted by the Third Reich. In the eugenic utopias envisioned throughout the centuries, women, being responsible for the continuity or selection of the species, are subjected to very strong persecution, ranging from the foolish precepts (concerning food, morality, etc.) imposed on pregnant women up to the higher morality required in order to have control of the progeny.

The emphasis on the mother, this time subordinated to her fertility, becomes a macroscopic theme within fascist policy at the beginning of twentieth century. The great fear of a decrease in the birth rate, which led to drastic anti-Malthusian measures, is at the center of Mussolini's policy. At the end of 1926 the institution of the tax on unmarried people anticipates the new political trend of the "demographic battle," in which the power of nations is identified with the number of their inhabitants or soldiers engaged in war. Thus is confirmed the feminine mission: to be devoted to a Stakhanovistic reproduction of children within a utopian, precapitalistic family. The woman is required to be proud of "serving the country as the greatest *Mamma*, the mother of all good Italians."[4]

This ideology of motherhood in the service of the state resulted in Italy—and even more so in Germany—in a massive expulsion of women from the labor force (above all from the service occupations) in an attempt to save the institution of the family and in a reaction to the crisis of the patriarchal authoritarian model.

This policy seems to be inspired, in spite of some differences which have to be stressed, by the utopian design of the main exponents of the futurist movement. According to the project outlines in *Democrazia Futurista* (1919), the woman is no longer the private property of man; however, far from reaching real autonomy, she becomes the property of the future and of the development of the race. "We—Marinetti says—speak in the name of the race, which requires aroused males and impregnated women. Fertility, for a race like ours, is, in case of war, its primary defense."[5] It is precisely from this esthetics and ideology of war—which is the most regressive aspect of futurism—that emerges the myth of Marinetti's superman, who knows only a genital eroticism that is totally directed toward procreation.

> Nothing is natural and important except coitus, which has as its purpose the 'futurism' of the Species . . . The carnal life will be reduced

exclusively to the function of maintaining the Species. And that will
be an enormous gain for the growing stature of the man.[6]

The emphasis placed by futurism on the rejection of family, marriage and above all feeling does not provide a solution for woman.
She, free from coercive monogamous mechanisms, is still a slave to
the imperial mission of Italy as well as to the need of Italian men to
prove their virility. In this sense the statements of the futurist Antonio Blangino seem to anticipate the demographic policy of fascism:
"Regard every drop of his [the male's] vitality as a seed of a coming
life, and in this way the state will never lack human material for defending itself and for using its wealth . . . ."[7] Though the unmarried
mother is rehabilitated (her illegitimate sons may be useful), the sterility of "ignoble" females is doubly despised. Furthermore, Blangino
says: "Do not let the fertile seed of the male be wasted in a sterile
and rotten uterus . . . ."[8]

In spite of the strong sentiments expressed by futurism against
the church and authority and its support of the extension of suf-
frage to women and the abolition of domestic slavery, the depiction
of woman that basically arises from this utopian manifesto affirms
again her absolute subordination to the aims of the state, aims which
are unrelated to her autonomy and freedom.

The examples outlined above give us an indication of the persistence of chauvinism even when the authors want to challenge existing society with projects of social renewal. Essentially, it is only
with the birth and the development of a women's movement that a
feminist utopia—as well as a real transformation of life—can be
created and strengthened.

MILAN, ITALY

Notes

[1]Between the seventeenth and the nineteenth centuries, many utopian communities developed, above all in the United States. They were essentially characterized by
new forms of sexual relationships and by different patterns of organization of social
life. These pre-marxist experiments range from the puritan sect of the Shakers, where
celibacy was strictly imposed, to the community of the Oneida Perfectionists, where
complex marriage was established in order to overcome monogamous bonds. These

communities, either religious or lay, were almost always characterized by respect for women and by a new definition of their role.

²See, for example, Dom Léger Marie Deschamps, *Le vrai Systéme ou le Mot de l'enigme métaphisique et morale*, 1771-74; or Charles Fourier, *Théorie des quatre mouvements et des destinées générales*, 1808, and *Le nouveau monde amoureux*, 1835.

³The *Malleus Maleficarum* was a basic text of the German and Spanish Inquisitions during the sixteenth century. It helped and supported the "mission" of the prosecutors of witches by providing detailed descriptions of the "crimes" of women.

⁴*I fasci femminili* (Milan: Libreria d'Italia, 1929), p. 20.

⁵Filippo Tommaso Marinetti, "Contro il matrimonio," in *Teoria e invenzione futurista*, ed. Luciano De Maria (Milan: Mondadori, 1968), p. 128.

⁶Ibid., p. 131.

⁷Antonio Blangino, "La tassa di filiatico e gli Istituti di allevamento della prole," in *Teoria e invenzione futurista*, p. 142.

⁸Ibid., p. 143.

FOUCAULT'S FANTASIA
FOR FEMINISTS:
THE WOMAN READING

Marcelle Thiébaux

I would like to ask you to imagine—quite apart from one another—
two figures. One is a man reading, bending in deep concentration
over his book. The "other" (and I ask you to think of that word in
Beauvoir's sense, too) is a woman reading, bending in deep concentration over her book. My principal interest, as this is to be a foray
in feminist criticism, is in the woman reading. I shall be referring to
Michel Foucault's "Fantasia of the Library" [*La Bibliothèque Fantastique*],[1] in which the central figure of a man reading, a saint to be
exact, allows Foucault to develop his metaphor for the accumula-
tion of discourses—books mirroring books to infinity. Out of the
saint's holy book rise up the lurid ghosts of other books, which in
turn yield up further books. These book-engendered visions are
seen to acquire a remarkable solidity. the solidity of discourse, and
discourse becomes an "event" that leaves the original act of reading
far behind. As my focus is to be on the discourses that may be constructed upon woman reading, I shall return to her shortly.

But first, let us consider Foucault's method and ask what it is
that we can learn from Foucault, those of us who would formulate
a feminist approach to literature. Foucault does not after all address
himself very often to the situation of women. Nor is he a "masculinist" critic whose philosophy is a "male-female biological model,"
like the Christian, Freudian, or Jungian systems of thought, in
which a binary opposition is set up between "man as self, or norma-
tive, and woman as other, or deviant."[2] When, however, he refers
in *The History of Sexuality* to the "hysterization" of women—that

is, the redefinition of the feminine body morally, emotionally, and medically as a womb,—he applies his method to illustrate the deprivation of power of "women, adolescents, children, patients" by "men, adults, parents, doctors."[3] With respect to women he demonstrates that whatever their condition, women are apt to be controlled by the weight of discourses about them.

For Foucault teaches us to look for the complex network, the "grid" of discourses, which societies, scholars, experts, poets, physicians, are capable of constructing upon acts, experiences, and events. Such discourses displace what they refer to and are themselves events of considerable power. In *The History of Sexuality*, for instance, Foucault argues that the multiplication of discourses about sex—from the confessional and the penitential manual to the psychiatrist's couch and the orgasmic notations of Masters and Johnson—have succeeded in displacing the sexual act. More seductive than sex, talking about, writing about, "discovering truth about sex" becomes itself a sexual activity. A *scientia sexualis*, whose aim is the formation of knowledge, displaces an *ars erotica*, whose aim is pleasure.[4] Sex is transformed into discourse. So, too, do the discourses about women displace what women are, do, or feel.

To illustrate Foucault's method in another of his works, that on punishment and prisons,[5] we may point to the discourse that proliferates on the matter of crime. This discourse comprises prison records, tables, statistics, classification of types of crimes, plans for prison architecture, daily routines for convicts, theories of recidivism, psychoanalytic assessments—all of which are the product of an "army of technicians," wardens, doctors, chaplains, magistrates, psychiatrists, educators, and penal personnel. Such experts can create a whole "verbal machinery," which may range from the trivial to the elaborate, acquiring autonomy and eventually the solidity of a monument.

Discourse or verbal machinery may achieve considerable distance from the crime, from the act or event. A wide division occurs between the thing itself and the thoughts or utterances about it. "Things and words [are] separated from one another"; the dissolution of "the profound kinship of language with the world" is a phenomenon that Foucault identifies as modern.[6] The sign is then capable of detaching itself from the thing it purports to signify—the discourse from the event—and this "grid of language" gains a more powerful reality than that event. As Edward Said observes, writing of Foucault, "the signifying power of language far exceeds, indeed overwhelms, what is being signified."[7] There does not even have to be an explicit subject upon which to erect a network of discourses. The so-called subject may be an old unexpressed assumption; it can simply be the elusive thing we are trying to find out about, the mystery. In this pursuit, one discourse can lead to another. Upon a "possible corpus of knowledge" we construct concepts (to paraphrase Foucault), carve out domains of analysis, and proceed to build further "scientific techniques and discourses."[8]

Discourse can be visual as well as written or spoken. Foucault describes the old public spectacles of punishment: chain gangs cleaning the streets, criminals doing penance in the market place, carrying the instruments of their crimes, while authorities distribute signs, placards, and posters. All constitute a "legible lesson," "an ever-open book," a discourse, a "permanent lexicon of crime and punishment" that can be "consulted" by the law-abiding and law-fearing populace.[9]

Here, it will be noted, Foucault uses the "book," the "lesson," the "lexicon" metaphorically to represent decipherable discourse, whether verbal or visual. It is to this metaphor of the book, multiplied into the library in which rows of "murmuring" books mirror other books, that I would like to draw our attention. For Foucault, the library is a repository of discourses, floating free. Edward Said points out that "A library is a total, infinitely absorptive system, infinitely self-referential (think of the catalog, of the unlimited possibility of cross-references there and in the books), numerically vast in its elements, and impersonal." And, "the library holds together, in ways Foucault tries to specify, the staggeringly vast array of discursive formulations, an array whose essence is that no source, origin, or provenance, no goal, teleology, or purpose can be thought through for it."[10] In "The Fantasia of the Library" Foucault analyzes Flaubert's *Temptation of St. Anthony*, which he calls (perhaps not entirely accurately) "the first literary work whose exclusive domain is that of books."[11] Here he unravels his theory of discourses.

We open Foucault's book, then; he is just opening Flaubert's novel. At the center of that work is a man reading. The man, St. Anthony, sits before his cave in a kind of theater surrounded by hills. His posture is familiar in medieval iconography: we have seen such a St. Jerome, a St. John of the Apocalypse. Now Anthony in turn opens *his* book, a Bible over which he pores in an effort to banish evil thoughts that menace. "Far from being a protection [the book] has liberated an obscure swarm of creatures and created a suspicious shadow through the mingling of images and knowledge."[12] The very pages seem to dissolve, yielding concrete images. Flaubert writes that the table supporting a book filled with black letters becomes a bush covered with nightingales. The black and white of print upon page turns into the black network of streets on a white uniformity of houses, streets and houses that Anthony has known. The book, although it is sacred scripture, releases foul shapes: "orgiastic palaces, drunken emperors, unfettered heretics, misshapen forms of the gods in agony, abnormalities of nature—arise from the opening of the book, as they issued from the libraries that Flaubert consulted."[13]

For this is Foucault's point: the fantasies crowding upward from the pages were not dreamed or imagined by Flaubert, the result of hallucination or sleep, but the fruits of carefully documented research into histories of Manichaeism and Gnosticism, studies of obscure heresies and ancient religions, ecclesiastical memoirs, bestiaries, and the Patrologia Latina. "Fantasies are carefully deployed in the hushed library, with its columns of books. . . . The imaginary now resides between the book and the lamp." Art is erected within the archive. The treasures of the fantasy "lie dormant in documents. . . . The imaginary . . . grows among signs, from book to book, in the interstice of repetitions and commentaries."[14]

The Temptation of St. Anthony, insists Foucault, is not a work of scholarship but of art that "exists by virtue of its essential relation to books. . . . It opens a literary space wholly dependent on the network formed by books of the past."[15] When he writes that "the Bible has become a bookstore" he means that one book can generate a world of books, each of which generates yet others, to infinity. The autonomy, the substantiality of these worlds of print attest to the solidity and independence of discourses built upon discourses and exerting the power of authentic events. Foucault's "Fantasia of the Library" provides a visualization of discourse. As for St. Anthony, his frenetic visions form a wreath-like interplay together with our own several perceptions (of the text, of him, his book, his visions) as reader-spectators. Like discourse, this "wreath" sustains "the simultaneous existence of multiple meanings"[16] which displace and outweigh the initial figure of man reading.

We have seen how the man as reader, or the figure of Reader/Book, has been analyzed and developed by Foucault to illuminate his metaphor of the library as a mirroring, echoing repository of discourse, discourse that ultimately envelops the Reader/Book. We should like as feminist critics to appropriate for ourselves the figure of Reader/Book in female terms. We must revise Reader/Book to Man/Book and Woman/Book. Our task will be to discover a figure of woman reading whose reading gives rise to a discourse experienced by herself as well as by us as readers and upon this entire complex investigate the possibility of further discourse. This must be the work of a female author who has used to similar advantage the figure of Woman/Book, wringing from the simple act of reading a stream of fantasies and discursive events that "take over." Eleven years before the first fragments of Flaubert's *St. Anthony* began to appear, Charlotte Brontë published *Jane Eyre* (1846). In her first chapter we encounter a woman reading, a figure that will prove useful for our explorations.

We know that Charlotte Brontë was herself a reader, one who did not assimilate her sources tamely but who tended to improve vastly upon them. Unable to accept Milton's Eve, for example, as a charming inferior whipping up dulcet creams in Eden, Brontë revised her upward as a Titan, large and strong as the hills, one from whose body Titans would spring.[17] Elaine Showalter tells us that the Brontës did not feel congenially inspired by their female literary predecessors either, forerunners like Jane Austen, Hannah More, or Maria Edgeworth, and cites Charlotte Brontë's letter expressing a preference for looking into her own heart, writing "what throbs fast and full, though hidden, what the blood rushes through, what is the unseen seat of life."[18] It must rouse our curiosity therefore to know what book it is that keeps young Jane Eyre in retirement in the window seat while the others are out for a stroll in wild wet weather. Separated from them by her "physical inferiority," she retreats to the window alcove, gathers up her feet and sits cross-legged like a Turk within the drawn red curtains. Thus is she withdrawn, "shrined in double retirement," the scarlet drapery closing her in at the right side and the clear gray-lighted window panes affording her light at the left. The framed, absorbed figure of the reader suggests the exotic and bookish iconography of the reading saint. Jane is, of course, no saint, but anti-saint, "like a Turk." Not only is "Turk" the medieval enemy of Christendom but a term used of a barbarously behaved child. No saint, nor is this a book of devotions any more than it is a novel of Maria Edgeworth's. It is Bewick's *History of British Birds*, a favorite of Charlotte Brontë's, it is said. Unlikely though this seems, Bewick may as well be a book of Jane's future, for it proposes a shadowy map of the terrain, both interior and physical, that she is to traverse. First, the book presents a collection of desolate northerly landscapes and seascapes, with verses and captions. Wrecked boats, eerie moonlight, a grave, a moonrise are among them. The only suggestions of actual birds are the statement that these are birds' haunts and the image of a "black, horned thing [a bird?], seated aloof on a rock" (chap. 1). Out of these Jane will elaborate her sketchbook pictures of the haunted mind. When she eventually shows her portfolio to Rochester, her fanciful pictures will stir his deep interest in her and provide setting and imagery for the main events of her life. In her sketchbook the drowned female corpse, the gold begemmed bracelet in a cormorant's beak; the wild-eyed female head with electric hair and a lunar reflection on its neck; rising into the landscape; another giant head and bloodless hands thrusting hugely against an iceberg—all indicate the personal discourse that Jane has drawn into the chill spaces of Bewick's *British Birds* (chap. 13).

Landscape is always before the reader's eye throughout the novel. What happens in *Jane Eyre* is a child's passage to womanhood. From a girl of ten to a woman of thirty, Jane journeys through a landscape of the passionate soul, projected in the narrative through storm-beaten wintry wastes; bleak frosts and drear, blood-red or glaring white moonlight nights; iron skies; fever-soaked fens, the dream garden of a midsummer night; and tranquil, tree-sheltered Ferndean. Place-names provide clues to stages in her progress: at the Dantesque entrance to Lowood, into which she follows her guide, she notes that "we descended a valley, dark with wood" where there is heard "a wild wind rushing amongst the trees." Gloomy Thornfield is the scene of crucifying passion, its meaning reinforced by the mad wife's tearing of Jane's bridal veil, an echo of the passion in Luke 23:45 ("And the sun was darkened, and the veil of the temple was rent in the midst"). She is an outcast in penitential Whitcross. At the last the wanderer finds a home and love in pleasantly named, sylvan Ferndean. The dark and storm-ridden stretches of that journey seem to roll up, much intensified, out of the dreary pages of Bewick's *British Birds*, while the "pleasances" evoked are their contraries. Bewick not only provides descriptions of landscape, both inner and outer, but anticipates the names and natures of Jane's lovers. The death-white reservoirs of frost and snow offer the material of the icy wastes of loveless love that will be held out by St. John Rivers, whose motifs are ice and water. Out of Bewick's solitary rocks and promontories—"the rock standing up alone in a sea of billow"—will emerge Rochester, the man of earth, the rock, whose "granite-hewn" features Jane observes at Thornfield. As the terrain indicates Jane's wandering life and her lovers, her tempestuous nature is pointedly noted by a speech of Rochester, who builds a further unwitting discourse on Bewick's terrain. Accusing her of having never felt love, of being possessed of an unawakened soul, he lashes out:

> Floating on with closed eyes and muffled ears, you neither see the rocks bristling not far off in the bed of the flood, nor hear the breakers boil at their base. But I tell you—and you may mark my words—you will come some day to a craggy pass of the channel, where the whole of life's stream will be broken up into whirl and tumult, foam and noise: either you will be dashed to atoms on crag points, or lifted up and borne on by some master wave into a calmer current—as I am now (chap. 15).

Yet, soon realizing love, Jane continues in a similar vein of imagery with an erotic undertow:

> Till morning I was tossed upon a buoyant but unquiet sea, where billows of trouble rolled under surges of joy. I thought sometimes I saw beyond its wild waters a shore, sweet as the hills of Beulah; and now and then a freshening gale, wakened my hope, bore my spirit triumphantly towards the bourne: but I could not reach it, even in fancy,—a counteracting breeze blew off the land, and continually drove me back (chap. 15).

If Rochester is "rock" and "earth," and Rivers "water," Jane is of course "air"—her name Eyre occuring in English as an early variant spelling of that light element. From the beginning Jane sees herself and is seen by Rochester as a sprite (spiritus, breath, air), a phantom, an elf, half fairy, half imp, a changeling. Is she "substance or shadow," "dream or shade?" "Mademoiselle is a fairy," declares Rochester, "a little thing with a veil of gossamer on its head" whom he will take to the moon.

A sprite is a thing of air, and so is a bird. Despite its promising title, Bewick's *British Birds* is, as we have noted, empty of birds—at least in the pages we are invited to glimpse in chapter 1. Birds frequent these places, "the solitary haunts of sea-fowl." But the bird must be another discursive event out of Jane's life that is wrought upon the pages of Bewick. And birds do abound. Midsummer days are "as if a flock of glorious passenger birds had come to the cliffs of Albion from the south." The mad wife's cry is more terrible than that of "the widest-winged condor on the Andes." Hunger, the vulture, sinks beak and talon into the fugitive Jane. But the chief denizen of air is Eyre herself. Rochester sees Jane as "a curious sort of bird through the close-set bars of a cage: a vivid, restless, resolute captive is there; were it but free, it would soar cloud high" (chap. 14). "You open your eyes like an eager bird, and make every now and then a restless movement" (chap. 27). "Jane be still, don't struggle so, like a wild, frantic bird that is rending its own plumage" (chap. 23). Her other lover, Rivers, observes how his sisters take her in and cherish her as they would "a half-frozen bird some wintry wind might have driven through their casement" (chap. 29). Jane contrasts herself to the birds, "emblems of love" "faithful to their mates," while abhorring herself as she flees from Thornfield (chap. 27). "I am no bird" (chap. 23), protests Jane, yet we see her frequently engaged in flight, and there will be nesting. "Eyre" is a noble bird's nest, from the older form eyrie or airie.

Again, Jane's sketchbook constitutes a further discourse on Bewick, for we see within its happier pages her drawings of "birds picking at ripe cherries, of wrens' nests enclosing pearl-like eggs, wreathed about with young ivy sprays" (chap. 8). Elsewhere she draws "a glimpse of the sea between two rocks; the rising moon . . . a group of reeds and water-flags, . . . an elf sitting in a hedge-sparrow's nest, under a wreath of hawthornbloom" (chap. 21). At arboreal Ferndean, journey's end, Jane achieves love and peace. But not before she finds the blinded Rochester with "a desperate and brooding look" of "some wronged and fettered wild beast or bird," looking as if he belonged in Bewick: "The caged eagle, whose gold-ringed eyes cruelty has extinguished, might look as looked that sightless Samson." His raven-black hair yet reminds her, like Nebuchadnezzar's, "of eagles' feathers; whether your nails are grown like birds' claws or not, I have not yet noticed." He appears "a royal eagle chained to a perch," beseeching her, "a sparrow" (chap. 37). In fact this noble bird at last can nest in his Eyre, for the inherited fortune, the nest-egg is hers.

Bewick's *British Birds* offers the woman as reader—both Brontë and Jane—the sourcebook of her own life's sketchbook, the landscape of her wanderings, its principal personages metamorphoses of air, water, rock and birds. This web of imagery and events has been constructed upon the several pages of Bewick that lay open on the young reader's lap in the first chapter. Shadowy footnotes of yet another book, the Bible, superimpose themselves on the edge of Bewick: the land of Beulah, the temple veil, Samson, Nebuchadnezzar. In Bronte's novel, then, the woman reading becomes the woman creating the book *Jane Eyre*, which in turn contains the sketchbook of her emotional life. (For Bronte, Jane's continual pencilling of drawings is a surrogate for the writer's real business of writing, as it is with Chopin's artist-protagonist in *The Awakening*.) We may observe that in both *Jane Eyre* and *The Temptation of St. Anthony* the figure of Reader/Book constitutes a fictive event upon which the author has multiplied discourses. It is these discourses, visions, adventures, wanderings, image-clusters, books within books mirroring other books, that displace the original act of reading and thus become principal events of the narrative. Another of Foucault's ideas demonstrated here is that books change their meanings depending on the use and reading they are subjected to. Patristic writings become the stuff of forbidden fantasies; ornithology turns into an emotional and passional landscape.

Woman/Book is absolutely at the center of the novel, just as is Man/Book at the center of the saint's visions. In both works the visions rippling up from the pages are validated by the centrality of the reading figure who is so immersed. We read over their shoulders, their visions become our visions, the words and images of their books take on the concreteness of experience. But what if the author were to put Woman/Book somewhat off-center, where she must inevitably be found in a work where the perspective is masculinist or patriarchal? The patriarchal perspective (whether it is a man's or a woman's) of a woman reading judges her to be not engaged in anything of importance: she may certainly be interrupted to attend to a more appropriately female task. In Mary Gordon's *Final Payments*, the heroine Isabel Moore tries to work out a life that embraces whatever of secular sainthood is possible (though anachronistic) in our time. She sees herself as a Mary, a Teresa of Avila, learned saints of Christian parable and history, rather than a Martha or a Thérèse of Lisieux, saintly, domestic women. But when her tormenter, the housekeeper, finds her reading, she breaks in: "I ask the child to put down her blessed book for one moment and pick up her room and she does not, does *not* give me the courtesy of looking up from her book even" (p. 28). When the perspective is entirely patriarchal, we as readers are not allowed to look over the reading woman's shoulder and into the pages of her book (thus sharing and validating her reading experience) but may only observe her off-center through a fictional observer or the patriarchal author himself. The fictional observer can thus construct a personal discourse upon the figure of Woman/Book, and we find that the substance of that discourse will be sexual. We may even choose to adopt Foucault's term from another context and say that the discourse "hysterizes" the woman reading. Reader/Book and Man/Book may be sexually neutral events, but Woman/Book is susceptible to discourse that is sexually charged. Flaubert's Emma Bovary as woman reading is addicted to novels that induce erotic dyspepsia and help her to destroy herself. The temptations of Emma are weak inglorious things compared to the cosmic temptations of St. Anthony to become one with all being. In writing of his heroine, Flaubert (says Foucault) simply drew upon the "prodigious reserve" of *The Temptation*, transforming "its inexhaustible treasure into the grey provincial reveries of *Madam Bovary*."[19] Patriarchal permission is given to women to be readers provided their reading limits them to their role and status as sexual beings.[20] Where patriarchal discourse addresses itself to the fictive event of woman reading three elements will be contained in that discourse: *rupture, redirection, incorporation.* In the figure Woman/Book, a *rupture* must be effected between Woman and Book: a woman reading a book shall be compelled to put it aside. A woman reading does not continue to read; she has a temporary look. Either she is interrupted by the author, the circumstances, the fictional observer, or she interrupts herself to take up a more "natural" female activity. This is the second element of the discourse, the *redirection* of her energies, their rechanneling into sexual conduits. The discourse then *incorporates* the woman reading into the destiny of a book like the one she has been reading, some other book, the observer's or patriarchal author's further discourse about her, and so on. In this third phase woman loses her autonomy as reader, as agent, and becomes read *about;* she is reduced to the status of text, incorporated *into* the book.

Dante records Francesca's own story of how reading about adultery stirred her and her lover's passion. The fateful kiss interrupts the reading: "That day we read no further."[21] Now she is a text in hell. Or we may refer to a famous procuring scene in English literature, in which Pandar visits his niece Criseyde on the morning of May 3rd to talk her into bestowing her sexual favors on that deserving young man Troilus. He finds her with her maidens engaged in that most futile of temporary acts for her: reading a book. He interrupts her, politely asking her what it is. It is the book of Thebes, a fallen city whose destruction prefigures the fall of her own city Troy. Her laughing answer is that it concerns a certain bishop who fell through the earth and into hell. Hell is the place to which Criseyde's later oaths condemn her. (And notice how women laugh to show that they *know* that what they are doing is unserious.) Now they both laugh; Pandar the pimp tells her to put aside the book and they will dance. When Criseyde demurs that as a widow she should be sitting in a cave and reading holy saints' lives, there is further merriment. The unspoken message, but one that will emerge in the patriarchal discourse of the poem is: "you are no reader of books; by your laughter you acknowledge this, but you shall be the subject of books." This Criseyde recognizes in her sorrowful address directly to the readers: "Alas until the end of the world, no good word shall be written or sung about me, for these books will destroy me. I shall be rolled on many a tongue!"[22] Like Criseyde, Chaucer's Wife of Bath achieves her sole identity as a mosaic of texts, a composite of hostile male utterances upon women. Even her language is textual/ sexual. One of her words for sexual intercourse is "to glose," as one writes glosses on a text: "My husband, so fresh and gay in bed, could glose me there so well that even if he beat me in every bone, I loved him."

Both Criseyde and the Wife become discursive events that displace their one time status as women readers. They are "women" no longer but have become worlds of patriarchal discourse, much as is the carefully manicured Queen of Sheba when she slithers from between the pages of St. Anthony's book and announces: "I am not a woman but a world!" Real women, as Virginia Woolf has relayed to us, may have been "locked up, beaten and flung about the room." But "if woman had no existence save in the fiction written by men, one would imagine her to be a person of the utmost importance; very various, heroic and mean; splendid and sordid; infinitely beautiful and hideous in the extreme; as great as a man, some think even greater."[23] Such is the woman of patriarchal discourse.

If a woman reading in her paved parlor in medieval Troy, or today in her bedroom in Queens, New York, can properly be interrupted to do more important things (and observe how in both places she would legitimize her reader status by connecting reading with sainthood), perhaps she can hope for sanctuary in a library. Let us use a modern example. Philip Roth's *Professor of Desire* is a work of fiction in which textual support is given to male desire, a literary autobiography which, as Foucault might say, transforms sex into discourse. The young narrator observes girls reading and tells us that for picking up or picking out girls, the library is

> a place comparable to the runway of a burlesque house in its power to stimulate and focus my desire. Whatever is imperfectly suppressed in these neatly dressed, properly bred middle-class American girls is immediately apparent (or more often than not, immediately imagined) in this all-pervasive atmosphere of academic propriety. I watch transfixed the girl who plays with the ends of her hair while ostensibly she is studying her History—while I am ostensibly studying mine. Another girl . . . will begin to swing her leg beneath the library table where she idly leafs through a *Look* magazine, and my craving knows no bounds. A third girl leans forward over her notebook, and with a muffled groan, as though I am being impaled,

I observe the breasts beneath her blouse push softly into her folded arms. How I wish I were those arms![24]

The autoerotically suggestive motions of the reading girls—hair twisting, leg swinging, breast squeezing—indicate that they are not, of course, wholly involved in reading. The fictional observer sees that at least one of them is ripe for interruption, and his interruption includes the effort to redirect her thoughts wholly to her sexual nature, as she studies "her History":

> I tell one of the girls how the sight of her breasts pressing against her arms had led me to wish I were those arms. And is this so different, I ask, pushing on with the charm, from Romeo, beneath Juliet's balcony, whispering, 'See! how she leans her cheek upon her hand: / O! that I were a glove upon that hand, / That I might touch that cheek.'[25]

Not only does young Kepesh attempt to redirect her energy, but he incorporates her into a literary text of Shakespeare's, a text surely to be found in this very library and mirrored in his interruption, his own narrative constituting a discourse on both.

The masculinist fictional observer peering over the shoulder of the woman reading is not concentrating upon Reader/Book with the same reverence as are we, the readers, when we look over the shoulder of Jane Eyre reading or St. Anthony reading. We acquiesce in the rights of those focally important readers and dreamers, and we place our confidence in their visions. But the fictional observer planted in his text by the patriarchal author is generally there to ravish away the woman reader's book and substitute his own. Both fictional observers in Chaucer's and Roth's narratives construct their own discourses on Woman/Book which include the three elements of interruption, redirection, and incorporation. Pandar persuades Criseyde to fling aside her book, writes her a new scenario in which she will play the fallen leading role, and forces her to sing lamentably about it to the audience. She will be banished to the realm of books, rolled bawdily about on tongues there. Roth's David Kepesh substitutes his own erotic discourse for whatever the girl in the library may be reading. She has been made alien. Having been reduced to the status of a patriarchal discourse, she has been effectively removed from the library by the fictional observer, who informs her that she is now a text among texts to be read by himself. Well may she poignantly reflect, with Virginia Woolf, should anyone care to listen, "upon the shut doors of the library and how unpleasant it is to be locked out."[26]

Of course, the most classically violent of interruptions of a woman reader is found in the first chapter of *Jane Eyre*. On hearing the others return from their walk, Jane reflects: "I feared nothing but interruption, and that came too soon." Her cousin tormenter, John Reed, upbraids her for reading "his" book, and crowns the whole business by striking her with the very book and felling her with a bleeding cut. All this is the prelude to being locked in the red room. Jane's immediate revenge is to incorporate *him* into Goldsmith's *History of Rome*, where he keeps company with Caligula and Nero. Furthermore, he is eventually incorporated in the novel as a rake and a suicide, having associated with "the worst men and the worst women."

The only possible library for a woman is one invented by herself, writing herself or her own discourse into it. A little-known admirer and imitator of Brontë, an American nineteenth-century writer named Julia Caroline Ripley Dorr, created a tension between her heroines and their surroundings that only their books and their libraries could assuage. The young women in *Farmingdale* (1854), *Lanmere* (1856), and *Sibyl Huntington* (1869) are would-be readers in the midst of punishing housework. Claustral space presses tightly around them in the kitchen, the bedroom, and the parlor. There is a wealth of documentation about woman's daily round in these female spaces—washing dishes, setting a sponge, peeling turnips, drying apples, scalding the milkpans, getting the tubful of laundry on the clothesline before the neighbors do theirs, overhauling the closets, spinning and weaving, tatting purses, counting lost stitches in a sampler that is always soft with sweat. From time to time as a special harrassment, a huge carpet-rag basket is brought down from the attic for a sorting, clipping, piecing chore.

The heroines of these novels are readers who hoard every scrap of print they can find, while grim-lipped mothers, aunts and older sisters levy fierce prohibitions. Books are locked in cupboards. In *Farmingdale* the girl is denied permission to attend the village school, "for the more she goes to school, the worse it'll be." Her aunt promises to teach her at home, but as the exultant girl looks about for books and writing paper, her aunt makes it plain that she means to teach her the arts of domesticity. Referring presumably to paper linings, she tartly raps out, "I've got all the paper she'll want this winter in my bureau drawer." In *Lanmere* the heroine is compelled to read the only books the household boasts: "The Duties of the Convalescent" and "How to Derive Spiritual Benefit from Personal Afflictions." Her mother sternly advises, "Read them without becoming interested."

Dorr's novels contain ongoing discourses about books, the art of composition, the "craving for utterance," what women poets feel or do not feel, the values of novel reading. The woman as thwarted, starving reader is a central figure of these domestic novels; her release will be found in schoolroom or library. Sibyl Huntington, a stormy young woman, longs for learning with hunger and thirst. Like Jane Eyre, she finds reprieve from the tyrannies of home by going away to school. At Oakwood an inspiring headmistress (modelled on Jane's Miss Temple) befriends her; through study she experiences an unprecedented "joy of conscious mental growth." The emblem of this growth is a dead-seeming fuchsia plant, brought up from the cellar, whose barren stalks Sibyl nurtures back to green life with water, care, and sunlight.

> Just so sudden and rapid was my growth during that never-to-be forgotten term. Perhaps my fuchsia was not aware how suddenly it burst into bloom and beauty. . . . But I felt the new influence at work upon me in every fibre of my frame. I laid down every night and rose up every morning with a thrill of delight that I shall never attempt to describe. It would be nothing less than profanation to lift the veil from so sacred, so profound a mystery.[27]

The fuchsia suggests Sibyl's release and intellectual flowering and will recur at a later point in the novel in Dorr's rhapsodic account of the library in which Sibyl will find her ultimate refuge.

As a governess at Greyhurst in her "quakerish" (like Jane's) dress, Sibyl discovers the library, "enchanted ground to me."

> In the library there were treasures that seemed to be beyond all price—costly books of which I had read, but which I had never hoped to see with mortal vision, huge folios of engravings,—a whole art-gallery in themselves,—which opened to me a world of new delights.[28]

In the schoolroom, with its "well-filled bookcase," orrery, globe, and other delights including a chair and table for Sibyl, two iconic figures are to be seen which provide the necessary clues to what a woman's library needs, as much as it needs books:

> Upon the table stood an exquisite figure of Silence, with her finger on her lip; and above it, in a simple frame, hung a lovely picture of a young girl poring over a large book, that might have passed for a missal.
> I looked around with brightening eyes.
> "How convenient and pleasant it is!" I exclaimed.[29]

Forced by family illness to return home to take up the domestic burden once again, Sibyl finds herself "starving for books." Salvation proves to be a position tutoring the niece of a new neighbor, an industrialist-philanthropist named Mark Halsey. Sibyl reflects, "Maybe it will appease my hunger a little if I can but breathe the atmosphere of a library once again. I have felt for many months the same prolonged torture, the same 'hungering and thirsting' that I felt before I went to Oakwood."[30] It is worth noting that Dorr allows Sibyl to reserve her expressions of thirst and hunger, her beating heart, her ardent transports, for Mr. Halsey's library, rather than for the Mr. Halsey whom she will marry. Their courtship is handled swiftly and discreetly, unruffled by ecstasy.

While Mr. Halsey's mother, a sweetly dotty old lady, makes continual preparations for an imagined pilgrimage to Jerusalem, complete with sandals and penitential garments, Sibyl's yearning guides her to her own shrine, the library. Mr. Halsey's library is as rich and verdant as a forest:

> The wood-work was of dark oak, well polished; the wall paper a soft neutral tint, threaded with a delicate arabesque of green and gold. The carpet was a mat of green and brown mosses, flecked here and there with a dash of sunshine. Just opposite the door at which we entered was a large bay window, around and over which luxuriant ivies were making haste to clamber; and within the recess, upon a light Chinese table, bloomed a large scarlet geranium, one mass of brilliant coloring, a white rose, and two or three graceful, drooping fuchsias. All the brightness in the room seemed centered there. On the right and left the walls were lined with books from floor to ceiling. An oval table stood in the centre of the room, and here and there in the large apartment were grouped great, comfortable looking chairs, cozy lounges, and low, cushion-like ottomans.[31]

The female tutelary geniuses that preside are two statues, one of " 'dreamy-lidded' " Psyche, the other "a Diana with bended bow, severe, calm and self-contained." The figures precisely body forth the rapt and inward beatitude of a woman free to be alone in a library.

Several observations may be made concerning the three passages quoted from *Sibyl Huntington*. First, despite the fact that books are said to be contained in libraries and schoolroom, their pages are not literally opened for us or for Sibyl. Books are mentioned, but their texts remain dark, unrevealed. What is emphasized is the library as significant space. The confined, mortal space of kitchen and parlor, contracting to even smaller spaces—the milkpan and the workbasket, the inside of the bureau drawer and the locked cupboard—has miraculously opened out into a new book-beatified space in which the discourse on reading and writing can establish itself and continue to reflect and reproduce itself. All that is contained in this space shines forth to constitute a visible discourse. One library is a treasury; another is penetrated by sunlight, a place for growth: the presence of fuchsia, Sibyl's emblem of intellectual and emotional burgeoning, appears as a sign to her. The very carpet is like the moss of a forest floor. Although the library is permitted to exist only within the patriarchal space of the husband's house, yet it appears to be detached—out of doors, in nature.

Library space also has a sacral aura. The Greyhurst library is something that might not have been hoped for "with mortal vision." Having become new female space, the Greyhurst schoolroom and the Halsey library are protected by female divinities or icons. The Greyhurst schoolroom is watched over by a figure of Silence; above it broods an image of a girl with a missal-like book. The Halsey library has two female divine presences: Psyche, the self-absorbed self and soul, and Diana, sternly chaste. Fuchsias bloom. Interruption, sexual redirection, incorporation into a patriarchal discourse could not violate such spaces. The library instead of being a repository of explicit books (from which other books, visions, or discourses might arise) is itself a sheltered and eloquent discourse. It is a "theater"—another image of Foucault's— in which meaning shines forth through displacement. The books are silent but the discourses of the female icons have displaced those of the books, just as the flowering fuchsia has displaced the woman reader and the entire library has displaced the husband himself.

For although this is the husband's library, we do not see him in it. The husband is relegated to the outside, to domestic space elsewhere in the marriage. All the signs *within* the library are subversive: the fuchsia of intellectual female flowering; the self-contemplating goddess of the psyche, the self and soul; and Diana, the severely chaste goddess. Instead of building a discourse arising from books that might have been based upon earlier male discourses, Dorr displaces books as completely as she displaces the husband. The library is the subject of the discourse of love. The discourse of love is wrought upon the library, not upon the husband.

Foucault's "Fantasia" has been fruitful for us because of his poetic style of thought. He has provided us with a provocative metaphor of the library as a treasury of discourses, capable of being converted to an instrument of literary criticism. The figure of Reader/Book is for Foucault a metaphor for man in relation to knowledge. This knowledge continually alienates and eludes him, as each book generates further books in an infinity of discourses. Just so do signs replace actions and become in turn replaced by further signs. Of course, we have exploited the metaphor to show how a work of fiction generates discourses that acquire lives of their own in a grid or network of images, finally separating themselves from the original books and the original act of reading. When the female reader is not central—as is usual in masculinist writing—the patriarchal discourse embraces the whole Woman/Book image and incorporates it into a further discourse of its own, wrenching the woman from the book and creating a realm of knowledge from which the woman is excluded, shut out of the library entirely. The only way for woman to create her own discourse is to create her own library.

Did any Victorian woman realistically enter marriage to contemplate herself as a growing plant in a library, as a dreamy-lidded Psyche under the protection of the virgin goddess Diana? It is as if in *Sibyl Huntington* the author has hardly dared to depict the woman reading in the library. Instead a visual discourse is generated upon the absence of woman reading, although woman reading has pervaded the entire novel as an elusive mystery, a thing to be sought for, hoped for, like knowledge itself. Sibyl stands with one foot on the sill, on the threshold of the temple, in love with the books within it. But her books are not seen giving rise to libraries-full of words, visions, and fantasies. She is content to take in the mysterious radiance of the place. The library is rich with images and icons that eloquently convey the rebel's legible lesson (which may, after all, be also contained somewhere in one of the books) that woman's place must be in the library of her own invention, and man's place is out of it. The true "fantasia" here is in the theatrical space of the library itself, which provides the setting for those icons, that flower, legible lessons of subversion.

ST. JOHN'S UNIVERSITY

Notes

[1]"La Bibliothèque Fantastique" served as the preface to Flaubert's *La tentation de Saint Antoine* (Paris: Gallimard, 1967), 7-33. This paper will refer to the translation, "The Fantasia of the Library," by Donald F. Bouchard and Sherry Simon, in Michel Foucault, *Language, Counter-Memory, Practice: Selected Es-*

says and Interviews, ed. Donald F. Bouchard (Ithaca: Cornell University Press, 1977), pp. 87-109.

[2]Dorin Schumacher, "Subjectivities: A Theory of the Critical Process," in J. Donovan, ed., *Feminist Literary Criticism: Explorations in Theory* (Lexington: The University Press of Kentucky), p. 34.

[3]Foucault, *The History of Sexuality*, Vol. I: *An Introduction* trans. Robert Hurley (New York: Pantheon Books, 1978), pp. 104, 99.

[4]Ibid., p. 71.

[5]Foucault, *Discipline and Punish: The Birth of the Prison*, trans. Alan Sheridan (New York: Vintage Books, 1977).

[6]Foucault, *The Order of Things: An Archaeology of the Human Sciences* (New York: Pantheon Books, 1970), p. 42.

[7]Edward W. Said, *Beginnings: Intention and Method* (Baltimore: The Johns Hopkins University Press, 1975), p. 285.

[8]Foucault, *Discipline and Punish*, p. 111.

[9]Ibid.

[10]Said, *Beginnings*, p. 302.

[11]Foucault, "The Fantasia of the Library," p. 92.

[12]Ibid., p. 94.

[13]Ibid., p. 95.

[14]Ibid., pp. 90-91.

[15]Ibid., p. 91.

[16]Ibid., p. 98.

[17]Sandra Gilbert cites this from *Shirley*, in "Patriarchal Poetry and Women Readers: Reflections on Milton's Bogey," *PMLA*, 93 (1978), 371.

[18]Elaine Showalter, *A Literature of Their Own: British Women Novelists from Brontë to Lessing* (Princeton: Princeton University Press, 1977), p. 103.

[19]Foucault, "Fantasia," p. 88.

[20]Examples can be found in ancient literature of women permitted to be "writers" as well, so long as they *literally* weave their stories (*texo*, weave, is also the word for literary fabrication, as in "text" and "context"), and so long as their stories refer to their condition as sexual beings. Helen in the *Iliad* weaves her guilt into a tapestry; Philomena's rape is woven into her handiwork when her tongue is cut out; Penelope's woven and unravelled web represents her temporizing with her suitors.

[21]*Inferno* V. 127-38.

[22]*Troilus and Criseyde*, Book II, lines 78-119; Book V, lines 1058-1061.

[23]Woolf, *A Room of One's Own* (New York: Harcourt, Brace and World, 1929, 1957), p. 45.

[24]Philip Roth, *The Professor of Desire* (New York: Farrar, Straus and Giroux, 1977), p. 14.

[25]Ibid., p. 15.

[26]Woolf, *A Room of One's Own*, p. 24.

[27]Julia C. R. Dorr (1825-1913), *Sibyl Huntington. A Novel* (New York: G. W. Carleton; London: S. Low & Son, 1869), p. 37.

[28]Ibid., pp. 82-93.

[29]Ibid., p. 91.

[30]Ibid., p. 209.

[31]Ibid., p. 214.

EL ANGEL DEL HOGAR: THE CULT OF DOMESTICITY IN NINETEENTH-CENTURY SPAIN

Bridget Aldaraca

> La mujer es mucho más buena de lo que
> generalmente se la juzga; es un ángel
> creado por Dios para sufrir con nosotros,
> enjugar nuestro llanto y producirnos las
> únicas felicidades que hay en la tierra: el
> amor y la familia.
>
> Antonio Fernández García,
> *El Correo de la Moda* (1877)

Introduction

In Victorian literature, the female stereotype known as "The Angel in the House" has survived in such familiar characters of Dickens' novels as Little Nell (*The Old Curiosity Shop*), Esther Summerson (*Bleak House*), and Little Dorrit. In American literature, perhaps the most famous angel of all is still Louisa May Alcott's Beth in *Little Women*. If the twentieth-century reader still remembers Little Nell or the self-effacing, child-like Little Dorrit it is not because of their stature within the novels. Dickens' angel-women are not powerful and dramatic heroines like Anna Karenina or Jane Eyre, or intelligent and lively like Elizabeth Bennet of *Pride and Prejudice*. If we remember Dickens' world, the evil of the London streets and tenements, we tend to forget the insipid goodness and homogeneity of his Victorian angels.

In Spain, it would be difficult to call to mind a comparable set of Dickenesque heroines because the best novelists, Galdós, Pardo

Bazán and *Clarín*, writing in the 70s, 80s and 90s, have no place in their novels for the sentimental heroines in vogue in the first half of the nineteenth century. Perhaps only Marianela (possibly an accolade to Dickens' Little Nell, who leads her grandfather around the pitfalls of vice) can be said to be truly an Angel out of the school of Dickens and Mrs. Gaskell. Readers of Spanish literature must turn to such sentimental hacks as Pilar Sinués de Marco, Angela Grassi, or coming up the scale slightly, Fernández y González, in order to find the equivalent Martas and Marías.

Our purpose here is not to relocate in literary history the countless *ángeles del hogar* whom posterity has quite rightly relegated to oblivion, but rather to comment on the fact that an ideal of womanhood which can be synthesized in the phrase *el ángel del hogar* lived and breathed in the pages of the women's and family magazines which abounded in Spain from the 1850s on. In articles written for *La Moda Elegante Ilustrada, El Correo de la Moda, La Guirnalda, El Museo de la Familia*, and others, the growing public of Spanish middle-class women were instructed in minute detail on how to be and act, what to do and think, and, especially, what they as superior beings might never aspire to.

The conflict that results from women's inability to realize this male ideal is the motor force that activates the plots of many of the great nineteenth-century realist novels. Emma Bovary, Dorothea in *Middlemarch* and Galdós' Fortunata have in common the fact that they will not fit into the prescribed mold of the submissive and self-abnegating *ángel del hogar*. The absence of this literary stereotype in the pages of Galdós and Pardo Bazán does not signify an absence of the cultural attitudes expressed in the refrain, "La mujer en casa y con la pata quebrada" (so much more threatening and arrogant than the relatively colorless English equivalent, "A woman's place is in the home"). The ideology of domesticity, which limited a woman's social existence to a sphere of activity within the family institution gained in strength throughout the nineteenth century and Spain is no exception. The following study documents and analyzes the ideological content of *el ángel del hogar* in order to throw light on the novelists of the same period who criticized, dissected, and as often as not defended in their novels the values which this literary stereotype embodies.

The definition of separate spheres of interest

The exceptional importance given to the social function of the moral education of children by their mothers in the home forms the nucleus of the doctrine of separate spheres of influence. The doctrine raises, at least theoretically, the social status of women, but it also becomes a new justification for the indispensability of women in the home and exercises much more suasion over women themselves than does the coercive stance of the church fathers.

In Spain during the period between 1845 and 1900, the manifestation of the doctrine of separate spheres of influence is characterized by an important contradiction. On the one hand, the relation of the family to the total social structure is constantly emphasized: "¿Qué es el *Estado*, sino la exacta imagen de la familia? ¿Qué es la *Patria*, en su más primitiva acepción, sino la reunión o asociación de los padres?"[1] On the other hand, the intimacy of domestic life is placed in opposition to the activities that take place in the public sphere. The institution of the family and the public sector are perceived as separate social spaces, theoretically complementary and interdependent, but more often depicted as antagonistic and mutually exclusive.

> En la familia residen la virtud, el amor puro y la calma del espíritu; en los salones de grande reunión y en los espectáculos públicos están el vicio, el oleaje de las pasiones y el incentivo de los deseos impuros.[2]

Such phrases as "el contacto letal del mundo," "esa puerta llena de sombras que se llama *negocio*," and "la política . . . forma social de la revolución"[3] are used to paint an image of a world given over to materialism and the primary law of self-interest. The public sphere of finance and politics is portrayed as corrupt, unstable, chaotic and, perhaps most important of all, to a great degree unfathomable. The following quote from an early women's magazine, *El Pensil del Bello Sexo*, exemplifies the process by which a perception of the public world as materialistic and threatening provokes in turn an idealization of the supposedly isolated sphere of female domesticity as a timeless spiritual refuge, a stable locus outside the turbulent flow of history.

> Si como vosotros los que habláis de la emancipación de la mujer, no sabéis que esa sola palabra puede cortar el único eslabón que nos sostiene en la cadena de los tiempos, que detrás de la profanación de la mujer está el abismo. Vosotros los que queréis asimilar la mujer al hombre, los que queréis llenar su corazón de sus pasiones con mil ensueños de hiero y oro, no sabéis que si desnaturalizáis los únicos seres en que se hallan algunos rastros de la gracia primitiva, nos vamos a

encontrar perdidos en el mundo, sin nada que nos ate a lo pasado y
nada que nos encamine al porvenir.[4]

As this passage demonstrates, the language which is used to discuss the two social spaces is characterized by a certain vagueness, a
tendency to hyperbole and a reliance upon the clichés of the period.
The author expresses the idea that the role of women is to provide spiritual support for men and that to do so they must themselves remain pure, "unprofaned" by any contact with the world.
Women, and by extension the place where they reside, are filled with
primitive grace, an image reminiscent of the biblical Eden prior to
Adam's fall from grace, after tasting the apple from the tree of knowledge. Innocence is thus organically linked with ignorance. In the
nineteenth century, however, an image of "primitive" grace also suggests the Rousseaunian debate on "natural" versus "civilized" man
and woman. And we are reminded that *Émile* and *Sophie* must not
be evaluated by the same yardstick. The idea that the female is more
natural than the male, that is, uncorrupted by the pernicious influence of urban civilization, effectively designates the former as a
kind of noble savage and provides the justification for isolating
women from modern history under the guise of protecting and preserving the purity of their natural nobility.

The lack of specificity in describing the social space allocated to
women results in part from the fact that what is being described is
the "space" within the institution of the family. It is a metaphorical
space which describes the role of women within a particular set of
social relations rather than the physical occupation of the house,
be it a mansion, a room, or the rose-covered cottage of Dickens and
Michelet. Thus we find, given the subjectivism inherent in the process
of idealization, that the world of domesticity and the family can in
turn be described as "sweet slavery" or "a vast theatre," depending
upon whether the author wishes to emphasize the inevitable submission of women to their social role or the influence which this role
exerts upon society.[5]

An important consequence of this basic contradiction involving
social spheres that are theoretically interdependent but consistently
depicted as mutually exclusive manifests itself in the different relationship of the individual to the sphere he/she occupies. Although
man is the natural occupant of the public sphere, he is in no way responsible for the corrupt environment in which he must move. He
survives in this hostile element by virtue of his superior strength, intelligence and moral character. The home, defined not as a physical

space but as a spiritual atmosphere, is, on the contrary, the creation of the woman who occupies this domain. She is, says one writer for *La Moda Elegante Ilustrada:* "... el vínculo de los más nobles afectos, la reguladora del orden y de la economía, el iris de paz, la inspiradora del contento y buen estar de todos."[6] *Order*, the preservation of the status quo (a concept which includes economy, i.e., living within one's means but also in accordance with the social position occupied); *peace*, generally defined as harmony, i.e., the absence of strife; and *happiness* or well-being: herein are expressed the social values to which the rising Spanish bourgeoisie aspires.[7]

The symbiotic relationship between the house and the woman who occupies it had been emphasized by Fray Luis de León:

> ...porque la casa forçosamente, y la limpieza della oliera a la muger, a cuyo cargo está su aliño y limpieza: y quanto ella fuera asseada, o desasseada, tanto assí la casa como la mesa y el lecho, tendrán de suzio o limpio.[8]

Fray Luis emphasizes, in language worthy of Zola, the concrete, physical relationship between the woman and her surroundings. While cleanliness certainly remains a virtue in the nineteenth century, of greater importance is the capacity of women to engender a holy light of peace and contentment which nurtures and pacifies not the house but the members of the family: "La mujer tiene una misión principalísima en la vida, la de ser el encanto y la alegría del hogar...."[9] The precise details of how women are to accomplish their life mission often dissolve into a diffuse rhetoric in which, logically, that virtue which is the antonym of the self-interest ruling the public sphere is acclaimed as the supreme virtue: negation of self, self-denial, abnegation.

> ¡La abnegación! Qué bella palabra; cómo realza la corona de la mujer y embellece su misión sobre la tierra. Sin la abnegación de la mujer no existiera la felicidad doméstica ni llegaría a veces el hombre a los grandes destinos a que le llama la sociedad. ¡Qué sentimiento tan rico en beneficio es la abnegación!... La abnegación es la fortaleza del espíritu, el olvido del bienestar propio para pensar en el ajeno, y por eso esta virtud es necesaria sobre todo al ama de casa....[10]

The generally accepted notion that women exist to please men, which is given additional legitimization in nineteenth-century Spain by the popularity of Rousseau's treatise on education, *Émile*, is a key to our understanding of the creation of the ephemeral *ángel del hogar*. In a period of history in which the social individual is acquiring a new definition and importance, "woman" is often perceived not as an individual but as a *genre*: "Respecto al carácter y aun al espíritu, encuéntranse menos diferencias de mujer a mujer que de hombre a hombre: apártanse menos de su naturaleza las mujeres, que nosotros de la nuestra."[11] The negation of any possibility of a conflict of interests between husband and wife, the primary tenet upon which ideal (harmonic) family life is predicated, results in a consequent lack of need to address the topic of daily domestic life in problematic terms. It is therefore the conscious or unconscious negation of real experience that creates the conditions under which women may be idealized. It only becomes possible to understand the image of woman as muse, inspiration, pure spirit, and the concomitant lack of specificity in the rhetoric surrounding the *ángel del hogar* within the context of the idealization process, by takin as a starting point the negation of the real presence of woman as individual, i.e., as an autonomous social and moral being. The idealized woman gains in spiritual strength to the degree that she loses in physical concreteness, becoming a Dulcinea-like omnipresent spiritual force characterized as much by her corporal absence as she is by her capacity to inspire. Dulcinea, given substance and personality, becomes Teresa Panza.

The primary rationalization for the restriction of non-working class women to the home continues to be, in the nineteenth century, a belief in female weakness, now lauded as an enchanting "feminine" characteristic. The weakness of women, which Fray Luis defined as moral weakness and righteously condemned, is transformed into graceful feminine frailty. The despised womanly softness becomes tenderness and vulnerability, inspiring in men the noble instinct of protection. Fray Luis, with unselfconscious misogyny, insisted that women be restricted to the home in order that they not contaminate the men with whom they might come in contact.[12] Now, however, it is women who must be protected from the contamination of a corrupt *mundo*.

Beneath the cover of an egalitarian marriage contract, that is, one supposedly entered into freely by two parties of equal legal status, the *modus operandi* of bourgeois marriage is the feudal formula of service in return for protection, the wife tied to her husband by bonds of total fealty. The Catholic traditionalists insist that women must accept male protection within marriage for the simple reason that they have no alternative. The emancipation of women "son palabras que no sientan bien a las que han de vivir siempre, o casi siempre, bajo la dependencia de otro sexo, porque así lo dispuso *el* que todo lo puede."[13] Considerable effort is required to sustain the inherent disjunction between an ideology which pretends to worship women as morally superior beings and a social structure which reasserts the right of *patria potestad* through the imposition of the Napoleonic Code and, consequently, maintains a legal and economic sexual hierarchy within the family. In the case of Fábreques as well as many other propagandists of the feminine ideal, there are curious and sudden lapses from the chivalric posture. Fábreques concludes his article on a clearly threatening note as he makes clear to his reader that male protection is not something freely sought and granted (or bought), but rather a permanent aspect of the "natural" condition of women. Rebellion against the divinely ordained condition of female dependency must be paid for by social ostracism: ". . . vale más depender del hombre, llámase éste padre, hermano o marido, que vivir abandonada a la ignominia . . ."[14]

While it is safe to say that the economic and legal restrictions on middle-class women, reinforced by a long tradition of female decorum, provided a strong motive for internalizing the dogma of female dependency, clothed as it was in the seductive garb of romantic chivalry, one can still find buried in the myriad of articles that finally overwhelm the reader in their triteness and pomposity an occasional voice which takes exception to the conventional position. In an article entitled "No hay sexo débil," the author pinpoints how an insistence on female weakness may serve to mask the reality of male depotism within the family.

> El hombre quiere débil a la mujer para ejercer en su hogar un predominio tiránico que le permite calmar, ya que no extinguir, la febril ansiedad, la ardiente sed que siente de una dominación más vasta sobre el universo. El hombre quiere débil a la mujer para hacerla su juguete, para explotar su debilidad . . .[15]

Much of the wrath of those who adhere to the doctrine of separate spheres is logically directed against the feminist position that is unwilling to accept the false status of equal but separate. The following commentary, written by a regular contributor to *La Moda Elegante Ilustrada*, is an excellent synthesis of the reaction of the middle-class male (and quite often the female as well) to the provocative phrase, "women's emancipation."

> Para la generalidad de los hombres, la palabra "emancipación de la mujer", significa la resistencia del sexo débil contra el fuerte, el abandono de los deberes, la ausencia de toda virtud, de todo decoro, el desenfreno, el libertinaje en fin.[16]

The argument of the traditionalists that Christianity had freed woman from her position as slave and concubine and raised her to a status of equality with men in her role as *esposa y compañera* is used to explain away feminist demands for equal political rights and access to the productive sector. Equal rights for women, which despite the lack of a feminist movement in Spain is the subject of heated debate,[17] signify primarily the right of middle-class women to a degree of economic independence. And it is at this point that the bourgeois origins of our image are most clearly revealed. The material preconditions for the realization of the ideal of *ángel del hogar* are obviously a house in which the Angel can perform her duties, be it the father's, brother's or husband's, and a man who will support the Angel at a level of middle-class decency throughout her life. For the lady of the house to work, especially given the absence of genteel occupations for women in Spain, is a manifestation of the husband's lack of economic power and consequently an overt sign of downward class mobility. Thus, the *señorita* or *señora*[18] cannot work if class status is to be maintained; it is her position as a lady, not as an angel, which binds her to the economic fortunes of the head of the household.

The propagandists for the *ángel del hogar* consistently refer to woman or women without any apparent class distinction. The problems of working-class women—be they factory workers or engaged in domestic service—who are forced to "abandon their children" are seldom if ever mentioned in the women's and family magazines which are directed to an aspiring bourgeoisie whose principal concern is to draw a sharp line between itself and the lower class. The fact that "woman" is referred to as a homogeneous universal is a sharp departure from the practice of writers prior to the nineteenth century. For the earlier writers, awareness of class and of the fact that lower-class women do not share in the privileges of the upper classes or have the same social obligations is their distinguishing trademark. In the case of the nineteenth-century ideologues, the linguistic eradication of class lines is, in part, a result of the failing prestige of the aristocracy as a model for the community. But the creation of an ideological world in which men and women become universals, with no personal history grounded in class origins, also reflects the tendency of the dominant bourgeoisie to impose its ideology upon the rest of society. One could say that in the process of fabricating their image of the ideal wife and mother, the propagandists fall victim to their own illusion of an egalitarian society.

The moral banner of the bourgeoisie, still steeped in the tradition of patriarchy, is religion, private property and the family. Our analysis of the ideological significance of the *ángel del hogar* is greatly clarified by underlining the fact that it is the family which is on the pedestal, high up and out of the mire, rather than a lone Venus or *Pieta* figure. The image of the Angel is never presented in isolation, but always with the necessary accoutrements that bring her into existence: the cradle, the thimble and sewing box, and, if not a spinning wheel in the late nineteenth century, perhaps a sewing machine. But above all, she is surrounded by the family members, for she exists *only* to serve them.[19]

The movement for women's rights must therefore necessarily be perceived by the Catholic traditionalists as a direct threat to their position, which links together Christianity and the sanctity of the bourgeois family. The following quote from an article entitled "La emancipación de la mujer" exemplifies the tautological reasoning essential to any perception of the world that sees in the status quo its own justification.

> Jesucristo vino al mundo porque la mujer, para cumplir la misión generosa que Dios le tenía fijada, necesitó que viniera Jesucristo: esclava, guardó en su seno, como el santuario guarda la divinidad, su propia redención: y como para merecerla títulos debía exhibir a la faz de las generaciones, Dios le dio el título de Madre: esa es la dignidad suprema de la mujer; Ahora bien: en el seno de nuestra sociedad cristiana, acaso por completar la serie de las aberraciones dolorosas, se vio a la luz del progreso esa amenaza de emancipación impía que hasta de pensamiento ofende: y aunque contrario a todos los preceptos cristianos, también esa funesta idea, como otros delirios del Siglo XIX, cuenta con entusiastas defensores en paises que se tiene por muy cultos, ¿qué voluntad satánica rasga así, al pie de la cruz, la bandera del cristianismo, ni qué puede esperarse más que eso de la filosofía moderna? . . .

And in an unusually straightforward style, the author concludes by defining precisely the limits of women's equality to men: ". . . la mujer no debe ser nunca igual al hombre en derecho social, sino su compañera."[20] The strident tones used to defend the inviolability of home and motherhood may be said to serve as a linguistic barometer that measures the gap between the projected male ideal of the perfect wife and mother and the inevitable failure of women to realize it. The quaintness of the author's use of theological catch-phrases ("qué voluntad satánica," etc.) does not, however, detract from the very modern attempt to professionalize housewifery and motherhood, making this activity the only possible career open to women. Men will earn degrees as doctors and lawyers; women, to realize their social role, must fulfill the title imposed upon them by Christ.

Until they enter into the sacred state of motherhood, there is no space for them in modern Christian civilization.

Traditional education of women and the concept of modesty

The basic contradiction between the perception of the public and domestic spheres as two antagonistic worlds and the belief that the family is the primary cell in an organic whole which is, in turn, the State, the nation or, in the case of the Krausists, the harmonious community of nations, is resolved at the level of rhetoric by the allocation to women of the social responsibility for exerting a civilizing influence on the members of the family within the structure of the Christian home. Female influence is embodied in the husband and male children and only through them is it able to transcend the home. In an article entitled "Instrucción y educación" from the popular family magazine *El Museo de las Familias*, which was published from 1843 to 1870, the author begins by asserting that: "La educación puede decirse que es la institución moral del hombre . . ." and concludes with, "Nada más moral, nada más instructivo y provechoso para la humanidad que la escuela del cristianismo."[21]

The school of Christianity is what defines and shapes women's attitudes and actions. The author leaves no doubt as to the content of woman's influence in the home, as well as the status of female influence in relation to patriarchal authority.

> Sin solicitarlo, estamos recordando la saludable influencia del cristianismo, porque el cristianismo dio a la mujer su dignidad, y la concedió el maravilloso derecho de servir de vínculo a la sociedad. En cuanto a la marcha gradual de la educación, la mujer participa de la influencia moral del hombre. El niño crece y se forma en el seno de la familia, bajo la autoridad del padre, pero también bajo las tiernas caricias de la madre; . . . En esta distribución de deberes para la educación, es preciso reconocer que ambas influencias marchan de consuno en busca de la unidad. La influencia del padre por la imagen de la autoridad, la de la madre por la imagen de la sumisión. . . .[22]

Throughout the nineteenth century, the traditionalists' concept of an adequate female education never really transcends a knowledge of the basic *labores*, elementary literacy, and all of this crowned with a firm indoctrination in Catholic dogma, since

> esta compañera angelical, después de Dios la debemos al cristianismo . . . Sin esta virtud la sociedad conyugal sería un laberinto funesto erizado de espinas, que lastimarían el corazón y tormentarían el alma.[23]

One of the most widely repeated clichés of the period, that men make the laws and women the customs (which is, in part, a statement of the failure of attempts from the Counter-Reformation through the eighteenth century to codify social behavior through the Sumptuary Laws),[24] also reflects a growing awareness of the family institution as a socializing agent in which dominant values, such as women's submission to male authority, are or are not perpetuated.

Education, conceived of as *moral* education, therefore centers around the correct development of instincts and sentiments manifested by the children in socially approved comportment, rather than the development of the intellect, the capacity to reason.

The arguments emphasizing women's superior authority in the terrain of sentiment evolve from an extrapolation of the belief in the basic intellectual inferiority of women with respect to men. Since the rationalization of separate but equal spheres precludes the notion of inferiority, the realm of sentiment, of emotions, must be elevated and dignified in order to provide a balance of power between mind and heart and thus maintain the illusion of equality. "Nególe el cielo a la mujer la fuerza y la energía física e intelectual que concediera al hombre; pero dotóla en cambio ricamente de una imaginación vivaz y creadora, de un corazón sensible y generoso . . ." writes one of the contributors to *El Correo de la Moda* in 1877.[25]

Yet by defining women as brainless creatures ruled by an instinctive need to love and be loved, by sensibility rather than sense, a kind of Frankenstein's monster is created over whom the master may, at any given moment, lose control. One of the controlling agents used to keep women within defined limits of socially accepted behavior is the perpetuation of the ideal of "innate" womanly modesty. The idea that modesty is a natural (i.e., an ontological) characteristic of women is a reiteration of the belief in the essential difference between the male and female nature. But it is to Fray Luis de León, unencumbered as he is by nineteenth-century romantic chivalry, that we must turn in order to see, in the clarity of his logic, how the image of the demure woman rises out of a profound belief in women's intellectual inferiority or in man's superiority.

> Porque, assí como la naturaleza, como diximos, y diremos, hizo a las mugeres para que encerradas guardassen la casa: assí las obligó a que cerrassen la boca . . . Porque el hablar nasce del entender, y las palabras no son sino como imágenes, o señales de lo que el ánimo concibe en sí mismo: por donde assí como a la muger buena y honesta, la naturaleza no la hizo para el estudio de las sciencias, ni para los negocios de dificultades, sino para un solo officio simple

y doméstico, assí les limitó el entender, y por consiguiente les tassó las palabras y las razones . . . El estado de la muger en comparación del marido es estado humilde: y es como dote natural de las mugeres la mesura, y verguença. . . .[26]

For Fray Luis the manifestation of female modesty through silence is a logical result of the fact that women have nothing to say worth hearing by any man. If Saint Paul ordained that women be silent in God's house, man, imitating the deity, follows suit in his own. The ideal of the wife's humble submission to male authority in the home remains intact in the nineteenth century, in spite of such cover-up phrases as "equal influence," "women's sphere" and the "companion-wife." But the form that this affectionate and grateful submission takes does change as a result of the new model of family life: the ideal of bourgeois domesticity which provides not only physical shelter but the private society of wife and children for the husband to enjoy. The ideal wife, *la mujer ilustrada*, who should adorn not only her body but also her mind in order to supply companionship to her husband, is defended by traditionalists and progressives alike, although the content of her *ilustración* is conceived of in very different terms. Nor is it surprising, given the fact that a modicum of education is equated with urbanity (that is, with gentle breeding), that an educational varnish should be defended on the grounds that "una mujer ilustrada hace más suave y fácil la vida del hogar."[27] Submission to one's husband can now be defended as a manifestation of decorous behavior; fighting, arguing, any form of defiance is uneducated, improper comportment.

In addition to the definition of modest and proper female behavior in the home as silent, or sweetly vocal, obedience to male authority, the question of prescribed female comportment in the public sphere forms an essential element of the canons of decorum.

La virtud más necesaria en una doncella, es la modestia: y conviene que por extremada, a todos sea notorio . . . para que si en el barrio sucede un escándalo, de la doncella tan recatada nadie crea cosa mala.[28]

The idea that a woman's modest behavior is her only protection against public opinion and that her own self-restraint is all that prevents society's watchdog, *el qué dirán*, from consuming her emphasizes again two previously noted elements of the public sphere: 1) it is a male terrain; women who leave the home forfeit the right to male protection, and 2) men are not responsible for what occurs in their terrain. The ultimate social authority, public opinion, is an impregnable power; nameless and faceless, the public voice emanates from no definable source. Free to create and destroy reputations, it cannot be controlled.

Proper behavior or decorum defined as obedience to the prescribed social convention of a given historical period is necessarily a question of style or *moda*. One might ask if there was a particular style of decorum to which the proper young woman of the middle and upper classes aspired in the nineteenth century that distinguished her from her predecessors.

> La modestia . . . es de mayor precio si se retrata en una mirada tranquila y honesta, en una boca por donde vaga la sonrisa de la inocencia, y en unas mejillas que tiñe el carmín infalsificable del pudor[29]

writes Severo Catalina, who together with his French counterparts Legouvé and Michelet is one of the most widely read and quoted "authorities" on women in Spain at this time.

Well and good, we may say, but what does a smile of innocence look like? The very vagueness of the description tightens the author's control over his image. The modest woman wears an ephemeral smile recognizable only to its creator. That the signs of proper comportment are as much dependent on the interpretation of the individual receiver as they are on a supposedly objective norm is revealed by two passages from the ecclesiastical authority Fray Antonio Arbiol.

> La maldad de la mujer se conoce en la mutación de su rostro . . . y pues tienes la señal, no te descuides en lo que tanto te importa . . .
> Que guarden modestia en sus ojos, para mirar con encogimiento, y rubor . . .[30]

And the same arbitrary subjectivity that permits our eighteenth century moralist to read the female blush as both innocence and guilt continues to function in the nineteenth century. In a widely read medical text that circulated in an abbreviated form from 1843 to 1870 and then appeared in an updated and complete edition, Catalina's "carmín infalsificable del pudor" is cited as one of the possible symptoms of incipient nymphomania, the dreaded disease known as *el furor uterino*.[31]

This antithetical interpretation of a presumably standard sign which should lend itself to only one single reading agreed upon by social convention undermines the argument that decorous comportment will defend women against the ultimate arbiter and censor, public opinion. Women can control, within the financial and educational resources available to them according to their class, certain exterior signs: their apparel or the sedate gait and lowered voice directly associated with the demure and sheltered lady who need not leave her house to quarrel with the fishmonger or butcher because she can send a servant in her stead. But she does not have the power to define herself as a good and modest woman; this power rests ultimately in those who will arbitrarily interpret her appearance and actions: the collective and anonymous judge, public opinion.

When Severo Catalina insists that "la mujer es un ser indefinible, porque es un ser ineducado, . . ." and then goes on to say that "El principal secreto de la educación no consiste en formar mujeres sabias: debe consistir en formar mujeres modestas"[32] it is evident that education for women is consciously perceived as an additional means of control over them and, perhaps, as a *modus operandi* for realizing at last that all too evasive ideal of the perfect wife.[33]

The idea that women do not exist in their own right, that they are undefined (Catalina), genre rather than individual, clay upon which man places his imprint, becomes, as in the case of Monlau, a means of reassuring the bourgeois patriarch that his world and woman are still under control.

> *El hombre hace a la mujer* . . . la naturaleza de la mujer es esencialmente buena, dócil y simpática: por poca educación que haya recibido, es fácil completarla: *el hombre hace a la mujer* . . .[43]

But the fact that men will control the process of education and therefore its results does not reassure a certain segment of reactionary thought that has long relied on the premise that the principal weapon of control over women is their own ignorance. The duty of the mother is to "conservar dos cosas en sus hijas: la ignorancia de la inteligencia y la bondad del corazón"[35] writes Fernán Caballero to Teodoro Guerrero in a letter published posthumously in 1877.

The ambivalent attitude of the traditionalists toward female education is revealed concretely in the results of the pedagogical congresses held throughout the nineteenth century, which have been carefully documented by G. Scanlon in the work previously cited. Education, perhaps, but within limits: "Lo que no ofrece duda es que no debe fomentarse, ni menos excitar en ella, las aspiraciones a salir de su propia esfera."[36]

Middle-class women who dared to aspire to enter the liberal professions would seem to have been aware that their goals posed a threat to their male counterparts. One woman, writing in *El Correo de la Moda* in 1882, warns her readers: "Una mujer ilustre necesita ser muy humilde para que no le denominen pedante. ¡Sed estudiosas y modestas, lectoras mías! Haced simpático el tipo de la mujer médico."[37] And Catalina declares that "La modestia no es la humillación; pero está tocando con la humildad."[38] Modesty, then, is seen to be the awareness and gracious acceptance of the *estado humilde* which defines women by reason of their sex. But as the pitifully servile and ingratiating manner of the majority of Spanish women who defended their right to education and work effectively demonstrates, humility, when forcibly imposed by external forces, does indeed become humiliation.

Female sexuality and the praise of motherhood

One of the reasons that even lip service can be paid to the idea of education for women is that the traditionalists have at their disposal a whole new set of arguments dressed in "liberal" scientific language. These arguments serve to still their fears that they may be losing control of the *sexo débil* even while they foment an image of women as possessing animal instincts that may drive them to repulsive, barely imaginable extremes.

Our previous discussion has shown that the feminine ideal—the gentle and frail woman composed not of flesh and blood but of sweetness and light—masks in reality a profound and unchanged disdain for women's intellectual and physical weakness as well as a long, historically rooted male-female relationship of antagonism and distrust. This disdain is made explicit, forming the other side of the Janus head, in the medical literature, both in the textbooks and in family magazines such as *La Medicina Popular, La Salud* and the more professional journal, *El Siglo Médico.*

The following passage exemplifies the eagerness and satisfaction with which the arbiters of women's destiny accepted the contemporary biological rationalization of female dependency.

> Nunca la mujer se impondrá al hombre, según se teme, porque tantos siglos en que nuestra compañera fue toda amor y humildad, toda abnegación y desinterés, son suficiente garantía contra el caso expuesto; además, sean cuales fueran las condiciones sociales en que viva el sexo hermoso, jamás se podrá eximirse de las leyes de la naturaleza, que le arrojan en nuestros brazos.[39]

One of the most important distinctions between the rhetoric that idealizes women as angels and spiritual guardians of morality and the language of the physicians is a more frequent and overtly expressed disgust and fear of women by the latter. Their scientific vocation imposes upon them the obligation of defining women on at least an apparently materialist basis. Such a definition would be reached through empirical observation and consequently would supposedly be free of superstition and prejudice. Thus we find that while the doctors concur in the general opinion that women are all love and sensibility, the physical center of woman is not the heart but the womb.

> La matriz es el órgano más importante en la vida de la mujer; es uno de los polos de la organización feminina . . . En la matriz retumban indefectiblemente todas las afecciones físicas y morales de la mujer, el útero hace que la mujer sea lo que es.[40]

There is no question of what women may or may not want. Their reproductive potential defines and limits them to a unique social role, that of motherhood. So adamant is Monlau on this point that he insists: "A las mujeres no se les debiera permitir el matrimonio sin que previamente contase su aptitud física para el parto."[41] Staunchly defending the doctrine of separate spheres, Monlau would also impose what is a middle- and upper-class ideal onto working-class women as well: ". . . que la mujer sea una mujer, que sea una verdadera *madre* y no una obrera."[42]

The scientific explanation elaborated in the second half of the nineteenth century to explain women's supposedly greater emotional sensitivity (which in turn provides the justification for the belief that women lack emotional control) rests on the "fact" that the female nervous system is weaker and more vulnerable than the male's because it is linked somehow to the reproductive organs.

> La maternidad, que es la función principal de las mujeres, determina en ellas condiciones predisponentes del estado nervioso. La aparición del flujo menstrual, la preñez, el parto, y la lactancia . . . la conducen a este estado.[43]

The idea that certain physical types were predisposed to insanity had wide circulation in Spain and throughout Western Europe during this period,[44] and it naturally followed that women, with their congenitally inferior nervous system, must exist in a condition of habitual nervousness or neurasthenia,[45] a state which borders on madness. In a long article printed in *La Guirnalda*, the author underlines the precariousness of women's emotional stability and again reminds the reader that women are not unique individuals, but rather a single genre.

> Por último, existe encarnada en la organización de la mujer la condición histérica, que es normal en ella; es resultado del alto

desarrollo de lo emocional en su sistema nervioso, y ha existido desde que la mujer fue mujer, en todos los grados de civilización, y en todas sus variedades físicas y mentales. Está en continuo peligro de estallar desenfrenada e inesperadamente en paroxismos producidos por el menor acontecimiento . . . Esta condición histérica puede compararse a un paquete de dinamita: inofensivo mientras sus partículas están en equilibrio, terrible cuando se conmueve.[46]

The statement that women are naturally hysterics may seem merely a crude manifestation of male prejudice, but the overwhelming appearance of real hysterical symptoms among the women of the Victorian Era—partial paralysis; loss of sight, hearing or the other senses; and, especially, the presence of the choking contraction of the throat muscles known as the *globus histericus*—partially explains such an assumption.[47] Ilza Veith links the presence of hysteria and the form it takes to the social mores of a given period.

. . . The manifestation of this disease tended to change from era to era quite as much as did the beliefs as to etiology and the methods of the treatment. The symptoms, it seems, were conditioned by social expectancy, tastes, mores and religion, and were further shaped by the state of medicine in general and the knowledge of the public about medical matters . . . Furthermore, throughout history the symptoms were modified by the prevailing concept of the feminine ideal. In the 19th Century, especially, young women and girls were expected to be delicate and vulnerable both physically and emotionally, and this image was reflected in their disposition to hysteria and the nature of its symptoms.[48]

The reified image of the hysterical female as a potentially harmful weapon, "un paquete de dinamita" capable of maiming and killing, is an obvious expression of the author's fear of women. But what do men have to fear from the gentle sex? Certainly there exists a global presentiment on the part of the traditionalists that both working-class movements and the push for women's rights constitute real obstacles to the future maintenance of the status quo, the state of order and harmony to which the rising Spanish bourgeoisie aspires in order to more efficiently exert its power. But male fear of losing control over women also stems in part from empirical evidence of a female sexuality completely divorced from the glorified function of childbearing. So entrenched is the belief that a good woman does not know sexual desire that "indecorous" manifestations to the contrary were often recorded as symptoms of insanity, i.e.,of nymphomania. The theory of a hyper-sensitive nervous system is extrapolated to include greater sensitivity of the female sexual organs. *El furor uterino* is the explanation for something so repulsive and unseemly that its presence can only be rationalized by categorizing it as a mental (moral) aberration.[49]

En las ninfomaníacas se observa de ordinario una especie de incomodidad epigástrica, sugestión uterina, angustias e inquietud, arrumacos graciosos, miradas muy tiernas y expresivas, solicitaciones bajo todas las formas, actitudes provocadoras, familiaridades insólitas, ruegos y caricias lascivas, posturas lúbricas, viniendo a parar al fin a una desnudez completa y sin rodeos, y *el furor uterino* se declara con gestos y gritos desordenados, que revelan la grande exaltación de los órganos genitales. Si hay satisfacción con la cópula o sus suplementos sobreviene la calma, sin apagarse los mismos deseos, pero a la primera ocasión se reproduce el parasismo erótico, y exige nuevos actos, y se entrega el sujeto a nuevos excesos, sin que se satisfaga jamás. Cuando la castidad y el pudor no enfrenan a la mujer, los placeres venéros son en ella mucho más estrepitosos . . . Si la mujer llega a perder el freno del pudor que tanto la embellece, nadie es capaz de presentar los actos lúbricos y obscenos a que la arrastra su mayor sensibilidad sexual.[50]

What is of particular interest to us, following as it does on our discussion of the concept of modesty, is the lack of specificity in what is apparently a list of exact, and therefore concretely identifiable, symptoms of mental disturbance. The image of the obscene woman is painted in a crescendo of accumulated details, beginning with certain manifestations of unease—*angustias, inquietud*—which would certainly be socially permissible under ordinary circumstances but which become contaminated by their insertion into the total picture. If we separate out the nouns from their qualifying adjectives, the nouns per se—*mirada, solicitación, actitud, ruego, caricia, postura, gesto, grito*—provide no information concerning mental or physical health. The burden of defining and describing *el furor uterino* rests solely upon a series of adjectives—*provocador, insólito, lascivo, lúbrico, desordenado, estrepitoso*—which in turn are judgments or evaluations ruled not by the laws of medical science but rather by contemporary canons of decorum. Only the first symptom, *incomodidad epigástrica*, a reference to the previously described *globus histericus*, falls into the category of a physiological disorder. Even the apparent objectivity of "una desnudez completa y sin rodeos" could conceivably signify, given the standard of modest dress for women during this period, no more than the removal of the outer garments or the appearance of a woman in her night dress.

While it comes as no surprise to learn of the author's disgust for the disease of nymphomania (leprosy, syphilis and smallpox also provoked fear and disgust), it is important to understand why the categorization of unfortuitous sexual desire as an emotional-mental aberration, as an illness, does not protect the sufferer from a disapproval that implies a more than limited degree of guilt—that is, of responsibility—for the disease.

The work of Pinel, *Traité medico-philosophique sur l'alienation mentale* (1809), introduces the possibility that hitherto incurable mental disorders, perceived as having a functional rather than an organic etiology, could at least be controlled, if not completely cured.[51] The classification of mental illness as a *moral* disturbance (Veith points out that "moral" is used in the nineteenth century as the equivalent of the modern term *functional*) reflects the belief that the etiology of non-organic mental disorders lay in the emotional excesses provoked by some factor in the patient's environment. Thus we have the constant strictures against certain stimulants, spices, or meats; forbidden books; hot climates or cold; soft beds or sedentary occupations.[52] But this concept of mental disturbance went hand in hand with the belief in the inherited predisposition to insanity of certain physical types. *All* women belonged to this category because of an organic capacity for excessive emotion as well as a latent susceptibility to factors in the environment that provoked emotional excesses. Women were vulnerable, women were weak. Men could not control women, and they concluded that women were incapable of controlling themselves.

In 1792, Josefa Amar y Borbón sounded the warning note for women of succeeding generations: "Ultimamente se reprende a las mujeres de que son extremadas en todos sus afectos, ya de amor, ya de aborrecimiento, de enojo, de ira, de pensar, etc. . . ."[58] Excessive emotion, then, becomes passion, and Dr. Angel Pulido, in his *Bosquejos médico-sociales para la mujer*, reflects the prevalent abhorrence of passion as excess when he says:

> Yo miro el estado de pasión como una transición entre la cordura y la locura.
> Para mí, el individuo muy apasionado tiene un pie en un campo y el otro en otro.[54]

The problem of determining what is excessive (i.e., unacceptable) social behavior inevitably stumbles over the essential subjectivity involved in defining standards of feminine comportment.

> Dijimos que la mujer está más sujeta al estado nervioso que el hombre, y como más impresionable, todas las acciones físicas y morales deben ser para ella más moderadas, pues de otro modo serían excesivas.[55]

Although it may seem obvious that the medical description of the female nervous sytem as weaker and more fragile than the male's is merely a particularized version of the general belief that women are morally and physically defective, the importance of the role that medical scientists play in giving new credence to old prejudices cannot be overestimated. The scientific arguments that provided a spurious materialist explanation for women's different and inadequate physiology are cited again and again to justify women's confinement to the domestic sphere, while their radius of influence is radically abridged by their supposed incapacity to function with any degree of physical or emotional stability. As one doctor exclaims, in a lecture entitled "Carácter moral de la mujer": "*Todo* ejerce un influjo poderoso sobre organización tan frágil y delicada, sobre fibras tan débiles y profundamente irritables . . ."[56] This statement is a total negation of the possibility that women could exert influence in any situation whatsoever. They are perceived as raw, skinless material, completely at the mercy of their environment. Their capacity to act as subject rather than object is nonexistent.

The process of idealization implies reification and functions to achieve control over the idealized subject. Nowhere does this become more evident than in the physician's prescription for proper bedroom behavior. Monlau's advice to the newly wedded husband reads as follows: ". . . Que no abuse de su reciente posesión, como harto generalmente sucede. . . ." In his customary aseptic style, he explains the role of women in sexual intercourse: "El oficio de la mujer en la copulación casi está limitado a sufrir la intromisión mecánica del órgano copulador masculino."[57] This physical description is, of course, a totally dehumanized image of what is usually thought of as a human activity, but even when infused with the degree of emotion permissible to women, the restraint of decorum prescribes definite limits to active participation. The following warning is given to the readers of *La Guirnalda* en 1876:

> La mujer puede, debe amar tiernamente a su marido; pero hay límites de que no debe nunca pasar. Su título de esposa, de madre, su dignidad personal, la necesidad de hacerse respetar no deben nunca abandonarla.[58]

Tenderness but not passion is obviously the code for the modest wife, passion or lust being associated with the sexual activity that takes place between a man and his mistres or a prostitute.

But one passion, that of a mother's love for her child, is not only allowed but sanctified. "El amor materno es pues el único inagotable, el solo que nunca envejece . . ."⁵⁹ writes Doctor Jiménez. The exaltation of maternal love by the physicians is partially a result of their need to rationalize the contradiction between the negation of sexual desire in the pure woman and evidence of the disorders brought about by sexual frustration. But when Dr. Pulido says: "La fuente principal del amor es el instinto de la reproducción,"⁶⁰ the instinct to reproduce is not used as a euphemism for a desire for sexual intercourse. Women are seen as somehow satisfying whatever sexual needs they may have through pregnancy and childbirth. Thus the *need* to bear children becomes one of the few legitimate passions allowed to women. In his opening chapter, entitled "El árbol sin fruto," Pulido relates with tender compassion the heart-rending story of a modest young woman of the Lisbon aristocracy whom he visited in the insane asylum of Rilafolles.

> Padece una monomanía extraña. Cree hijos suyos cuantos niños ve. Se ha hecho necesario traerla aquí, porque a todos los besaba y quería llevar consigo, sufriendo horriblemente cuando se los separaba de ella.⁶¹

Given the fact that middle-class women were made to feel nonexistent, or at best *de trop*, until they married and bore a child, it is quite conceivable that some women would be obsessed with this idea to the point of madness. It is also possible to theorize, in light of the restraints on physical intimacy with their husbands which modest wives felt obliged to exercise, that women may frequently have turned to their children in order to enjoy a less inhibited relationship of affection and closeness. Certainly during this period the moral sanctions against kissing and caressing children were removed. Amar y Borbón, arguing against traditional parental severity, insists that a more benign attitude with children facilitates a correct moral upbringing.⁶² But her image of filial piety, a blend of respect, love, and the necessary fear of authority, is still many steps removed from the caressing, tender, angel-mother of the nineteenth century. In *El Museo de las Familias* we read:

> La naturaleza nos confía desde que nacemos al amor y a las caricias de una madre. Sus formas hermosas, su voz grata, hacen desde luego plácida nuestra existencia. Reposando entre su regazo, nos guía con su mirada cariñosa, y nos instruye con su ternura.⁶³

We have selected this passage for two reasons. First, it is an example of the typical style that relies on an enumeration of virtually synonymous and interchangeable nouns and adjectives: *amor-amoroso, cariño-cariñoso, hermosura-hermoso*, etc. And second, this particular passage highlights the extent to which the creators of the image of the angel-mother identify with the product of their fantasy. The point of view is not that of the father observing the mother with *his* child on her lap but rather that of the man-child himself, gazing up into the eyes of his mother. This same phenomenon, the identification of the adult male with the role of the child rather than that of the father, is found in an exceptionally beautiful and sensual passage in Fray Luis, where he attempts to persuade the perfect wife of her obligation to nurse:

> Porque, ¿qué trabajo no paga el niño a la madre, quando ella le tiene en el regazo desnudo, quando él juega con la teta, quando la hiere con la manezilla, quando la mira con risa, quando gorgea? Pues quando se le anuda al cuello y la besa, paréceme, que aun la dexa obligada.[64]

What is utterly foreign to the nineteenth-century image of mother and child is the erotic quality of this description, the strong overtone of sexuality.

Even though nursing was proclaimed by moralists and physicians alike to be the mother's sacred duty to her child, our general impression is that working-class women nursed not only their own but the majority of upper-class children as well. In an article entitled "Amas de cría" (1863), the author protests the fact that many middle-class women and almost all those of the upper class refused to nurse because it circumscribed their social life or because they feared it would ruin their beauty. Whether a middle-class woman nursed or not, according to this author, would seem to have depended entirely on her financial and social status, on having the resources to imitate and thus enter into the society and customs set by the bourgeoisie, who in turn imitated the ladies of the aristocracy.[65] As a result, the criticism leveled against women who employed a wet nurse became, in part, a criticism of the vain and frivolous mores of upper-class women who preferred the seductions of a *té-dansant* to those of their legitimate offspring. The antagonism expressed toward the aristocracy is paralleled by an enumeration of the vices of lower-class women employed as wet nurses: drunkeness, sexual promiscuity, greed, and slovenly personal habits. Thus we see that the insistence that "women" nurse their children represents a rejection of both upper and working class; that is to say, it is a reaffirmation of the author's own middle-class status.

It would appear that while ideally the mother should nurse, feminine weakness was considered an acceptable excuse. The repressive attitudes toward sexuality may have made nursing seem too onerous a burden to demand of so spiritual a creature. Certainly Pulido, who insists that "los pechos no son órganos de adorno," backs off from any physical contact in his description of the mother and child.

> La casta matrona que vela al lado de la cuna por el fruto que el cielo la ha concedido, que la adormece con dulces cantos y suaves balanceos, y que deposita sobre su blanca frente un amoroso ósculo . . . representa a Jesucristo . . . .[66]

We will let this final image of the ideal mother speak our concluding remarks. It is an image entirely devoid of sensuality, almost inert. The woman, faceless, without any identifying physical characteristics, hovers over the crib like the guardian angel in the penny *estampitas* of the period. And like them, she can safely be put away and forgotten.

UNIVERSITY OF MINNESOTA, MINNEAPOLIS

Notes

[1]Pedro Felipe Monlau, *Higiene del matrimonio*, 3rd ed. (Madrid: 1865), pp. 292-93.

[2]Angel F. Pulido, *Bosquejos médico-sociales para la mujer* (Madrid: 1876), p. 30.

[3]R. de Latorres, "Estudios filosóficos sobre la mujer," *El Pensil del Bello Sexo*, 18 enero 1846. Pilar Sinués de Marco, "Contra el lujo," *El Correo de la Moda*, 2 sept. 1883, p. 258. Juan de Luz, "Una receta casera," *La Margarita*, 30 julio 1871.

[4]R. de Latorres, ibid.

[5]A. P., "Influencia de la mujer en la sociedad," *El Museo de las Familias*, 21-22 (1863), p. 126. "En efecto, mientras que nosotros aspiramos a la independencia, ellas desean dar y recibir una dulce esclavitud." Ruperto García Cañas, "Sobre la influencia de las mujeres en nuestras sociedades modernas," *El Museo de las Familias*, III (1845), p. 73. ". . . Seguramente en el seno de la familia hay un vasto teatro donde la madre, la esposa, la hermana y demás que se hallan ligados con el vínculo de la sangre ejercen poderoso influjo en el porvenir de la sociedad. . . ."

[6]A. Pirala, "De la influencia e instrucción de la mujer," *La Moda Elegante Ilustrada*, 30 abril 1873, p. 125.

[7]Of such great importance is social order that peace and happiness are perceived only as a function of the maintaining of order. See José Luis L. Aranguren, *Moral y sociedad* (Madrid: Editorial Cuadernos para el diálogo, S.A., 1967), p. 94.

[8]Luis de León, *La Perfecta Casada*, reimpresión de la tercera edición, con variantes de la primera, y un prólogo (first published in Salamanca in 1583) ed. Elizabeth Wallace (Chicago: University of Chicago Press, 1903), p. 110. Although written during the Counter-Reformation, this treatise on domestic economy was read steadily up to and throughout the nineteenth century.

⁹"Algo para las mujeres," *El Correo de la Moda*, 2 julio 1881, pp. 195-98.

¹⁰Baronesa de Olivares, "La vida en familia," *El Correo de la Moda*, 2 dic. 1884.

¹¹A. P. (cf note 5), p. 126. See also Monlau, pp. 164-65. "En la mujer, la individualidad está mucho menos pronunciada que en el hombre: éste es más egoísta, menos sufrido. La mujer vive más para la especie que para sí misma."

¹²Luis de León, pp. 98-99. "Y assi es que en sus casas cerradas y occupadas las mejoran, andando fuera dellas las destruyen. Y las que con andar por sus rincones ganarán las voluntades y edificarán las consciencias de sus maridos, visitando las calles, corrompen los corazones agenos: y enmollecen las almas de los que las veen, las que por ser ellas muelles se hizieron para la sombra, y para el secreto de sus paredes."

¹³S. M. Fábreques, "La mujer casada y San Pablo," *La Moda Elegante Ilustrada*, XXX, 27 (1871), p. 215.

¹⁴Ibid.

¹⁵María de la Concepción Gimeno, "No hay sexo débil," *La Moda Elegante Ilustrada*, 22 junio 1874, p. 187.

¹⁶Robustiana Armiño de Cuesta, "La mujer emancipada," *La Moda Elegante Ilustrada*, XXX, 2 (1871), p. 15.

¹⁷See Geraldine M. Scanlon, *La polémica feminista en la España contemporánea: 1868-1974* (Madrid: Siglo XXI de España, 1976). This seminal study is a thorough documentation of the traditional and so-called liberal viewpoints on the subject of "the woman problem." Of particular value is the author's careful reconstruction of the historic circumstances within which the middle-class women attempted to live out the myth of the ideal woman.

¹⁸The concept of the "Lady" refers to class origin regardless of the married state. While the image of the Lady and the Angel in the House overlap at certain points (asexuality, frailty, gentleness and, of course, modesty), the Angel is more specifically a model for middle-class women. While she may not work *outside* the house, she is expected to service the men and the children and to maintain the house in order.

¹⁹The hyperbolic praise of women tends to mask the fact that the ideal wife exists only as a function of the family. The family as an institution did not suddenly gain importance in order to provide an occupation for the bored *ama de casa*. That it is the family and not the housewife that is the focus of the ideology of domesticity has become much clearer in the twentieth century. The family is still rigorously defended as the ultimate and sacred preserve of the individual, at the same time that prestige for the role of housewife and mother has radically declined in part as a result of women's growing importance in the work force.

²⁰A. P. A., "La emancipación de la mujer," *El Correo de la Moda*, 2 nov. 1875, p. 321.

²¹J. A. Bermejo, "Instrucción y educación," *El Museo de las Familias*, XII, feb. 1854, pp. 25, 28.

²²Ibid., p. 26.

²³Cañas, p. 73.

²⁴The Sumptuary Laws are defined by Sempere y Guarinos as laws, "para contener los excesos en la comida, y las demasías en los trages, muebles, modas, y demás ramos de luxo," See *Historia del luxo y de las leyes suntuarias de España* (Madrid: 1788), pp. 8-9. Attempts to regulate those aspects of daily life which by the 18th century were no longer considered to be the rightful domain of the State resulted in the revolt of the people against Prime Minister Esquilache in 1766. For one account,

see Charles E. Kany, *Life and Manners in Madrid: 1750-1800* (Berkeley: U. of California Press, 1932), pp. 220-24.

²⁵Fermín Gonzalo Morán, "La mujer," *El Correo de la Moda*, 10 nov. 1877.
²⁶Luis de León, pp. 93-94.

²⁷Concepción Gimeno de Flaquer, "La mujer estudiosa," *El Correo de la Moda*, XXXVI, 45 (1886), p. 358.

²⁸Antonio Arbiol, *La Familia Regulada con Doctrina de la Sagrada Escritura, y Santos Padres de la Iglesia Católica* (written in 1715; Madrid: 1783), p. 493. This work, a Counter-Reformation defense of the institution of matrimony, was a stock item in the libraries of the Catholic traditionalists. The Baronesa de Olivares, in the article previously cited, emphasizes that "women's rights," defined primarily as the right to exist without being slandered or physically harmed, are dependent on the woman's virtuous (modest) behavior. ". . . los *derechos de la mujer* son teorías hechas para los espiritus débiles o las imaginaciones pobres: *los derechos de las mujeres los aseguran sus propias cualidades.*"

²⁹Severo Catalina, *La mujer*, title page missing (1858?), Ch. II, "La Modestia," p. 116.

³⁰Arbiol, p. 488.

³¹Fabre y D'Huc, *Tratado elemental de las enfermedades de la mujer y del niño*, ed. & tran. Rogelio Casas de Batista, 3rd ed. (Madrid: 1872), p. 421.

³²Catalina, pp. 106, 115.

³³For further discussion of "la mujer ilustrada" see Scanlon, Ch. 1, "Educación."

³⁴Monlau, p. 129.

³⁵Fernán Caballero, *El Correo de la Moda*, 2 mayo 1877.

³⁶Mariano Carderera, *Actas del Congreso Nacional Pedagógico* (Madrid: 1882), p. 317, quoted in Scanlon, p. 27.

³⁷Concepción Gimeno de Flaquer, "La mujer médico," *El Correo de la Moda*, 2 dic. 1882, p. 358.

³⁸Catalina, p. 117.

³⁹José Moreno Fuentes "Reparos y obligaciones acerca del destino natural de la mujer," *El Correo de la Moda*, 26 sept. 1885, p. 286.

⁴⁰Monlau, p. 164. José Lopez Piñero calls Monlau ". . . el más importante higienista español contemporáneo." And he goes on to say, "En las sucesivas ediciones de sus tratados de higiene pública y privada se educaron los médicos españoles durante más de medio siglo. . . ." "El testimonio de los médicos españoles del siglo XIX acerca de su tiempo," in *Medicina y sociedad en la España del siglo XIX* (Madrid: Sociedad de Estudios y Publicaciones, 1964), p. 131.

⁴¹Monlau, p. 33.

⁴²Monlau, p. 579.

⁴³Juan Drumen, *Tratado elemental de patología médica*, vol. 2 (Madrid: 1850), p. 385. See also Pulido, p. 335.

⁴⁴On Drumen, see Trino Peraza de Ayala, *La psiquiatría española en el siglo XIX* (Madrid: Consejo Superior de Investigaciones, 1947), pp. 80-87. For an important contemporary source see Pedro Mata Fontanet, *Tratado de medicina y cirugía*, 5th ed., vol. II (Tetuán de Chamartín: 1874), p. 289.

⁴⁵The term neurasthenia *per se* does not come into use until the latter part of the 19th century. It refers to what was previously called a nervous condition, *un estado nervioso*: one of hyper-sensitivity, exhaustion, irritability, depression, fits of crying and insomnia. See Peraza de Ayala, p. 83. See also Ilza Veith, *Hysteria: The History*

of a Disease (Chicago: University of Chicago Press, 1965), pp. 242-43, for a chart of symptoms.

[46]"La mujer y la política," *La Guirnalda*, 20 agosto 1883, pp. 125-26.

[47]The most comprehensive and accessible treatment of the subject for the lay person is the work of Ilza Veith cited in note 44, especially chapters 8 and 9.

[48]Veith, p. 209.

[49]Veith, p. 172. See also Fabre y D'Huc, ch. VIII, pp. 403-24, for a contemporary discussion of hysteria versus nymphomania.

[50]Mata Fontonet, p. 373.

[51]Veith, pp. 174-79.

[52]Fabre y D'Huc, pp. 420-21.

[53]Josefa Amar y Borbón, *Discurso sobre la educación física y moral de las mujeres* (Madrid: 1790), p. 240.

[54]Pulido, p. 338.

[55]Drumen, pp. 394-95.

[56]Justo Jiménez de Pedro, "Carácter moral de la mujer" (Madrid: 1854), p. 12.

[57]Monlau, p. 209.

[58]Condesa Dash, "De la castidad conyugal," *La Guirnalda*, 20 marzo 1876.

[59]Jiménez de Pedro, p. 26.

[60]Pulido, p. 221.

[61]Pulido, pp. 2-3.

[62]Amar y Borbón, pp. 252-54.

[63]A. P. (cf. note 5), p. 126.

[64]Luis de León, p. 106.

[65]Carlos Frontaura, "Las amas de cría," *El Museo Universal*, 1 feb. 1863, p. 39.

[66]Pulido, p. 30.

MIS BRUJAS FAVORITAS

Luisa Valenzuela

As a bridge to the next section, we are including a paper by Luisa Valenzuela (Argentina) written especially for this volume. To her reflections on the function and use of language in the works of women writers she has added impressions of Margo Glantz's Las mil y una calorías, *a book that she considers illustrative of the subversive quality of women's writing today.*

Luisa Valenzuela presently resides in New York City. Her works include the novels Hay que sonreír *(1966),* El gato eficaz *(1972), and* Como en la guerra *(1977), and the short story collections* Los heréticos *(1967),* Aquí pasan cosas raras *(1976), and* Libro que no muerde *(1980). Translations of her works into English include* Clara (Los heréticos *and* Hay que sonreír; Harcourt Brace Jovanovich, 1976) *and* Strange Things Happen Here (Como en la guerra *and* Aquí pasan cosas raras; Harcourt Brace Jovanovich, 1979).

La indagación se plantearía desde el punto de vista de la posible existencia de un lenguaje femenino. La respuesta habría que tratar de concretarla por el lado de las brujas: aquello en lo que no se cree—o quisiera no creerse o no se pudiera creer—pero que las hay, las hay. Más adelante y por vías igualmente irreprochables, postular la seguridad de un lenguaje femenino en absoluto emparentado con aquellas azucaradas palabras con las que hemos sido recubiertas a lo largo de siglos. Abrillantadas, bañadas en colores sonrosados como torta barata (¿*tart* como podría decirse en inglés? ¿Disfrazadas de putas baratas, las mujeres que manejan la palabra? He aquí otra de las inconfesables caras).

De los tantos velos que habrá que ir rasgando en lo posible (desvirgamiento de los mitos, fuerza que debemos asumir): el que oculta la dicotomía puta/santa, establecida por el hombre. La mujer colocada en uno de los dos extremos de esta oposición, y en el medio la nada. Como nada hay entre las piernas femeninas, la célebre ausencia del falo que el discurso masculino nos enrostra como carencia generadora de envidia.

La ausencia fálica—a la que volveremos—es apenas un incidente entre esos dos extremos, un encasillamiento que nos limita y empobrece. Entre la santa y la puta tenemos espacio sobrado para desplegar, de atrás para delante, al costado y en profundidad, todas las posibilidades del mundo que sospechamos son las nuestras. La gloriosa de dar vida y la otra no menos gloriosa de quitarla. Prerrogativa esta última que parecería pertenecer al campo masculino—el campo de batalla—y sin embargo es nuestra por obra y gracia del lenguaje. Analicemos por ejemplo el temor supersticioso al número 13. Cifra de la letra M, inicial de *muerte* y también de *mujer*. Como todos los nombres que se le dan a la muerte y son nombres femeninos: la pelada, la segadora, la igualadora, la tiznada, la pálida, la huesuda. La última de las parcas, por lo tanto, otra de las nuestras, armada con la hoz que siega vidas.

Amenazadora posibilidad, es cierto, pero también posibilidad muy novelística que se nos ha venido amputando al someternos a un lenguaje impuesto desde fuera, desde ese territorio organizado, tabulado, del discurso masculino.

Cierto es que el lenguaje se origina en el inconsciente humano, esa convención de neutralidad identificada por Freud. Pero en su afloramiento el lenguaje debe atravesar el filtro del consciente, laberinto contaminado de hormonas sexuales. Y allí te quiero ver, porque las connotaciones y las asociaciones y las digresiones y las entonaciones coloran las palabras y pueden llegar a cambiarles la carga. El célebre deslizamiento del significado por debajo del significante—hoy tan vital como lo fue en su momento el encuentro fortuito del paraguas con la máquina de coser—no es necesariamente el mismo para cada individuo, y con mayor razón para individuos de distinto sexo.

Por ese lado también se nos ha ido castrando meticulosamente. Una dama no debe proferir injurias, una dama no dice malas palabras—y las malas palabras son sólo tales para la mujer; el hombre no es para nada maniqueo en lo que a su propio lenguaje respecta. Con el padre Freud a la cabeza, dándole bendición casi científica a estas iniquidades, ubicando a la mujer tan sólo como catalizadora de la comunicación entre hombres cuando del juego de palabras se trata.

Sin poder permitirse interiormente los malabarismos verbales, venero de los grandes hallazgos, la mujer aún hoy se deja atrapar en la red de los convencionalismos del lenguaje. Ese espejo de alondras. Todo porque le falta a la mujer ese rollito de carne mal llamado falo por quienes quieren obnubilarnos con el mero símbolo. Jacques Lacan fue quizá el único que lo vio claro, y no sé si los hombres en general han leído bien el ensayo lacaniano titulado *La significación del falo*. En su interpretación estructuralista de Freud, Lacan apunta que el falo como significante es en realidad el lugar de una ausencia. Tanto para la mujer como para el hombre, dado que el bebé humano atribuye el falo a la madre, la gran protectora. Al crecer, el bebé descubre con enorme decepción que no existe tal falo materno, apenas una representación carnal no demasiado confiable que el padre esgrime—simbólicamente—como emblema de poder. Resultado de lo cual la humanidad en pleno gira en torno a una carencia, con cada sexo instalado en ubicación opuesta en lo que al falo como hito se refiere. Razón por la cual se impone que la mujer refuerce su posición y recree su discurso. Para reorganizar su territorio.

Territorio donde imperan otros órganos, otras sangres.

En muchas culturas primitivas y otras que no lo son tanto, el hombre ha estructurado un tabú alrededor de la sangre menstrual y la primera menstruación de la mujer. En la India sólo los parias pueden acercarse a la mujer durante su período; en el Amazonas y en ciertas zonas del Africa los ritos de purificación para las adolescentes son demasiado ricos y complejos para ser relatados en pocas palabras. ¿Y por qué existen? ¿Por miedo a la sangre, por impurezas del menstruo? En absoluto. Pienso que la situación es menos directa pero más comprensible: porque el hombre siente un reclamo insoslayable a su virilidad, con la primera menstruación su tarea de fecundador empieza. Y su tarea de fecundador (que la mística masculina suele confundir con el poder viril) debe toparse con sucesivos fracasos ante cada nueva menstruación.

Otra sangre, dije, otro órgano. Este hueco negro, señal de los orígenes y amenaza, simultáneamente, por eso mismo. Algo que quizá en algún profundo rincón del inconsciente recuerde a los otros huecos negros, aspiradoras del universo hacia la antimateria. O no tanto, apenas una proyección de ese otro hueco femenino tan cargado de amenazas: la boca. De la cual no deben emerger las culebras de las malas palabras; las palabras malas, aquellas que podrían perturbar el preestablecido orden del discurso masculino. El mismo que siempre se encargó de amordazar a las mujeres, muchas veces acusándolas de brujas. Brujas primero, histéricas más tarde: las que por sus bocas descargan todas las frustraciones impuestas a su sexo que es también su lenguaje. Brujas como aquella a la que hace referencia Pennethorne Hughes en el libro *La brujería*:

> El ama de llaves de Alice Kyteler, Petronilla de Heath, confirmó los cargos por lo cual fue necesario azotarla seis veces más siguiendo las instrucciones del obispo. Cuando lo poco que quedaba de ella fue de nuevo llevado a prisión para que se la azotase por séptima vez confirmó todo lo que los jueces quisieron. Fue conducida a la ciudad y quemada públicamente, mientras juraba contra el clero y despreciaba y maldecía a los verdugos.

Es decir, sólo un momento de libertad para expresarse con toda fuerza antes de la muerte. Después, eso sí, de haber emitido las palabras que le habían sido impuestas y que habrían de condenarla. Pobre Petronilla de Heath y tantísimas otras. Pobre todas nosotras. Sin ir más lejos, hay en Cartagena una balanza de tiempos de la Inquisición, gracias a la cual se establecía quiénes eran en verdad brujas: toda aquella desnutrida o grácil que pesara menos de 100 libras.

Esta balanza sigue siendo usada por nuestros críticos, por nuestros editores, por tantos que nos rodean. Eso sí, ahora no se trata de comer más porque el peso es aleatorio. Todo lo contrario, a veces cuanto más peso, peor. Al peso moral me refiero, al peso de la erudición o de la inteligencia, o de la gracia y el sentido de libertad. Por eso se impone descompaginarles las escalas, sacar a relucir otros valores que no puedan ser medidos con las antiguas varas. Investigar profundamente, por ejemplo, las posibilidades de este lenguaje hémbrico (por oposición y no por desvalorización ante el llamado lenguaje viril). Del que ya hay muchas pruebas. Dos novelas me vienen enseguida a la mente: *El buzón de la esquina*, de Alicia Dujovne Ortíz, y *Entrada libre* de Inés Malinow. Pero haré el análisis de un tercer y muy extraño libro para que no se diga que soy parcial, que sólo pienso en mis compatriotas, y porque creo que esta *novela dietética* de la mexicana Margo Glantz, por eso mismo, por dietética y no-novela, es de las que mejor pueden empezar a trabar el mecanismo de la vieja, eterna balanza de Cartagena.

Pecados que redimen del pecado de la gula

A propósito de *Las mil y una calorías. Novela dietética* de Margo Glantz (México: Editora Premiá, 1979).

En la lectura puede darse la voracidad desenfrenada, la gula, o la sutil suavidad del paladeo. Están aquellos que dicen: me tragué la novela en una noche; la engulleron, sí, y quizá sabrán el qué sin jamas alcanzar los arcanos del cómo (lo dijo Joyce: "No me importa qué se dice, sino cómo se dice"). Y están los otros lectores, los que dan vuelta bajo la lengua cada palabra, cada frase, y se detienen en un goce puramente sensual que no despièrta resonancias ni logra ser asimilado por los profundos intestinos (las intestinas profundidades, las insondables) de la mente.

Contra la gula y también contra el refinado gourmetismo de la lectura, Margo Glantz establece una nueva propuesta gastroliteraria: la novela dietética. El título—*Las mil y una calorías*—define ya las pautas del sustancioso libro; el subtítulo advierte lo que le espera al osado lector que abra la entelada tapa, es decir que pegue el primer mordisco.

Nóvela dietética, hecha de mínimas dosis que alimentan más que los vastos discursos fofos, los inconsistentes. Porque nadie es inocente en este proceso de digestión, que por carácter transitivo va de la escritura a la lectura. El que escribe está prestando la boca de su mente para emitir esa cosa bastante subversiva que llamamos ideas, y el que lee—el que en verdad sabe *leer*—presta una oreja atenta que paulatinamente se convierte en manzana (como lo demuestra el asombroso dibujo de Ariel Guzik), y la manzana es el consabido fruto del pecado.

Un pecado que, en manos de Margo Glantz, es del todo original aunque pocas veces haga referencia a aquel confuso episodio que, según ciertas mitologías en vigencia, nos privó casi desde un principio de los monótonos placeres del paraíso terrenal.

Otros, y muy sutiles, son los pecados a los que nos remiten las páginas de este libro. Porque Margo Glantz ha alcanzado una forma muy personal del conocimiento, enraizada en el sentido del humor y en la crítica exacta. La suya es una sabiduría sólida, redonda como un garbanzo que germina y cada tanto da los frutos más inesperados, insólitos. Semillas que a su vez se siembran en el lector proclive para transformarse en otros frutos distintos pero hermanos en asombros. Las metamorfosis constantes, deseadas, provocadas, aterradoras y a la vez fascinantes. La manzana—si uno la mira bien —puede a su vez convertirse en un culo lustroso y ese culo en un corazón o en un veneno del que surge Blanca Nieves. El pecado, por lo tanto, reside en la trasgresión del estatismo, en la aceptación de las transformaciones. MG va más allá; *suscita* las transformaciones, las provoca en los dos sentidos del verbo provocar: las gesta y a la vez las incita.

Textos brevísimos que lo dicen todo, o al menos proponen una multiplicidad de sentidos que pueden convertirse en un desliz motivado por el puro gozo. Gozo que en este caso consiste en descubrir las secretas connotaciones, los nudos que se pueden ir atando a pesar del texto, a pesar de la autora, por obra y gracia de una cierta forma de masticación a la que el texto instiga. Porque esta novela dietética está elaborada con una receta tal que requiere a cada página el aporte de los jugos gástricos de aquél que la está ingiriendo. Y pensar que Margo Glantz intentó con este libro escribir su biografía. . . . Y pensar que de alguna manera muy secreta lo h. logrado, biografía de todo lo que fue asimilando a lo largo de años entregados al estudio profundo de la literatura ("Yo soy en realidad lo que he leído" expresó Borges alguna vez):

> —Entregué buena parte de mi vida a la autocompasión. Pero ahora me he vuelto corrosiva, quizá sarcástica. Claro que el sarcasmo lo vuelvo contra mí misma, contra el estereotipo de la femineidad, el lírico. Escribiría cualquier cosa con tal de destruir el arquetipo de la madre.

Dicho así con aparente impunidad pero sabiendo que tarde o temprano la cazadora es cazada, que como bien dice el tango se da el juego de remanye. Que el inconsciente tiene razones que la razón no querría aceptar. Es decir que todo empezó, según confesión privada de la autora, con un mínimo cuento sobre una oveja negra que no figura en el libro. ¿Autobiográfico? Sí, en la medida en que esta mujer extrañamente bella se sintió la oveja negra de la familia, la distinta, la desclasada. El cuento confesional no forma parte de estas calorías, pero otros ovinos de igual calaña afloran en las páginas de *Las mil y una calorías*. Por ejemplo, la numerada 46, "Historia banal", dice así: "las ovejas negras suelen salir de sus rediles para regresar transformadas en las madres de los hijos pródigos". De las ovejas negras a la serpiente hay un solo paso: el que transita por el misterio, "el que realiza el paseo perpetuo por el corazón mismo de la zona prohibida" (Breton). Margo Glantz tiene la enorme valentía de hacer su nido en esta zona y aceptarla como propia. De allí su afinidad con Georges Bataille a quien ha traducido y prologado en otras publicaciones. Como Bataille, también MG se encuentra en "el techo del templo desde lo alto del cual aquel que abriera los ojos plenamente y sin vestigio de miedo captaría la relación que mantienen entre sí todas las posibilidades opuestas". Es en el techo de este preciso templo donde se enrosca la serpiente, la gran desprestigiada. MG, por lo tanto, asume su defensa, y así concluye un texto: "para lograr que sobreviva como especie

literaria es necesario conservarle toda su falicidad....." Conservarle
la falicidad con toda felicidad, naturalmente, porque el pecado que
Margo Glantz reconoce como propio no es aquel de Adán y Eva al
que hice referencia antes, lo que ella misma se encarga de iluminar:

> hundidos en la inocencia, nuestros primeros padres vivían en el
> silencio. cuando probaron el fruto del árbol prohibido conocieron
> simultáneamente el pecado y el ruido, al oír los pasos de dios que se
> aproximaba para castigarlos ("Historia de la acústica").

No, no, nada de pecado original sino del otro, el más humano,
reiterado, familiar y casero.... Pobre Edipo, pobres pies cansados.
MG lo tiene cogido por todas sus posibilidades de escape o de entrega: las que distorsionan las palabras y las que les arrancan sus
significados prohibidos: "edipo, rey del fandango, acudió al oráculo
de belfos para liberarse de la sifila de cumas" ("Historia secreta").
Podríamos establecer una lista de las distintas regiones (anató-
micas e imaginarias) valiéndonos de las cuales la autora organiza el
cerco.

(1) *Los pies.* Reconocida debilidad de Edipo y que MG a menudo
coloca bajo su personal microscopio, que al reducir todo a su más
ínfimo tamaño le devuelve su máxima intensidad, su verdadera definición. Pies edípicos o piececitos femeninos que harían la felicidad
de los fetichistas: "las extremidades femeninas dan pie a reflexiones
y a coplas de pie quebrado" ("Historia púdica"; historia ilustrada
con un gran seno, porque ¿qué otra cosa es el seno sino una extremi-
dad femenina, sobre todo en los casos de opulencia?).

(2) *El conocimiento.* Es sabido que, con la ceguera, Edipo no pagó
el pecado del incesto sino el de haber descifrado el secreto de la es-
finge. Toda escritora conoce el riesgo que corre al poner la punta del
pie (precisamente) en las cenagosas aguas del conocimiento. MG,
más que muchas, porque suele adentrarse con fruición en estas aguas.

(3) *El incesto.* O más bien su oscuro, siempre latente deseo (no por
más reconocido hay que olvidarlo): "la conjunción copulativa en-
gendra monstruos" ("Historia incestuosa").

¿Y? Y tantas posibilidades de apertura, tantas vías a otras líneas
de pensamiento gracias a esta *Mil y una calorías.* Fábula a veces,
a veces evidentes verdades, distorsiones de una realidad que puede
ser más real que esta otra distorsión a la que estamos acostumbrados.

El humor negro es un cristal que permite observar al sol de frente y asistir a los eclipses sin arriesgar ceguera. MG pule este cristal
hasta darle las facetas de un diamante. Las múltiples posibilidades

del humor negro no desdeñan todas las otras coloraciones que van hasta las más rosadas, las más en apariencia insoslayables, y entonces la fábula asoma a menudo sus narices o la Bella Durmiente va sufriendo mutaciones y envejece, o se convierte en príncipe durmiente, que se convierte en sapo para trastrocar la irrealidad en la que vivimos desde niños.

Un juego sí, un artefacto del todo lúdico, este libro. Se forman las figuras más inesperadas y ¡reales!: "en el alto nilo viven los nuers que adoran a las vacas y ordeñan las nubes" ("Historia del origen de la vía láctea"). O los títulos señalan los caminos de la lucidez:

> *Historia con espinas*
> la japuta es un pez comestible bastante apreciado

Irreverentes asociaciones y verdades ocultas ("la ciática es a la vez un árbol y un dolor, como Dafne"), dosis homeopáticas de inteligencia afloran en *Las mil y una calorías* y corresponde dejarlas bajo la lengua (es decir el lenguaje). Lenguaje que da nacimiento al mito que lo recrea, eterno retorno del que Margo Glantz es muy consciente. Por eso comienza su llamada novela con la siguiente advertencia: "cualquier semejanza con el mito es realidad", frase que se espeja en otra, casi al final del libro: "para los hombres de poca fe los mitos son invisibles". Lo que de ninguna manera significa inexistentes ya que Margo Glantz sabe, como el artista Tao, que su misión consiste en hacer visible lo invisible. O, mejor aún, volver nutritivo todo aquello que contenga el germen de lo insólito.

II. Critical Applications:
The Works of Female Writers

IDEOLOGY AND
THE MYSTERIES OF UDOLPHO

Mary Poovey

The system of "values, ideas and images" that cemented the position of the upper middle class within the social and political hierarchy of eighteenth-century England was based on what contemporary poets and philosophers called the "sentimental virtues."[1] "Sentimentalism," with its close kin "sensibility," was the ideology derived from the theory of moral sentiments proposed by Shaftesbury in his *Characteristics* in 1711. As subsequently elaborated by such theorists as Francis Hutcheson, David Hume, and Adam Smith, sensibility was generally understood to include both consciousness—the ability to feel strongly—and conscience—the capacity for *rational* feeling.[2] Thus the values associated with sensibility for most of the century were both aesthetic (sensitivity, responsiveness) and moral (benevolence, generosity). The interdependence of these categories helps explain how sensibility could constitute the foundation for an ethical as well as an aesthetic theory: virtue was held to be its own reward because generous behavior automatically returned aesthetic pleasure.

In the course of the century, the values associated with sensibility were used by the powerful middle classes to ennoble and justify almost every kind of behavior—not only aesthetic and ethical, but economic and political as well. Theories based on sensibility were advanced, for example, to support the American revolution, charity for the poor, and the liberation of enslaved Negroes. Together, the theories of sentimentalism described a utopic society in which individual desires and collective needs participated in perfect reciprocity, where "natural" inequality was robbed of its sting by the unforced benevolence of the "well-bred gentleman." But while its hierarchy of duties and responsibilities helped control potential religious and political unrest, sentimentalism was also underwriting both laissez-faire capitalism and the weak central government the aspiring middle classes desired. And in the last decade of the century, the soothing myth of the happy society finally collapsed. Partly because the gulf between the laboring poor and the purportedly "well-bred" gentleman yawned ever wider with the advance of capitalism, and partly in response to the theories and turmoil brewing in France, during the 1790s the contradictions inherent in sensibility became increasingly obvious. From the periodic minor crowd disturbances at Tyburn to the mob action of the Gordon riots in 1780, from that supposedly religious outburst to the undeniably political gatherings of the Corresponding Societies in the 1790s were short but profoundly significant steps—undeniable signs that the ideology of sensibility did not account for, and could not control, all of English society. Despite the threat that the consequences of increased capitalistic activity eventually posed to sensibility, however, the ideology itself actually fueled this challenge from below: not only did sensibility lack theories to account for such social unrest, but its paradigm of innate benevolence initially sanctioned the laissez-faire individualism that gradually transformed England from a paternalistic hierarchy to a modern class society.[3]

A study of the ideology of sensibility, its power and the challenge to it, is essential to our understanding of one underprivileged subgroup within the dominant class.[4] For with the gradual blurring of class lines between the aristocracy and the middle classes and the simultaneous, rapid growth of agrarian, then industrial capitalism, "the Third Estate of the Third Estate," as one French pamphleteer called women, also began to experience a loosening of the mortar that had secured its place within the traditional order. The challenge posed to sensibility, in fact, had a profounder significance for women than for any other group. For although the ideology rationalized the economic and political powerlessness of women, it also constituted the basis for their peculiar but undeniable power. In the course of the eighteenth century, those sentimental virtues that contemporary philosophers initially considered innate in all men were increasingly characterized as specifically feminine virtues. By the end of the century, it was customary for authors of conduct books for "women of rank and fortune" to describe women's "natural" characteristics as a version of (and justification for) sentimentalism: "the most amiable tendencies and affections implanted in human nature, of modesty, of delicacy, of sympathizing sensibility, of prompt and active benevolence, of warmth and tenderness of attachment."[5] According to Rousseau and his numerous followers, these feminine qualities compensated for the "inequality of man-made laws" by assigning women very specific social responsibilities, thereby assuring them of very specific powers.[6] Thomas Gisborne, whose *Enquiry into the Duties of the Female Sex* is quoted above, describes women's unique contributions to social stability as follows:

> First, In contributing daily and hourly to the comfort of husbands, of parents, of brothers and sisters, and of other relations, connections, and friends, in the intercourse of domestic life, under every vicissitude of sickness and health, of joy and affliction.

> Secondly, In forming and improving the general manners, dispositions, and conduct of the other sex, by society and example.

> Thirdly, In modelling the human mind during the early stages of its growth, and fixing, while it is yet ductile, its growing principle of action; children of each sex being, in general, under maternal tuition during their childhood, and girls until they become women.[7]

From our perspective we can see that the most crucial "power" of middle-class women actually resided in their ability to preserve in the home the sentimental values and behavior traditionally associated with paternalistic society.[8] By providing men a retreat from what Gisborne called "the sordid occupations and degrading profits of trade," women were able to perpetuate these values even after developments in the "real world," made up of marketplace and mob, challenged them. Not incidentally, however, by keeping the theatre of humane values separate from materialistic activity, this feminine illusion inadvertently contributed to the eventual success of the marketplace values it appeared to counteract.

It is not surprising that at the end of the eighteenth century the debate about woman's proper place and her particular power intensified, for as the French revolutionaries challenged the neat order of the paternalistic system, women sensed the imminent destruction of both their dependent status *and* their power. Their response, predictably, was a deeply divided one. On the one side, Mary Wollstonecraft insisted that women's dependence was not "natural" but acquired and exhorted her sisters to protect themselves against the threat she anticipated by learning new habits of genuine strength:

> I wish to persuade women to endeavor to acquire strength, both of mind and body, and to convince them that the soft phrases, susceptibility of heart, delicacy of sentiment, and refinement of taste, are almost synonymous with epithets of weakness, and that those beings

who are only the objects of pity and that kind of love, which has been termed its sister, will soon become objects of contempt.[9]

On the other side, Hannah More replied with Rousseau's argument for innate characteristics. The "original marks of difference stamped by the hand of the Creator," More reminded women, dictated their "natural," their "proper" and therefore their "right" place, and to defy this order would not only pervert the natural law but invite absolute powerlessness.

> Is it not then more wise as well as more honorable to move content-edly in the plain path which Providence has obviously marked out to the sex, and in which custom has for the most part rationally confirmed them, rather than to stray awkwardly, unbecomingly, and unsuccessfully, in a forbidden road? to be the lawful possessors of a lesser domestic territory, rather than the turbulent usurpers of a wider foreign empire? to be good originals, rather than bad imitators? to be the best thing of one's kind, rather than an inferior thing even if it were of an higher kind? to be excellent women rather than indifferent men?[10]

Mary Wollstonecraft and Hannah More, in their polemical zest, take extreme and particularly clear positions. In the fiction written and read during this period by middle-class women these two antithetical attitudes more frequently lie side-by-side, causing competing tendencies that rupture the bland optimism their narrators assert. The novels of Ann Radcliffe, "the Great Enchantress," provide a particularly good example of the tensions the challenge to paternalism and its values caused such women, for in her romances Radcliffe investigates specifically the paradoxical role sensibility plays in simultaneously restricting women and providing them power and an arena for action. Moreover, in the process of her investigation Radcliffe uncovers the root cause of the late eighteenth-century ideological turmoil, the economic aggressiveness currently victimizing defenseless women of sensibility. Despite her claims that her romances are set in the distant past, then, the psychological situations Radcliffe dramatizes belong to late eighteenth-century England and to the ideological complexities I have been describing. Only distancing the story, in fact, permits Radcliffe to unmask the implicit threat sensibility poses without actually challenging its contemporary importance. For in spite of her penetrating insight, Radcliffe does not abandon sentimental values. Instead, she retreats from the terrifying implications of her discovery and simply dismisses the threat sentimentalism cannot combat. Rather than proposing an alternative to paternalistic society and its values, she merely reasserts an idealized—and insulated—paternalism and relegates the issues she cannot resolve to the background of her narrative. Thus, in the dynamics of Radcliffe's romances we have an excellent example of an ideology *in practice*, a testing of its images and values by one member of that class which had most at stake in it. In the tonal and structural dissonances, the competing ideas that characterize even Radcliffe's most successful novel, we see the conflicts within the ideology realized—acted out, as it were, in one woman's attempt to imaginatively resolve the instability that threatened her. And in her return to the very values she has questioned we see the way in which her investment in these values delimited the range of her response.

I

In *The Mysteries of Udolpho* (1794), sensibility is introduced in the first volume as an element integral to an ideal, paternalistic society. In this society, and within a series of protective enclosures (the chateau of the patriarchal estate, La Vallée, and her father's paternal care), Emily St. Aubert is able to cultivate and then indulge sentimental virtues—a quick responsiveness to nature and an unreflecting generosity to others. Radcliffe clearly believes that these virtues are valuable, for, initially at least, she sets them up as a counter to that lust for material gain threatening both Emily's society and her own. In Volume One Radcliffe explicitly establishes an opposition between sentimental virtues—"tenderness, simplicity, and truth"—and their materialistic counterparts—"selfishness, dissipation, and insincerity." Only by exercising the first can one earn the true "luxury" of aesthetic gratification, as the chevalier Valancourt learns when he donates his last coins to the poor. Valancourt's enrichment is immediate: "his gay spirits danced with pleasure; every object around him appeared more interesting, or beautiful, than before."[11] Beside this, Radcliffe suggests, the "frivolous" pleasures of material wealth are artificial, cold, and unsatisfying.

In her descriptions of sensibility, Radcliffe preserves the marriage of ethical and aesthetic components we saw in earlier theories: "Virtue and taste are nearly the same," Emily's father explains, "for virtue is little more than active taste, and the most delicate affections of each combine in real love" (I, V, 49-50). But aesthetic rewards automatically follow virtuous actions only so long as sensibility operates in an environment regulated by a moral authority. Emily's youthful pleasures and Valancourt's aesthetic delight are possible only in the gentle French countryside, where "the sublime luxuries" of God's natural world always greet the questing heart. In order to be effective, sensibility needs some such external governance, for, as Radcliffe is quick to note, sensibility itself is inherently unstable: it is susceptible to "excess." And "all excess is vicious," as St. Aubert warns Emily.[12] St. Aubert's dying words convey his deep suspicion of indulged sensibility:

> "Above all, my dear Emily . . . do not indulge in the pride of fine feeling, the romantic error of amiable minds. Those, who really possess sensibility, ought early to be taught, that it is a dangerous quality, which is continually extracting the excess of misery, or delight, from every surrounding circumstance. And, since, in our passage through this world, painful circumstances occur more frequently than pleasing ones, and since our sense of evil is, I fear, more acute than our sense of good, we become the victims of our feelings, unless we can in some degree command them" (I, vii, 79-80).

The "painful circumstances" St. Aubert describes are those anarchic situations beyond the purview of paternalistic guardians, where the feeling heart is exposed to the tyranny of others or the riot of its own excess. Emily St. Aubert soon experiences both of these dilemmas, for when her father dies she is exiled from her protected childhood home and taken to the city, where there is no moral protector. Instead, Emily is placed in the custody of her aunt and Signor Montoni, Italian incarnation of excess itself. Subjected to Montoni's unprincipled tyranny, Emily learns the terrible meaning of her father's words: without external protection the creature of sensibility has no power over herself or others. In the avaricious anarchy of Montoni's circle, feelings do *not* become principles and thus the sentimental heroine is helpless before both real and imaginary villains.

Radcliffe's twofold critique of sensibility achieves its clearest articulation in the episodes that take place within Montoni's decaying Alpine retreat, the castle of Udolpho. Udolpho is the sinister inverse of La Vallée, an enclosure whose boundaries oppress rather than protect, a prison that shelters hatred rather than love, a bastille that excludes both law and moral nature itself. Within Udolpho Emily is totally helpless: Montoni dictates her confinement and her virtual isolation. But the external tyranny is, on the surface at least, less oppressive than the terror generated by Emily's own undisciplined imagination. There is, as time will tell, nothing supernatural in Udolpho's winding corridors, but there are evil agents; and Emily's overly sensitive imagination, deprived of external guides, all too readily converts the unnatural into the supernatural. Thus Radcliffe's first critique of sensibility focuses squarely on the imagination itself.

For Radcliffe, as for Adam Smith, the imagination is the faculty responsible for the aesthetic—and thus the ethical—response of sensibility. A capacious faculty, the imagination prompts the feeling heart to project itself into another's situation; by transforming the beneficiary's gratitude into the benefactor's pleasure, the imagination therefore presides over that reciprocity between virtuous actions and aesthetic rewards we have already seen. But Radcliffe insists that the imagination may also be the principal agent in victimizing its vessel, for the imagination is not inherently moral; it is merely susceptible. Only as long as Emily is protected by a moral environment can her imagination receive the divine benefits embodied in the natural world.[13] And only as long as her own feelings are calm can she trust her imagination even to extend itself outward toward that comforting landscape. Within Udolpho, Emily is persecuted by "those mysterious workings, that rouse the elements of man's nature into tempest" (II, xi, 329), and consequently her senses become "dead" to the awe-inspiring scenery outside the castle. Repeatedly during her imprisonment Emily laments the "irresistible force of circumstances over the taste and powers of the mind" (III, v, 383). In "painful circumstances" such as these, a cruel new reciprocity is established: the imagination turns back upon itself and exudes demons that feed its own excess.

The interior of Udolpho is a maze of dimly lit corridors, murky recesses, and obscure stairways. This darkness only exacerbates Emily's condition, for Udolpho's gloom completely baffles perception. In such complete obscurity the imagination is cut loose from all governing images, moral or otherwise. Aroused yet unguided, its innate susceptibility becomes an aggressive force, rushing to fill the void with its own projected images and creating, in effect, an external "reality" as idiosyncratic as the psyche itself. Just beyond the responsiveness of feeling, Radcliffe warns, there lurks this completely amoral, uncontrollable force: "the wild energy of passion, inflaming imagination, bearing down the barriers of reason and living in a world of its own" (II, xi, 329).

Like many women novelists of this period, Radcliffe is using the spectral arena of the Gothic castle to dramatize the eruption of psychic material ordinarily controlled by the inhibitions of bourgeois society.[14] It is revealing that she explicitly links this "energy" with "passion," for Emily's response, like those of her numerous sisters, enacts what we now think of as the seesaw of liberated desire and repression. Vacillating between curiosity and fear, Emily is bold enough to explore the castle's darkest recesses, but when she imagines a corpse "crimsoned with human blood," she retreats from confrontation by fainting. Again, she boldly lifts the forbidding veil of an ominous painting, but falls senseless to the floor before she can identify its contents. Within Udolpho, desire wrestles with dread, even though the heroine is too discreet to recognize the sexual component of her energy.

Radcliffe, however, does acknowledge the kinship between imaginative responsiveness and sexual desire. Through the character of Sister Agnes, Radcliffe suggests that—given slightly different circumstances—Emily's intense susceptibility could have taken a more destructive incarnation. Because Agnes is rumored to be Emily's real mother, her anguished cry implicates her astonished listener:

> "Sister! beware of the first indulgence of the passions; beware of the first! Their course, if not checked then, is rapid—their force is uncontroulable—they lead us we know not whither—they lead us perhaps to the commission of crimes, for which whole years of prayer and penitence cannot atone!—Such may be the force of even a single passion, that it overcomes every other, and sears up every other approach to the heart. Possessing us like a fiend, it leads us on to the acts of a fiend, making us insensible to pity and to conscience" (IV, xvi, 646).

The crime of Sister Agnes, born the Lady Laurentini, was giving in to passion, agreeing to become the mistress of the Marquis de Villeroi. In Radcliffe's world, the devastation Agnes describes inevitably follows such liberation of feminine feeling, for as Patricia Meyer Spacks has noted, "to submit to passion means to abandon the controls by which women even more than men—given their social conditions—must live."[15] Abandoning the "controls," those moral feelings internalized as "principles," catapults a woman into the anarchy of sexual desire and tears from her the last remnants of her social power, even her identity. This, then, is at the heart of Radcliffe's critique of sensibility's affinity to "excess": the amoral energy beyond responsiveness is the "fiend" of sexual desire, whose crimes neither prayers nor regrets can undo.

Despite her undeniable responsiveness, however, Emily's curiosity never becomes full-fledged sexual desire, largely because Radcliffe presides over her situation. For Radcliffe does not stop with uncovering the internal instability of sensibility: beyond a woman's

natural susceptibility to passion she intuits an even more threatening fiend. Sensibility *is* dangerous, as Emily's hysteria shows, because it encourages imaginative and libidinal excesses. But its more
telling liability resides in its inability to resist the masculine version
of desire—the lust of unregulated avarice.[16]

For most of the two central volumes of *The Mysteries*, Emily's
external circumstances are almost completely controlled by Montoni. The Italian has the power to tyrannize her helpless virtue
because his position is protected by law and, more importantly, because his energy is a purely aggressive force, immune to the socializing reciprocity of sensibility.

> Delighting in the tumult and in the struggles of life, he was equally
> a stranger to pity and to fear; his very courage was a sort of animal
> ferocity; not the noble impulse of a principle, such as inspirits the
> mind against the oppressor, in the cause of the oppressed; but a con-
> stitutional hardiness of nerve, that cannot feel, and that, therefore,
> cannot fear (III, ii, 358).

Montoni's calculating passion is the most powerful force Radcliffe
dramatizes in *The Mysteries*, for his purely materialistic appetite
scorns the aesthetic rewards of sensibility. Through her depiction
of Montoni and in the network of economic themes centering on
him, Radcliffe delivers her second, and most telling, critique of sensibility: *this* is the viper its assumptions have allowed—the masculine
passion of unregulated, individualistic, avaricious desire. This monster operates wholly outside the moral universe, and sensibility's
amiable "principles" will never take root in its icy heart. The surfac-
ing of this force as a figure in Radcliffe's fiction attests to her remarkable ability to penetrate the surface of the sentimental ideology, to
see through to its economic base. Yet even as she unmasks the hideous incarnation of capitalistic energy she returns to the very values
she has just proved inadequate. For Radcliffe can imagine no force
apart from sensibility's feminine principles to control this masculine force.

In what Robert Kiely has called "the male world of Udolpho,"[17]
the most significant confrontation is that between Emily's sentimental virtues and Montoni's materialistic desire. Money, in fact,
lurks behind every turn of *The Mysteries*' plot. Emily's hysteria within Udolpho is ultimately a consequence of her legal dependence on
Montoni: as an orphan, she is penniless and powerless; as a female
she has no legal rights. Her immediate poverty, however, will soon
be replaced by comparative wealth, for upon coming of age Emily
stands to inherit several valuable estates in Gascony. This situation—

not sexual desire—motivates Montoni's original interest in Emily: as an imminent heiress, she is a potentially valuable commodity on the marriage market, and, quite simply, he needs her estates to pay off his gambling debts. Emily is shocked to learn the truth from Count Morano, her would-be purchaser: " 'You hear, that Montoni is a villain,' exclaimed Morano with vehemence,—'a villain who would have sold you to my love!... Emily! he has no principle, when interest, or ambition leads' " (II, vi, 262). Morano himself, although he seems to Emily to pose a sexual threat, is also motivated by mate-rialistic desire. "A man of ruined fortune," Morano has plotted to defraud Montoni of Emily's estates. In fact, it was the discovery of this design that prompted Montoni to imprison Emily in Udolpho in the first place (II, vii, 273-74).

In a society in which a single woman's value is intimately tied to both sexual purity and endowed property, the consequences of sex-ual and economic exploitation are effectively identical: either would curtail Emily's chance of attaining social identity through the only avenue open to her—marriage. But Radcliffe depicts masculine ava-rice as more powerful than lust because she recognizes that the "un-feeling" energy Montoni embodies is actually a denial of feeling. It therefore threatens to undermine the entire system of social values that protects the vulnerable woman.[18] Montoni's passion "entirely supplie[s] the place of principles" (III, viii, 435), and once such femi-nine, sentimental principles as sensitivity, responsiveness, decorum, and generosity are no longer also considered "manly," there will be no governing code to socialize aggressive energy. Radcliffe dia-grams this lesson explicitly in Valancourt's experience in Paris where, despondent over his separation from Emily, the susceptible young man falls prey to the charms of salons and the temptations of the gaming table. Artificial beauties and the lure of a quick fortune con-spire "to dazzle his imagination, and re-animate his spirits," and the passion he develops for gambling displaces his feeling for Emily, leads him into debt, and culminates in imprisonment. Only when in-carcerated—protected, that is, from his own passion—can Valan-court benefit from Emily's socializing image:

> In the solitude of his prison, Valancourt had leisure for reflection, and cause for repentance; here, too, the image of Emily, which, amidst the dissipation of the city had been obscured, but never obliterated from his heart, revived with all the charms of innocence and beauty, to reproach him for having sacrificed his happiness and debased his talents by pursuits, which his nobler faculties would formerly have taught him to consider were as tasteless as they were degrading (IV, xv, 652).

If Valancourt's passion had been left to pursue its natural course, the chevalier's "nobler faculties" would presumably have become as unresponsive as Montoni's. And without "taste" to principle his behavior, Valancourt's desire for Emily would hardly have remained virtuous. In this lesson Radcliffe implies that the feminine values of sensibility *could* socialize masculine energy *if* there were some sure way to enforce them—if, in other words, there were some authority strong enough to keep masculine energy from becoming Montoni's fatal power.

II

The "solution" Radcliffe offers in Valancourt's story obviously does not resolve the problem of Montoni or his materialistic desire. For the sentimental ideology, delegating responsibility for moral action to the individual's own aesthetic taste, provides for no institutional watchman to discipline the "unprincipled" man. In fact, the absence of this provision virtually invites such calculating fiends to prey on sensibility's defenseless creatures. But even more frightening is the possibility that in yoking self-interest to the desire for sympathy, sensibility has actually assisted in the birth of this beast. Hydra-like, its antithesis emerges from the sentimental ideology, promising to devour it as it grows.

Radcliffe's insight that economic forces underlie the challenge to feminine values is, therefore, potentially subversive to those values themselves. But Radcliffe does not pursue this insight to its logical conclusion. Although by the 1790s the social and ideological revolution that conservatives had feared was clearly underway, compelling Radcliffe to respond to sensibility's limitations, the attendant possibility of complete social and ethical chaos was simply too disturbing for Radcliffe—or her largely middle-class female audience—to confront.[19] Rather than sacrifice the sentimental virtues, therefore, Radcliffe tries to manage these anxieties by imaginatively insulating the ideology's feminine virtues from the masculine threat of material self-interest. Radcliffe insists, first of all, that despite all evidence, passion *can* be governed by principles. And in order to ensure their victory, she simply abolishes the "painful circumstances" that undermined their power. By taking Emily out of Udolpho, restoring her to nature's inspiring influence and to a moral, paternalistic society, Radcliffe is able to substitute ethical dilemmas for the unresolvable threat of avarice and to return the plot complication to a harmless encounter between virtue and error. Radcliffe's strat-

egies are conspicuous and, more than anything, they call attention
to the difficulties materialism posed for sentimental values, but her
very insistence attests to her investment in saving the sentimental
ideology from itself.

The first of these substitutions occurs even before Emily is liberated from Udolpho. Having imagined that the recurring sound of
a French ballad must mean that Valancourt is imprisoned in the
castle, Emily is shocked senseless to discover that the hidden singer,
into whose arms she has thrown herself, is a complete stranger. This
dilemma, of course, is one which sentimental principles *can* resolve.
Upon regaining consciousness, Emily assures Monsieur du Pont
that she mistook him for someone else and appeals to his virtue to
pardon her indecorous behavior. Emily is correct in judging du
Pont to be a harmless creature of sensibility like herself. Du Pont is
so responsive, in fact, that his impassioned apology brings Montoni's ruffians crashing into their secluded hiding place.

Emily escapes from Udolpho with surprisingly little trouble,
given Montoni's previously absolute power. But she must still endure
two important dilemmas which take the place of and, by implication,
are meant to resolve the anxieties generated within Udolpho. First,
rumors of Valancourt's behavior in Paris endanger Emily's future
happiness; then the suggestion that her beloved father might have
nursed an illicit affection threatens to undermine the authority of
her cherished sentimental education. Radcliffe invests these possibilities with enormous thematic and emotional significance, for Valancourt's passion for gambling and St. Aubert's promiscuity seem to
be embryonic versions of the destructive energy Montoni embodies.
By dramatizing the socialization of passion—or denying its presence
altogether—in these good characters, Radcliffe simultaneously con-
structs a model of how excess can be contained and attempts to negate the disturbing suggestions Montoni aroused.

Valancourt's rehabilitation, which I have already described,
demonstrates Radcliffe's strategy most clearly. By permitting him
to be infected and then cured of the same "unnatural," avaricious
passion that characterizes Montoni, Radcliffe offers the possibility
that this disruptive force *can* be controlled *if* it remains sufficiently
responsive to the aesthetically gratifying principles of feminine virtue. With some kind of infallible external control, perhaps even the
male possessed of the more dangerous energy can be taught to in-
ternalize virtue, to attune his desires to the principles dictated by his
"nobler faculties."

Neither Emily nor the reader learns of Valancourt's reformation until very late in the narrative, however, for Radcliffe uses this uncertainty to demonstrate the wisdom of St. Aubert. Emily believes Valancourt has fallen; therefore she must choose between the restraint advocated by her father and the special pleading of her own desire. When she resolutely follows her father's advice, subduing her implicitly sexual passion by means of principled feeling, she proves herself capable of managing her own sensibility—in strictly benign circumstances such as these, of course. Radcliffe immediately rewards Emily with both the "rational happiness" of marriage and the knowledge that St. Aubert's loved one was, appropriately, his own sister.

Radcliffe completes her strategy of substitution by sustaining the mystery of Valancourt's fall and the identity of St. Aubert's other love for almost 500 pages. Just as the perceptual obscurity of Udolpho jeopardized Emily's self-command, so the opaqueness of ignorance threatens her ethical security. By having Emily overcome the second trial, Radcliffe attempts to eradicate the ominous implications of the first. Radcliffe's notorious revelations contribute to this same strategy: just as time can erase the apparent moral failings of Valancourt and St. Aubert, so the narrator can provide natural explanations for most of Udolpho's apparently supernatural horrors. Even if these explanations do not successfully offset the anxieties that Udolpho and Montoni originally generated, Radcliffe clearly wants to create the *effect* of having resolved the ideological complexities by working through the less intractable, newly centered moral problems. She disposes of the remaining loose ends with equal ease: Montoni is arrested and dies mysteriously and offstage in prison (presumably a victim of evil's natural attrition), Emily regains her father's and her aunt's estates, Valancourt's brother gives him entail to his family's "rich domain," and Udlpho passes into the possession of a female relative—thus, we assume, into socializing control.

Not surprisingly, the new order ushered in at the end of the romance simply restores the traditional, paternalistic community of Emily's childhood, with the social contract of marriage now presiding in St. Aubert's place. Marriage sanctifies and socializes the desires of Emily and Valancourt, and they retire to Emily's reclaimed ancestral estate to bask happily ever after in the glow of virtue rewarded. The undisputed possession of property protects them from the temptations of avaricious desire, and perfect reciprocity is reestablished between the aesthetic charms of moral nature and the ethical responses of a sympathetic but principled heart. The subversive traces of sexual and materialistic passion engendered in Udolpho might almost vanish in the mist of this protective, pastoral harmony. In the last paragraphs of the novel, Radcliffe cannot help but applaud her artful contrivance:

> Oh! how joyful it is to tell of happiness, such as that of Valancourt and Emily; to relate, that, after suffering under the oppression of the vicious and the disdain of the weak, they were, at length, restored to each other—to the beloved landscapes of their native country,—to the securest felicity of this life, that of aspiring to moral and labouring for intellectual improvement—to the pleasures of enlightened society, and to the exercise of the benevolence, which had always animated their hearts; while the bowers of La Vallée became, once more, the retreat of goodness, wisdom and domestic blessedness! (IV, xix, 672).

The aura of fantasy that enchants this final arrangement suggests that it does *not* constitute a convincing solution to the problem of how virtue is to be protected from internal or external threats. Radcliffe dramatizes no "enlightened society" to offset the power of Montoni's tyranny; she has emphatically shown this harmony not to be "secure"; and the retreat to the domestic comforts of La Vallée hardly illuminates the darkness of the castle Emily has left behind. The anxieties generated by Montoni's avarice simply continue to haunt the formulaic resolution Radcliffe presents. Having admitted the genuine specter of aggressive, individualistic energy into her fiction, Radcliffe cannot effectively disarm its threat. Having uncovered the material forces that actually endanger the sentimental ideology, she cannot successfully contain their subversive threats without abandoning those sentimental values she cherishes. The dissatisfaction registered by generations of readers testifies to the discrepancy between the complexities Radcliffe has raised and the simplistic solution she proposes. "Curiosity," as Coleridge remarked of *The Mysteries*, "is raised oftener than it is gratified; or rather, it is raised so high that no adequate gratification can be given it."[20]

One point still needs to be made. Despite the fact that Radcliffe dramatizes, in no uncertain terms, the inherent liabilities of the sentimental ideology, she nevertheless suggests that there is a positive as well as a defensive reason for preserving feminine values. Even at the moment of Emily's greatest victimization within the oppressive walls of Udolpho, Radcliffe attributes to her a very real, if indirect, power. Much of the interest of the romance centers, in fact, on how

Emily will be able to exercise this power given the extremity of her "painful circumstances."[21] Radcliffe postpones Emily's marriage to Valancourt, promised early in Volume One, not primarily so that the young chevalier can prove himself or make his fortune but so that the young woman can have an opportunity to test her power, to enjoy an intense (if harrowing) adventure before settling into her "proper sphere." Udolpho obviously poses unexpected psychological complexities for Emily, but it also offers her this chance to exercise an ingenuity that the rules of propriety will soon deny her. Exploring the labyrinthine corridors virtually at will, penetrating into secret passageways and eavesdropping on Montoni's midnight revels, Emily answers the Italian's blatant bravado with a quiet resourcefulness that eventually enables her to elude him. Even at her moment of greatest danger, when Montoni demands the transfer of her ancestral estates, the girl demonstrates a remarkable power in denying him his desires. The root of her strength lies in that particularly feminine gesture of passive aggression, but Montoni's frustration is no less for the delicacy of his antagonist.

Thus we can see in *The Mysteries* that Radcliffe at least partially affirms the sentimental values because they do provide women power, even if it is only the indirect or negative power of influence and resistance. By elevating women's dependent position, their victimization, to the status of myth, she is even able to suggest a degree of heroism in these gestures. Emily's ability to frustrate Montoni's designs retards, if not actually undermines, his triumph, and in so doing she proves an important agent in protecting the status quo against the threat of encroaching materialism. But, significantly, Radcliffe allows Emily such extraordinary power only within Udolpho. After her escape Emily returns to a more typical position of dependence, ward first of du Pont, then of the father-surrogate Count de Villefort, then of the exonerated Valancourt. In the realm of banditti and political intrigue outside the castle, men once more take the initiative, and the tension and complexity of the narrative diminish proportionately. Like Emily, Radcliffe is only willing to elaborate the feminine potential for power within definite boundaries; only the extremity of Udolpho's oppression sanctions such unorthodox fantasies of resistance become heroism. Radcliffe's final moralistic apologia returns her romantic dreams to their appropriate, humble dimension:

> And, if the weak hand, that has recorded this tale, has, by its scenes, beguiled the mourner of one hour of sorrow, or, by its moral, taught

him to sustain it—the effort, however humble, has not been vain, nor is the writer unrewarded (III, xviii, 672).

The legacy Ann Radcliffe bequeathes us is neither a singleminded call to abandon the sentimental values nor a wholehearted endorsement of them. Rather, hers is a complex, even contradictory response that reveals, most significantly, the power of sentimentalism and the competing tendencies within the ideology. Her romance reminds us that sensibility was not just a minor literary movement but a set of values and images that legitimized economic and political behavior as well and that it, like any system of values, was never monolithic but harbored and even nurtured its ideological opposite. As the foundation for the decidedly ambiguous power granted women in the late eighteenth century and as one theory hospitable to capitalism before its triumph, sensibility deserves more careful attention than it has yet received.

Radcliffe's romance also reminds us that all art—even specifically non-political art—constitutes a response to material conditions and the systems of ideas they generate. *The Mysteries of Udolpho* is, on the surface, merely an escapist fantasy, providing vicarious thrills for thousands of homebound, altogether proper ladies. But these very fantasies announce the frustrations and desires of an important social group at an important historical moment. Responding to the threat revolutionary turmoil posed to sentimentalism, Radcliffe sees to the heart of the sentimental code by which she lives; she sees its price and its rewards; she sees its bitter economic root and its beautiful flowering in feminine virtue. Even her refusal to explore the implications of her insight is an important aspect of her response, for it tells of the shelter sentimental values offered their middle-class proponents. *The Mysteries of Udolpho* reminds us, in short, that the imagination's response to reality involves testing, rejecting, and affirming values, and that in the process of creating meaning it may offer insights into changes deep in the social system itself.

SWARTHMORE COLLEGE

Notes

[1]My use of "ideology" as a lived system of values follows the definition of Terry Eagleton in *Marxism and Literary Criticism* (Berkeley: Univ. of Calif. Press, 1976), pp. 16-17. "Ideology is not in the first place a set of doctrines; it signifies the way men live out their roles in class-society, the values, ideas and images which tie them to their social functions and so prevent them from a true knowledge of society as a whole." In this sense, an ideology is largely class-specific, although even the dominant ideology must contain values meaningful to other classes if it is to retain its position of power. See also Raymond Williams, *Marxism and Literature* (Oxford: Oxford Univ. Press, 1977), pp. 55-71, for a discussion of the history, ambiguities, and limitations of this term. Following Williams' critique of critics' tendency to limit ideology to separable *concepts*, I try here to show how, even for its proponents, it necessarily involves a *process* of producing meaning, the lived experience of testing, rejecting, and affirming that system of values which defines one's position within a culture.

[2]In his *Keywords: A Vocabulary of Culture and Society* (New York: Oxford Univ. Press, 1976), Raymond Williams explains that the word *sensibility* was, throughout the eighteenth century, informed by its root affiliation with *sensible* and that it was closely associated with both *sentimental* and *sentiments*. "The significant development in 'sense' was the extension from a process to a particular kind of product: 'sense' as good sense, good judgment, from which the predominant modern meaning of *sensible* was to be derived. . . . *Sensibility* in its eighteenth century uses ranged from a use much like that of modern 'awareness' (not only 'consciousness' but 'conscience') to a strong form of what the word appears literally to mean, the ability to feel. . . . The association [of *sentimental*] with *sensibility* was then close: a conscious openness to feelings, and also a conscious consumption of feelings." See *Keywords*, pp. 235-38. In this essay, I use *sensibility* and *sentimentalism* interchangeably.

[3]For discussions of the turmoil of the late eighteenth century and the ongoing resistance of urban and rural poor to the values of paternalism, see Douglas Hay, "Property, Authority, and the Criminal Law"; Peter Linebaugh, "The Tyburn Riot Against the Surgeons"; and E. P. Thompson, "The Crime of Anonymity"; in *Albion's Fatal Tree: Crime and Society in Eighteenth-Century England*, ed. Hay et al. (New York: Random House, 1975), pp. 17-118, 255-308. For a discussion of the challenge posed to paternalism and the development of a class society, see Harold Perkin, *The Origins of Modern English Society 1780-1880* (London: Routledge & Kegan Paul, 1969; paper ed., 1972) and E. P. Thompson, *The Making of the English Working Class* (1963; New York: Random House, 1966). However, the ideology that had rationalized and defined paternalistic society persisted—even after the development of class society—as a rationalization for women's continued powerlessness. Even after the lower classes achieved sufficient consciousness and cohesion to explode the paternal social practice, women continued to be subordinant and, in fact, to embrace sentimental values. The Victorian ideal lady or "angel of the house" is in reality a reincarnation of sentimental values.

[4]Although some of the values and attitudes of middle- and upper-middle-class women were emulated by lower classes, my discussion of the values of sensibility is confined to those middle-class women who largely made up the female reading public.

⁵Thomas Gisborne, *An Enquiry into the Duties of the Female Sex*, 4th ed. (1797; London: T. Cadell, 1977), p. 23.

⁶Jean-Jacques Rousseau, *Émile*, trans. Barbara Foxley (1792; New York: Dutton, 1911), p. 324.

⁷Gisborne, pp. 12-13.

⁸See Nancy F. Cott, *The Bonds of Womanhood: "Woman's Sphere" in New England, 1780-1835* (New Haven: Yale University Press, 1977), pp. 64-74.

⁹Mary Wollstonecraft, *A Vindication of the Rights of Women with Strictures on Political and Moral Subjects* (1792; New York: Norton, 1967), p. 34.

¹⁰Hannah More, *Strictures on the Modern System of Female Education with a View of the Principles and Conduct Prevalent Among Women of Rank and Fortune*, 2 vols. (London: T. Cadell and W. Davies, 1799), 2:23.

¹¹Ann Radcliffe, *The Mysteries of Udolpho: A Romance, Interspersed with Some Pieces of Poetry*, ed. Bonamy Dobrée (1794; London: Oxford Univ. Press, 1970), vol. I, book v, page 53. All future references will be to this edition and will be incorporated into the text by volume, book, and page numbers.

¹²A common adage, even in the last decade of the century. Cf. Edmund Burke, *Reflections on the Revolution in France* (1790; Garden City: Anchor Press/Doubleday, 1973), p. 179.

¹³Before entering Udolpho, Emily's experiences with nature are decidedly religious. For example: "From the consideration of His works, her mind arose to the adoration of the Deity, in His goodness and power; wherever she turned her view, whether on the sleeping earth, or to the vast regions of space, glowing with worlds beyond the reach of human thought, the sublimity of God, and the majesty of His presence appeared. Her eyes were filled with tears of awful love and admiration; and she felt that pure devotion, superior to all the distinctions of human system, which lifts the soul above this world, and seems to expand it into a nobler nature; such devotion as can, perhaps, only be experienced, when the mind, rescued, for a moment, from the humbleness of earthly considerations, aspires to contemplate His power in the sublimity of His works, and His goodness in the infinity of His blessings." *Mysteries*, I, iv, 47-48.

¹⁴See especially Robert Kiely, *The Romantic Novel in England* (Cambridge, Mass.: Harvard Univ. Press, 1972), pp. 72-78, and Norman N. Holland and Leona F. Sherman, "Gothic Possibilities," *New Literary History*, 8, no. 2 (1977), pp. 279-94.

¹⁵Patricia Meyer Spacks, *Imagining a Self: Autobiography and Novel in Eighteenth-Century England* (Cambridge, Mass.: Harvard Univ. Press, 1976), p. 85.

¹⁶Nelson C. Smith, in his article "Sense, Sensibility and Ann Radcliffe," (*Studies in English Literature*, 13, no. 3 [1973], p. 577), also observes that Radcliffe was critical of sensibility. "Far from being an advocate of sensibility, she, like Jane Austen two decades later, shows its weaknesses and flaws." But Smith, and most of the critics who have followed him, asserts that the cure for indulged sensibility is simply a "return to reason." Radcliffe's insight that sensibility is intimately bound to sexual and avaricious passion clearly makes such a solution, while attractive, impossible.

¹⁷*The Romantic Novel*, p. 75.

¹⁸It is interesting to note here the reversal in priorities that has occurred since Richardson's *Clarissa*. In the earlier novel, the threat to Clarissa's virginity was foregrounded and the economic "rape" by the aristocrat Lovelace was subordinated. Richardson's Christian plot focused specifically on the spiritual dimension of the heroine's physical fall. For Radcliffe, on the other hand, otherworldly consolation is intimately linked to earthly conditions; without sufficient money to protect her-

self, Emily's physical integrity would always be in danger. Thus Radcliffe foregrounds the economic threat as endangering both sexual *and* spiritual security.

[19]Radcliffe's was not, of course, the only possible fictional response to this situation. Other middle-class women novelists, most notably Mary Wollstonecraft, explicitly repudiated both the sentimental ideology and the emergent capitalism that threatened it. But we should remember that Radcliffe's romances found a much larger audience than did Wollstonecraft's *Maria*—no doubt because Radcliffe voices the fears and fantasies of a majority of the female reading public.

[20]S. T. Coleridge, "Review of *The Mysteries of Udolpho, A Romance*," in *Coleridge's Miscellaneous Criticism*, ed. Thomas Middleton Raysor (Cambridge, Mass.: Harvard Univ. Press, 1936), p. 357.

[21]Robert Kiely also discusses this point. See *The Romantic Novel*, p. 73.

LA POUPÉE PERDUE:
ORDRE ET DÉSORDRE DANS
LES PETITES FILLES MODÈLES
DE LA COMTESSE DE SÉGUR

Sylvie Mathé

A mi-chemin du conte de fées et du témoignage réaliste sur son temps (cf. l'étude de Pierre Bléton, *La Vie Sociale sous le Second Empire, un étonnant témoignage de la Comtesse de Ségur*),[1] l'oeuvre pour enfants de la Comtesse de Ségur née Sophie Rostopchine se présente comme une entreprise d'instruction de la jeunesse au même titre que de divertissement. Si sa vocation littéraire est née d'une contingence (le départ de ses deux petites filles, Camille et Madeleine, pour Londres et son désir de continuer à leur raconter des histoires, par écrit cette fois), elle n'en a pas moins rapidement évolué d'une relation familiale de type affectif et pédagogique en une relation artistique professionnelle et rémunérée. L'oeuvre de la Comtesse de Ségur, qui a fait les beaux jours de la Bibliothèque rose de la Maison Hachette, n'a cessé d'être lue par des générations successives de petites filles du Second Empire à nos jours. La persistance d'un tel succès conduit à s'interroger sur les ressorts de cette littérature enfantine, sur la représentation du monde qui y est donnée, ainsi que sur l'idéologie qui la traverse.

Le cas des *Petites Filles Modèles* s'avère particulièrement intéressant pour une étude de type féministe sur l'importance des conditionnements dans l'éducation des petites filles et dans la formation du rôle féminin dès la petite enfance. Le titre, en effet, peut être renversé et se lire Les Petites Filles Modèles: modèle pour les petites filles. En d'autres termes, il ne s'agit pas seulement de représenter des petites filles exemplaires par leur qualités, leur conduite etc., mais de faire de cette représentation un modèle précisément, une sorte de guide pratique et théorique à l'usage des petites filles, un manuel social et spirituel de bonne intégration aux moeurs et à la morale de son temps, ainsi que de préparation à la vie adulte. Le récit devient source d'édification morale et sociale et par là-même moteur d'un conditionnement féminin dont nous étudierons ici les modalités.

Les Petites Filles Modèles se présentent comme une parabole sur le thème de l'ordre et du désordre, c'est-à-dire que le récit procède d'une représentation idéalisée d'un ordre établi menacé par l'irruption plus ou moins contrôlable des forces du désordre. Sa fonction édificatrice se double donc d'une fonction thérapeutique, puisque la menace est finalement écartée ou intégrée pour aboutir à un réconfort final. Le récit est ici proche, à bien des égards, des contes de fées dont le rôle thérapeutique a été remarquablement analysé par Bruno Bettelheim dans son livre *Psychanalyse des Contes de Fées*: "ils informent des épreuves à venir, des efforts à accomplir. Mais ils s'achèvent toujours par le succès ou le réconfort. L'enfant, en s'identifiant au héros ou à l'héroïne, exige cette fin heureuse."[2]

Nous essaierons dans un premier temps de dégager les éléments de l'ordre établi présenté dans le récit comme un ordre idéal à préserver et à perpétuer. Puis nous étudierons les irruptions du désordre sous ses trois formes essentielles: le désordre social et moral, le désordre des instincts et des passions, enfin le désordre physique et naturel. A partir de cette dualité de forces, nous analyserons la démonstration littéraire qui permet à la Comtesse de vaincre le désordre et de triompher des épreuves, pour faire de ses petites filles des modèles et les fixer ainsi dans un rôle d'autant plus tenace qu'elle aura montré les dangers à vouloir y échapper. Démonstration, comme nous le verrons, qui n'est pas sans ambiguïtés.

I. L'ordre établi

Le récit s'ouvre sur un portrait des deux petites filles "modèles", Camille et Madeleine, qui à lui seul résume, englobe et transcende la dualité ordre/désordre pour garantir un état de bonheur idyllique où toutes les contradictions sont déjà résolues:

> Madame de Fleurville était la mère de deux petites filles, bonnes, gentilles, aimables, et qui avaient l'une pour l'autre le plus tendre attachement... Jamais on n'entendait une discussion entre Camille et Madeleine.

Pourtant leurs goûts n'étaient pas exactement les mêmes. Camille, plus âgée d'un an que Madeleine, avait huit ans. Plus vive, plus étourdie, préferant les jeux bruyants aux jeux tranquilles, elle aimait à courir, à faire et à entendre du tapage... Madeleine préférait au contraire à tout ce joyeux tapage les soins qu'elle donnait à sa poupée et à celle de Camille qui, sans Madeleine, eût risqué souvent de passer la nuit sur une chaise, et de ne changer de linge et de robe que tous les trois ou quatre jours. Mais la différence de leurs goûts n'empêchait pas leur parfaite union... Elles étaient parfaitement heureuses, ces bonnes petites soeurs et leur maman les aimait tendrement.[3]

Telle est bien l'image du bonheur parfait, celui où l'altérité n'est pas source de mésentente mais où, bien au contraire, la bipolarisation des types (vif/calme) apparaît comme une dualité intégrée, réconciliée dans l'ordre et l'équilibre. Tous les éléments du bonheur sont là: deux petites filles et une maman unies par le plus tendre amour dans une éternité idyllique. L'imparfait de ce premier chapitre le situe hors temporalité; nous sommes ici en plein conte de fées, comme en témoignent les premiers mots du deuxième chapitre: "Un jour..."[4]

Pourtant la Comtesse insiste dans sa Préface sur la vérité du portrait: "Mes *Petites Filles Modèles* ne sont pas une création; elles existent bien réellement: ce sont des portraits, la preuve en est dans leurs imperfections mêmes."[5] La suite du récit sera donc consacrée aux "ombres légères qui attestent l'existence du modèle", prouvant par là une intention réaliste. La Comtesse entend enraciner son oeuvre dans la réalité de son temps, et l'intemporalité féérique du premier chapitre fonctionne comme représentation idéalisée d'un monde statique dont la Comtesse redoute la disparition. Comme le souligne Marc Soriano dans son *Guide de la Littérature enfantine*, "les professions de foi politiques et sociales sont fréquentes dans l'oeuvre de notre auteur",[6] et bien qu'utilisant certains procédés littéraires à la manière des contes de fées, ses récits sont si profondément ancrés dans l'histoire de son temps qu'ils ont pu servir de base à Pierre Bléton dans son étude sur *La Vie Sociale sous le Second Empire*. Le cycle des Fleurville qui se déroule autour de 1857 est bien un "étonnant témoignage" sur la vie de l'époque, du moins sur la vie d'une certaine aristocratie provinciale, qui était le monde de la Comtesse de Ségur dans son domaine des Nouettes, en pleine campagne normande entre Argentan et le Pays d'Ouche. Tel est le cadre géographique de ses récits, telle est aussi son implantation historique et sociale. Sophie Rostopchine, née à Saint-Pétersbourg en 1799, dont le père, gentilhomme beau parleur et mythomane, fut ministre de Paul 1er et se vanta d'avoir incendié Moscou à l'arrivée des troupes napoléoniennes (cf. *Guerre et Paix*), est bien l'héritière d'un monde féodal, celui du Moyen-Age de la Sainte Russie tsariste, malgré sa venue en France dans un milieu aristocrate et mondain imprégné des idées philosophiques du dix-huitième siècle sur une société plus juste et plus conforme à la "nature".

Son mariage (malheureux) au Comte de Ségur, sa fréquentation d'un milieu sceptique mondain, ne l'empêchèrent pas de rester Sopholetta, la petite aristocrate russe convertie au catholicisme par une mère austère et porteuse d'un idéal féodal suranné où aux classes sociales sont substitués des ordres irréversiblement séparés: l'aristocratie et le peuple. Elle retrouve ici un courant de pensée contemporain, de l'aristocratie foncière conservatrice, opposée à l'usurpateur Napoléon III, celui du monde légitimiste et ultramontain, où l'aristocratie se considère comme de droit divin, où tout individu est respectable en tant qu'élément de l'ordre auquel il appartient, pourvu qu'il accepte de rester à sa place. De même que les pauvres doivent accepter leur condition et leur rang, "un duc, une comtesse ne doivent rien commettre qui soit indigne de leur rang".[7] Pour la Comtesse le pire mal n'est pas un pauvre qui s'accepte dans sa condition, mais un parvenu qui prétend transgresser son rang. Telle est bien la tare profonde de Madame Fichini dans *Les Petites Filles Modèles*, dont l'absence de particule est en elle-même hautement symbolique, et dont la tenue extravagante est longuement décrite au chapitre IX comme signe de vulgarité et de déclassement. "Quelques instants avant l'heure du dîner, Madame Fichini arriva avec une toilette d'une élégance ridicule pour la campagne."[8] Suit une longue description des "ruches, dentelles, velours, et des mille enjolivures" qui bariolent sa toilette:

> La calèche était découverte; la société était sur le perron. Madame Fichini descendit, triomphante, grasse, rouge, bourgeonnée. Ses yeux étincelaient d'orgueil satisfait; elle croyait devoir être l'objet de l'admiration générale avec sa robe de mère Gigogne, ses gros bras nus, son petit chapeau à plumes de mille couleurs couvrant ses cheveux roux, et son cordon de diamants sur son front bourgeonné. Elle vit avec satisfaction secrète les toilettes simples de toutes ces dames... Aucune n'avait ni volants, ni bijoux, ni coiffure extraordinaire. Madame Fichini ne se trompait pas en pensant à l'effet que ferait sa toilette; elle se trompa seulement sur la nature de l'effet qu'elle devait produire: au lieu d'être de l'admiration, ce fut une pitié moqueuse.[9]

Et comme dans un vaudeville, au moment de s'asseoir, "la largeur de sa robe, la raideur de ses jupons repoussèrent le fauteuil... et l'élégante Madame Fichini tomba par terre." La leçon est claire: qui veut s'élever s'abaisse. Il importe d'être modeste, même dans les rangs les plus élevés, car la modestie rend compte de l'authentique conscience que l'on a de son rang. Ainsi les petites filles modèles sont-elles toujours sobrement habillées: "Camille et Madeleine n'étaient jamais élégantes, leur toilette était simple et propre."[10] De même Elisa, la bonne Elisa (dans les deux sens du mot) hésite avant de porter l'habit de fête que les petites ont choisi pour elle: "Ce n'est pas pour moi, tout cela; c'est trop beau! Je ne mettrai pas une si élégante toilette; je ressemblerais à Madame Fichini."[11] Les "bons" domestiques sont bien ceux qui ont conscience de leur rang et ne cherchent pas en sortir. Les rapports économiques sont ainsi définis que les maîtres commandent et vivent de leurs rentes, tandis que les serviteurs travaillent pour mériter des bontés que les "bons" maîtres ne peuvent que témoigner envers les "bons" serviteurs. Lorsque les petites veulent emmener Elisa en promenade, celle-ci refuse: "J'ai autre chose à faire que de m'amuser... Une bonne est une bonne et n'est pas une dame qui vit de ses rentes; j'ai mon ouvrage et je dois le faire."[12]

La représentation de la réalité est donc ici strictement calquée sur l'idéal politique et social de la Comtesse. Chacun est à sa place, laquelle est reflétée par la langue que parlent les différents personnages. Si Elisa, qui est une "bonne bonne", parle un langage châtié, la Comtesse varie souvant le style en fonction de l'appartenance sociale du personnage, non pas tant en vue d'un effet réaliste, mais davantage pour des préoccupations idéologiques. Une lettre à sa fille, citée par l'abbé Cordonnier dans son ouvrage La Comtesse de Ségur, est particulièrement révélatrice:

> Chère petite, j'ai fini et je n'ai pas fini. C'est-à-dire qu'ayant lu à Gaston Jean qui Grogne et Jean qui rit, nous avons trouvé, indépendamment des incorrections de langage, une réforme à faire sur le ton trop familier des domestiques et trop amical des maîtres. Ils sont trop camarades. C'est tout à revoir. Peu de pages à réécrire, mais une foule de mots, d'expressions à changer.[13]

Le monde de la Comtesse est donc bien un monde d'ordre, fondé sur l'acceptation de classes sociales rigides et sur l'irréversible rapport du maître et de l'esclave. La justification en est bien sûr quasi théologique: l'aristocratie est de droit divin, Dieu a ainsi fixé l'ordre extérieur qu'il est pour les classes inférieures une nécessité et pour les classes supérieures un devoir. La responsabilité des riches envers les pauvres consiste essentiellement à pratiquer la charité, la philanthropie étant conçue comme une justification ontologique des privilèges. Les petites filles modèles, qui ont déjà l'étoffe de petites saintes, ne manquent jamais de secourir les pauvres pourvu qu'ils soient bons et méritants. Projetant une promenade du côté de la grande route "pour voir passer les voitures", les petites filles n'oublient pas de prendre quelque argent:

> Madeleine: "Si nous voyons de pauvres femmes et de pauvres enfants, nous leur donnerons de l'argent. Je vais emporter cinq sous."
>
> Camille: "Oh oui, tu as raison, Madeleine; moi j'emporterai dix sous."[14]

Cette émulation charitable ne cessera à travers le récit. Seuls les mauvais pauvres comme Jeannette la voleuse (Chapitre XI) qui, refusant d'avouer qu'elle a volé la poupée, sera privée du "joli fichu de soie et du beau tablier pour les dimanches" que lui destinait Madame de Fleurville, ne bénéficient pas de leur charité chrétienne. Les priorités sont néanmoins très nettes: dans l'épisode de l'accident de la diligence, les premiers secours vont à la dame et à son enfant; ce n'est qu'après qu'on songe au postillon "aussi": "Et le malheureux postillon, écrasé par la voiture, ne fallait-il pas aussi lui porter secours?"[15] La bonne Elisa est d'ailleurs la première à avoir intériorisé ces hiérarchies sociales et à condamner en particulier les méchants pauvres. Dans le code déontologique de la Comtesse, toute faute en soi est pardonnable, pourvu qu'on la reconnaisse, qu'on se repente et que cette expiation serve à renforcer l'ordre établi. La religion vient donc donner une justification transcendante à un ordre immuable.

Ainsi les rôles de la femme sont-ils parfaitement définis: les femmes sont des mères qui aiment tendrement leurs enfants et les petites filles sont de futures mères qui jouent à la poupée. Elles s'occupent de l'organisation domestique et les petites filles font de même avec leurs poupées:

> Un jour Madeleine peignait sa poupée; Camille lui présentait les peignes, rangeait les robes, les souliers, changeait de place les lits de poupée, transportait les armoires, les commodes, les chaises, les tables. Elle voulait, disait-elle, faire leur déménagement: car ces dames (les poupées) avaient changé de maison.[16]

Mères et filles, d'autre part, exercent la charité de conserve. Elles sont modestes quant à leur apparence physique, mais conscientes de leur rang. Elles vivent une existence paisible, retirée et sédentaire, loin de l'agitation du monde, à exercer les vertus du travail et de l'ordre ainsi exaltées par Madame de Fleurville:

> Mes chères enfants, si vous voulez me rendre toujours heureuse

comme vous l'avez fait jusqu'ici, il faut redoubler encore d'application au travail, d'obéissance à mes ordres et de complaisance entre vous.[17]

Voilà le modèle proposé aux petites filles. Encore faut-il qu'il résiste aux sollicitations du désordre.

II. L'irruption du désordre

Dans *Les Petites Filles Modèles*, le désordre social et moral est principalement incarné par le personnage ridicule et odieux de Madame Fichini. Dès l'abord, l'absence de particule suggère la roture, elle-même associée à la vulgarité puisqu'elle s'accompagne d'une volonté de transgression. Madame Fichini, belle-mère de la petite Sophie de Réan (des *Malheurs de Sophie*) présente toutes les caractéristiques de la marâtre des Contes de Fées. Elle n'est pas la vraie mère de Sophie, ce qui rendrait inconcevables les mauvais traitements qu'elle lui fait subir et son manque d'amour; elle n'est que sa belle-mère et par là-même la marâtre par excellence. Bruno Bettelheim dans sa *Psychanalyse des Contes de Fées* a insisté sur le "fantasme de la méchante marâtre", artifice fondamental qui permet à l'enfant de réconcilier deux entités distinctes de sa mère; "celle qui aime et celle qui menace": "La mère qui est le plus souvent la protectrice infiniment généreuse, peut se transformer en une marâtre cruelle si elle a la méchanceté de refuser au bambin ce dont il a envie."[18] Le rôle de Madame Fichini est donc essentiel comme pendant à celui de Madame de Fleurville: la vulgarité de l'une atteste la noblesse de l'autre, la méchanceté de l'une fait valoir la sainteté de l'autre. Madame Fichini a l'avantage d'allier en sa seule personne un mal social, puisqu'elle est parvenue, un mal moral, manifesté par sa cruauté aveugle et son impitoyable méchanceté, ainsi d'ailleurs qu'un mal esthétique, puisqu'elle est "la grosse Madame Fichini". Pareil repoussoir est bien sûr idéal. Elle n'a pas plus de réalité qu'un pantin grotesque et finit par disparaître à Naples dans d'autres aventures, ayant définitivement abandonné Sophie à sa "vraie" mère, Madame de Fleurville, et étant devenue entretemps Comtesse Blagowski. Comme dans les contes de fées, la marâtre n'est donc bien qu'un "avatar passager" qui permet aux petites filles de "cristalliser" leur haine de la mauvaise mère, tout en les réconciliant avec une image favorable intacte de la mère admirable, émanation parfaite d'un ordre harmonieux.

A ce désordre extérieur vient s'ajouter un désordre intérieur, qui est l'objet premier du récit, le désordre des instincts et des passions. Dans son intention d'instruire la jeunesse et de l'orienter vers la foi, la Comtesse de Ségur n'a pas manqué d'accorder une importance primordiale aux défauts du caractère et aussi, plus profondément, aux sollicitations du désir—en termes psychanalytiques, aux manifestations du "ça". La plupart des épisodes des *Petites Filles Modèles* sont des variations sur le thème des désordres du "ça": le public auquel elle s'adresse étant enfantin, les appétits sont limités et la gourmandise, en particulier, y prend souvent une signification symbolique. Ainsi ce désir subit et effréné de poires, qui conduit la petite Sophie à voler sur l'arbre (Chapitre IX) les quatre seules poires "d'espèce nouvelle, d'une grosseur et d'une saveur remarquables",[19] l'envie qu'a Marguerite de couper toutes les fleurs du jardin de ses amies, "oeillets, giroflées, marguerites, roses, dahlias, réséda, jasmin, enfin tout";[20] enfin le désir plus sadique, plus obscur, d'enfoncer ces "pauvres petits hérissons" que le garde ("vilain Nicaise") a jetés dans la mare, ce afin de les noyer plus vite—autant de sollicitations de l'inconscient qui sont ici dénoncées. Chaque épisode entraîne ses conséquences tragicomiques: si l'on mange trop de cassis, on sera malade; et si l'on s'approche de la mare défendue, on tombera dedans et on recevra le fouet pour avoir désobéi. Cet épisode aux connotations directement sexuelles est particulièrement symbolique. Les interdits sont donc à chaque fois renforcés par leur transgression même. C'est précisément lorsqu'on veut désobéir qu'on éprouve à ses frais la résistance de l'interdit. La fonction édificatrice du récit bat ici son plein grâce à l'opposition qu'introduit la Comtesse entre les petites filles: les petites filles "modèles", Camille et Madeleine, toujours sages à une ou deux ombres près vite chassées, incarnent parfaitement le surmoi de l'enfant. En revanche, les deux autres petites filles, Marguerite, plus jeune et plus irréfléchie, et surtout Sophie, incorrigible victime de ses mauvais penchants, se partagent les degrés du ça. Ce sont elles qui, en suivant leurs impulsions aux dépens de la raison, font temporairement triompher le principe de plaisir sur le principe de réalité, ce qui immanquablement suscite une répression plus ou moins féroce ou une catastrophe plus ou moins grave, qui leur serviront comme autant de leçons dans l'acquisition du surmoi. Et comme un tel récit pour enfants ne saurait être qu'optimiste, elles finiront par s'amender progressivement et par tenter de se mouler sur le modèle de Camille et Madeleine, vivantes incarnations de l'intériorisation du surmoi. Là encore, la Comtesse se sert de procédés proches du conte de fées: ainsi la mare qui attire irrésistiblement Sophie, son envie de hérissons, et surtout l'épisode de la forêt (Chapitre XXII), où pour avoir voulu exercer toutes seules la charité, Sophie et Marguerite s'embarquent dans la forêt primitive des contes de fées et se perdent entre les loups et les sangliers:

Marguerite: "Sophie, je crois que nous sommes trop petites pour nous en aller toutes seules dans la forêt."

Sophie: "...Tu crains peut-être que le loup ne te croque?"
Et elles se mirent en route, ne prévoyant pas les dangers et les terreurs auxquels elles s'exposaient.[21]

Cet épisode de peur et d'errance dans la forêt à lui seul résume les autres transgressions pour leur donner un impact symbolique archétypal:

Immobiles de terreur, les pauvres petites avaient peine à respirer; le froufrou approchait, approchait; tout-à-coup, Marguerite sentit un souffle chaud près de son cou... L'animal qui arrivait droit sur elles était un sanglier... Si elle étaient restées sur son passage, il les aurait déchirées avec ses défenses.[22]

La transgression prend ici un caractère ouvertement sexuel. Et c'est curieusement un homme qui les retrouvera—le seul homme du récit—pour mourir quelques chapitres plus loin. La démonstration est claire: malheur aux petites filles déobéissantes et curieuses.

Enfin, après les sollicitations du désir, le dernier type de désordre qui fait irruption dans le récit est cette fois physique, de l'ordre de la nature et de la destinée. Il s'agit de la maladie, de la souffrance et de la mort. Une série d'épisodes illustre ces malheurs: un chien enragé mord Marguerite, la petite vérole frappe successivement Camille et la bonne Elisa—deux épisodes qui se terminent bien. Ces malheurs n'ont pas tous une fin heureuse néanmoins: des animaux meurent, de par la cruauté des hommes (les hérissons), ou de par leur propre entêtement (?) (le rouge-gorge puni d'avoir voulu quitter sa cage). Enfin et surtout, le destin frappe parfois aveuglément: ainsi périt le sauveur de Sophie et Marguerite, le "bon boucher Hurel," qui tombe de cheval et se noie dans la rivière. Le malheur, cette fois, est sans rémission; qui plus est, il reflète l'injustice et l'aveuglement du destin. Les voies de Dieu sont impénétrables...

III. Démonstration littéraire

Ainsi se fait l'apprentissage de l'ordre du monde. Le désordre est précisément ce qui permet au récit d'exister et de progresser. Il fonctionne à la fois comme élément thématique et comme élément dramatique. Il ouvre les yeux des petites filles sur les dangers qu'elles encourent à vouloir résister à l'ordre établi, et il sert aussi de moteur à l'intrigue. La démonstration littéraire de la Comtesse consiste à produire du désordre pour mieux le vaincre et pour aboutir à une soumission complète à l'ordre du monde. Les épreuves sont des occasions de repentir, d'expiation et de rachat. Elles servent aussi d'initiation à la souffrance, au malheur et à la mort. La fonction ultime d'une telle révélation ne peut être que de rassurer en dernier ressort. Les vrais malheurs ne frappent que les pauvres, et le désordre momentané débouche sur un ordre. Le récit fonctionne donc comme une opération d'exorcisme du désordre. Voyons quels sont les procédés littéraires dont se sert la Comtesse pour effectuer sa démonstration.

Le premier de ces procédés consiste à répéter certains événements sous forme de jeux. Ainsi, l'accident de la diligence, qui est d'abord présenté dans le récit comme une mini-tragédie particulièrement traumatisante pour Marguerite qui l'a vécue, est répété sous forme de jeu quelques jours plus tard; alors que sa mère est encore alitée à la suite de cet accident, Marguerite s'amuse avec ses amies:

> Enfin elle prit la petite diligence attelée de quatre chevaux et elle demanda à Camille et à Madeleine de sortir avec elles pour mener la voiture dans le jardin. Elles se mirent toutes trois à courir dans les allées et sur l'herbe; après quelques tours, la diligence versa. Tous les voyageurs qui étaient dedans se trouvèrent culbutés les uns sur les autres; une glace de la portière était cassée.[23]

Mais dans le monde des jouets, tout est réparable:

> Marguerite: "Si les voyageurs ont mal à la tête, comme Maman?"
> Madeleine: "Non, non, ils ont la tête trop dure. Tiens, vois-tu, les voilà tous remis, et ils se portent à merveille."

La répétition de la scène en jeu permet donc à la petite fille de revivre le drame de la vie, et ainsi de l'intégrer en se l'appropriant. Le rôle des jeux, et en particulier des poupées, est particulièrement intéressant à étudier dans ce récit, car ils servent de miroir de la réalité à l'échelle enfantine et par là-même de lieu de passage du principe de plaisir au principe de réalité. Par ailleurs, la nature même des jeux reflète le conditionnement des petites filles et joue un rôle fondamental dans la formation des modèles féminins: "Ce jour-là et les jours suivants, elles employèrent leur temps à habiller, déshabiller, coucher et lever la poupée."[24] Dans son livre *Du Côté des Petites Filles*, la psychologue italienne Elena Gianini Belotti insiste sur l'importance du choix des jouets et des jeux: "Dans les jeux des enfants et dans l'utilisation qu'ils font des jouets, la reproduction de la réalité sociale dans laquelle ils vivent est plus évidente que jamais."[25] Ainsi la répétition ludique des événements ou des attitudes sert-elle à enraciner les données de la réalité dans la vie et dans la mentalité des petites filles. Rien n'est innocent, les voies sont tracées dès l'enfance. A un autre niveau, le conditionnement à un rôle féminin donné est encore renforcé par un phénomène d'emboîtement des rôles. En effet, dès le début du récit, les deux petites filles modèles sont investies de la responsabilité d'être les mères de l'autre petite fille:

Marguerite: "Eh bien, vous serez mes petites mamans. Maman Camille et Maman Madeleine."[26]

Cette investiture spontanée sera d'ailleurs sanctifiée par les vraies mères, Madame de Fleurville et Madame de Rosbourg, qui s'en remettent à Camille et Madeleine pour l'éducation de la plus jeune:

Marguerite est plus jeune que vous. C'est vous qui serez chargées de son éducation, sous la direction de sa maman et de moi. Pour la rendre bonne et sage, il faut lui donner toujours de bons conseils et surtout de bons exemples.[27]

C'est ici que la signification des petites filles modèles joue à plein. Non seulement sont-elles des filles modèles mais elles deviennent même des modèles de mères, exemple dont la valeur est à la fois présente et future. Elles s'empressent d'ailleurs d'exercer leur autorité sur Marguerite et de reproduire ainsi les schémas maternels:

Madeleine: "Camille a la bonté de t'écouter, mais cette fois nous *voulons* que tu sortes. Il faut te montrer obéissante."[28]

Cette délégation des rôles de la mère à la fille est le plus sûr moyen de perpétuer la situation de la femme comme mère. Elle fonctionne comme un carcan destiné à enfermer la petite fille dès l'enfance dans sa vocation de mère. Comme l'a écrit Simone de Beauvoir:

On verra plus loin combien les rapports de la mère à la fille sont complexes: la fille est pour la mère à la fois son double et une autre, à la fois la Mère la chérit impérieusement et elle lui est hostile; elle impose à l'enfant sa propre destinée; c'est une manière de revendiquer orgueilleusement sa féminité et une manière aussi de se venger.[29]

Cet emboîtement des rôles prend d'ailleurs l'allure d'une poupée gigogne: Madame de Fleurville est la mère de Camille et Madeleine qui sont les mères de Marguerite qui est la mère de sa poupée. Celle-ci est d'ailleurs perdue dans la forêt, puis volée, et Marguerite pleure sa maternité frustrée... La démonstration est ici solidement étayée: point de salut hors de la maternité!

Enfin, le procédé littéraire qui est dominant dans *Les Petites*

Filles Modèles est celui du redoublement: la Comtesse de Ségur multiplie les rappels, les analogies, les échos sur un autre mode et les renversements. Ce système de symétries et de renvois suscite des effets de profondeur qui à chaque fois redoublent la démonstration. Ainsi au vol de poires de Sophie font écho le vol de la poupée de Jeannette et le vol du vin de Palmyre injustement attribué à Sophie. Sophie sera fouettée par sa marâtre et Jeannette de même par sa mauvaise mère. En revanche, Sophie fouettée par sa marâtre ne le sera plus par Madame de Fleurville: la Comtesse de Ségur, dont le sadisme a fait couler beaucoup d'encre, dépense ici beaucoup d'énergie à condamner pareille répression "barbare", pour lui opposer les bienfaits du "Cabinet de Pénitence". (Il est intéressant à cet égard de noter que son oeuvre illustre le passage d'une punition corporelle à une punition morale. Dans son livre *Surveiller et Punir*, Michel Foucault a longuement analysé ce tournant du dix-neuvième siècle qui "s'émerveillait de ne plus châtier les corps et de savoir désormais corriger les âmes".[30] Sophie hurlant sous la verge de sa marâtre et Sophie faisant pieusement ses écritures dans le Cabinet de Pénitence illustrent bien ce débat central au dix-neuvième siècle de l'enfermement contre les châtiments corporels.) A la pénitence de Sophie dans sa prison fait alors écho le chagrin de Mimi dans sa cage, Mimi le rouge-gorge humanisé qui, pour s'être échappé, périra "mangé par un vautour ou par un émouchet": "Ci-gît Mimi, qui par sa grâce et sa gentillesse faisait le bonheur de sa maîtresse jusqu'au jour où il périt victime d'un moment d'humeur."[31] De même la poupée perdue dans la forêt annonce l'aventure malheureuse des petites filles égarées dans une forêt noire de symboles. L'épisode de la mère Lecomte et de sa fille s'explique aussi par la disparition du père sur le même vaisseau que commandait Monsieur de Rosbourg, disparu lors du même naufrage. A la noyade tragicomique de Sophie fait écho la noyade, fatale cette fois, du bon boucher Hurel. Enfin, la longue maladie d'Elisa qui, contaminée par Camille, faillit périr de la petite vérole, se termine par un joyeux épilogue, celui de la Fête au Château où, nouvelle analogie, le spectacle présenté raconte le dévouement d'une "bonne Négresse":

> Le sujet de la pièce était l'histoire d'une bonne Négresse, qui, lors du massacre des Blancs par les Nègres à l'île Saint-Domingue, sauve les enfants de ses maîtres, les soustrait à mille dangers et finit par s'embarquer avec eux sur un vaisseau.[32]

Cette construction par redoublement est systématique dans tout le récit. La Comtesse ne laisse rien au hasard dans une démonstration qu'elle veut infaillible.

L'ordre du monde finit donc par triompher des forces du désordre. La Providence sanctifie les riches. Le mal aveugle et irrémédiable n'arrive qu'aux autres, de préférence aux pauvres, et, curieusement, à un homme. La fonction thérapeutique du récit consiste à reporter les possibilités de malheur sur autrui, et, dans cet univers presqu'exclusivement féminin, sur le seul être masculin actif de l'histoire. Il est intéressant de constater que l'univers de la Comtesse est un gynécée, d'où les hommes sont absents: Monsieur de Fleurville a péri dans un combat contre les Arabes et Monsieur de Rosbourg a disparu en mer dans le naufrage de la Frégate. Cet univers clos exclut les hommes, que la Comtesse tenait généralement pour veules, et apparaît comme un monde autarcique parfaitement idyllique. Au Chapitre IV Madame de Fleurville et Madame de Rosbourg décident de se mettre en "ménage" et tout se joue dans un théâtre de femmes. La Comtesse n'hésite pas à supprimer le seul homme, boucher de surcroît, et à se donner bonne conscience en faisant mourir sa veuve de chagrin et trouver la paix au Paradis (alors que Madame de Fleurville et Madame de Rosbourg survivent fort bien dans leur veuvage!).

Conventions du récit qui, on doit le dire, sont peu conventionnelles et qui amènent le lecteur à s'interroger sur les implications d'un tel matriarcat: il apparaît alors que, derrière les très forts conditionnements féminins que recèle le récit, et derrière le maternalisme sentimental exalté à chaque page, se dessine une autre figure de la Comtesse, celle d'une femme hantée par "l'incurable blessure de son enfance",[33] dont les absences et les silences visent secrètement à un bouleversement des rapports sociaux, où la femme serait revalorisée et retrouverait sa juste place. Les petites filles modèles angéliques de la Comtesse ne sont certes pas des féministes militantes, mais leur existence bienheureuse loin des hommes atteste le féminisme inconscient de leur auteur, sur un mode allusif "qui n'est pas celui de la revendication mais bien celui du parti pris des choses".[34]

WELLESLEY COLLEGE

Notes

[1]Pierre Bléton, *La Vie Sociale sous le Second Empire* (Ed. Ouvrières, 1963).

[2]Bruno Bettelheim, *Psychanalyse des Contes de Fées* ("Réponses", Robert Laffont, 1976).

[3]*Les Petites Filles Modèles*, Nouvelle Bibliothèque Rose (Hachette, 1958), pp. 7-8.

[4]Ibid., p. 9.

[5]Ibid., p. 5.

[6]Marc Soriano, *Guide de la Littérature Enfantine* (Flammarion, 1975), pp. 476-86.

[7]Ibid.

[8]*Les Petites Filles Modèles*, p. 64.

[9]Ibid., p. 65.

[10]Ibid., p. 64.

[11]Ibid., p. 236.

[12]Ibid., pp. 246-47.

[13]Chanoine Cordonnier, *La Comtesse de Ségur* (Paris, 1925).

[14]*Les Petites Filles Modèles*, p. 10.

[15]Ibid., p. 11.

[16]Ibid., p. 9.

[17]Ibid., p. 23.

[18]*Psychanalyse des Contes de Fées*, p. 93.

[19]*Les Petites Filles Modèles*, p. 68.

[20]Ibid., pp. 26-27.

[21]Ibid., p. 190.

[22]Ibid., p. 195.

[23]Ibid., p. 19.

[24]Ibid., p. 77.

[25]Elena Gianini Belotti, *Du Côté des Petites Filles* (Des Femmes, 1974), p. 121.

[26]*Les Petites Filles Modèles*, p. 16.

[27]Ibid., pp. 23-24.

[28]Ibid., p. 25.

[29]Simone de Beauvoir, *Le Deuxième Sexe* ("Idées", Gallimard, 1949), tome I, p. 305.

[30]Michel Foucault, *Surveiller et Punir* (NRF Gallimard, 1975).

[31]*Les Petites Filles Modèles*, p. 157.

[32]Ibid., p. 238.

[33]*Guide de la Littérature Enfantine*, loc. cit.

[34]Ibid.

THE FICTION OF FAMILY: IDEOLOGY
AND NARRATIVE IN ELSA MORANTE

Annette Evans

The much-heralded and highly politicized appearance of Elsa Morante's *La storia* in 1974 brought to a close her literary production.[1] It is the last of her three novels,[2] novels which were written over a span of thirty years and encompass a startling range of narrative techniques. Generally, the questions raised about Morante's work focus upon her use of Freudian psychological theory and her elaborate exploration of the mythic, fabulous atmosphere of childhood innocence, or they concentrate on the relationship of the narrative to a factual base.[3] I should like to propose instead that an examination of Morante's conception of the institution of the family may be of a higher degree of pertinence to the ideological significance of her work.

Indeed, Morante focuses upon family relationships as one of the central superstructural elements of the contemporary bourgeois order of Italian society. Furthermore, her condemnation of the bourgeois Italian model is even more concentrated because she enters the code of family with a steady view of the female component and shows again and again that culturally induced roles are doomed to produce insanity in women and cruelty and weakness in men. Thus, although she attacks bourgeois values from the same base as Moravia,[4] she shifts the emphasis to the illness of the family as a central metaphor for the cultural decay and the concomitant global disaster represented in modern history. In this way, her analysis of family structure creates a negative dialectic against the whole system of society as it now stands.

The first novel, *Menzogna e sortilegio*, is a theoretical abstraction of all the possibilities of family life, a textbook of the struggle and disillusionment inherent in the family roles developed within a class society. The theme itself is the destruction of a family of the lower classes, one whose members attempt to align themselves in various ways with a family of the lower nobility in Sicily. Morante covers three generations of women, giving to each a different way of approaching the dilemma of self-fulfillment within society. The grandmother attempts through education to insert herself into a higher class: she becomes a governess and then snares the heir of the Massia house in a marriage of ambition. He, however, is on the brink of financial ruin and is subsequently disowned by the family. Their daughter, Anna, perhaps because of the aristocratic weakness that she inherits from her father, is lazy and unwilling either to be educated or to work; she becomes a kind of useless parasite on society. Finally, she falls disastrously in love with her cousin, who she knows will not marry her, and accepts society's disapprobation for his sake. Anna's attempt to live by the irrational concepts of self-negating love do not, of course, end in the salvation that she seeks; instead, she is forced to marry another man in order to rescue herself and her mother from starvation. The irrationality of her first love has led her into an irrational union sanctioned by society. It is her daughter, the recluse Elisa, who narrates the story of the family. With her, the family ends in sterility, an indication of the sterility of the family as an institution.

Morante uses these three women to explore the condition of women in a society that puts such a premium on caste, and not the least of the tragedies is the lack of sympathy and sense of community between mother and daughter. Indeed, the isolation of the women from any consolation or self-realization is acute. Only the last character, cut off entirely from family ties, can accomplish anything, and she must endure the heroic isolation that creates art.[5]

There are no happy marriages in *Menzogna e sortilegio*, there are only various pairings for convenience or for gain. In this way, marriage becomes homologous with the structure of capitalist society: the emphasis within the institution is on the fetishism of money rather than the productive nature of human relationships. The institution of marriage is also seen as a kind of recapitulation of the patriarchal state, for the men in the novel need marriage for status and they use their authority in an absolute and capricious manner. It is only by resignation that women can recover a bit of dignity and peace in such a relationship. Thus, marriage becomes a place where the false consciousness necessary for the hegemony of the capitalist state is produced.

The only relationship that seems promising in the novel is that between mother and son, because the son is the over-determined sign of the unfilfillable ambitions of the mother. Concetta, the mother of the young heir of the noble Massia family, is a harsh and religious woman with an extravagant weakness for her beautiful son. Their relationship is physical, bordering on the incestuous. At the same time, the institution of religion allows her to picture herself as a Madonna, giving a legitimacy to the all-devouring passion that she has for her son. Because she can see herself as thus ennobled through her offspring, she supports his self-indulgence and cunningly courts his favor. When he dies of tuberculosis, she goes mad.

The second mother of a son is the peasant Alessandra, who brings forth and adores her male child in a "natural" way. The innocent idyll of this woman with her bright and loving son lasts until he is forced to leave home for his formal schooling. Then she too is forced to accept the child's integration into the paternalistic world and to suffer subsequent humiliation and deprivation because of his follies in society. Alessandra is the character in the novel who has strength because she knows her place in this scheme: she must provide and suffer and survive, for that is the natural order of things for mothers.

The ultimate dissolution of these several branches and alliances of the Massia family is a case study in the internal pressures that bourgeois aspirations and false expectations bring to bear on the structures of trust and sympathy upon which the family must depend. The topoi that Morante establishes in *Menzogna e sortilegio* reappear in the other two novels, frequently in minor re-evocations, but this novel is basic in formulating the ideological base against which the others must be read.

Arturo's Island, which appeared in 1957, shows the clearest kinship with Moravia's work—especially with *Agostino*—and critics have frequently remarked on this.[6] But the Freudian myth is here given a much fuller and more structurally complex treatment. The novel is a reconstruction of the world of adolescent prelapsarian innocence. At the beginning of the work Arthur's realm seems devoid of the evils of society: he has almost complete freedom as the son of a wealthy, mysterious, often absent father.[7] His mother is dead, and the usual enveloping care that mothers represent has been replaced by an almost solitary existence; his physical needs are overseen by a sympathetic old manservant who in no way impairs Arthur's free wanderings about the island.

However, it is with his father's remarriage that the central motif of family relationships is introduced into the novel. Indeed, what Morante proposes here is an examination of the superstructural phenomenon of family relationships as seen in Italian society, but entirely severed from the economic base. This procedure gives a quality of abstraction to the work that has often been noted and debated by critics.

Arthur's crisis—his father's remarriage—introduces both the mother-surrogate and the motif of incest into the story. The new bride is young, only two years older than Arthur, and his love for her is the most exaggerated representation of the incest taboo in Morante's work. Arthur must renounce this love for Nunziata and must also suffer her bearing a new son to his father.

In this novel, Morante has taken the basic nuclear family and has so stretched and extended the relationships as to create a parody. Two characters inform Arthur's world, his father and his new stepmother. Because we must follow the story from Arthur's viewpoint, much of the mystery of the work is in the character of the father. Where does he go when he leaves the island? Why does he suddenly appear with a new wife whom he does not seem to love? The revelation that his father's deeper commitment is to another man on the mainland and that his father is totally absorbed in this passion is Arthur's last lesson in the workings of the adult world.

Morante has shown in this work that the familial roles which are so frequently exaggerated in bourgeois society inevitably lead to a crisis of caring, and that this crisis is particularly acute in the relationships between sons and mothers. The ambiguities attendant on the mother-son relationship, especially in the overidealization of the mother, lead to sons who are weak, if not homosexual. In any case, it produces men who are incapable of establishing a fulfilling relationship with a woman.

The character of Nunziata, who rejects Arthur but continues to mother her own son in those "natural" ways that are the province of the peasant or lower-class woman, is the only untortured one of the book. As long as she is willing to substitute the joys of animal motherhood for the unattainable joys of wifehood, she can at least survive this distorted triangle.

Morante's most recent work, *La storia*, is an attempt to capture the pathos of history through the depiction of World War II. Thus, although the location of the novel is Rome, 1941-1947, the war itself is a metaphor for the victimization of people by history. In order to incarnate this sense of the victim, the novelist returns to the motif of the family, here further reduced to its skeletal and moribund form both in an institutional and in a narrative sense.

The central character is Ida, the Other that Italian society has conspired to destroy. She is a half-Jewish widow, retiring, diffident and defenseless. She is also the prototypical mother who feels at home only in the company of children. She has one legitimate son, Nino, who is the embodiment of the assertive, irresponsible, adored male. The other son, Useppe, is the fruit of the book's opening rape scene; his father was a passing German soldier who in Morante's portrayal is himself a victim of History.

Although the flashbacks of the novel establish Ida's parentage and the projections of the final sections show a continuation of the line through Nino's son, the focus is rigidly and strictly upon this reduced family unit of mother and two sons.

Ida follows Morante's topos of the all-giving mother. She suffers the insults, vagaries, and small humiliations that Nino's adolescence imposes upon her. When she and Useppe are bombed out of their apartment, she scavenges for food and steals for him; in the end she virtually stops eating in order to provide some small nourishment for him.

Ida is also a Madonna in what seems a conscious parody of the Christian story. Although she has borne one child and buried a husband, at the time of the rape she is experientially a virgin. The rape takes on an almost supernatural aura, for not only does Ida faint dead away, she awakens after the fact to feel a miraculous compassion for the German soldier who raped her. But the clearest sign that she is a parody of the Madonna is Useppe himself, a magical, innocent and wonderfully precocious child who is attuned to the good of the world. However, in the modern world a Christ-like figure such as Useppe has no place; his redemptive powers are to no avail and he suffers an early death.

What is absent in Ida that Morante has explored in the two earlier works is the seductive and incestuous relationship between mother and son. Ida gives birth to and nurtures Useppe in crisis, in the dangers and deprivations of war. She has no strength or inclination to dote on him in the usual fashion of the mothers of the previous novels. Rather, Ida must become father as well as mother to Useppe and see to his material well-being. He is left alone from a very early age, while she goes out to forage; in her place she leaves the family dog, who understands his needs and protects him. In the most lyrical extension of the narrative technique, the magical child and the dog even have a language and can communicate in words.

In the middle section of *La storia* there is another animal whose story even more perfectly parodies Morante's scheme of family. Rossella, the cat, bears one tiny kitten who cannot nurse because her mother has been so undernourished during her pregnancy. Rossella seems to understand that the kitten has no chance for life, and in a natural and merciful way she abandons the kitten to die. Ida, on the other hand, cannot preserve her being as separate from that of her child; no matter what the cost or the logic, she must alienate herself in his service. Her whole role as mother within the institution of the family demands that she reduce herself to the agent of her child. Thus, when Useppe dies Ida goes mad, for without the existence of the child there is no longer the rationale of motherhood.[8]

The three novels present a rather interesting set of narrative progressions: the time shifts ever closer to the present and the scene moves from abstracted southern settings to the hard facts and clear geographical locations of the Second World War. This progression is also marked by the choice of the narrator of each piece: *Menzogna e sortilegio* is told by the last remnant of the Massia family; *Arturo's Island* is recounted by the main character, while *La storia* has an omniscient and puzzlingly intrusive narrator.[9] This change to an impersonal extra-familial narrator marks the last stage of the crisis of the family, one which is interwoven with the cultural crises inherent in the war.

The possibilities of the family so carefully explored and found to be wanting in *Menzogna e sortilegio* are repeated as distillations in the succeeding two novels. The narrowing of family structures from the extended family of *Menzogna e sortilegio* through the over-determined portrait of the nuclear family in *Arthuro's Island* to the reduced family of *La storia* can be seen as a deliberate pattern: the family as a bourgeois institution can no longer bear the pressures of history.

UNIVERSITY OF MASSACHUSETTS

Notes

[1]*La storia* (Turin: Einaudi, 1974). Before its appearance, Morante indicated that it was to be her last novel. Cf. Angelo Pupino, "Elsa Morante," *I Contemporanei* (Milan: Marzorati, 1969), p. 716. The general excitement and controversy surrounding the publication of the book has been amply documented by Gian Carlo Ferretti, "Il dibattito su *La storia* di Elsa Morante," *Belfagor*, 30 (1975), pp. 93-97.

[2]The other two novels are *Menzogna e sortilegio* (Turin: Einaudi, 1978) and *L'Isola di Arturo* (Turin: Einaudi, 1957).

[3]Among the most useful of these studies are Giacomo Debenedetti, "*L'Isola di Arturo*," *Nuovi argomenti*, 26 (1957), pp. 43-61; Franco Ferrucci, "Elsa Morante's Limbo without Elysium," *Italian Quarterly*, 27/28 (1963), pp. 28-52; Angelo Pupino, *Strutture e stile della narrativa di Elsa Morante* (Ravenna: Longo, 1967); Luigina Stefani, "Elsa Morante," *Belfagor*, 26 (1974), pp. 290-308; Mario Boselli, "Dalla storia della menzogna alla menzogna della storia," *Nuova corrente*, 67 (1975), pp. 313-29.

[4]Morante was married to Alberto Moravia for a short time, a fact which most biographers mention prominently. It is clear that the two authors have a literary background in common and share, to some degree, a political vision.

[5]Elisa reconstructs the reality of her family through their lies ("menzogna") and through witchcraft ("sortilegio"). The question of fictional reality is one that concerns Morante in all her work: cf. her article "Risposta a nove domande sul romanzo," *Nuovi argomenti*, 38/39 (1959), pp. 17-38, and Boselli's study of her novels, "Dalla storia della menzogna."

[6]Angelo Pupino, "Elsa Morante," p. 732.

[7]Debenedetti, "*L'Isola di Arturo*," shows the mythic dimensions of this novel in his Proppian analysis.

[8]This outcome, of course, echoes the fate of Concetta, but Ida has much greater reason.

[9]Morante explains her adherence to the "io" philosophically: ". . . nel momento di fissare la propria *verita* attraverso una sua attenzione del mondo reale, il romanziere moderno, in luogo di invocare le Muse, è indotto a suscitare un *io* recitante (protagonista e interprete), che gli valga da alibi. Quasi per significare, a propria difesa: 'S'intende che quella da me rappresentata non è *la* realtà; ma una realtà relativa all'io di me stesso, o ad un altro io, diverso in apparenza, da me stesso, che in sostanza, però, m'appartiene, e nel quale io, adesso, m'impersono per intero'. Così, mediante la prima persona, la realtà nuovamente inventata si rende in una verità nuova." "Risposta a nove domande sul romanzo," pp. 24-25.

THE OFF-CENTER SPATIALITY
OF WOMEN'S DISCOURSE

Rosette C. Lamont

In his review of two books on Jane Austen that appeared in *The New York Times Book Review* of May 6, 1979, Tony Tanner, the author of *City of Words*, begins by quoting Austen herself: "Men have had every advantage of us in telling their own story. . . . The pen has been in their hands." Tanner agrees with this statement and goes on to say: "The pen *had* been mainly in the man's hand: It was the male who effectively owned and controlled the discourses within which women had to move and have (or fail to have) their being."

If this awareness is not new, it has never been more clearly realized and given expression than today. In the words of Hélène Cixous, women must "write their own selves into writing."[1] This is no easy task, but it is important for women today not to ape the stance of men, not to wear male masks or masculine attire, not to swagger, not to hide. Women must invent their own style, both new and rebellious, and thereby emerge from the restricted spaces assigned them for their existence. Their discourse will then take flight on the wings of words that grow out of their flesh, like those of birds and angels, instead of appendages affixed to their backs. In French the word fly (*voler*) is the same as the word to steal, and Cixous makes much of this ambiguity, stressing the fact that women have had to steal moments of time, steal off and away in order to rise up.

> To fly is the gesture of woman, to fly in language, make it fly. All of us have learned the innumerable techniques of the art of taking off since for centuries we could accede to having only by stealthily taking. We lived by stealth, stealing off, finding narrow, hidden, crossing passages. Stealing is a taking and a taking off, played out between two interdictions, both enjoyed as the avoidance of the

police of common sense (meaning). It is not pure chance then that woman has something of the bird and the thief, as the thief has something of woman and bird: they pass, flee, enjoy the scrambling of orderly space, of disorientation, changing the place of furniture, things, values, breaking in, out, voiding structures, turning own and ownership upside down. . . .A feminine text cannot be anything but subversive: if writing itself, it does so by the volcanic raising of ancient, established, encrusted surfaces (pp. 178-79).

Cixous is not unaware of the libidinal component of the dream of flight as well as that of the itch to steal, to take possession of the forbidden. This militant feminist speaks of writing, of what she calls "la prise de la parole" (p. 170), in the same terms as Jean Genet speaks of committing a theft. Women and thieves, Cixous claims, share the same algebra of the imagination, that of marginal, peripheral people condemned by society to *relative* being. In Sartrian terms, they are the Other. Precluded from touching, grasping the real, they are doomed to transgression. Thus a feminine text must be subversive in order to make its way toward a new freedom.

The road to this liberation is not necessarily a straight path. Cixous sees it as a sinuous exploration that begins within, at the very center of the female body that "has been confiscated, made into a disquieting stranger" (p. 179). Nor is this in-dwelling narcissistic, for woman's libido, according to Cixous, is "cosmic" (p. 162), and her erogeneity "heterogeneous" (p. 164). She takes in the world, feels it grow inside her like a child within her womb. Only when women learn to write from this inner place, the core of their being, will they, according to Cixous, give rise to "the other language made up of a thousand tongues" (p. 162). Women's discourse, coming from the most private recesses, will assume its place in an "elsewhere," a space other than "the territories subject to the philosophico-theoretical domination" (p. 170) exercised by male speech and writing.

The attack upon phallocentric thinking voiced in *La jeune née* is directed against Occidental cultures. As a "gauchiste," Cixous compares the situation of women in her society to that of colonized peoples, slaves, Blacks, Jews. She would agree with the writer Aimé Césaire's definition of his country as not only underdeveloped but "peripheral," and thus unable to develop normally.[2] And yet, this marginality can be made into a source of power, one that is perhaps greater than the brute strength of the central reigning powers. Speaking of the shock created in his native Martinique by the encounter between two systems of thought, two philosophies—that of the European colonizer and that of the African—Césaire suggests that a synthesis might come out of this "Sociéte en Sursis."[3] On the one hand, the writer explains, we have in the Antilles the world of the white man, based on aggression, the dream of conquest, and domination; on the other there is the universe the slaves brought with them, the Bantu longing for cosmic integration, for reconciliation, harmony, the insertion of man and society into the infinite. Whether this declaration is to be taken as myth or reality, it is fascinating to watch the great poet from Martinique build his meditation upon culture on concepts which he tells us have been developed and systematized by a Third World economist, Samir Amin, concepts of the differences created between the *central* and the *peripheral*. In order to escape from being imprisoned in the latter, Césaire speaks of "UN SURSAUT COLLECTIF, galvanisateur et salvateur. . . ."[4] What is suggested here is that salvation will come when a new consciousness develops from the peripheral, the marginal, travelling back to the central.

Speaking at the 1979 Barnard conference on "The Future of Difference," the poet Audrey Lord seems to address herself to the same problems in almost identical terms when she states: "Poetry is the language of difference whereby we give name to the nameless. . . and issue from a dark, inner sphere. . . the hidden place of power."[5] For Cixous, woman is the Stranger who speaks a "pre-language she has never stopped hearing."[6] This tongue might be that of the mythic isle of her sisters the Amazons or that of the dark continent whence all life sprang. In a passage of pure poetic incantation, Cixous exclaims, addressing all women: "We, the precocious, by culture repressed, lovely lips lagged, gagged breath, we, labyrinths, ladders, trampled spaces; usurped, robbed—we are 'black,' and magnificent."[7] If Cixous identifies with African women it may well be because of her Algerian origins. As a Jew, a "Pied Noir," and a woman, she felt thrice excluded from patriarchal French culture. Thus it is with a good deal of defiance that she defines herself in *La jeune née* as "Juifemme" (p. 187).

This parallelism between the female sex and the Jewish people had already been noted by Tolstoy. Like the Jew or the Black, women are excluded from the human *mitsein*. For women, however, there is no return to a motherland; no state of Israel expects or accepts them. Mutilated in Africa and the Orient (clitoridectomy, bound feet), burnt as witches by the thousands for centuries in Europe and even in the United States, imprisoned within the confines of the home, deprived of all rights, derided and feared, women have had to survive by the most enduring will to live. No wonder, then, that many now prefer to assert their difference and to invent spaces of expression in the lacunae of official discourse.

Julia Kisteva was the first to make the claim that women are perpetual dissidents. Indeed, like camp inmates or prisoners, women make do with limitations of time and space. For them creation of an artistic order comes either before or after a long day of chores and duties. It is achieved out of the remnants of sapped vitality or as a spurt of repressed energy. Although survival is an intimate, personal struggle, comfort can be derived from the fact that women, again like camp inmates or lifers, are not alone: they belong to a community of outcasts and misfits. Like the latter they must weave a tapestry of sounds made from their voices blending together, voices "from the chorus."[8]

Today's women are dissidents who will no longer be silenced. They have come to realize that woman—her sexuality, her inner life, her imperatives, and indeed her whole self—has been the victim of planned censorship and, worse still, that like the artist working under the repressive conditions of a dictatorial regime she has often had to impose self-censorship upon her efforts. It is up to women, however, to assist in what Cixous calls "the circulation of discourse."[9] As Elizabeth Janeway declared recently: "It is incumbent upon women to create a framework of significance and to invent the future by giving rise to their own language, their own symbols."[10] Women's dissident discourse will reinvent society, or at least create a parallel mode of existence.

A question is sure to arise: Isn't every work of art—whether that of a man or of a woman—an autonomous universe, parallel to our own but self-consciously different from it? Perhaps it must be said at this point that a number of male writers have also been concerned with the creation of an "elsewhere." Cixous is aware of this, and in *La jeune née* she names Kleist (particularly as the author of *Penthesilea*, the story of the Amazon queen); Baudelaire, the androgynous poet par excellence;[11] Flaubert, whom Sartre calls in his famous study "the family idiot"; Joyce; and Shakespeare, who according to Cixous "was neither man nor woman but a thousand beings."[12] One is tempted to add Thomas Mann, Proust, Eugene Ionesco, Beckett, and quite a few others. The great poets—and this includes certain novelists and dramatists—the visionaries who were free enough to surrender to their subconscious, situate themselves outside the norm. They also make a virtue of being peripheral, marginal. On the other hand, a number of women writers take pride in making their stand at the center of things, of mounting an assault on "the center of action." There is nothing marginal about Madame de Staël save for the fact that Napoleon forced her exile to Switzerland whence she continued her campaign against his tyranny. The same holds true for George Sand, who must be credited with playing an important role in the awakening of the liberal imagination of her time—an achievement due to her pamphleteering rather than to her artistic production. And when Monsieur Willy did the great Colette the favor of leaving her, she promptly stepped into the center of all the stages of art and life. Obviously there are no simple answers. The writer of this essay will attempt to analyze those instances of female discourse which, like those of some male writers, have attempted to develop an aesthetic of marginality. Two contemporary writers have been chosen, one French, the other American: Marguerite Duras and Elizabeth Hardwick.

In a book of informal conversation taped with the journalist Xavière Gauthier, *Les Parleuses (Women Talkers)*, Marguerite Duras ponders a revealing device that she used in one of her films, *Nathalie Granger*. A group of women have just cleared the table at which they were having a meal. Now they are in the kitchen, washing dishes. One knows this from the clatter of plates, the tinkle of glasses, the voices rising over the splashing water, but the women are not shown on the screen. Instead, the camera lingers on the empty table, cleared, wiped clean. It seems to stay there forever, almost aimlessly. Trying to come to grips with her peculiar brand of realism, Duras wonders, thinking aloud:

> It is a realism pushed to the extremes; it turns into the unreal. Perhaps this is due to a kind of insistence, duration. In my script I have not written: "She clears the table," but "Hands clear this table," and then, as though starting a new paragraph: "The table has been cleared." I never show the clearing of the table itself, simply a table cleared. There is a slight break, a displacement of reality. Had I wanted to be realistic I would have placed the camera in the kitchen and waited for the women to enter from the dining-room, carrying dishes. That's what film makers usually do. Instead, I have the camera stay on the table. It's a battering of the realistic code."[13]

The word "displacement" is a key to the universe of Marguerite Duras. Not that it is an alienated world, although it can also be called that, as I will later show. What is striking is that Duras attaches a tremendous importance to things being quietly there, physically present. Why does the camera linger on the empty table? It accounts for life itself at its most primitive level. "The bare table is pure magic," says Duras, "it has a life of its own, one apart from that of the women. It says something about the house, about space, about cinematographic space" (p. 96). The physicality of cinematographic vocabulary that seems so important to Duras has been stressed by more than one filmmaker. Most recently, Andrei Serban, the avant-garde Rumanian director, having been invited by British television to film a fragment of a play written by Jane Austen when the novelist was a child of twelve, tried to compare his work as a director of plays with this new assignment. He made the following declaration: "Theatre touches a more invisible reality. Film is more concrete, it catches real objects in the camera."[14]

Duras' space, whether filmic, novelistic, or dramatic is a hollow, rich, passive void, pregnant with possibilities and expectations. Words whirl around this hole which is a whole: they fail to fill it. Even words of love, of erotic passion—for Duras, as she often affirms, there is no difference between the two—are unable to disguise the ever-present, ever-renewed hunger of desire. Eros and Thanatos touch, intertwine. Duras traces her own transformation as a writer and a thinker to a crisis arising from an overwhelming erotic experience, one which she tried to transmit in *Moderato Cantabile*. In *Les Parleuses*, a book which resulted from days and days of intimate conversation taped in her home, she speaks with complete frankness of the depth of that enslavement and of a temptation to take her own life or have that life taken from her by the man she loved:

> For a long time I'd go out in society, having dinner at people's homes, attending cocktail parties. All that time I was writing my first books. All of this formed a kind of totality. And then, one day I had this love experience, a very, very violent erotic experience. I went through a crisis . . . a suicidal temptation . . . that's what I tried to tell in *Moderato Cantabile*, the story of a woman who wants to be killed. I lived through that, I lived it, and from then on my books changed. The turn in the direction of sincerity took place then . . . A break occurred in the very depths of my being . . . It is true that in *Hiroshima* I had already written: "You kill me! but I had never, never experienced it before (pp. 59-60).

For those who think of Duras as a writer with a cool, almost detached style, this is a very revealing analysis. Clearly, for her the erotic universe is the dark side of the moon. Nor is this apprehension the prerogative of the female sex, but, Duras suggests, women are perhaps more receptive to this awareness. Xavière Gauthier suggests: "I believe there is a strength in feminine desire, in female sexuality, that man does not wish to know," and Duras echoes:

"Men are not strong; they are turbulent" (p. 39). For men the quenching of desire is direct, fairly simple; for women there is a persistent erotic tension. The latter creates its own inner space, vast, uncharted. Perhaps this is why Duras states so firmly: "Each and every woman is more mysterious than a man" (p. 50). This all-pervasive presence of erotic consciousness is in itself, Duras says, a form of transgression. Society has always tried to bridle this passion, to enclose it safely within the marriage relationship. This is a travesty, and Duras is not afraid to say that "women have a Medieval fear of infidelity" (p. 41). Only "plural experience" (ibid.) can break these bonds. Nor must erotic plurality be confused with sexual looseness; it is rather the form that love takes when it is divorced from the capitalistic needs of ownership. Duras' sexual politics are in harmony with her libertarian, anarchist stance. As a sexual being and as a political creature she posits herself off-center, in those zones that have not been colonized.

In Conversation Two of *Les Parleuses*, Duras discusses what she calls four books, and then redefines as three books and a film (clearly it is almost impossible for her to separate one genre from the other; since all express what she needs to say, all form a single discourse): *L'Amour, Le Vice-Consul, Le Ravissement*, and *La Femme du Gange*. She and Gauthier notice that there are no heroes in these works, only anti-heroes, and that there is no heroic will or intention either expressed or implied. Everyone in these works seems to "undergo" events and even sentiments. Identity has disappeared and yet existence is all the stronger. Desire is not concretized upon a single being; it circulates freely from one to the other, like blood flowing through a vast social body. The latter is not that of society as we know it but rather the kind of anti-society wrought by the very young, the hippies, the dropouts. Not that Duras ever portrays hippies. On the contrary, she often describes and films society people, *des mondains* living in hauntingly empty houses as though some revolution were about to take place or had occurred leaving them stranded, intact and yet deeply wounded. They move through official fêtes, balls, receptions, or sit in the gardens of decrepit yet still beautiful luxury hotels, what the French call *palaces*. They are "dislodged" from society, out of time, out of place. Something has happened to them all, something that might have been described and explained in an earlier book. The book, however, has not been written, does not exist. The unwritten book is like the invisible women in the kitchen, off camera range. In this book that has never existed Duras says she would have described her characters' separation from society, the facts and reasons for this separation. It is all conditional, a condition that has not been fulfilled since everything is suspended. Yet the people of Duras' films or plays or novels are present in their *thereness* ensconced in their refusal of existing conditions, submerged but not annihilated. This refusal to will, to make decisions, this stubborn being in the world is as political as revolutionary action—political if not concerted. The surface of the characters' expectation is passive, but under the surface there is an urgent tension, an almost erotic pulsation.

Duras' subversive approach is strictly personal. If she identifies with anti-heroes, dropouts, and even hippies, it is because she wishes above all not to be caught in the trap of single-minded, simple-minded ideologies. In the margin of her transcribed conversations with Gauthier, the writer notes:

> A man who would view himself as nothing more than a Marxist consciousness, who would wish himself to be that and that alone, would be the simplified model proposed as the ideal Stalinist. This is more than a dangerous concept, it is a terrifying one. Simplification is the basis of both Hitlerism and Stalinism. Every simplification fosters a form of fascism (*Les Parleuses, Notes en marge*, p. 236).

When the other dialoguist, obviously more *engagée*, presses her interlocutor to side with Marxism, particularly as a way of emerging from the dilemma of female repression, Duras draws back with great firmness:

> Hitlerism and Stalinism touch, fuse. . . . A party member always elects to accept a certain lack of complexity. To freeze leftist ideals is to aid in their disappearance. . . . Every true revolutionary is his own leftist. One must always continue to explore the wild spaces of one's contradictions, and the true communist will preserve these within. If the Chinese fail to understand this truth, if they come to believe that everything in man is reducible, then their revolution is dead (ibid.).

For Duras the revolutionary attitude is perpetually alive and must renew itself. She learned her independence and her Eastern passive resistance from her childhood in Indochina and from her indomitable mother, an impoverished, widowed schoolteacher who, having purchased a piece of land from crooked speculators, devised an extraordinary scheme to erect a self-made barrage or dam against the flooding ocean. It was an absurd, heroic endeavor, one doomed to failure. Duras describes it in a novel, *La Barrage du Pacifique*, and a recent play, *Eden-Cinéma*. Because the family was poor they had no access to the colonialist elite despite the fact that they were French and Caucasian. About the old woman of *Le Barrage*, Duras says with pride and affection: "She invented a personal dialectic" (p. 184), and although this individual form of rebellion may not have been unconnected with what is known as revolutionary dialectic, it was not Marxist but simply a brave woman's "own brand" (p. 184) of resistance and protest.

By having grown up in Indochina among the native population, sharing the plight of the colonized, Marguerite Duras made the apprenticeship of difference. It was a lesson she never forgot. India, as she portrays it in fiction and film, is for her "the world's flaming core of absurdity, a senseless agglomeration of famine and illogic" (p. 177). Some of her films are conceived as a shout of protest or as the vengeance of the East. It is, she explains in *Les Parleuses*, as though the boats traveling down the Mekong, bringing the tithe-payers to the colonial administrator, had suddenly crossed the Atlantic to land on the fashionable beaches of Trouville. Her works are those boats, and they have reached our shores. Yet, this is also what makes them so strange. Duras often complains in the course of these conversations of her solitude, of the complete lack of understanding her work meets with in France. Not unlike Cixous, she feels that she is a foreigner in her own country. She states: "I live off my British and German copyrights. In France it's almost a total blackout" (p. 35). She is in fact reduced, she claims, to a kind of clandestine literary existence.

Like Aimé Césaire, Duras spent her formative years in a "peripheral," "marginal" culture. Her mother taught French, and in the home contact was maintained with the *patrie d'origine*, but Duras felt more in tune with the exotic, free life of her mother's pupils. With them she ran barefoot through the jungle, unafraid of snakes, miraculously untouched by them. The miracle seemed to persist as the girls swan in the river full of caymans. Recalling these years Duras speaks of "a kind of collective grace" (p. 143), an "elemental receptivity" (ibid.). Surrealist images constituted the everyday reality: Tigers and monkeys watched the girls in the rain forest where fish swam high above the ground, spawning in pools held by the naturally woven baskets of centuries-old, clustered creepers. Once Duras caught a glimpse of a black panther a few feet away. But the road to the Bokor was a *via dolorosa* of Vietnamese slaves interred alive up to their necks for non-payment of taxes. Beauty and horror existed side by side.

Even before Duras came to Paris to complete her studies she was aware that the Occidental illusion that man is the master of his fate, a belief grounded in Cartesianism and the Kantian dream of the superman, was a foolish way of looking at existence. In *Les Parleuses* she explains: "Asiatic philosophy does not live by this illusion; in the Far East people believe that destiny is stronger than we are, and that it runs through us" (p. 141). Duras defines this view as "informed passivity" (p. 146), and she is convinced that in our society it is women, and women alone, who can communicate this apprehension to the rest of the community. "This refusal, this passivity, is a mode of self-knowledge, as strong and fecund as communication through speech in a close and closed society" (p. 149).

Although some theoreticians of feminism may be surprised to see Duras equate feminine with passive, an old stereotype, it is important to note that all along the writer has been speaking in praise of a certain patience, a passive waiting. In this she is not unlike the Beckett of *Waiting for Godot*, who opposes the Gogo/Didi couple, the friends who are waiting for Godot—waiting, hoping— and the Pozzo/Lucky pair of master and slave who travel back and forth on the road of life, one whipping and driving the other until, made weary and weak by all this activity they return in Act II to stumble and fall at the feet of the two knights of "choiceless awareness."[15] Duras belongs to the race of the Gogos and Didis of this world—androgynous, vulnerable beings who try to avoid violence and help those who are close at hand and in need.

A displaced person in France, an inner exile of the mind, at eighteen Duras was sent by her mother to complete her last class at the lycée (Philosophie) and enter university. The capitalist society based on production and consumption that met her eye did not seem to have anything to do with the reality she had left behind. But back in Indochina there existed other forms of horror imposed upon a gentle, contemplative people by colonial administrators. Clearly, in Yeats' words, "the centre cannot hold."[16] Many of her works seem to record the falling apart of things prophesied in "The Second Coming." Thus, early in life Duras began to develop that off-center aesthetic which characterizes all her work.

Perhaps it is in her most recent dramatic work that Marguerite Duras has demonstrated most clearly her unorthodox approach. To Xavière Gauthier she explains her position in terms of her dramaturgy:

> You have the theatre space, that's where the public is sitting. Facing them there's the stage. And then there's another space. It is in that other space that events are lived, experienced. The stage is only an echo chamber. . . . It is also the darkroom of the spectators. Where

does the real action take place? Not on the stage where nothing is happening, or being said, but in that other space where it is all taking place. . . . The stage is an antechamber, a transparent consciousness (pp. 190-91).

In Duras' *Eden Cinéma* actors go soundlessly through motions and emotions while their story is being narrated by off-stage voices. The latter come from the wings or from one side of the stage, reaching the audience sideways. Thus, the public does not receive the text as though it were spoken at it, but as a recitation, something read rather than said. The intent is to "de-realize" the action, an effect Duras seeks to achieve on the sound track of her films by using voices that sound dubbed or daubed. At a performance of *Eden Cinéma* the audience is neither lured into the action nor lulled into identification with the characters; it is made to feel that it is reading a novel or that it is being read to and that the images presented on the stage arise from the consciousness of readers of a book who, by dint of their intellectual activity, also participate in the writing of the story. The audience is acting rather than being acted upon.

The title, *Eden Cinéma*, is ironic: it suggests a fake paradise, that of a house of dreams, the movie theatre of a small provincial or colonial town. The title provides a clue for the viewing of the play. It is as though we were shown a film, a silent flick with captions.

The character of the main heroine is split into two women, played by two actresses,[17] one on the stage, the other, older, functioning as the reader. This device also suggests the situation of an older woman thinking of her past. In a program note Duras explains: "I'd like the play to be read as much as heard, to be heard as much as seen, to be made as much as viewed."[18] Since Duras is not only telling her own story—that of the girl—but also the story of her mother,[19] the play/story acquires the quality of a dream, of a remembrance of something past. The play, like all of her previous plays, issues, Duras tells us, "from the night that precedes the act of writing."[20]

Many of Duras' voices emerge from the same shapeless, sensual night. They do not coincide with the images presented on the screen, nor are they supposed to parallel the action. They are like nature sounds used for the soundtrack. In discussing *La Femme du Gange* with Gauthier, Duras makes the point that these disembodied whispers speak for the characters or for some kind of action which may be part of a collective past. The images and sounds form what she calls "a bi-film." The voices keep on filtering through, crowding into the spaces left by images that are not close together. Perhaps recalling her playmates in the jungle, Duras imparts shape and color to the voices: "They wear white, tattered clothing and inhabit the top floor of the hotel, a floor where instead of windows there are only high transoms. . . . They see and are seen in different ways" (p. 89). The girls' whisperings inhabit the filmic space, fluttering through it like wild birds, making holes with their wings for air to enter. Duras states that her film breathes through these holes and that the viewers are also able to catch their breath. Here also her intentions are clearly in opposition to the traditional techniques of filmmaking in which off-film voices comment on the action shown or about to be shown. "Commentaries fill the void," she explains in *Les Parleuses* "whereas in my film the voices perforate the surface, making holes, or spaces" (p. 89). Not unlike the symbolist poet Stéphane Mallarmé, with whom Duras has a great deal in common, the maker of *La Femme du Gange* plans to leave blank spaces upon the page, even if the latter is celluloid.

The reiterated statements about the importance of the void, the impossible fulfillment, the slow rhythm of film action that approximates the time of waiting, of expectation and remembrance—all of these remind the modern viewer of some of the works of Samuel Beckett. But Duras also suggests to Gauthier that there is something specifically feminine about this aesthetic (in a positive sense, of course), that time does not pass in the same manner for men and women. Women experience time the way prison inmates do, living from chore to chore, meal to meal. Does this imply that women are perpetually jailed in our society, held prisoners? Probably. At any rate, Duras claims that women feel more comfortable among marginals (homosexuals, dropouts) because, like them, women have special antennae that allow them to detect the telltale signs of the death of our society. Marginals and women, then, share the same off-center discourse, which may express itself through the semiotics of a nihilistic pantomime (unconventional attire, sexual attitudes and preferences) or, if they are creators, through the aesthetics of marginality Duras explores in so many different ways.

In her "Conversation" on her book *Sleepless Nights*, published in *The New York Times Book Review* of April 29, 1979, Elizabeth Hardwick seems to echo Marguerite Duras' thought on the subject of the almost instinctive rapprochement between women and marginals when she declares:

> I guess I'm very much drawn to drifters, to frauds, to working-class people, waitresses, 10-cent clerks, bus stations. . . . I don't like cruelty

or indifference. . . . I just like to think about the flow of life of the unsteady, think about all those people in automobiles, driving about with their debts. Sometime I hope to write about trailer parks.

In reviewing *Sleepless Nights* for the daily *New York Times* (Friday, May 4, 1979), John Leonard wrote: "So the center didn't hold. Perhaps there is no center. Perhaps the only center is the past. Perhaps the past doesn't hold either, and is merely the history of damages." Hardwick's work of fiction—if indeed it can be called that—can be compared in its fragmentary aesthetic to Montaigne's essays, Pascal's *Pensées*, La Bruyère's *Portraits*, or, to bring it closer to the twentieth century, Sinyavsky's *A Voice from the Chorus*. Julia Kristeva would no doubt recognize in Hardwick a quiet, discreet, but determined dissident, one whose mind strains to recover the blank spaces of history and comes up instead with "little splinters of memory that seem to have been personal."[21]

Who are the damaged, the discarded, the disregarded that Elizabeth Hardwick turns to with affection, understanding, and compassion? First, her "tireless mother" who had "nine children" (p. 24). Her "femaleness was absolute, ancient," endowed with "a peculiar, helpless assertiveness . . . the old, profound acceptance of the things of life" (p. 25). What the writer remembers most vividly about her is an "ineffable femininity, tidal" (ibid.). Although she never left the South—her wanderings took her from Kentucky to Virginia or Tennessee—she is described as "having the nature of an exile" (p. 92). And yet there is little doubt that her home was her center, even if the night led to days full of "drudgery and repetition" (p. 94). This oceanic mother must have taught her daughter to look into the secret selves of the flotsam and jetsam of our civilization: the vanquished derelicts of the Hotel Schyler, "deserters from family life, alimony, child support, from loans long erased from memory," (p. 44), who lived in the center of Manhattan as in a burglarized house, "wires cut, their world vandalized, their memory a lament of peculiar losses" (p. 32). They lived in insolent hope, drinking, fornicating, making brief connections with one another, running up bills, lying to others but mostly to themselves, always hoping to make it, to get into the big time. They are not unlike Gorky's characters in *The Lower Depths* or the habitués of the bar in O'Neill's *The Iceman Cometh*.

Out in the streets of New York, Elizabeth Hardwick's eye picks out the bag ladies, "hugging their load of rubbish so closely it forms a part of their own bodies" (p. 52). This is the end of the line, but in between there are the old maids and house maids, the anonymous inhabitants of rooming houses, the young prostitutes. Most of these

derelicts are women: Miss Lavore, who is embraced only by her dancing partners at the Arthur Murray Dance School where she goes
every night of the week, all dressed up as though for a first date; Miss
Cramer, the failed mezzo, once endowed with a voice, a mother, a
mannish felt hat, a shining black convertible, then quite quickly
losing voice, mother, car, courage, all; Judith, a handsome woman
with a Ph.D., harem silk pants, Afro hair, a mixed-up son, an absent
lover, the victim of chronic ill-luck or bad judgment; Marie, the lovely society girl, adored by her parents, turned communist, who takes
ugly, fat Bernie, her lover, into her white, lacy, girlish bedroom only
to lose him to "a militant, sexy, talkative comrade" (p. 85); Josette,
the courageous cleaning woman, who loses a breast to cancer and a
husband to untimely death; Ida, the cheerful laundress, who lets
Herman, a would-be fisherman in Maine, rob her blind; Juanita,
who turns to prostitution for no clear economic reasons and dies of
venereal disease "in unbelivable suffering" (p. 23). All of these lives
seem to "obey the laws of gravity and to sink downward, falling as
gently and slowly as a kite, or violently breaking, smashing" (p. 15).

Another such fall is that of the great, dark comet, the singer Billie
Holiday. About her the narrator says that she was headed from the
start for grand destruction. When she was not singing in night clubs
she could be found in the Federal Women's Prison in West Virginia,
or in hospitals, or dingy hotel rooms, filling all these spaces with her
"stinging, demonic weight" (p. 40). Not like a real person, but a kind
of "bizarre deity" (p. 34), she unleashed malevolent forces, those of an
archaic Great Mother. Her own mother, who had hoped to work for
her, was kept at arm's length, and when the old lady died her daughter did not make the funeral on time. Billie Holiday, the marginal par
excellence, turning her marginality into her statement and her art,
glows at the core of this collage of fragments. Hardwick writes:
"Somehow she had retrieved from darkness the miracle of pure style"
(p. 36).

Is this a woman's book, a book written by a woman, for other
women to read? The author does not like to be defined in this manner, refuses in fact to let this be her self-definition,[22] and yet few
works in recent years would fit this category—if one needs categories—better than *Sleepless Nights*. The persona writing these fragments is "a broken old woman in a squalid nursing home" (p. 3). On
a day in June she begins to gather a bunch of fading, distorted memories. No order, no organizing intellect makes sense of them. They
flow like the waters of life, at times in a trickle, at times gathering
speed, in turbulent falls.

The style is simple, direct, almost transparent. Some images seem to issue from the daily chores of a quiet life: "The bright morning sky that day had a rare blue and white fluffiness, as if a vacuum cleaner had raced across the heavens as a weekly, clarifying duty" (p. 47). Perhaps Hardwick's angels are not sexless but female, winged housewives with cheerful dispositions.

At other times clouds gather. One can feel the rage and scorn of the narrator when she evokes the Goncourt brothers' judgment upon their loyal servant Rose who, having served them for twenty-five years, had the indecency to die on the evening they were going out to dine at the home of their friend Princess Mathilde. There they were told of the poor woman's "nocturnal orgies" and realized that they ought to be suspicious of womankind, a sex given to lying. A lifetime of devotion was dismissed in one second. Elizabeth Hardwick reveals here a horror of male prejudice, showing how easy it is for well-established men, sure of their place in society, to *uncreate* a woman, returning to non-being one who lived for them until the end.

Uncreation is also the subject of a vignette of an abortionist, a "cheerful, never-lost-a-case black practitioner" who, the narrator tells us, "smoked a cigar throughout" (p. 46). No more need be said to suggest the pain and the isolation of the patient. There was a time when even this kind of abortion was for most an unattainable luxury.

Anger is a rare emotion in *Sleepless Nights*. Elizabeth Hardwick does not like to waste her emotions. She says that she prefers the word "compassion" to the word "rage."[23] There are, however, archaic, anarchic pulsations in this spare, quiet book. Perhaps they are all the more powerful because the voice of the narrator is, like that of the author, a "lady-like," gentle one. Her tones may be that of a Cordelia, but she does not hesitate to reveal the underside of life: Little girls allow a clean old man to ply them with chocolates and take them to the movies to caress their thighs throughout the performance; the narrator loses her virginity to a literary snob who initiates her first to James Branch Cabell before driving her on a Saturday to a seedy part of town and leading her into a house still redolent of the owner's cheap perfume, where he firmly comes down on top of her, "smiling, courteous, determined" (p. 17); unmarried schoolteachers lose their life savings to drifters and ex-convicts with the sex-appeal of the unwashed; a murdered man may have "chosen to put [himself] in the path of a murderer" (p. 142). A couple of words, half a phrase open a door upon a yawning abyss. Nothing is easy, nothing is truly simple, and the virtue of Hardwick's perspective is that her narrator will neither explain nor explain away. The only statement one can glean from these subtle, allusive and elusive pages is that "it is better to be exploited by the weak than by the strong" (p. 7).

Who are the weak? Certainly not the women we meet in *Sleepless Nights*. Nor are they the exploiters. Like the voices in Marguerite Duras' films or plays, Elizabeth Hardwick's message is not delivered at us directly, but comes in a whisper from the wings of the theater of the mind. And, to return to Cixous with whom we started, one is inclined to say that it is a winged message, one that flutters in the dark, softly, then begins to circle slowly, then rises, circles, soars, finally letting us contemplate life from on high. Suddenly, the shattered memories fall into place and there is harmony and wisdom. The tentative tone of the old woman narrator, so much like the hesitant mode of Elizabeth Hardwick's speech, is only the supreme politeness of the searching mind. The latter, whose "insomnias are filled with words" (pp. 49-50), puzzles out "the transformations of memory" (p. 88), knowing that "the concordance of truth . . . like an extra pair of spectacles . . . is . . . a hindrance" (p. 151). There is time on "sleepless nights" to turn with love to all the people one has buried. At the end of the novel, the old woman, close to death as she is, wonders:

> At times I am not certain who is imagining the working people living in their clashing houses, lying in their landscape, as if beneath a layer of underclothes. Or those gathering rubbish, dear indeed to them as relics. Or those threading through love, missing the eye of the needle (p. 150).

"The eye of the needle," a woman's image? Certainly one that comes from the patient daily work of women, what Adrienne Rich calls "world-protection, world-preservation, world-repair—the million tiny stitches . . ."[24] As to Elizabeth Hardwick herself, she has indeed pulled her thread through the delicate eye, the shimmering thread of a story which is hers but also that of us all; it will be strong enough to hold our world together.

In the Indian village of Mithila, little girls, under the direction of their mothers, learn to paint and draw. They use the materials at hand: rice water for the whites, dry cow dung for the ochres, indigo gathered in the fields. With a cotton thread dipped in the color obtained they make refined, elaborate drawings that fill the surface at their disposal. Most of these works are not meant to be preserved. They cover the decorative papers meant to wrap a wedding gift or, on feast days, the walls of the simple houses. Soon the rains wash off the paint, the wrapping paper is torn and crumpled, and the process must be repeated. What counts, however, is not that the work endure, but that it be performed. There is great pleasure in ritual repetition since the very act is considered a form of prayer or at least meditation. If the men of the village of Mithila are all its "priests," the women can be said to be its embodied "writing." They are the scribes of the sacred history of their culture. As mothers and daughters work in harmony with their God and themselves they feel at one with the entire community. Their ground paintings, the *aripanas*, are altars designed for the accomplishment of domestic duties that are not chores but other forms of worship or, one could say, another form of discourse. The creative ritual of the women of Mithila places them at the very core of the village's spiritual existence. Their space is indeed the center of things, and, in being where they are, doing what they do, they define where the center is.

At this moment in the history of the Western world women are far removed from this ideal. Many over the centuries have tried to establish themselves and their concerns at the center of their culture; others have found it easier to start on the periphery hoping to attract to these marginal zones those with greater sensitivity and understanding. Soon, perhaps, they will begin to move in. When they do they will bring with them the secret knowledge they have gained from resistance and from triumphing over so many visible and invisible interdicts.

THE GRADUATE CENTER OF
THE CITY UNIVERSITY OF NEW YORK

Notes

[1]C. Clément/H. Cixous, *La jeune née* (Paris: Union Générale d'Editions, Collection 1018, 1975), p. 170. All quotations from this book have been translated by the writer of this essay. Subsequent references will not appear as separate notes unless other citations intervene, but will be given as page references in the text.

[2]Aimé Césaire, "La Martinique telle qu'elle est," *The French Review*, Vol. LIII, No. 2 (December 1979), p. 183.

[3]Ibid., p. 188.

[4]Ibid.

[5]Saturday, April 21, 1979. The writer of this essay attended the conference and was able to note this down. The Barnard Conference is not followed by publication.

[6]Cixous, p. 162.

[7]Ibid., p. 126.

[8]I am referring here to the book of "pensées" by Andrey Siniavsky entitled *A Voice from the Chorus*, which was written in slave labor camp and sent in the form of letters to his wife.

[9]Cixous, p. 292.

[10]Monday, April 30, 1979. This was the first of four symposia on "American Women in the Arts: The Dialectic between Public and Private Spaces" organized by the writer of this essay at the Graduate Ceter of CUNY.

[11]The unpublished Ph.D. dissertation of Annette Shaw, *Baudelaire, The Androgynous Vision*, Graduate School of CUNY, 1979. A section of this thesis was published in Centerpoint, The Interdisciplinary Journal of the Graduate Center of CUNY (Special issue on Women: Public and Private Spaces, Spring 1980).

[12]Cixous, p. 227. Cixous wrote her Doctorate d'Etat on Joyce, and she also translated some of the stories from *The Dubliners*.

[13]Marguerite Duras et Xavière Gauthier, *Les Parleuses* (Paris: Les Editions de Minuit, 1974), p. 94. All quotations have been translated by the writer of this essay. Subsequent references to this book will not appear as separate notes but have been incorporated into the text.

[14]Richard F. Shepard, "Serban, in Film Debut, Meets Jane Austen," *The New York Times*, Monday, January 28, 1980 (C11).

[15]I am referring here to my own essay on *Waiting for Godot*, "Beckett's Metaphysics of Choiceles Awareness," in *Samuel Beckett Now*, ed. Melvin J. Friedman (Chicago: University of Chicago Press, 1970).

[16]William Butler Yeats, "The Second Coming," *Michael Robartes and the Dancer* (1921), *The Collected Poems of W. B. Yeats* (New York: The Macmillan Company, 1945), p. 215.

[17]In Jean Louis Barrault's October 25, 1977 production, Suzanne was played by two actresses: Bulle Ogier played the young Suzanne, the one at the center of the stage, while Catherine Sellers was Suzanne's voice. Both actresses were seen by the audience, but Sellers was reciting the text played by Bulle Ogier.

[18]Remarks made by Marguerite Duras and transcribed by Jean Louis Barrault in his *Cahiers Renaud Barrault, 96*, p. 57.

[19]The role of the mother was played by Madeleine Renaud.

[20]Lecture delivered by Marguerite Duras on October 7, 1975, at the French Institute/Alliance Française.

[21]Elizabeth Hardwick *Sleepless Nights* (New York: Random House, 1979) p. 35.

[22]Elizabeth Hardwick spoke at The Graduate Center of CUNY on Monday, May 7, 1979. This was the second of the four symposia on "American Women in the Arts: The Dialectic Between Public and Private Spaces," (Women Writers). Her appearance coincided with the recent publication of *Sleepless Nights*.

[23]Ibid.

[24]Adrienne Rich, "Conditions for Work: The Common World of Women," foreword to *Working it Out*, ed. Sara Ruddick and Pamela Daniels (New York: Pantheon Books, 1977), p. xvi.

NARRADORAS HISPANOAMERICANAS: VIEJA Y NUEVA PROBLEMATICA EN RENOVADAS ELABORACIONES

Gabriela Mora

La década del setenta marca, creemos, el fin de las concesiones, excusas y explicaciones que se daban cada vez que se consideraba la escritura de las hispanoamericanas, carente, se presumía, de grandes figuras (las excepciones confirmaban la regla).[1] Fundada o no esa opinón—una historia del desarrollo de la literatura escrita por mujeres está todavía por hacer—es indudable que hoy el número de autoras de calidad permite una selección amplia de nombres que bien se pueden situar entre los que han contribuido al prestigio de las letras del continente.

En estas páginas nos proponemos revisar ciertos cambios y y constantes que se destacan al examinar los asunto elaborados por sobresalientes narradoras contemporáneas. La perspectiva feminista que guiará nuestra búsqueda se interesa, obviamente, en observar los códigos culturales en que se inserta la obra literaria.[2] Por esto, nos parece útil constatar las variaciones en relación a esos códigos, a la luz de las transformaciones que van ocurriendo en la situación de la mujer.

Estamos conscientes de que la invención artística resulta de un complejo acto que une habilidades técnicas y creación imaginativa, y de que el juicio estético se apoyará sobre todo en la destreza con que la autora supo manejar su instrumento—el lenguaje—para construir su obra. Con todo, antes de proceder a constatar la calidad del objeto artístico, se deberá contar con el texto. Esto que parece una perogrullada, no lo es en relación a la escritura femenina. La verdad es que muchos no se han enterado todavía de la

existencia de trabajos muy dignos de atención escritos por mujeres.
Aquí comienza una de las tareas feministas, y otro modesto fin de
estas líneas: evidenciar la presencia de valiosas producciones, y
subrayar, cuando sea pertinente, su incidencia en los puntos que
interesan a tal perspectiva.

El enfoque panorámico que nos hemos propuesto no da cabida
para tratar otros aspectos cuya riqueza y variedad requeriría extensa detención en cada obra. Trataremos sí de señalar ciertas
particularidades como medio de llamar la atención sobre algunos
textos y sus creadoras. Una ojeada a trabajos representativos de
las décadas pasadas servirá como iniciación a este propósito.

I

Antes de los sesenta, la narrativa de las hispanoamericanas,
con pocas excepciones, presentaba una problemática que se distinguía poco de la que mostraban las escritoras de otras latitudes.
Las barreras geográficas se borraban ante el igualador sexual que
había confinado a la mujer al ámbito doméstico y a la búsqueda
del amor como única posibilidad de realización personal. María
Luisa Bombal resumió muy bien este estado de cosas en palabras
de una de sus protagonistas:

> ¿Por qué, por qué la *naturaleza* de la mujer ha de ser tal que tenga
> que ser siempre un hombre el eje de su vida? Los hombres, ellos,
> logran poner su pasión en otras cosas. Pero el destino de las mujeres
> es remover una pena de amor en una casa ordenada, ante una tapicería inconclusa[3] (subrayado mío).

Centradas exclusivamente en el amor, las vidas femeninas tenían
como contorno social el perímetro casero que, generalmente, se
presentaba como una prisión que ahogaba a las heroínas dotadas
de imaginación y sensibilidad. Si tomamos como punto de partida
el año 1924 que vio la publicación de *Ifigenia* de Teresa de la Parra,
obra de clara intención feminista, seguida en los treinta por las
obras de la Bombal, en los cuarenta y cincuenta por las exitosas
novelas de Silvina Bullrich en Argentina y de Elisa Serrana en
Chile, las escritoras coinciden en el retrato de un tipo de protagonista de familia pudiente—como sus creadoras—de gran sensibilidad, casada muy joven por razones socioeconómicas ocultas en
el espejismo de un amor juvenil, que termina en matrimonio desgraciado. Encerradas en la monotonía doméstica (pues estas mujeres
nunca trabajan fuera del hogar y en el hogar generalmente tienen
criadas), el mundo exterior al propio sufrimiento apenas existe.

Por esto, los personajes que las rodean son como desconocidas sombras, o caen en el franco estereotipo en el que el del marido insensible e infiel es el más repetido.[4] El cambio que se advierte en la década del cincuenta estriba mayormente en la presentación del amor. Del sentimiento devastador, casi místico, que se daba en las obras de la Bombal o en Teresa de la Parra, las autoras posteriores descubren la fuerza del sexo, poderosa, pero insuficiente también para satisfacer los anhelos de las protagonistas. La traída del sexo a la luz pública, especialmente en relaciones extramaritales, contribuyó a éxitos de venta. *Bodas de cristal* y otras novelas le permitieron a Bullrich ganarse la vida con la pluma. *La brecha* de Mercedes Valdivieso se consideró un libro escandaloso, y llegó a cifras record en número de ediciones.[5]

La clase media o baja comienza a aparecer con mayor frecuencia en obras escritas por mujeres hacia la mitad de los cincuenta, y estas heroínas comparten con las de clases sociales más elevadas un destino que parece estar sellado por la desgracia. La novela *Enero* de Sara Gallardo, valiosa por su estructura y su lenguaje, tiene como protagonista a una campesina demasiado joven e ignorante para siquiera imaginar un destino diferente al que sus padres le imponen. *María Nadie* de Marta Brunet ofrece uno de los pocos retratos de mujer que trabaja para ganarse la vida, pero ella, como las demás, es víctima igual del amor y de los prejuicios sociales. *Ciudad Real* de Rosario Castellanos muestra una galería de mujeres cuya dependencia económica hace del matrimonio o el concubinato una manera única de sobrevivir, sobrevivencia que conlleva toda clase de abusos y violencia.[6]

Los acontecimientos mundiales que marcaron la década de los sesenta de manera tan particular, especialmente en relación a la reactivación de los movimientos feministas que siguieron a otros de carácter más general, inician para la escritura tanto femenina como masculina un período nuevo. En Hispanoamérica, la revolución cubana, entre otros procesos, con el extraordinario despertar de una conciencia cada vez más lúcida sobre los problemas de la dependencia, afianzaron la obra de las escritoras en la huella inquisidora de los problemas políticos, sociales y económicos, rasgo caracterizador de la literatura latinoamericana.[7] De este modo, en la narrativa de los sesenta la vida de la mujer formará parte de un contexto social general, sin énfasis especial en la condición femenina, nota diferenciadora del trabajo de las hispanoamericanas vis à vis sus compañeras de USA y otros lugares.[8]

El distinguido grupo de escritoras argentinas que se inspiraron en la situación nacional pivoteada por la figura de Perón, ilustra bien esta corriente. Bullrich cambió la visión específica del destino particular de una mujer por una crítica generalizada a toda una clase social.[9] Beatriz Guido siguió de cerca algunos hechos históricos en su retrato de la decadencia de la aristocracia de su país, y Marta Lynch se inspiró directamente en la dictadura de Perón para construir sus mundos de ficción.[10]

El trasfondo social con una clara comprensión de la división de clases y de razas llegó a ser factor importante en la elaboración de las obras de escritoras mexicanas. El fracaso de la revolución—constante en la literatura del país—es vertebral en *Los recuerdos del porvenir* de Elena Garro. El hecho de que Garro muestre ese fracaso especialmente a través de la violencia ejercida sobre las mujeres, hace de la novela—dada su calidad—una obra feminista de primer orden. *Oficio de tinieblas* de Castellanos crea una protagonista india con hechuras de verdadera heroína en un libro que expone con mayor y profunda complejidad el choque de grupos divididos por factores socio-económicos, raciales y sexuales.[11]

La censura al sistema socioeconómico en las obras de las hispanoamericanas a partir de los sesenta incluye naturalmente un examen crítico de la institución familiar. Un modelo en este terreno es el cuento "Días dorados de la señora Pieldediamante" de Silvia Lago, pionero de la sátira despiadada con que las escritoras atacarán más tarde tabúes tradicionales de la familia. Por su calidad, y por ser una especie de puente que lleva a las características que se darán posteriormente, señalaremos algunos aspectos relevantes en nuestra búsqueda.

El asunto del relato es el mismo que había elaborado De la Parra en *Ifigenia*: el matrimonio como transacción comercial para elevar la posición de una familia, en que la joven narradora sirve de víctima vendida al mejor postor. Ambas protagonistas comparten una sensibilidad artística no desarrollada en profesión, el miedo a la pobreza y a la soltería, y la debilidad para resistir las presiones familiares. Muy diferente es, por otra parte, el tono usado por las narradoras. La elegante ironía de María Eugenia en la novela se transforma en mordaz sarcasmo en la Laura del cuento. En una interesante creación al nivel del lenguaje, Lago maneja el estereotipo recargado para esbozar situación y personajes. En la escala animal que enmascara rasgos de los habitantes de la casa (Linceagudo Gerifalte, el marido; Esteban Picorreal, un amante; Tiranosaurio, el suegro) la madre de la protagonista es "la gran mofeta

carnicera", la "zorra", la "rapazuela", cuya hipócrita moral sólo
sirve sus intereses. En oposición a María Eugenia de la novela, que
es incapaz de romper convenciones y comprender su destino más
allá del ámbito personal, Laura entiende que su vida es el resultado
de un brutal mecanismo económico en que la virginidad, la belleza,
la docilidad, son propiedades que realzan el valor de la mujer como
objeto de intercambio.[12] A esta concientización que significa des-
nudar la falsedad de los valores que guían a su grupo social, se agrega en la protagonista el franco enfrentamiento con su propia responsabilidad:

> Hija de puta. Hija de tu madre, . . . vas a disimular ahora ante
> vos misma . . . "Simamá . . ." como si ella hubiera tenido la culpa,
> como si ella te hubiese impuesto el matrimonio a vos, la niña-dócil;
> como si no supieras lo que elegías, solamente vos, mucho, mucho
> más puta . . .[13]

La lucidez de este personaje para analizar su situación vital es
un paso adelante en la caracterización de personajes femeninos en
la narrativa del momento escrita por ambos sexos. Por otra parte,
el suicidio de la joven, a pesar de su belleza, posición, marido e
hijo, a la vez que apunta a vicios y debilidades de una específica
clase social, socava mitos tradicionales adscritos a la "felicidad"
de la mujer.

Este horadar más profundo en los problemas, y el empleo del
humor para construir incisivas sátiras a la manera del cuento citado
o de *Album de familia* de Castellanos,[14] será la tónica de la escritura
actual de las hispanoamericanas, como veremos en el próximo
apartado.

II

De manera general, se puede advertir en las obras publicadas
en los setenta una abierta posición política de oposición a los go-
biernos represivos, y una conciencia de las raíces socioeconómicas
de la particular situación de dependencia de América latina. Esto
no significa que a las escritoras no les interese explorar la específica
condición de la mujer. Al contrario, en número creciente ellas se
van preocupando de destacar el sitio desmenguado de su sexo como
parte de la crítica al sistema social imperante que presentan en sus
obras.

Esta crítica social que en los años previos se dirigía casi siempre
a señalar la corrupción de las clases en el poder, ahora socava las
estructuras socioeconómicas a un nivel más profundo, mediante

textos que subvierten algunos de los principios básicos en que se apoyan esas estructuras. Los lazos sanguíneos, antes férreos, muestran su vulnerabilidad ante el golpe de los intereses económicos. El respeto por los mayores se rompe con el descarnado retrato del viejo como epítome del egoísmo y de la pequeñez de mira. El sagrado mito de la maternidad se convierte en blanco favorito de las corrosivas sátiras favorecidas por las autoras de hoy.

Por otro lado, al mismo tiempo que se evidencia en las creadoras una práctica más profesional de la literatura en cuanto a la continuidad de la producción, al esfuerzo meditado de la composición y al resultado total más eficaz de la obra, los mundos inventados ofrecen algunos cambios señaladores de la mayor participación de la mujer en otras funciones que las meramente señaladas por la tradición.

En los espacios novelescos, ceñidos como antes a mimetizar de preferencia las acciones y actitudes de las clases media y alta (con raras excepciones), los personajes de Luisa Valenzuela, Albalucía Angel o Antonieta Madrid se mueven de Barcelona a México o a Buenos Aires (*Como en la guerra*), viven en Greenwich Village de Nueva York (*El gato eficaz*), recorren las calles y los parques londinenses (*Dos veces Alicia*), o se mueven cómodamente entre París y Caracas (*No es tiempo para rosas rojas*).[15]

Pero el referente específico al medio nativo sigue imperando. Los policías especialmente adiestrados en Brasil que llenan las calles de Buenos Aires en *Como en la guerra*, aluden a la Argentina de hoy. El acuciante problema de la tortura política es el centro organizador de *La última conquista del ángel*, obra que se aparta espectacularmente de los escritos anteriores de Elvira Orphée.[16] La tortura aparece en el contexto histórico de los años cincuenta de Colombia que dibuja *Estaba la pájara pinta sentada en el verde limón* de Angel, y ha sido motivo recurrente en los trabajos de Peri Rossi desde el 69.[17]

Entre las nuevas funciones que permiten las nuevas experiencias, encontramos a la guerrillera que dirige una operación armada (*Puebloamérica*[18]), a la universitaria que piensa tanto en filosofía como en teoría política (*No es tiempo para rosas rojas*), a la escritora tan preocupada de la creación de su obra como sus colegas masculinos (*Dos veces Alicia, A cada rato lunes*).[19]

Sin embargo, a pesar de la existencia de estas aperturas—y en esto la literatura estaría a tono con la realidad de cambios estructurales mínimos de la sociedad—muchos de los asuntos usados por las escritoras siguen siendo los mismos que se trabajaron en décadas pasadas. La divergencia, y muy significativa, está en las perspectivas y procedimientos diferentes que se adoptaron para elaborarlos. Estas divergencias y algunos de los asuntos y motivos incorporados en la narrativa actual, es lo que pasamos a examinar ahora.

La pasividad, atribuida como "natural" en la mujer por tanto tiempo, puede servir de pauta para iniciar nuestro objetivo. Si se recuerda, la pasividad de la protagonista de *La última niebla* no se cuestionaba, aparecía más bien como inherente a su índole soñadora y, en cierto modo, causa de la vida inventada que se construye para sobrellevar su existencia desgraciada. La pasividad casi vegetal del personaje central de *Enero* se dibuja como "natural" de su condición de campesina. Pasivas son la mayoría de las mujeres de *Los recuerdos del porvenir*, y cuando Garro crea una figura femenina con ánimo rebelde, generalmente la rebelión lleva a la soledad o al suicidio.[20]

Buen ejemplo de la manera diferente con que se trata el asunto hoy es el relato "La mujer ignorada" de *A cada rato lunes* de Ulalume González de León. Utilizando la exageración para satirizar el rasgo de la pasividad, la autora crea una situación hiperbólica de incomunicación en que la no-existencia de la mujer hace que el hombre camine, literalmente, sobre ella, sin verla. La cita siguiente ilustra la manera juguetona en que González de León construye el momento después del atropello, burlándose de la sacrificada, de la que lo perdona todo. De paso, nótese en el trozo la huella de la *Alicia* de Lewis Carroll, autor que junto a muchos otros forma parte del espesor intertextual que caracteriza el volumen:[21]

> Todavía de espaldas contra la alfombra, disculpaba a José con instinto de náufrago: —Después de todo no me lastimó.— Levantó una pierna, luego otra, como si estuviera haciendo gimnasia. . . . Ni siquiera rompió mis medias nylon cuando pasó por mis rodillas.— Entonces se fue nadando piso arriba hasta el dormitorio, trepó como un caracol a la cama, se derramó sobre el colchón, líquida, y se durmió para ignorarse, en un último intento de solidaridad con José, quien obviamente la ignoraba (40).

La práctica masculina de buscar una "mujer ideal" inexistente, viejo motivo literario, se satiriza en la narración paralelamente a la de la pasiva que acepta acomodarse a ese papel. Fuera del humor con que se trató un asunto antes favorecido por el melodrama, la decisión final de la esposa de abandonar el hogar—después de comprender su posición de fantasma creado y destruido por el narcisismo del hombre—es sin duda expresión de una toma de conciencia nueva sobre la situación de dependencia femenina.

La imagen de una muñeca, como metáfora exagerada de la pasividad, sirve en *El libro de mis primos* para cuestionar con cáustico humor el rasgo que comentamos, además de la virginidad y otros mitos adscritos al sexo. En un enfoque decidadamente político, Peri Rossi fustiga a las mujeres que se dejan convertir en obstáculos para los cambios sociales al desempeñarse como "dulces Marías" que acechan a los hombres "para protegerlos y someterlos a un orden inalterado".[22] En *Indicios pánicos*, que la autora concibió como un detonador para activar conciencias en su país,[23] la uruguaya va más lejos aún cuando pone en boca de un personaje la reflexión de que la pasividad es rasgo que afecta a todos, ya que se trasmite por generaciones:

> Esta era una triste enfermedad que les venía desde la infancia: progresivamente, y debido a un nefasto envilecimiento de nuestros cromosomas hereditarios, la pasividad de los padres se encarnaba en los hijos, en los hijos de los hijos de aquellos, y así sucesivamente, hasta convertirnos en un pueblo de mansos.[24]

Peri Rossi, de extraordinaria capacidad poética, ilustra el caso de la joven escritora hispanoamericana cuya obra, a la vez que exhibe una gran pericia técnica, se inserta con fuerza en una línea de creación que concibe el arte y la política como un solo quehacer inseparable. Dentro del pensamiento político, la liberación sexual, especialmente de la mujer, es para la autora un imperativo de cualquier movimiento que se califique de revolucionario.[25]

Relacionado con la pasividad está el problema de la necesidad y capacidad de la mujer para poder expresarse, motivo de estudios feministas especiales por ser área que ejemplifica bien su situación social desfavorable.[26] La frecuencia con que las latinoamericanas han elegido presentar la ficción a través del yo de una narradora ofrece un amplio campo para examinar este fenómeno. Recordemos de paso el lenguaje no asertivo de las mujeres bombalianas; el estoico silencio de Nefer, la campesina de *Enero*; el ensimismamiento del personaje femenino de "La soledad de la sangre", el bien construido cuento de Brunet; o la mudez de Conchita, de *Los recuerdos del porvenir*, que aparece en la novela diciendo: "¡Qué dicha ser hombre y poder decir lo que se piensa!".[27]

La repetición de conductas originadas en antiguos modelos culturales en un personaje contemporáneo con un radio experiencial mucho más amplio que el de sus congéneres anteriores, lo representa bien la protagonista de *No es tiempo para rosas rojas* de Antonieta Madrid. Perteneciente a la burguesía acomodada, uni-

versitaria y activista política, la innombrada narradora es una
típica joven de una gran metrópolis, expuesta tanto al rock y a las
drogas como a la creencia de que bastan la buena fe y un poco de
Marx para cambiar el mundo. Desde el punto de vista feminista,
interesa ver cómo la muchacha, a pesar de su educación y comprensión de fenómenos sociales, sigue ajustándose a comportamientos
de mujer tradicional:

> Hablaban de asuntos serios y yo los oía . . . Calladamente los
> miraba mientras ustedes hablaban de la revolución . . . yo callaba
> y pensaba que yo también podía hablar de todo eso, pero . . . prefería estar callada y me ponía a pensar en que yo también militaba
> en una célula de la facultad, que yo también militaba en el partido,
> en la base del partido. No había forma de salir de la base, siempre
> en la base, no ascendía, siempre contra el suelo, pegada a la tierra.[28]

Dejando de lado la observación crítica de que aun los partidos
revolucionarios no cambian en la práctica arcaicas actitudes sexistas, cuestión importante en la obra, es claro que lo que el personaje
ve como sus propios deseos de silencio, es en realidad la respuesta
a un proceso de socialización que no la alentó a exteriorizar sus
opiniones:

> pero, lo que era hablar sola, intervenir, o pedir un previo, eso
> jamás, me moriría antes de que me saliera la voz, por eso era que
> más bien yo estaba como resignada a mi posición, resignada de
> por vida a permanecer en la base de la pirámide (21).

Por medio del fluir de la conciencia de la narradora, Madrid
crea un personaje complejo que tanto puede representar a la niña
privilegiada que al jugar a la política obtiene su merecido, o a una
joven capaz de ver más allá de los eslóganes fáciles y las posturas
seudo-revolucionarias. Su autodestrucción al final, espoleada por
una existencial angustia, señala la persistencia del motivo del
suicidio en la escritura femenina (índice a la vez de la persistencia
de una situación intolerable), pero difiere de los anteriores cuyo
único resorte era el amor desgraciado. Aquí, al fracaso amoroso
se añade el desengaño sobre la familia, la amistad, y sobre todo,
de la acción política, factor que requiere un análisis cuidadoso,
además de los usuales en el estudio literario, para la comprensión
cabal del libro.

Pero el suicidio también se trata con mofa hoy. El humor es
la tónica con que González de León lo maneja en dos de los cuentos
de *A cada rato lunes*, ninguno de los cuales ve consumado el acto.

La narradora de "Suicidio", después de prepararse un trago para "disfrutar lúcida su desesperación", comienza así el proceso:

> La última vez pensé: quiero morir, y me pareció que la postura adecuada a tan grave determinación era sentarme en una silla pequeña con los pies juntos y la cabeza entre las manos . . . decidí mientras pensaba, recorrer primero la mitad de la fatal distancia, luego la mitad de la mitad, etcétera, método que deja mucho tiempo para pensar (8).

Esta mujer es sólo una de las varias que se utilizan en la obra para indagar en el tema de la incomunicación, central en el volumen. El diestro manejo de la lengua poética de su autora da a los relatos una retozona liviandad y una lectura superficial pudiera ocultar las acertadas observaciones sobre problemas derivados de la convivencia entre los sexos. Por ejemplo, la cuestión de la infidelidad y el doble estándar cultural, que González de León trabaja con gracia y humor en "E.S.V.M. y un miriápodo, arácnido o insecto". El juego en torno al poema "The penitent" de Edna St. Vincent Millay, significativo pero no único entre los numerosos textos que se integran en la narración, es catalizador de la fábula. De los frecuentes detalles que acentúan una perspectiva claramente feminista, sobresale la manera cómo se resume la infidelidad para cada sexo. En el de ella leemos:

> Crimen: pecado terapéutico./ Causa: inseguridad patógena./ Consecuencia: recuperación de la confianza en sí misma . . . / Consecuencia: Comprendí que todo había sido un juego idiota./ . . . Tiempo para cobrar esa conciencia: aproximadamente una semana./ Epílogo: presentación voluntaria de la delincuente ante el juez (116).

En el soliloquio masculino, el hombre juzga su acción de la siguiente manera:

> Crimen (que no se persigue de oficio entre los representantes del sexo masculino): aventura consumada./ Causa: Fatalidad cultural./ Consecuencias: ninguna./ Epílogo: esto no amerita confesión (123).[29]

Como una exploración en una más amplia gama de reacciones afectivas de la mujer, se da en cambio la infidelidad en *No es tiempo para rosas rojas*. Divergente del amor arrasador y totalizante del pasado, la narradora de la novela a la vez que está enamorada de uno, se siente poderosamente atraída hacia otro. La experiencia sexual placentera con el que ella llama "mitad amigo-mitad amante" termina, sin embargo, con los clásicos golpes del macho posesivo, no contra el amigo traidor, sino contra la mujer insolente

(143). Que el amante revolucionario sea casado y tenga querida permanente, es punzante comentario agregado al cuadro de la posición de inferioridad de la mujer que presenta la novela.

Se mencionó al comienzo que la maternidad es tópico favorecido por las escritoras de hoy para atacar las presentes estructuras sociales. Rasgos caricaturescos se burlan de las madres deformadas por el capitalismo en *El libro de mis primos, No es tiempo para rosas rojas* y *Estaba la pájara pinta sentada en el verde limón,* todas ejemplos de la consumidora por excelencia. La figura central de *Dos veces Alicia* de Angel nos servirá para ilustrar el caso. Usando los trucos de la ficción detectivesca, la novela plantea misterios en el seno de una familia burguesa contemporánea que puede pertenecer a cualquiera ciudad grande del mundo occidental (Londres aquí). Disfrazada de Sherlock Holmes, la narradora principal, descendiente tanto de Doyle como de Lewis Carroll, empuja al lector con juego y misterio a desentrañar los hilos de la narración a la vez que el secreto de los personajes. El misterio se crea principalmente en torno a la Sra. Wilson, quintaesencia de la mujer con pretensiones aristocráticas, manías domésticas y adquisitivas, racista e hipócrita. Llamada "madre a medias" por sus hijos, el personaje se utiliza para cuestionar incisivamente en el mito de la maternidad. El mundo social externo a la casa familiar y ésta, están unidos por el motivo de la agresión, constante en el libro. El suspenso y el humor que surgen especialmente de la manera desenfadada del lenguaje de la narradora, no disminuyen la fuerza del aguijón crítico contra la familia, microcosmos que reproduce la violencia del mundo.[30]

Otra manera novedosa de subvertir los patrones tradicionales de la familia se da en el trastrueque de los rasgos que caracterizaban a las generaciones. Los viejos, vistos como seres mezquinos, cerrados a los cambios, no tienen en la ficción de las narradoras de hoy ni visión ni sabiduría. El carácter metafórico que se le atribuye al adjetivo "viejo" para una actitud mental más que un dato cronológico, lo subrayan González de León al hablar de "viejos de cara lisa jugando engañosas partidas de tenis" (*A cada rato lunes*, p. 92), y Elena Portocarrero, que creó en *La multiplicación de las viejas* una alucinante parodia de la posición conservadora en el Perú.[31]

Peri Rossi alude constantemente a la complicidad de los viejos con el poder establecido, y se refiere a ellos en insólitas formas:

todos los viejos son iguales, como los recién nacidos: todos babean, todos ven poco, todos oyen de un solo lado . . . todos pierden la memoria, todos caminan arrastrando los pies todos son torpes todos gimen todos dicen desear la muerte todos se aferran impúdicamente a la vida (*Indicios pánicos*, pp. 53-54).

En la narrativa de Peri Rossi, los niños son los que toman los puestos de sabios y visionarios antes ocupados por los ancianos. El niño adolescente narrador principal de *El libro de mis primos* es el que sabe mirar con claridad y hacer las preguntas fundamentales.[32] En el relato "La influencia de Edgar A. Poe en la poesía de Raimundo Arias", además del hecho inusitado de que es la madre la que combate en la guerrilla, la encargada de guiar al padre en la dureza del exilio es su hijita.[33] El adolescente de "La rebelión de los niños" cuestiona la complacencia con que los padres trasmiten a los hijos conceptos ya vacíos en el contexto social en que viven, preguntándose: "y el día que los padres no sirvan como intermediarios para que un convencionalismo se trasmita generacionalmente, ¿me pueden decir qué sucederá con las nociones de autoridad, respeto, propiedad, herencia, cultura y sociedad?"[34]

La aceptación del placer erótico de la mujer, y la puesta en solfa del sexo como mero instrumento reproductor, es también una modalidad nueva entre las escritoras. Una discreta seriedad en el enfoque del asunto, que en la mayoría de los casos se presentaba en la narrativa como fuente de dolor y desastrosas consecuencias para la mujer, fue la tónica anterior.[35] Hoy día, en cambio, el goce sexual femenino se muestra en forma franca en *No es tiempo para rosas rojas, Dos veces Alicia*, y *Estaba la pájara* . . ., esta última una especie de *bildungsroman* en que el despertar erótico se agrega al aprendizaje de las diferencias socio-económicas en el contexto de la política y la violencia colombianas.[36]

Que el sexo se toma hoy más a la ligera lo ilustra bien *El gato eficaz* de Luisa Valenzuela, obra ejemplificadora de la nueva novela en que la fábula y los personajes se hacen secundarios como estructuras centrales para dejar al lenguaje mismo como sostén principal de la creación. En el fragmento número 8 del libro, la gata/narradora termina una reflexión sobre el poder del sexo para transformarla en persona (cambio que por lo general provoca la huida del amante) con estas palabras: "Tiene razón, qué cuernos. No hay que volverse épico cuando sólo se quiere pasar un buen momento. Un coito . . . no es excusa ninguna para ahondar en las almas."[37] En la sección del mismo libro titulada "Juguemos al fornicón", traviesa descripción del acto sexual, los consejos para intensificar el placer de los participantes terminan con la siguiente advertencia:

> Lamentablemente como el fornicón es también un trabajo que se realiza para propagar la especie, se aconseja asesorarse antes en los negocios del ramo sobre las precauciones a tomar para darle un carácter verdaderamente lúdico (70).

La calidad de la elaboración poética, común a todas las escritoras que vamos nombrando, sostiene sin desdoro atrevidas alusiones sexuales, inimaginables en años anteriores, como puede ilustrar *Papeles de Pandora*, de Rosario Ferré. El pasaje que transcribiremos a continuación pertenece al relato "Cuando las mujeres quieren a los hombres", ingeniosa elaboración sobre el tema del doble, que integra la colección. En él, la negra Isabel recuerda cómo a instancias de su amante Ambrosio, el marido blanco de la otra Isabel, ha perfeccionado su arte de iniciar sexualmente a los temerosos hijos de los ricos:

> arrodillándomeles al frente como una sacerdotisa oficiando mi rito sagrado . . . bajando la cabeza hasta sentir el pene estuchado como un lirio dentro de mi garganta, teniendo cuidado de no apretar demasiado mis piernas podadoras de hombres, un cuidado infinito de no apretar demasiado los labios, la boca devoradora insaciable de pistilos de loto . . .[38]

Los viejos motivos literarios de la virgen y de la prostituta, que intentaban encapsular desde polos diferentes manidas esencias de lo "femenino", se utilizan en la narración, a la par que se cuestionan trasnochadas nociones sobre comportamientos sexuales:

> Pensando que no era por ellos que yo hacía lo que hacía sino por mí, por recoger algo muy antiguo que se me colaba en pequeños ríos agridulces . . . , para enseñarles que las mujeres no son sacos que se dejan impalar contra la cama, que el hombre más macho no es el que enloquece a la mujer sino el que tiene el valor de dejarse enloquecer . . . (36).

La objeción, posible, de que a través del personaje de la prostituta se suscriban otros tipos igualmente nefastos de cartabones de conducta sexual, es parte de la variedad de significados de las diferentes lecturas a que invita la riqueza del texto de Ferré.

La experiencia del sexo viene aparejada, por supuesto, con los mismos problemas derivados de su práctica en la realidad, y representados en la literatura. El embarazo indeseado, terminado en aborto, que se asomó contadas veces en obras anteriores, se trata hoy abierta y críticamente. Víctima todavía de viejos moldes culturales, la protagonista de *No es tiempo para rosas rojas* decide provocarse un aborto para no perturbar la labor revolucionaria de su amante. La decisión no es fácil por la angustia de desear el hijo y por el riesgo de la operación clandestina. La novela da cuenta no sólo de los detalles desagradables del examen ginecológico, sino que muestra además la actitud sexista del médico:

> ¡Ay!, eso es muy grande, doctor, le dije. No mijita, no es tan grande, me contestó mientras me sonreía y me metía la aguja, como queriéndome decir, ahora tienes que aguantar el dolor, si antes lo hiciste por placer, ahora toma, y me empujó la aguja con más fuerza (130).

La obra fustiga con fuerza el hecho de que sea la mujer la que debe solucionar el problema del embarazo, sin la cooperación o responsabilidad del varón, cuyas labores son miradas por el grupo social como de mayor importancia.[39]

Pero no es sólo en lo sexual que las escritoras van mostrando nuevas experiencias. Un área importantísima hoy atañe al quehacer literario mismo, en que las creadoras cuestionan su labor o se miran practicándola. Tanto en *Indicios pánicos* como en *El libro de mis primos* Cristina Peri Rossi plantea el eterno problema de la utilidad del arte y el compromiso del intelectual vis à vis los males del mundo.[40] *Dos veces Alicia*, que en uno de sus niveles puede verse como una alegoría sobre la agresión prevalente tanto dentro como fuera de la familia, en otro es principalmente una mirada al componer y escribir esa alegoría. La narradora de la ficción, que es al mismo tiempo la que supuestamente escribe el texto que se lee, revisa constantemente su tarea sobre la marcha de producirla, creándose así un personaje femenino enriquecido con nuevos intereses y problemas.

Las dificultades que enfrenta una escritora que es también dueña de casa, son tratadas en algunos relatos de *A cada rato lunes* con característico humor, a través de mujeres golosas de la lectura y de la excitación que reciben del sonido y textura de las palabras.[41] En el titulado "Difícil conquista de Arturo" de dicha colección, el proceso de creación, cuyo desafío para la autora ficticia es lograr la simultaneidad de acciones separadas en tiempo y en espacio, resulta en una visión paralela de la mente creadora asaltada por el mundo doméstico: Por medio de cortes tipográficos y otros arreglos espaciales, el lector recibe la impresión del proceso mental cortado a retazos por los ruidos de voces, teléfono, barredora, etc. El conocido reproche de Virginia Woolf, incorporado al texto, no deja lugar a dudas de la intención seria detrás de la traviesa elaboración:

"Estoy casi en la situación a que atribuye Virginia Woolf la escasez de genios femeninos en la historia: falta de dinero propio y de un cuarto propio. Gano algún dinero, pero el cuarto deja mucho que desear" (15).

Al seleccionar obras que representaran constantes y cambios en la narrativa actual de las hispanoamericanas, buscamos doblemente en los asuntos y en los recursos empleados ejemplos de preocupaciones feministas y de un buen manejo de técnicas literarias. En cuanto a los primeros, los que tienen que ver con asuntos públicos (guerrillas, revoluciones, dictaduras represivas) se han agregado a los que tradicionalmente venían caracterizando la problemática de la mujer (matrimonio desgraciado, temor a exteriorizar deseos y sentimientos, amor no correspondido, etc.). El tratamiento humorístico de estos últimos, favorecido por la mayor parte de las autoras, unido a la franqueza con que se manejan motivos antes no tratados como el del placer sexual, la infidelidad o el aborto, son indicios de la influencia que van teniendo los cambios que poco a poco va experimentando la mujer en la sociedad. El enfoque paródico de muchas de las producciones contribuye, con el distanciamiento producido como efecto, a cuestionar las más arraigadas creencias sobre el "ser" femenino: su imputada pasividad, su abnegación maternal ilimitada, su incapacidad para el goce sexual, entre tantas otras.

Por otro lado, la toma de conciencia de las escritoras del cultivo de las letras como oficio y juego serio va produciendo cada vez un mayor número de obras destacadas por su factura poética. Como oficio, se revisa la finalidad del arte literario en un continente de tantas aflicciones, sin dejar por ello de afinar los instrumentos de la creación. Como juego, se rompen las tradiciones retóricas, se experimenta, se mira jugar. A la mezcla de géneros (verso/prosa, historia/ficción, periodismo/ficción),[42] la multiplicidad de perspectivas y códigos lingüísticos usados,[43] se añade una indudable calidad en la creación del lenguaje.

Fuera del alejamiento del viejo realismo, los trabajos de las narradoras evidencian la utilización de la fantasía no sólo para indagar más hondamente en ciertos problemas, sino para imaginar nuevas posibilidades en las relaciones humanas. La carga subversiva que conllevan estas creaciones en su examen de las instituciones que nos rigen, es precisamente uno de los rasgos que la lectura feminista asocia con la escritura afín a tal perspectiva.[44]

Lo que importa repetir es que estas creadoras, sin perder de

vista las condiciones prevalentes en Latinoamérica, han traído a la
luz, según los cánones literarios del día, nuevas formas de examinar
las viejas fundaciones culturales que vienen imponiendo por siglos
una situación desventajada para la mujer.

RUTGERS UNIVERSITY

Notas

¹La presunción de la carencia se demuestra en la omisión de narradoras en
las antologías o historias de la literatura hispanoamericana. Un ejemplo (y no de
los peores, pues la cantidad de mujeres incluidas es mayor que en otras obras):
A Dictionary of Contemporary Latin American Authors, comp. David William
Foster (Tempe: Center for Latin American Studies, Arizona State University,
1975), que incluye 260 autores y 30 autoras (entre poetas y prosistas). El campo
de las traducidas al inglés indica la misma indiferencia: El recuento hecho por
el Center for Interamerican Relations (New York, 1970) contiene 8 títulos de
escritoras entre los 130 de la categoría novela. Del grupo del cuentistas, de los
16 nombrados, ninguno es mujer.

²Usamos la noción de código cultural en el sentido explicado por Roland
Barthes en su *S/Z* (New York: Hill and Wang, 1974), p. 20. Para "perspectiva
feminista", veáse mi "Crítica feminista: Apuntes sobre definiciones y problemas",
pp. 2-13 de este volumen.

³María Luisa Bombal, *La amortajada* (Santiago de Chile: Nascimento, 1941),
p. 74.

⁴Por ejemplo, Gabriel, el amado de la protagonista de *Ifigenia*, es casado e
infiel. En la misma novela, la figura de César es un franco estereotipo de hombre
vano e insensible. En *La última niebla* de Bombal, los varones son siluetas apenas
entrevistas. La infidelidad del marido es la causa principal de la infelicidad de casi
todas las mujeres en la ficción de Bullrich, en su primera etapa.

⁵*La brecha*, que apareció en 1961, había llegado a su quinta edición en 1964,
un éxito de venta insólito en Chile. Entre los muchos comentarios que veían en
el libro un llamado al "libertinaje", véase el que publicó *El Diario Ilustrado* de
Santiago, el 27 de abril de 1961, titulado "Proceso a la morbosidad".

⁶Sara Gallardo, *Enero* (Buenos Aires: Sudamericana, 1958). Marta Brunet,
María Nadie (primera edición 1957), en sus *Obras completas* (Santiago: Zig-Zag,
1963). Rosario Castellanos, *Ciudad Real* (Universidad Veracruzana, 1960). In-
cluimos este título de Castellanos, a pesar de que apareció en 1960, porque obviamente los cuentos se escribieron antes. De esta colección el relato "Modesta Gónez"
es una de las mejores muestras de vida de mujer en el penúltimo peldaño de la
escala socioeconómica (el último corresponde a los indios, en el cuento).

⁷Juicio muy generalizado entre los latinoamericanistas. Tesis de Jean Franco
en *The Modern Culture of Latin America: Society and the Artist* (London: Pall
Mall Press, 1967).

[8]Las escritoras han mostrado en sus obras, igual que sus colegas masculinos, la intensa preocupación social que caracteriza la literatura latinoamericana. Preocupaciones y hechos políticos recientes han sido elaborados, para nombrar sólo algunas, en la narrativa de Marta Lynch (*El cruce del río*), Iverna Codina (*Los guerrilleros*), M. Esther de Miguel (*Puebloamérica*), Cristina Peri Rossi (*Indicios pánicos*), Antonieta Madrid (*No es tiempo para rosas rojas*), Elvira Orphée (*La última conquista del ángel*).

[9]En *Los burgueses* (1964), *Los salvadores de la patria* (1965), o *La creciente* (1966), por ejemplo.

[10]Beatriz Guido, *El incendio y las vísperas* (1964). Marta Lynch, *La alfombra roja* (1962) y *Al vencedor* (1965).

[11]Elena Garro, *Los recuerdos del porvenir* (México: Mortiz, 1963); Rosario Castellanos, *Oficio de tinieblas* (México: Mortiz, 1962).

[12]Aunque De la Parra enfatiza el asunto de la mujer/mercancía, le interesaba principalmente dibujar a una muchacha que se desconocía a sí misma. Sobre esto véase mi estudio "La otra cara de Ifigenia: una revaluación del personaje de Teresa de la Parra", *Sin Nombre*, VII, 3 (oct.-dic. 1976).

[13]Usamos la edición del cuento incluido en *Aquí la mitad del amor contada por seis mujeres*, selección de Angel Rama (Montevideo: Arca, 1966). La cita está en la página 22.

[14]Rosario Castellanos, *Album de familia* (México: Mortiz, 1971).

[15]Luisa Valenzuela, *Como en la guerra* (Buenos Aires: Sudamericana, 1977); *El gato eficaz* (México: Mortiz, 1972). Albalucía Angel, *Dos veces Alicia* (Barcelona: Barral, 1972). Antonieta Madrid, *No es tiempo para rosas rojas* (Caracas: Monte Avila, 1975). Las citas que usaremos más adelante, pertenecen a estas ediciones.

[16]Elvira Orphée, *La última conquista del ángel* (Caracas: Monte Avila, 1977). Muy diferentes a esta crónica ficcionalizada sobre la tortura, son las obras anteriores: *Uno* (1961). *Aire tan dulce* (1966), y *En el fondo* (1969).

[17]Albalucía Angel, *Estaba la pájara pinta sentada en el verde limón* (Bogotá: Instituto Colombiano de Cultura, 1975). El problema de la tortura es importante en *Indicios pánicos* de Peri Rossi, que aunque apareció en 1970 (Montevideo: Nuestra América), se escribió antes.

[18]María Esther de Miguel, *Puebloamérica* (Buenos Aires: Pleamar, 1974). Iverna Codina, que sigue de cerca los acontecimientos históricos argentinos en *Los guerrilleros* (Buenos Aires: Ediciones de la Flor, 1968), también muestra a mujeres activas en acciones bélicas.

[19]Ulalume González de León, *A cada rato lunes* (México: Mortiz, 1970). Citas posteriores son de esta única primera edición.

[20]En *Los recuerdos del porvenir* Isabel, inconformista y valiente para romper convenciones, se mata al final de la novela. La figura central del drama "La señora en su balcón" se suicida. La imaginativa y rebelde Titina de "Andarse por las ramas" se queda sola, después de intentar liberarse.

[21]La obra de Lewis Carroll, además de en *A cada rato lunes*, está presente en *Dos veces Alicia* de Angel y en algunos relatos de *La tarde del dinosaurio* de Peri Rossi, entre los numerosos latinoamericanos que muestran obvia admiración por el inglés.

[22]*El libro de mis primos* (Montevideo: Biblioteca de Marcha, 1969), p. 115.

[23]Declaración de la escritora en correspondencia particular con la autora de este estudio.

²⁴*Indicios pánicos* (Montevideo: Nuestra América, 1970), p. 91. Esta primera edición es inencontrable. La autora anuncia una segunda próxima a salir en España.

²⁵Véase declaraciones de la autora en una entrevista que le hizo John F. Deredita, *Texto Crítico*, IV, 9 (enero-abril 1978), p. 136.

²⁶El estudio más conocido es el de Robin Lakoff, *Language and Woman's Place* (New York: Harper and Row, 1975). En lo hispanoamericano, Naomi Lindstrom ha explorado este asunto en "The Literary Feminism of Marta Lynch", *Critique* XX, 2 (1978), 49-57, y "Clarice Lispector: Articulating Woman's Experience", *Chasqui*, VIII, 1 (1978), 43-51.

²⁷*Los recuerdos del porvenir*, p. 26.

²⁸Antonieta Madrid, *No es tiempo para rosas rojas* (Caracas: Monte Avila, 1975), p. 21. Todas las citas son de esta edición.

²⁹Sin querer restar méritos al indudable alto nivel creativo, un enfoque feminista de la obra de González de León tendrá que contender con el estereotipo de mujer que dibuja la autora. Por un lado, es cierto que sus criaturas femeninas son inteligentes, cultas y se atreven a independizarse si así lo requiere la situación (pueden hacerlo por su clase y preparación). Por otro, la graciosa irresponsabilidad que las hace tan atractivas si bien rompe el estereotipo de la mujer tradicional práctica, sostén del orden doméstico, sigue ajustándose demasiado al patrón literario de la intuitiva, pura imaginación y poco intelecto (como la Maga de Cortázar, por ejemplo), que continúa encasillando al sexo femenino en el viejo molde del "otro" con rasgos taxativamente opuestos a los del varón.

La larga tradición de la mujer como el Otro fue revisada polémicamente por Simone de Beauvoir en *El segundo sexo*, semilla de los incontables estudios que han seguido sobre el asunto. Un buen resumen de la cuestión lo ofrece el capítulo "Femininity: Definitions and Perspectives" del libro *Femininity and the Creative Imagination: A Study of Henry James, Robert Musil and Marcel Proust* de Lisa Appignanesi (London: Vision Press, 1973). En cuanto a Hispanoamérica, el retrato de la mujer graciosa, "cabeza de chorlito", abunda en las obras de los dos sexos y habría que estudiarlo como parte de la fijación de los modelos literarios.

³⁰Una reseña sobre la novela y una entrevista a la autora aparecerán en *Hispamérica* (1981).

³¹Elena Portocarrero, *La multiplicación de las viejas* (Buenos Aires: Sudamericana, 1974). Algunas características formales y la posición ideológica de esta novela son tratadas en "El conflicto generacional en dos novelistas hispanoamericanos: Adolfo Bioy Casares y Elena Portocarrero" de Ana María Barrenechea, *Anuario de Letras* (México), XIV (1976), pp. 201-13.

³²Véase mi trabajo "El mito degradado de la familia en *El libro de mis primos* de Cristina Peri Rossi", *The Analysis of Literary Texts: Current Trends in Methodology*, ed. Randolph D. Pope (New York: Bilingual Press, 1980), pp. 66-77.

³³Cristina Peri Rossi, *La tarde del dinosaurio* (Barcelona: Planeta, 1976).

³⁴El cuento fue publicado en *Eco* (Bogotá), XXVI, 6, 156 (1973), pp. 465-89. Se incluyó también en la colección recién aparecida *La rebelión de los niños* (Caracas: Monte Avila, 1980).

³⁵Fuera de *María Nadie* y *Enero*, citados aquí, véase *La culpa* de Margarita Aguirre (Santiago de Chile: Zig-Zag, 1964).

³⁶Llama la atención el silencio de la crítica colombiana sobre *Estaba la pájara . . .* , que tuvo gran éxito de público (se agotó la primera edición) y es una importante contribución a la narrativa sobre el período de la violencia.

³⁷Luisa Valenzuela, *El gato eficaz* (México: Mortiz, 1972), p. 60.

[38]Rosario Ferré, *Papeles de Pandora* (México: Mortiz, 1976), pp. 35-36.

[39]Sobre el aborto, interesa señalar como una actitud nueva de parte de las autoras, la falta de sentimentalismo para considerar al feto, que en esta novela se ve como "cosa fibrosa", apenas "un coágulo más grande" que la protagonista y una amiga examinan con un palo (131).

[40]En *Indicios pánicos* los trozos número 17, 18, 28, y especialmente el 30 titulado "Sitiado". En *El libro de mis primos*, es el poeta-guerrillero el que encarna estas inquietudes. Véase el estudio citado en Nota 32.

[41]Las palabras "excitan deliciosamente" a la escritora/personaje del relato "Difícil conquista de Arturo" y a la traductora de "A cada rato lunes".

[42]*Indicios pánicos* es una muestra notable de uso de diversas formas. La historia, la ficción y el periodismo entran en el tejido novelesco de *Estaba la pájara* . . . .

[43]Un tango se integra en el monólogo masculino del divertido relato "El trono" y un bolero popular en "El hombre que sube aprisa las escaleras", ambos de *A cada rato lunes*. Un buen uso feminista de avisos, para satirizar el comercialismo que hace presa de la mujer, se halla en el relato de Rosario Ferré "La bella durmiente" de *Papeles de Pandora*.

[44]Véase la definición de crítica feminista de Adrienne Rich en este volumen, p. 3.

ALIENATION AND EROS
IN THREE STORIES BY
BEATRIZ GUIDO, MARTA LYNCH,
AND AMALIA JAMILIS

H. Ernest Lewald

Alienation and Eros have been linked to the urban spirit of Buenos Aires since the Argentine capital became what Ezequiel Martínez Estrada called "la cabeza de Goliat" in a book of essays by the same name.[1] In fact, the growth of the city brought about the inevitable sickness of mind that this Argentine essayist termed "neurosis de las grandes ciudades," where the inhabitant is cut off from the nurturing spirit of the homeland.[2] But other factors entered into making this city uniquely problematical. In *Psicología de la viveza criolla* the Argentine parasociologist Julio Mafud quotes the vital statistics that were responsible for creating the social and psychological scenario for the women and men of Buenos Aires early in the century, when waves of European immigration, consisting largely of adventurous young males, brought about a terrible imbalance of the sex ratio.[3] Thus we find an infamous Buenos Aires filled with the red lights and white slaves so dramatically recorded by Manuel Gálvez in his novel *Nacha Regules* of 1919, a portrait that cast its shadow across the Atlantic.[4] While under these conditions sex was readily available for the lone male, affection, tenderness and intimacy were absent. Speaking about "orfandad amorosa," Julio Mafud states that "el hombre iba al prostíbulo a entregar su semen, no su alma."[5] Thus the *porteño* was apparently up to his ears in sex but at the same time failed to obtain the slightest glimpse of love.

Back in 1931 Raúl Scalabrini Ortiz published the volume of

essays *El hombre que está solo y espera* in which he focused on the lonely male standing at the street corner of Corrientes and Esmeralda in downtown Buenos Aires, outwardly cocksure of his virile attractiveness and male superiority but inwardly afraid of having overextended his projected ego ideal. José Ortega y Gasset made it his business to probe into this ego in the essay "El hombre a la defensiva," and in so doing he incurred the instant displeasure of his male hosts. Ortega y Gasset had dared to ask, among other things, whether the Argentine man of 1936, so preoccupied with his self-image, was capable of giving of himself freely in the love relationship. Apparently, he had reasons to be doubtful. Years later several native observers of the *porteño*'s psyche agreed that the Argentine male was not yet able to break his spiritual isolation grounded in the cult of manliness, a variation of *machismo*, when faced with the prospect of an open and genuine relationship with the opposite sex.[6] In *Geografía de Buenos Aires*, Florencio Escardó writes on this subject:

> El hombre porteño guarda frente a la mujer una permanente actitud sexual . . . él es el hombre y ella la mujer ajena o inaccesible; resulta entonces natural que todas las demás valencias humanas que la mujer ha adquirido no encuentren equivalente ni resonancia en él; su incapacidad de ser camarada, compañero, amigo, co-partícipe en la vida de la mujer es encogimiento, es timidez, es polarización de una actitud única y aljamiada ante el fenómeno femenino.[7]

Quite obviously the polarization has the effect of not allowing the *porteño* to approach the female on any basis but a sexual one, thus removing her emotive expressions and needs from his awareness and at the same time blocking any possibility of understanding the essence and totality of her womanhood.

While Escardó's analysis introduces the factor of a basic isolation between the sexes that can result in alienation, Domingo F. Casadevall in *Esquema del carácter porteño* traces the isolation of the male to a withdrawal that is based on erotic frustration and that carries overtones of narcissistic sulking:

> El frustramiento de los deseos [sexuales] encuentra refugio y consuelo en el aislamiento y la hurañez. Egoísta, sensible e impaciente, el sujeto ansía ser amado 'porque sí' y sin perder su independencia, y juzga 'traicionera' a la mujer elegida porque prefiere a otro y no a él.[8]

For Casadevall this male resentment is translated into what he terms a "fuente de soledad" that prompts the individual to harbor such feelings as "rencor, envidia, celos, venganzas" directed at the source of his resentment.[9] This gamut of male emotions has long found its expression in many of the classical tango lyrics that still serve as a vehicle of popular male *Weltanschauung*. Florencio Escardó views the tango as a ritual in which the male identifies with the protagonist or narrator who distrusts, rejects or even injures his female counterpart, the eternal feminine element whose hopes or needs he is incapable of understanding. "Apenas suena [la canción del tango], el porteño se va con ella al seno de su propio aislamiento, a la acentuación de su soledad. . . ."[10]

Unfortunately, the cultural interpretations of the male-female relationship and the resulting alienation process have been mostly presented from a male point of view. Alfonsina Storni's celebrated "hombre pequeñito" constitutes the sole exception back in the 1930s; it was the first important feminist statement belittling and accusing the male of failing to understand the need of the *porteña* to be accepted as a total person instead of as a pure sex object.[11]

Julio Mafud's "viveza criolla," in reality a regional modification of *donjuanismo* when applied to female-male relationships, continues to look to many *porteños* like a serviceable tactic for breaking down the defenses of the bourgeois-educated, reluctant and besieged female, but this "viveza" leaves little margin for a meaningful relationship between the sexes. Thus Scalabrini Ortiz can write in his subchapter "La ciudad sin amor":

> Hombres y mujeres se zanjaron en una rivalidad que ni el matrimonio salvaba. Por la presión del ambiente enrarecido, la mujer veía en el hombre al timador de su honestidad. El hombre, en la mujer, la enemiga de su lozanía instintiva. Los hombres quedaron desamparados.[12]

Again, the rivalry is based on pre-established social conditions, the "ambiente enrarecido," alluding to the cultural atmosphere heavily charged with male aggressiveness, female mistrust, and a mutual lack of understanding of the needs and motivations that perhaps were acting on a subconscious level and not even approaching a level of awareness in the minds of the opposing parties. The psychological consequences, however, seemed quite clear: solitude, isolation and most probably a general feeling of resentment. Although they had few advocates, women like Alfonsina Storni felt that their emotional and physical resources had no outlet in the Buenos Aires of Scalabrini Ortiz and thus these resources lay stagnant and thwarted, ready to be finally absorbed by the forces of isolation and alienation.

It was Roberto Arlt, the rediscovered novelist and chronicler of Argentine city life, who saw the potential of the new Argentine woman when he offered the reader of *Aguafuertes porteñas* two vignettes of the *porteña* around 1940: one, the wasted life of "la muchacha solitaria del balcón" who is hopelessly reduced to playing the role of a silent witness to life; and the second, the frustrated office secretary who rejects the possibility of marrying someone who would not treat her as an equal and who learns English in night school in order to become independent in a man's world.[13]

In the war of the sexes the battle lines remain drawn. Bernardo Verbitsky's youthful *muchachada* that populates the cafés and street corners of the *porteño* suburbs of Flores or Liniers in novels like *La esquina* or *Es difícil empezar a vivir* are boys or young men who talk and think about women as an unknown entity, a sort of complicated sex object.[14] Thus woman is still the antagonist or, if the boys are lucky, a conquest, never a companion. Julio Mafud makes two very pertinent observations concerning the relationship of love and sex in *Psicología de la viveza criolla*. He sees love in permanent danger of being displaced by sex; secondly, he thinks that the Argentine male equates sex with virility or dominance and love with weakness.[15] The *porteño* seems to sense that love might give the woman the upper hand; she might be more giving, understanding, sensitive, alive, and a danger to the insecure male ego. Love, then, becomes a woman's domain in which the male would feel inferior. Thus he recoils and seeks refuge in isolation, *machismo* and, if necessary, violence.[16]

In 1965 Juan José Sebreli's *Buenos Aires, vida cotidiana y alienación* appeared; in it he considers the problem of alienation in the light of class division and class consciousness. Apparently inspired by the Marxist tenet that literary expression is inevitably linked to the social awareness and *Weltanschauung* of the writer and his or her public, Secreli belabors the bourgeois nature of Argentine big-city fiction. He focuses especially on the protagonists of Eduardo Mallea, who like their creator appear aristocratically aloof but live in the void of an existential anguish that converts them into *hombres-isla* and *mujeres-isla*, incapable of giving of themselves.[17] Curiously enough, Mafud claims that the characters of the aristocratic Mallea and the proletarian Arlt share some basic traits. Talking about Erdosain in Arlt's *Los siete locos* and Chaves in the novel of the same name by Mallea, Mafud observes in *El desarraigo argentino*:

> Son los que se han aislado convergiendo hacia sí mismos después de haber sido excluidos desde afuera. El mundo de cada uno de estos personajes es cíclico: comienza y termina en su proprio yo.

Su encierro en ese círculo infernal es total . . . ninguno tiene la
posibilidad de la comunicación.[18]

It is probably no coincidence that the female protagonists in
the novels of Arlt and Mallea are almost interchangeable, show
little character development and seldom come to life. Mafud sees
this portrayal as reflecting a pattern that emerged from centrifugal
forces within Argentine society that predate the writings of both
Arlt and Mallea.[19] He might have included their male counterparts
when he speculates about the relationship between the literary hero
and the cultural tenets of his society:

> Nunca los héroes argentinos encuentran o descubren el vínculo
> que los ubique en la convivencia social; este hecho esencial los identi-
> fica. La sociedad se resiste por todos los medios a aceptarlos. Su
> primera actitud es de exclusión. La segunda, de rechazo. Arraigar-
> se y afincarse . . . les está vedado. Para el héroe argentino todas
> las metas que conducen a la sociedad estan dinamitadas. Las únicas
> viables lo llevan a la soledad.[20]

By the time Sebreli examined the lonely upper-middle-class
characters of Eduardo Mallea, he could already have included a
large number of novels and short stories produced by Argentine
women writers who explored male-female relationships within the
context of marriage, separation, adultery and divorce.

If alienation and Eros account for the passive rancor of the female protagonist in the early days of feminine writing, today the
overt form is that of refuting male dominance. One could easily examine the work of Silvina Bullrich, which spans over a quarter of a
century, and compare her female protagonist in *Bodas de cristal*
(1951) with the female narrator in *Te acordarás de Taormina* (1976).
While the former justifies her *status quo* as a neglected *mujer legítima* by celebrating her fifteenth wedding anniversary, the latter
caustically tells her mother: "A menudo a la mujer le toca elegir entre
la prostitución y la domesticidad, la elección ha de ser difícil."[21] Already in 1966 Julio Mafud, that indefatigable chronicler of *porteño*
society, registered in *La revolución sexual argentina* the image of
the modern *porteña* whose economic independence can give her the
luxury of defying the patriarchal bonds, although at the expense
of becoming "la mujer que está sola y espera." In fact, Silvina Bullrich presents us with a liberated yet frustrated woman in stories like
"La abnegación" in which a self-reliant airline stewardess loses her
lover to an ultrafeminine and traditional woman.

But the evolution of the *porteña*'s independence continues, perhaps on an erratic upswing, and is being recorded. In 1969 Mafud

brought out *Las rebeliones juveniles en la sociedad argentina*, in which he describes *la subcultura juvenil* as being in a state of frank rebellion against the bourgeois mores and values of the older generation. Possibly the girls who try to seduce their male teachers in a Buenos Aires Night School in Reina Roffé's youthful novel *Monte de Venus* (1976)—so far forbidden to be sold by the Argentine military government—are enacting the latest stage of feminine self-affirmation and sexual alienation in a city filled with eight million anonymous people in which women now outnumber men by a decisive margin.

The three stories considered in this article, "Diez vueltas a la manzana" by Beatriz Guido, "Campo de batalla" by Marta Lynch, and "Los trabajos nocturnos" by Amalia Jamilis, share some common denominators: the ambience of the big city, Buenos Aires; sexual intercourse as a substitute for an emotive relationship; a deep sense of instability; and the use of the automobile and the hotel room as the sole context for human experience.

In Beatriz Guido's story a young man and woman are hunting for a taxi that will take them to a hotel where couples can rent an hour or two of privacy for their amorous gymnastics. They finally catch an ancient taxi with an elderly driver who, upon hearing the destination, tries to convince them to spend the afternoon in a more simple, joyous pursuit. He offers Laura a piece of chocolate and stops to talk to a friend from the Salvation Army. The hotel's shutters are down and the taxi begins to circle the block as Pablo frets, Laura becomes more anxious and the driver continues with his evangelism. When a vacancy occurs Pablo and Laura find themselves in the furnished room, two strangers brought together for an ancient ritual. But now Laura panics, whereupon Pablo, lamenting his bad luck, takes her to her boarding house.

Within the framework of this fairly brief story Guido has managed to assemble a number of cultural and symbolic elements. Pablo and Laura do not express any feelings of tenderness, care or love toward each other. As her apprehension increases Pablo responds with the irritation of an anxious seducer. When Laura breaks down in the rented room, Pablo's angry reaction is one of sexual frustration. "Yo no tengo aquí a nadie a la fuerza. No quiero que me des explicaciones . . . todo por meterme con estudiantas de filosofía."[22] He is not interested in her fears or needs; neither is he concerned with her beyond the realm of sexual satisfaction. She exists as a category: the liberated university student itching for a taste of life. Thus

Pablo blames the taxidriver, the woman and his bad luck. "Eso sólo me pasa a mí," he moans as they leave, Eros defeated. Laura's experience is altogether different. Her agitation grows as the taxi keeps going around the block; the ride brings back memories of riding through childhood on a merry-go-round. She eagerly listens to the taxidriver's suggestions to spend the day elsewhere. It is the evangelist at the wheel who equates the *amueblado* with a trap. "Apenas salga un coche, abren. Es como una tramps."[23] The *amueblado* symbolizes a dehumanizing sex trap that swallows motorized couples every few minutes, catering to the rhythm of the big city's inhabitants who are deluding their spirit through their senses. As Laura enters the room, she desperately attempts to find some meaning in the depersonalized ambience. "Comenzó a recorrer la habitación; abrió los cajones que estaban vacíos; descorrió las cortinas que cubrían la pared simulando falsas ventanas."[24] The effect of total alienation is overwhelming and Laura bursts into tears of despair. After Pablo drops her at the *pensionado* she only has one thought: "Tengo que mudarme mañana mismo . . . no lo volveré a ver nunca más."[25] Then she finds the piece of chocolate and slowly puts it into her mouth, like an act of communion in which she regains a sense of spiritual strength and perhaps a belief in human kindness.

If "Diez vueltas a la manzana" implicitly allows for a meaningful relationship that might have resulted from the furtive trip to the *amueblado*, Marta Lynch leaves no doubt that "Campo de batalla" portrays two male and two female protagonists who are not even pretending to have a personal interest in each other. For them sex is the only game in town and they all know how to play it to their advantage. Adela, in her late twenties, and Mirta, nineteen, share a room and a modern dream: to triumph in the world of television and the movies. Their backgrounds are far from unique: Adela had been the mistress of a colonel and a somewhat successful model. Mirta had supported a young film director and made a few television commercials. Both are *veteranas*. They have met their share of promoters, sat on more than one casting couch, and have come to accept their daily bouts with the male world as just one more skirmish with fortune, although Adela, being older, shows some battle fatigue. Adela and Mirta share the inevitable obstacles in their hunting of the most elusive of goals:

> . . . las largas horas de pie en el probador, las poses para las fotografías y las changas en la televisión con el miserable café con leche de las dos y media . . . las malas compañeras, la directora de escena

lesbiana. Conocían el magro presupuesto, la necesidad de aparentar, la loca esperanza de las cámaras sobre sus caras maquilladas y bonitas, el ansiado ojo experto que las descubriría llevándolas a la riqueza. . . .²⁶

When they meet Senior and Tito, who claim to be influential TV executives, the obligatory scene follows. Late in the afternoon all four get into a Di Tella car and drive to a deserted street in Palermo where the exchange of favors takes place. As the men begin to display their ardor, the women accept their behavior with passivity and endurance. "Soy una mujer, decía Mirta, explicándose. Una terminología apta y precisa como un buen membrete de mercado."²⁷ Her only worry is "Se me romperán las medias."²⁸ Adela, older and more disillusioned than her friend, goes through the obvious motions with a saddened lassitude.

> Senior . . . era puerco y exigente. En aquellos trances, y como era la más vieja, siempre ocurría que su mala suerte la ponía cerca de lo peor. Suerte para Mirta, suspiró, dejándose llevar tan entristecida que entrevió la caída de las ramas sobre la ventanilla como una visión de lágrimas.²⁹

Once the act is finished, the predictable dénouement occurs. Senior and Tito turn out to be unimportant employees at the TV station who must rush back to take their places in the production room. They hurriedly drop the women off and naturally promise to put in a good word with the producer. "—Mañana llamaré seguro, hermosa —dijo el Senior besando la ancha boca de Mirta. Adela los miró con odio."³⁰ As the story ends, the two women are left standing at the street corner knowing full well that another skirmish has been lost. "—Che, qué hacemos —preguntó Adela . . . —yo tomaría un café —contestó Mirta impasible."³¹ The war is over for now but the "campo de batalla" will come to life again in a day or two.

In the last of the three stories, "Los trabajos nocturnos," the profession of the female protagonist automatically combines the essence of alienation and Eros. Mafud belabors the obvious when writing that by the very nature of her profession, the prostitute sets herself apart from any meaningful contact with her male partners; in other words, she offers Eros within the sole context of alienation.

> Toda prostituta representa para el argentino la exacerberación de lo sexual. Esta concepción nace en la psicología masculina de ver a la prostituta como ser enajenado por el sexo. La existencia de la prostituta para el argentino está absolutamente identificada con el sexo y excluye toda otra adjudicación de referencias y cualidades

femeninas. De ahí nace la característica deshumanización con que en muchos casos es tratada por el hombre que paga.[32]

But in Amalia Jamilis' story Olimpia is a prostitute who actually transcends that condition by unsuccessfully trying to establish a genuine interest in people and places around her. Jamilis has a penchant for portraying social outcasts such as the female shoplifter in the story "Las grandes tiendas." Olimpia could also be a kin to Luisa Valenzuela's Clara in *Hay que sonreír*, a novel that pits a naive prostitute against a picaresque and soul-destroying male *porteño* world.

Amalia Jamilis' protagonist steps out into the *porteño* night filled with lonely men behind the wheels of cars, crowded *amueblados* and cynical bystanders. Her first customer drives her to the hotel Eros. The place is crowded with waiting couples and Olimpia becomes fascinated with the blinking lights on the artificial Christmas tree in the lobby. But her attempts to share her feelings with the customer fail. When she exclaims, "—Querido, vení a mirar esto, estas luces que se encienden y apagan," the customer makes it clear that he does not intend to establish a personal relationship with her. Thus he scowls, "No me llames querido, no vuelvas a llamarme querido . . . Pero entonces . . . —empecé a decir. —Bueno . . . podría ser, digamos, Rodolfo."[33]

On their way to another hotel they meet a friend of Rodolfo's and Olimpia is told to deliver a package to a bar called La Cabaña on Arenales Street in the Barrio Norte. There a party of drunken men and women quickly make her the center of attraction, shouting "Es una verdadera puta, no puede irse. . . ."[34] Someone pushes a glass of champagne to her lips and makes them bleed. Everybody cries "suerte, suerte" and then she is lifted upon a table, every inch the streetwalker whose sordid existence makes the elegant crowd feel derisively superior. After being reunited with Rodolfo at another hotel the police take him to the precinct because he has left his *documentos* at home. When Olimpia solicitously returns with the papers to bail him out, Rodolfo's erotic barometer has fallen considerably. Thus he simply dismisses her and she reminds herself without bitterness that "los trabajos nocturnos" must continue. "Me di vuelta despacio, salí a la calle y comencé a caminar sin apuro. Caminé tres cuadras, entonces sentí el zumbido de un auto a un costado. Un hombre sacó la cabeza por la ventanilla y me invitó."[35] The protagonist bravely reenters the *porteño* night, her only weapon being the promise of some physical pleasure made viable in anonymous cars or impersonal hotel rooms. As a pure sex object she is ever ready to seek encounters instead of relationships, offering matter instead of spirit.

In the preface to his *Geografía de Buenos Aires* Florencio Escardó wrote "tal vez no haya en el mundo ciudad más necesitada de amor."[36] Within the context of *porteño* mass society and its motorized anonymity the concept of *amor* seems to have been substituted by the pursuit of sex, the illusion of pleasure and the cover of alienation. In varying degrees the female protagonists in these three stories share this experience. While novelists like Arlt, Gálvez, Mallea and Verbitsky have largely explored Eros and alienation from a male point of view, the female characters in these stories allow the reader to share their views, feelings and needs by coming alive through the eyes of women writers who with all sincerity attempt to offer us a woman's interpretation of a cultural reality.

UNIVERSITY OF TENNESSEE

Notes

[1]For Martínez Estrada, the cosmopolitan spirit of the huge capital represented the triumph of the contaminated European heritage that ignored the telluric forces and regenerative powers of the land, a position that clashed with Sarmiento's pro-European stand in both his politics and his celebrated book *Facundo*.

[2]*La cabeza de Goliat* (Buenos Aires: Nova, 1957), p. 33.

[3]Novels like *Le chemin à Buenos Aires* by the French writer Albert Londres contributed to giving the Argentine capital a terrible reputation in the Western world as late as the 1930s.

[4]In this semi-naturalistic work Gálvez seeks a solution to the problem of the sexual rapacity of the *porteño* as well as the excesses of laissez-faire capitalism by preaching spiritual love and understanding through the deeds of his protagonist Fernando Montsalvat, a Tolstoyan figure.

[5]*Psicología de la viveza criolla* (Buenos Aires: Americalee, 1965), p. 63.

[6]Mafud attempts to trace this *machismo* to an earlier gaucho prototype that supposedly served as a cultural model for the twentieth century Argentine male. Thus he writes: "El amor o el querer no era para el gaucho el eje de su vida. Otros 'amores' absolutos los desplazaban: el amor a la libertad, el amor al caballo, el amor al juego, cierto amor a la justicia." One of the gaucho's favorite mottos was: "Por hembras no me pierdo." *Psicología de la viveza criolla*, p. 60.

[7](Buenos Aires: Editorial Goncourt, 1968), p. 125.

[8](Buenos Aires: Centro Editor, 1967), p. 43.

[9]Ibid., p. 44.

[10] *Geografía de Buenos Aires*, p. 118.

[11] The Swiss-Argentine poetess was deeply concerned about the inferior role assigned to women in the context of *porteño* society. Her "Hombre pequeñito" is today a much-quoted poem in which the lines "ábrame la jaula, que quiero escapar; / hombre pequeñito, te amé media hora, / no me pidas más," portray her demands to be treated as an equal in a love relationship.

[12] *El hombre que está solo y espera* (Buenos Aires: Plus Ultra, 1964), p. 47.

[13] Novelist and playwright, Arlt also wrote a column for the *porteño* daily *El Mundo*. The two pieces "La muchacha solitaria del balcón" and "¿Existe la felicidad para la mujer que trabaja?" were first published in *El Mundo* and later incorporated into *Aguafuertes porteñas*. Both pieces portray Arlt's view of woman as a victim of a male-dominated society that tried to keep the female in a sheltered or inferior position.

[14] Verbitsky's earlier works mainly present lower or lower middle-class young males as a marginal group, alienated from the older generation and relying on the spirit of camaraderie at the street corner or the local café, which in turn deepens the hiatus between the sexes. See, e.g., *Café de los angelitos*.

[15] P. 69.

[16] Loc. cit.

[17] The typical characters in the novels and stories of Mallea show above all anguish and a feeling of alienation, produced partly by their hermeticism and partly by their unsuccessful search for the "invisible" Argentina with its telluric sway. See, e.g., *La bahía de silencio* and *La ciudad junto al río inmóvil*. Ernesto Sábato's protagonist in *El túnel*, the painter Juan Pablo Castel, would certainly qualify as an extreme case of a person totally alienated from his society and its values who vainly seeks to use sex as a medium to control and possess the woman he finally kills.

[18] (Buenos Aires: Americalee, 1959), pp. 101-02.

[19] Ibid., p. 103.

[20] Ibid., pp. 99-100.

[21] *Te acordarás de Taormina* (Buenos Aires: Emecé, 1976), p. 240.

[22] Beatriz Guido, *La mano en la trampa* (Buenos Aires: Losada, 1971), p. 116.

[23] Ibid., p. 114.

[24] Ibid., p. 116.

[25] Ibid., p. 117.

[26] Marta Lynch, *Cuentos de colores* (Buenos Aires: Sudamericana, 1970), p. 188.

[27] Ibid., p. 189.

[28] Ibid., p. 190.

[29] Ibid., p. 191.

[30] Ibid., p. 195.

[31] Loc. cit.

[32] *La revolución sexual argentina* (Buenos Aires: Americalee, 1966), p. 95.

[33] Amalia Jamilis, *Los trabajos nocturnos* (Buenos Aires: Centro Editor, 1971), p. 72.

[34] Ibid., p. 75.

[35] Ibid., p. 83.

[36] P. 7.

III. Critical Applications:
The Works of Male Writers

A FEMINIST READING OF
"LOS OJOS VERDES"

H. Patsy Boyer

"Los ojos verdes," a legend published in 1861 by Gustavo Adolfo
Bécquer, was included in the readings for a course on the images of
women in Spanish literature because of its striking male-female
polarity. It was very surprising that the class, comprised mainly of
women, unanimously interpreted the feminine principle drawn in
the legend as that of the devouring female, the negative force of destruction. I had long understood the archetypal figure as a positive
natural image of spiritual unification and rebirth. The disparity of
our readings indicated that the students had been schooled to read
from a masculinist perspective, remaining insensitive to the dynamic
feminine reality underlying the surface of works such as this one.
In this paper I propose to study the rich ambiguity of Bécquer's legend and to present both a masculinist and a feminist interpretation
of "Los ojos verdes" in order to show the contributions of and the
need for feminist criticism.[1]

The elements which contribute to the story's impact are the ambiguity of the setting, the characters, the structure and the style. The
legend appears to take place at some indefinite time during the late
Middle Ages in the wilderness of Moncayo, a specific region of
north-central Spain. There are three scenes: a hunt, a conversation
in the castle, and the encounter of male and female in a secluded
woods by a spring. There are likewise three characters. The protagonist is the noble young hunter Fernando de Argensola. The
antagonist is Iñigo, his old servant and huntsman. These two men
are placed in relationship with the mysterious woman with the green
eyes who dwells in the spring. The triangular tension derives from
the attitudes of the men toward the female.

The work opens with a brief introduction in which the author tells the reader directly that this is the sketch of a picture he plans to paint, a picture of the green eyes, the central image from which the legend is drawn. The legend itself consists of three separate episodes that succeed each other in an unspecified time sequence. Each episode occurs in the present and sketches a dramatic encounter. The first scene depicts the encounter of the young hunter with his quarry, the deer that leads him to the spring where he sees the green eyes. The second encounter consists of the conversation between Fernando and Iñigo that establishes the conflicting attitudes of the two men toward the woman with the green eyes. Fernando seeks and loves the mysterious being while Iñigo, as the voice of reason and experience, fearfully warns his young charge of the demonic danger of the spirit. The third encounter takes place when the woman engages in conversation with Fernando, telling him of her love and inviting him to join her in the nuptial bed which is the spring.

Stylistically, the legend does not take the form of a narrative but rather alternates between rapid dramatic dialogue, communicating a sense of immediacy and tension, and descriptive passages that are intensely poetic. These lyrical descriptions of nature create a sensual and emotional climate that envelops the plot developed in the dramatic encounters. As Bécquer stated in the introduction, the nature imagery is visual and "painterly." His language also has onomatopoetic and musical qualities that transmit a feeling of dynamic, luminous sonority in nature, as can be seen in Fernando's description of the forbidden place to Iñigo:

> Tú no conoces aquel sitio. Mira: la fuente brota escondida en el seno de una peña, y cae, resbalándose gota a gota, por entre las verdes y flotantes hojas de las plantas que crecen al borde de su cuna. Aquellas gotas, que al desprenderse brillan como puntos de oro y suenan como las notas de un instrumento, se reúnen entre los céspedes y, susurrando, susurrando, con un ruido semejante al de las abejas que zumban en torno de las flores, se alejan por entre las arenas y forman un cauce, y luchan con los obstáculos que se oponen a su camino, y se repliegan sobre sí mismas, y saltan, y huyen, y corren, unas veces con risas; otras, con suspiros, hasta caer en un lago. En el lago caen con un rumor indescriptible. Lamentos, palabras, nombres, cantares, yo no sé lo que he oído en aquel rumor cuando me he sentado solo y febril sobre el peñasco a cuyos pies saltan las aguas de la fuente misteriosa, para estancarse en una balsa profunda, cuya inmóvil superficie apenas riza el viento de la tarde.[2]

The powerful audio and visual qualities of Bécquer's prose incorporate different kinds of sensorial imagery, such as references to natural phenomena (wind, waves, sun, moon), vegetation (leaves, plants, flowers, algae) and minerals (rock, emeralds, gold, silver). This imagery elicits physical sensations that communicate a sense of motion, sound, light, shadow, hot, cold. The substance and symbolic value of the nature imagery produce an affective climate in which the underlying mythic patterns take shape.

At first glance, the nature imagery appears clear and transparent, but examination of its symbolic significance tinges "Los ojos verdes" with ambivalence. (I use the term ambivalence with its etymological meaning of 'dual value' in a positive sense, and particularly as it relates to myth.) The most striking instance is the legend's reminiscence of the metamorphosis of Narcissus. The classical myth serves as an essential point of departure for understanding Bécquer's work. According to Ovid, Narcissus never responded to Echo's love and wasted away because he was unable to relate with other than his own ephemeral reflection.[3] Fernando, on the other hand, seeks union not with his own likeness or mirror image but with the other, the anima, the feminine principle who is the spirit of nature. Fernando ultimately joins the object of his love. He enters into the spring, into the eye of nature, into the center and source of life.

The similarities between the myth and the legend in character and plot also occur in structure and style, especially in the pervasive presence of "Echo" in the legend. Virtually every image and action are duplicated. To cite a few examples: the hunt occurs on two levels (the literal pursuit of the wounded stag in the opening episode and the figurative search for the other that forms the plot); the falling drops of water described above anticipate the setting of the sun and the fall of the hero; the sound of the falling drops prepares for the sound of the falling body; the greenness of the eyes, water and place are of the same hue. Descriptions of sights and sounds are expressed in terms of reflections and reverberations:

> Las cuencas del Moncayo repitieron de eco en eco el bramido de las trompas, el latir de la jauría desencadenada, y las voces de los pajes resonaron con nueva furia, y el confuso tropel de hombres, caballos y perros se dirigió . . . (134).

This echoing assumes the form of waves of sound and light and of the watery silver circles that widen and spread across the surface of the round pool. Many other forms repeat roundness: the rocks, stones and boulders that surround the pool; the sense of the enclosing horizon and the mountains; the shape of the setting sun and the rising moon. These circles mirror and magnify the physiognomy of the eye encircled by golden lashes: "en el cerco de sus pestañas rubias brillaban sus pupilas como dos esmeraldas sujetas en una joya de oro" (140). The circle, perhaps the most complex of all symbols,[4] is the unifying and containing form of the legend.

Coupled with the circle imagery of "Los ojos verdes" is the frequent suggestion of triplicity, made graphic in the shape of the triangle.[5] In the legend, there are three places, three times, three characters, three encounters, and three primary circles: the eye, the pool and the moon with its three phases symbolic of the triune goddess.[6] Bécquer's style is similarly characterized by the traditional rhetorical tricolon or triple amplification: "La cabalgata se detuvo, y enmudecieron las trompas, y los lebreles dejaron refunfuñando la pista" (134). Throughout the legend the feminine principle occurs over and over in the forms of the triangular yoni and the circular womb, which are identified with the "eye" (also meaning *spring* in Spanish), the water, the source, ultimate oneness. They are manifestations of the unitary *matter-mater-matrix*, the substratum, superstratum and energy of change.[7]

Both the circle and the triangle rest upon accumulated oppositions that build up to the ambivalent climax of "Los ojos verdes." Fundamental to these oppositions is the hero's relationship with the other, presented in a variety of forms. Like Narcissus, Fernando pursues the remarkable stag to discover the pristine spring in the wilderness, the latter setting representing the realm of the unconscious. The dynamic opposition is introduced in the first episode in the configuration of hunter, hunted and hunt.[8] The hunt is the quest with spiritual, erotic or religious significance; the stag is a spiritual messenger whose antlers are associated with renewal and with the Tree of Life. The hunter, paradoxically, often turns into the hunted: they become one.

The second dramatic episode places the hero in open conflict with Iñigo, who represents the voice of reason, experience and societal law. Their conversation, which can be read as an inner dialogue, dramatizes the opposition and sets forth the dangers of this quest. Iñigo's explicit warnings clarify the sense of destiny and inevitability in Fernando's search: "te amaría como te amo, como es mi destino amarte" (140). In seeking psychic integration and individual fulfillment, the hero knowingly goes beyond social law to obey a higher principle of meaning. The spirit with the green eyes describes the nature of his goal: "soy una mujer digna de ti, que eres superior

a los demás hombres," and she promises to reward him with her love
in a mystical marriage, since he is "Un mortal superior a las supersticiones del vulgo" (140). As a result of his conversation with Iñigo,
Fernando's quest becomes a conscious affirmation of his being, dif-
ferentiated from the initial blind pursuit of the stag.

In the final episode, Fernando enters the abode of the feminine.
Virtually all of the imagery devolves from the feminine: the woman
with the green eyes is the sacred place; she dresses in the natural
phenomena and is the divine energy that animates. She breathes in
the breezes, speaks in the sounds, moves in the waves and grows in
the vegetation: "Yo vivo en el fondo de estas aguas, incorpórea
como ellas, fugaz y transparente; hablo con sus rumores y ondulo
con sus pliegues" (140). In describing the place to Iñigo, Fernando
has said:

> En las plateadas hojas de los álamos, en los huecos de las peñas, en
> las ondas del agua, parece que nos hablan los invisibles espíritus
> de la Naturaleza, que reconocen un hermano en el inmortal espíritu
> del hombre (137).

In this place, the waters spring forth from the breast, "seno," of the
rock and come to rest in the deep green pool. It is significant to note
that this pool is not the fearsome "bottomless lake" so attractive in
folk tales and romantic literature;[9] rather, it holds in its depths the
nuptial bed. All aspects of this place, all rhythms, derive from the
feminine as traditionally depicted.

The nature imagery, like the circle and the triangle, connotes
a participation, a merging, which implies the transfer of the hero
from the material earthly realm to the watery spiritual realm. Each
image of consubstantiation reflects the transformation of basic elements into water. The veil that shrouds the woman's form turns into
veils of mist, which is her breath become watery. When Fernando's
material body, like a stone, falls into the water, it becomes demateri-
alized. When he loses his footing, he loses touch with the earth. As
the body enters the water, sparks of light leap upward, and water
takes on the appearance of fire: "Las aguas saltaron en chispas de
luz y se cerraron sobre su cuerpo, y sus círculos de plata fueron ensanchándose, ensanchándose, hasta expirar en las orillas" (141).
Air, earth and fire assume the properties of water.[10]

Relating this to the psyche, Cirlot states that water is

> a symbol of the unconscious, that is, of the non-formal, dynamic,
> motivating, female side of the personality. . . . Whether we take water
> as a symbol of the collective or of the personal unconscious, or else
> as an element of mediation and dissolution, it is obvious that this

symbolism is an expression of the vital potential of the psyche, of the struggles of the psychic depths to find a way of formulating a clear message comprehensible to the consciousness.[11]

In "Los ojos verdes" everything returns to this primordial element; even the moon is seen only as a reflection on the surface of the water. In presenting the encounter between the masculine and the feminine, Bécquer relates them both to the stone. Fernando goes daily to sit on the boulder beside the pool wherein his beloved dwells. One day he finds her, part rock and part water, "sentada en mi puesto, vestida con unas ropas que llegaban hasta las aguas y flotaban sobre su haz" (138). In the concluding episode she again sits "sobre una de estas rocas, sobre una que parecía próxima a desplomarse en el fondo de las aguas" (139). Attracted by her invitation, Fernando draws nearer and nearer to the "borde de la roca"; finally, like a stone, he drops into the waters. Jung has written at length on the complex and paradoxical symbolism of the stone:

> The very concept of the "stone" indicates the peculiar nature of the symbol. "Stone" is the essence of everything solid and earthly. It represents feminine *matter*, and this concept intrudes into the sphere of the "spirit" and its symbolism.[12]

Basically, stone, the lapis philosophorum, is the mystery, the arcane substance, the beginning and the end of the alchemical process. It is triume—earthly, heavenly, divine—and the offspring of sun and moon. Curiously, another designation for the lapis is *cervus fugitivus*.[13] In describing the alchemical significance, Jung writes:

> Usually the coniunctio precedes the production of the lapis and the latter is understood as the child of Sol and Luna. To that extent the lapis exactly corresponds to the psychological idea of the self, the product of conscious and unconscious.[14]

The symbolism of the stone, water, triangle and circle is essential to a comprehension of the transformation that takes place in "Los ojos verdes."

Just as Fernando and the woman with the green eyes participate in the mystery of the stone, they share in their association with the sun. In the concluding episode, Bécquer repeats that the sun has fallen behind the mountains, that the shadows are spreading across the skirts of the mountain. The setting of the sun anticipates the fall of Fernando's body into the pool and marks the end of daytime. In describing the transcendent union of opposites, Jung writes of the sun:

> the winged youth is espoused to the "Central Waters." This is the

fountain of the soul or the fount of wisdom, from which the inner life wells up. The nymph of the spring is in the last analysis Luna, the Mother-beloved, from which it follows that the winged youth is Sol, the *filius solis, lapis, aurum philosophicum, lumen luminum, medicina catholica, una salus*, etc. He is the best, the highest, the most precious *in potentia*. But he will become real only if he can unite with Luna, the "mother of mortal bodies."[15]

Fernando's fall materializes the trajectory of the fiery sun, which daily plunges into the western waters.

The woman with the green eyes is likewise identified with the sun. The two descriptions of her imponderable beauty compare her golden hair and eyelashes to the rays of the sun. Indeed, when Fernando first glimpsed the green eyes in the depths of the pool, he thought he perceived a ray of sunshine. Hair and gold traditionally represent the radiant energy of the sun. At the end of the legend, the golden light of the sun gives way to the spreading shadows and fades into the pale silver reflection of the moon on the surface of the waters. The moon defines the spreading silver circles and accentuates the leaping sparks of water. The sun and moon are the eyes of heaven, just as the eyes are the proverbial windows of the soul. The climax occurs when both are present in the sky, although they are visible only in their effects, in the shadows and reflections. Their position and the contrary motions of ascent and descent express the union of opposites, the merging of hot and cold, day and night, gold and silver, fire and water, masculine and feminine.

The identifications and oppositions in "Los ojos verdes" zero in on that point in time which marks the transition, when one element merges with another. The mind can scarcely imagine this mystical moment of transformation. That point, the center of the eye and of the circle, "symbolise l'état limite de l'abstraction du volume, le Centre, l'origine, le foyer, le *principe* de l'émanation et le terme du retour. Il désigne la puissance créatrice et la fin de toutes choses."[16] In his picture of the green eyes, Bécquer captures the instant of passage; his revitalization of the myth of Narcissus reenacts the mystery of his metamorphosis.

The traditional masculinist reading of "Los ojos verdes" focuses on the three dramatic encounters. It requires reader identification with Iñigo, whose perspective rests on reason and conventional experience. He speaks for traditional religious and societal values that construe the unknown as fearsome and diabolical and consider the death of the individual as negative, tragic. Iñigo believes in the reality and the power of the evil spirit and fervently repeats the warnings his parents had told him "a thousand times." His perception of the power of evil seems Manichaean, which, interestingly, was the base for the development of alchemy with its goals of reconciling opposites and transforming matter.[17] Because of his fear of the unknown, Iñigo tries to restrain the hero and hold him within the bounds of conventional social behavior, for the sake of "all he loves most." Iñigo will see the death of the hero as a defeat at the hands of the diabolical feminine principle and a failure of the individual to control destiny. This corresponds to the archetype of the failed hero.

Iñigo's view is predicated on the supernatural attracting power of evil; his fatalism reinforces basic human fears of death, of the unknown and of the feminine.[18] Wolfgang Lederer, in *The Fear of Women*, studies in depth the age-old romantic fascination of the femme fatale, the lady of the lake, Lorelei, the mysterious woman who inhabits the waters and lures men to their destruction.[19] These tales typify the deep-seated Freudian fear of falling in, being swallowed, suffering castration. The masculinist reading rests on these fears, stressing the moral significance of the encounter: there are limits not to be transgressed. Iñigo assumes that the hero is irrationally attracted by the supernatural force of evil and consequently is punished, devoured by the *vagina dentata*.

The feminist reading of "Los ojos verdes" focuses on the whole mythic and symbolic climate containing the action. From this perspective, the feminine principle drawn in the legend is viewed as natural instead of evil. Nature transcends moral judgement. The impact of her image is mysterious rather than negative. Mysteries and secrets are awesome and fearsome by definition. This reading accepts the perspective of the hero, of the virgin hunter who pursues the stag that leads him to the pool, in whose depths he sees the compelling green eyes. He describes her as the spirit of nature, and she describes herself as pure spirit. The imagery communicates that she is nature herself and the cosmic energy that animates it. With a voice that sounds like music, she reveals her identity and tries to explain her "descent":

> yo te amo más aún que tú me amas; yo, que desciendo hasta un mortal siendo un espíritu puro. No soy una mujer como las que existen en la Tierra; soy una mujer digna de ti, que eres superior a los demás hombres. Yo vivo en el fondo de estas aguas, incorpórea como ellas, fugaz y transparente: hablo con sus rumores y ondulo con sus pliegues. Yo no castigo al que osa turbar la fuente donde moro; antes lo premio con mi amor, como a un mortal superior a

las supersticiones del vulgo, como a un amante capaz de comprender mi cariño extraño y misterioso (140).

This image of the feminine principle responds to every human fantasy of perfect love. But, true love, giving oneself to the other, is also fearsome, for it represents the abandonment of one's individuality. Whitmont, in *The Symbolic Quest*, explains that "Fear and attraction, in fact, always go together in the confrontation of the world of the absolutely other, the other sex. It is fear of the threateningly unknown and simultaneously a magnetic attraction of this same unknown."[20]

Contrary forces are also revealed in the attitudes of the two men toward the mysterious identity of the woman with the green eyes. Iñigo sees her as the diabolical. Fernando sees her as the infinitely desirable. She identifies herself as pure spirit. There is also a question about the meaning of the fate of the hero. He, like the stone and the sun, falls into the waters. His fall produces a series of circles of which he is the center. The nature imagery can imply that the circles of the eye and the pool and the stone come together in the living womb of nature as opposed to the contrary notion of the devouring maw. On entering into the source, the hero experiences a mysterious passage that can be understood as a death and as a rebirth.

Stated in different terms, this mystery refers to the magical function of the living eye: vision. The act of visual perception is essential to exchange; it is a basic mode of communication and is itself an act of creation. It establishes the relationship between, as well as the existence of, self and other. The mystery is the nature of perception, which is selective, which focuses. Correlative with the act of perception is the act of creation, which occurs in the utterance of the *verbum*, the word. Bécquer chose the vehicle of the word to paint his picture of the green eyes. This vehicle requires a perceiving subject, a perceived object and the imaginative exchange in order to come alive. Like seeing, reading is a dynamic communion. Whitmont stresses the importance of the dynamic vision of the archetypal image: "Integration of the archetypal image comes about through recognizing and experiencing it as a 'picture of meaning' (Sinnbild), as a symbol."[21] In his citation of Emma Brunner-Traut, he provides a basic definition of myth and its timeless reality:

> Myth is not definition, nor is it proof. It is self-evident. It is endowed with dignity and majesty, perfect in its inner power and validity and the only adequate language for that which we can grasp only through faith and through our action in the physical world.[22]

Bécquer was entirely conscious of his art. In his introduction to the *Leyendas*, written in 1868, he addresses, in a manner reminiscent of Goya, the children of his fantasy who struggle to be born from within his head. Here he makes reference to the fact that "entre el mundo de la idea y el de la forma existe un abismo que sólo puede salvar la palabra" (39). This statement recalls his introductory "cuento con la imaginación de mis lectores para hacerme comprender" (133), which in turn recalls the woman's description of Fernando as an "amante capaz de comprender mi cariño extraño y misterioso" (140). Depending on the act of comprehension, he admonishes his creatures: "Id, pues, al mundo a cuyo contacto fuisteis engendrados y quedad en él como el eco que encontraron en un alma que pasó por la Tierra sus alegrías y sus dolores, sus esperanzas y sus luchas" (41). The complex mystery he presents in "Los ojos verdes" is a confrontation with the self, the creative self.

Creation requires creator and creature. Northrup Frye, in dealing with myth as a visionary model, stresses the importance of reader re-creation:

> In human life creation and contemplation need two people, a poet and a reader, a creative action that produces and a creative response that possesses. . . . the message of all romance is *de te fabula*: the story is about you; and it is the reader who is responsible for the way literature functions, both socially and individually. . . . One's reading thus becomes an essential part of a process of self-creation and self-identity that passes beyond all the attached identifications, with society or belief or nature, that we have been tracing.[23]

Frye, like Bécquer and like the others cited in this study, seeks to identify, clarify and expand individual perception, vision, the meaning of the word.[24] In the process of creation and re-creation which is the theme of "Los ojos verdes," we readers and our comprehension of the words are the vital link in communication, communion. The mythic glimpse of an eternal verity must be intuited, experienced directly and actively through creative imagination; it must be felt.

Because myth deals with opposition, it is ambivalent. The fate of the hero in "Los ojos verdes" must be construed from the two perspectives simultaneously. It is both a tragic failure and a glorious marriage; above all, it is a vision of the green eyes "que reconocen un hermano en el inmortal espíritu del hombre" (137). The purpose of a feminist reading is to penetrate the mystery and to add another dimension; this reading stresses the author's stated intent to re-create a picture of the green eyes.

In closing, I shall comment briefly on the probable reactions of male and female readers to the masculinist reading. For the typical male reader who accepts the *vagina dentata* interpretation, the legend does not necessarily represent a negative experience. In recognizing the evil in the feminine principle, he may feel scintillated by the challenge. The power of the femme fatale is highly attractive to the male because it stimulates his aspirations to become a dragon slayer and a hero. This reading may prove very stimulating to the male fantasy. However, the female reader who interprets the legend as a portrayal of the devouring female archetype is confronted with a negative and fearsome picture of her own sexuality. This reading would restrict her imaginative response, leaving her little alternative but to acknowledge and accept one more statement of the age-old self image of woman as Terrible Mother, the one who castrates or devours her son. The masculinist reading would thus not tap the energy of the female imagination as it would unleash the male imagination.

Bécquer's conscious art and the symbolic ambivalence of "Los ojos verdes" depict a reality that incorporates and transcends death and destruction just as the moon waxes and wanes, spring follows winter, light follows darkness. Nature repeats herself in patterns of creation and destruction. A feminist reading of the legend offers a deep apreciation of Bécquer's conscious aesthetic even as it provides a transcendent image of the union of the masculine and the feminine in the green eyes, the circles on the pool, and the contractions of fertility and rebirth.

COLORADO STATE UNIVERSITY, FORT COLLINS

<h2 style="text-align:center">Notes</h2>

[1]By masculinist I mean that reading which focuses on the male protagonist and his fate, which often obviates serious consideration of the female character or casts her in a negative light. Masculinist does not refer to the sex of reader or critic. Similarly, feminist, as defined in this paper, means a perspective that focuses on the nature and role of the female character and clarifies the impact of this image on the male and female reader.

[2]Gustavo Adolfo Bécquer, *Obras completas* (Madrid: Aguilar, 1969), p. 137. All citations are taken from this edition and are indicated within parentheses in the text.

[3]"He fell in love with an insubstantial hope, mistaking a mere shadow for a real

body. . . . Unwittingly, he desired himself, and was himself the object of his own approval, at once seeking and sought, himself kindling the flame with which he burned." *The Metamorphoses of Ovid*, tr. and ed. Mary M. Innes (London: Penguin Books, 1955), p. 92.

[4]The psychoanalytic dimension of the rotundum is explained by Jung as symbolizing wholeness, the ultimate state of oneness which resides in the unconscious, the *anima*. Further, the unconscious is the feminine element of the psyche; thus the *rotundum* becomes associated with the mother as the place where the symbol of wholeness resides. C. G. Jung, *Mysterium coniunctionis*, tr. R. F. C. Hull (Princeton: Bollingen Series XX, 1963), pp. 355-57. It is significant that the Uroboric serpent, which symbolizes the primordial origin as well as the unity from which all oppositions emerge, is also a circular figure.

In his introduction to his study of male fear of the female, *The Fear of Women* (New York: Harcourt Brace Jovanovich, 1968), p. 3, Wolfgang Lederer points out that in Indic mythology the circular eye is associated with the yoni, also symbolized as a lotus blossom or as a triangle. Lederer asserts that man's fear stems from a fear of "the uncanny place which is nothing but the entrance to the old home of mankind, to that abode where every one of us was once and first at home." I include, here and elsewhere, references to Indic symbolism because it represents a very different world view from that of the West and also because it had a profound effect on Bécquer. See, for example, his last legend, "La Creación (poema indio)," which recounts the creation of the world by Brahma.

[5]Symbolically, in medieval alchemy, the four elements were drawn as four female figures, each containing a different triangle to signify the basic elements. The upward pointing triangle represents fire and the masculine principle; the downward pointing triangle represents water and the feminine principle. Conjoined, the two triangles form the six-pointed star of Solomon which symbolizes the soul, the union of masculine and feminine, of fire and water. Specifically referring to the universal symbol of the feminine, Lederer writes: "Buddhahood itself is said to abide in the female organ. In Yantric designs a downward pointing triangle is a female symbol corresponding to the yoni; and it is called 'shakti' (p. 139). Lederer had previously defined 'shakti' as "power, ability, capacity, faculty, energy; shakti is the female organ; shakti is the active power of a deity and is regarded, mythologically, as his goddess-consort and queen" (p. 136).

[6]One of the most thorough studies of the moon and its psychological import is M. Esther Harding's *Woman's Mysteries* (New York: Harper Colophon Books, 1976).

[7]Indian symbolism centers on the Two-in-One mystery stated in the mystical terms of sexual analogy: "This female figure is the essence, the creative energy, the shakti, of the phallic pillar." Heinrich Zimmer, *Myths and Symbols in Indian Art and Civilization* (Princeton: Bollingen Series VI, 1972), p. 199. Zimmer defines Shakti as "the Goddess, the feminine active principle, the efficient and material cause of our universe" (p. 205). He describes the original creation: "The God and Goddess are the first self-revelation of the Absolute, the male being the personification of the passive aspect which we know as Eternity, the female of the active energy (shakti), the dynamism of Time. Though apparently opposites, they are in essence one" (p. 139). Indeed, the name Kali is the feminine form of the word for time, *Kala*.

[8]"Le symbolisme de la chasse se présente assez naturellement sous deux aspects: la mise à mort de l'animal, qui est la destruction de l'ignorance, des tendances

néfastes; d'autre part, la recherche du gibier, la poursuite à la trace signifiant la *quête* spirituelle." Jean Chevalier and Alain Gheerbrant, *Dictionnaire des symboles*, 4 vols. (Paris: Ed. Seghers, 1973), I, 335.

[9]See Lederer, Chapter 26 ("The Bottomless Lake, and the Bottomless Pit"), pp. 233-39, and Chapter 29 ("Our Lady of Pain"), pp. 249-67.

[10]"The waters, in short, symbolize the universal congress of potentialities, the *fons et origo*, which precedes all form and all creation. Immersion in water signifies a return to the preformal state, with a sense of death and annihilation on the one hand, but of rebirth and regeneration on the other, since immersion intensifies the life-force." J. E. Cirlot, *A Dictionary of Symbols*, tr. Jack Sage (New York: Philosophical Library, 1962), p. 345.

[11]Ibid., p. 346.

[12]Jung, p. 450.

[13]Ibid., p. 159.

[14]Ibid., p. 371.

[15]Ibid., p. 166.

[16]Chevalier and Gheerbrant, IV, 36.

[17]Jung, chapter entitled "Alchemy and Manichaeism," pp. 37-41.

[18]Jung would analyze Iñigo's position as follows: "But the unconscious is also feared by those whose conscious attitude is at odds with their true nature. Naturally their dreams will then assume an unpleasant and threatening form, for if nature is violated she takes her revenge. In itself the unconscious is neutral, and its normal function is to compensate the conscious position. In it the opposites slumber side by side; they are wrenched apart only by the activity of the conscious mind, and the more one-sided and cramped the conscious standpoint is, the more painful or dangerous will be the unconscious reaction." (pp. 156-57).

[19]Cf. note 9.

[20]Edward C. Whitmont, *The Symbolic Quest* (Princeton: Princeton University Press, 1969), p. 192.

[21]Ibid., p. 30.

[22]Ibid., p. 79.

[23]Northrup Frye, *The Secular Scripture* (Cambridge, Mass.: Harvard University Press, 1976), pp. 185-86.

[24]Whitmont states: "Jung felt that the central meaning of our lives can be grasped only through a realization of our own individual myths. . . . When we confront the myth—the mythical (archetypal) core of our complexes—we confront the ultimate borderline of our place in transcendental meaningfulness. We confront that utterly essential and indispensable element of meaning in our lives which had hitherto clothed itself in personal experiences and associations in the form of the shells of our complexes" (p. 84).

"FOLLY AND A WOMAN": GALDOS'
RHETORIC OF IRONY IN *TRISTANA*

Edward H. Friedman

Quanquā si quid petulantius aut
loquacius à me dictum videbitur,
cogitate, & Stulticiam & mulierē
dixisse.

—Erasmus, *Moriae Encomium*

The ironic reading of a literary text may produce a circle of ironies, levels of interpretation in which one irony leads to another, *ad infinitum*. An ultimate irony, in terms of literary criticism, may be seen in the vastly different analyses of texts by those who read ironically and by those who do not. Acceptance of an ironic meaning forces rejection of a literal meaning; yet, as Wayne Booth has demonstrated in *A Rhetoric of Irony*, neither internal nor external hermeneutic clues are totally reliable for determining whether a given statement is accurate or misleading, to be taken literally or ironically.[1] The art of defining an author's perspective, both crucial and elusive, becomes one of learned intuition. At a certain point, the critic is called upon to make a decision that more often than not will be all right or all wrong, and the difficulties are heightened by the fact that there is no consistent pattern of irony.

One does not have to be flightily romantic nor overtly inclined toward symbolic interpretation to recognize that *Don Quijote* is a more complex, more sophisticated novel now than it was in 1615 because novelistic experimentation and the theory of the novel, on becoming more complex and more sophisticated, have illuminated aspects of the work which the seventeenth-century reader and critic could not have discerned. Similarly, *Tristana* is perhaps a more effective work now than in 1892 because the source of its irony has been more clearly elucidated and because its almost precognitive social stand has been verified. The novel focuses on a woman who must confront traditional and dogmatic social positions and who ultimately rejects accepted views regarding education, career potential, and feminine honor. The fact that Tristana is fighting a losing battle is not as significant as the battle itself, a battle which must be viewed in light of Galdós' system of absolute values. The self-conscious use of literature as a mediating factor (as, for example, the representation of Don Lope as a Don Quijote turned Don Juan, seducer of Tristana, whose name derives from the chivalric tradition) allows for the elaboration of a multifaceted analogic structure that illustrates Galdós' feminist position. The foundation of this structure is the ironic narrative voice of Galdós.

Simply put, Galdós the storyteller, the manipulator of the literary events—*el dios de la obra*—loads the deck. Galdós the narrator is in full sympathy with Tristana. The novel is not parodic, but ironic. The impossibility of realization of Tristana's goals is not due to her mother's mental instability and the inheritance of insanity, nor to the defiance of natural law (in which the amputation of the leg may be seen as nature's revenge), nor because she has an incomplete and unrealistic vision of society, nor because she is too given to idealism. For Tristana, there is no hope from the beginning, no possible way to act, no way to plan for the future, no realistic course of action. Galdós has created a blind alley and his subject, as in the early thesis novels, is intolerance and the cruelties of society, only here the treatment is more subtle, more ironic. Galdós the narrator is the judge of Tristana and her circumstances, with the added advantage that as both judge and creator he can manipulate character and situation. It is precisely the narrator's stance, the strength and nuances of his voice, which one must intuit to comprehend *Tristana*.

The tension between the narrative persona as observer and omniscient witness, his attitude toward the characters, the subtlety of his expression, the literary orientation of his rhetorical devices, and the elaboration of an external viewpoint put Galdós in full control of his material. He creates an internal or covert irony to replace the obvious or overt irony of the thesis novels.[2] By establishing an open and unlimited perspective, Galdós can work (and play) on a number of levels. The final effect is tragicomic because the tragic potential of the major social theme is countered by a resolution that initially seems anticlimatic and, perhaps more significantly, by a reduction of the "real" attributes of the characters. Linked to literary prototypes and increasingly dependent on the narrator, the characters are so fictionalized as to become indistinguishable from the storyteller. While recognizing Galdós as "the most complex presence in his novel," David I. Grossvogel believes that the characters of *Tristana* suffer at the hands of the powerful narrator, that "mocked and manipulated by the author, his people are prevented from achieving fully their fictional self-definition: a part of them exists as a function of his commentary."[3] For Grossvogel, the narrator's strength is the novel's weakness:

> From a surrealist point of view, Galdós is twice a prisoner of his words. He uses them not for themselves (as pure sound, or *objects*) but as signs (symbols), and he does so not in order to create an object that will stand separate from him, but to inform mere phantasms with his commenting (mental) presence.[4]

This reading negates an open structure, multiple sources of ambiguity, and all but the most bitter of ironies. For Grossvogel, "the author, having shaped his protagonists to his Procrustean bed, marries them off to each other without even the benefit of a bitter afterthought."[5]

One could argue that the effect is precisely the opposite. In *Tristana*, Galdós deals in literary terms with a social issue, on which he takes a definite stand. The social issue forms part of a work of art that is determined but not restricted by thematic elements. The novelist must treat reality differently than the essayist by working indirectly to make a statement and subjecting that statement to the rules of art. Thus, there can be seen a ricocheting effect between the social backdrop and the literary precedents, all within a newly created literary world. The narrator synthesizes the diverse elements and adds to them a commentary which, rather than closing the narrative by asphyxiating the characters, opens it by speaking ambiguously and by constantly changing the points of reference. In this system, the narrator (or the author controlling the narrator) makes no attempt to detach himself from his characters, in accord with the concept of a single vision in which the reader must take literary clues and discern the author's comprehensive perspective.

The fact that the character cannot be separated from the storyteller, like the proverbial dancer and his dance, in no way impedes Galdós' vision and to a certain extent makes it more forceful. The thematic aspect of this vision, then, derives from the creation of the literary analogue, and the fictional aspect of the vision lies in the subtlety of the presentation. The narrator is the source of the statement and the way in which it is communicated, and Galdós gives him the dual function of showing and telling. Hardly a prisoner of his words, he is the master of both situation and diction, playing all sides, arguing all points, exploring the infinite uses of language, and dominating the universe he has created by providing a means of decoding the novel's ambiguities. The decoding of ambiguities in this case is synonymous with defining the ironic structure of *Tristana*. The wedding of Tristana and Don Lope is far more than a weak allusion to the marriage ending traceable to Greek New Comedy; it is the final irony of the novel and the culmination of an intricate series of ironies.

The mode of presentation in *Tristana* is rhetorical, self-referential, impressionistic, and manipulative. The narrative persona takes charge from the opening passages of the novel and maintains full authority throughout. The Galdosian narrator relies heavily on a synthesis of perspectives, on establishing a literary compatibility between seemingly incompatible conventions. *Tristana* begins with a description of Don Lope and his milieu. The allusions to *Don Quijote* are clear and numerous: we have an *hidalgo*, confusion of names (Don Juan López Garrido becomes Don Lope, "composición del caballero"[6]), a quotidian schedule, and two female figures reminiscent of the housekeeper and niece of the Cervantine novel. Galdós has his narrator borrow a literary voice before his own voice can be heard, and we are once again in the Quijotesque realm of narrative ambiguity. An anachronistic (derivative) voice presents an anachronistic Don Quijote using anachronistic language, a linguistic correlative of both the narrative stance and object. The incongruity of the nineteenth-century *hidalgo* is conveyed in equally incongruous terms: the gentlemen, "de buena estampa y nombre peregrino," notable for his "catadura militar de antiguo cuño, algo así como una reminiscencia pictórica de los tercios viejos de Flandes," inhabits a "plebeyo cuarto de alquiler de los baratitos, con ruidoso vecindario de taberna, merendero, cabrería y estrecho patio interior de habitaciones numeradas" (p. 7).

The chivalric overtones of the introductory chapter are purely ironic, for this gentleman is the antithesis of Don Quijote. Like the monkey dressed in silk who remains a monkey, Don Lope is a despicable figure despite the knightly linguistic trimmings. The narrator, the creator of this language, is fully conscious of the discrepancy, in effect the basis of the novel's irony. The narrator's attitude toward Don Lope reflects the interplay between art and concept that characterizes Galdós' approach. The mock serious, ultimately burlesque, treatment of Don Lope makes a statement and makes it creatively. We see an egotist ("en afeitarse y acicalarse, pues cuidaba de su persona con esmero y lentitudes de hombre de mundo, se pasaban dos horitas," p. 9), a man who takes himself too seriously ("O había que matarle o decirle don Lope," p. 8), and a womanizer ("se preciaba de haber asaltado más torres de virtud y rendido más plazas de honestidad que pelos tenía en la cabeza," p. 8). The self-styled knight is portrayed as a gratuitous seducer of women, and the images from the tradition of courtly love, euphemisms that have lost their former prestige, make him appear ridiculous. Don Lope, who will victimize Tristana, here as throughout the novel falls victim to the narrator.

Just as he initiates the novel with a voice not entirely his own, the narrator gives himself what may be termed a false presence, that of uninformed observer. He writes in a tentative style of his acquaintance with the characters ("La primera vez que tuve conocimiento de tal personaje y pude observar . . . ," p. 7) and with studied uncertainty of the identity of Tristana and her relationship with Don Lope ("orejas hubo en la vecindad que le oyeron decir papá, como las muñecas que hablan," p. 11). During the course of the narration, the outsider looking in will become omniscient, and this narrative change will be matched by a change in the opening impression of the title figure. Tristana is presented as beautiful but lifeless, ironically detached from society ("Sus manos, de una forma perfecta . . . , tenían misteriosa virtud, como su cuerpo y ropa, para poder decir a las capas inferiores del mundo físico: la vostra miseria non mi tange," p. 10). The first chapter ends with a partial clarification of Tristana's role in Don Lope's household:

> no era hija, ni sobrina, ni esposa, ni nada del gran don Lope; no era nada y lo era todo, pues le pertenecía como una petaca, un mueble o una prenda de ropa, sin que nadie se la pudiera disputar; ¡y ella parecía tan resignada a ser petaca, y siempre petaca! (p. 11).

The passage is, of course, ironic. Tristana will hardly be immune from the world's misery, and she will refuse to resign herself to a negligible social role until the moment of her final and ambiguous conversion. The narrator is asking the reader to analyze the written word, to question the apparent, and to search for meanings; from the beginning, he is asking the reader to read ironically.

The examination of Don Lope continues in the second chapter, in which the narrator purportedly attempts to be truthful ("conviene hacer toda la luz posible en torno del don Lope, para que no se le tenga por mejor ni por más malo de lo que era realmente," p. 13). Echoing Jorge Manrique's *Coplas*, the narrator describes Don Lope as "muy amigo de sus amigos," "servicial hasta el heroísmo" (p. 15). The praise is straightforward until the reader is made aware that the specific case used to demonstrate Don Lope's generosity is that of Don Antonio Reluz, Tristana's father. Don Lope saves his friend, but destroys his friend's daughter; he frees Don Antonio from jail, and later imprisons Tristana. Don Antonio was deceived by "un socio de mala fe, un amigo pérfido" (p. 16), and the man who brings about his salvation ultimately proves himself to be an unfaithful friend. The case of Don Antonio follows a series of general statements concerning the character of Don Lope, all of which emphasize his hypocrisy. The motivating force in Don Lope's life is a resuscitated code of honor that is as shallow and dependent on appearances as its exponent. The industrial revolution is inimical to the views of the class-conscious Don Lope: "La sociedad, a su parecer, había creado diversos mecanismos con el solo objeto de mantener holgazanes y de perseguir y desvalijar a la gente hidalga y bien nacida" (p. 14). The narrative voice reaches its highest tenor in a consummately ironic passage that combines exposition and direct quotation to accentuate Don Lope's hypocritical nature while seemingly presenting him as an enemy of hypocrisy:

> Respecto a la Iglesia, teníala por una broma pesada, que los pasados siglos vienen dando a los presentes, y que éstos aguantan por timidez y cortedad de genio. Y no se crea que era irreligioso: al contrario, su fe superaba a la de muchos que hocican ante los altares y andan siempre entre curas. A éstos no los podía ver ni escritos el ingenioso don Lope, porque no encontraba sitio para ellos en el sistema seudocaballeresco que su desocupado magín se había forjado, y solía decir: "Los verdaderos sacerdotes somos nosotros, los que regulamos el honor y la moral, los que combatimos en pro del inocente, los enemigos de la maldad, de la hipocresía, de la injusticia . . . y del vil metal" (pp. 14-15).[7]

The narrator's message is playful but clear; subsequent affirmations of Don Lope's benevolence, even from the narrator himself, are not to be trusted.

In this chapter, Don Lope's view toward the past is contrasted with Tristana's bleak vision of the future ("sus ojos no sabían mirar al porvenir, y si lo miraban, no veían nada," p. 12). At twenty-one, Tristana's coming of age is characterized by a wish for independence and a recognition of the absence of possibilities. The narrator employs verbal humor to emphasize the incongruity of the matter ("Ejercía sobre ella su dueño un despotismo que podremos llamar seductor," p. 12), so that once again the conceptual analogue finds a linguistic counterpart. The lack of decorum and the ironic courtly imagery relate deceptive diction to the deceptive behavior of Don Lope and its effect on Tristana. A member of a society striving toward equality, Don Lope is seen as an unceasing opponent of absolute justice. He is served by an anachronistic and retrogressive code, and his opposition to progress is mirrored on an individual level in his seduction of Tristana, the figurative destruction of her future.

The Cervantine fictional world provides the backdrop for the third chapter, devoted primarily to Tristana's mother, Doña Josefina, a woman who finds release from the tribulations of the real world in the ideal world of chivalry ("Su niña debía el nombre de Tristana a la pasión por aquel arte caballeresco y noble, que creó una sociedad ideal para servir constantemente de norma y ejemplo a nuestras realidades groseras y vulgares," p. 20). After her husband's death, Doña Josefina enters a fantasy world in which she is dominated by two obsessions: moving from house to house and an inordinate concern for cleanliness. Before she dies, she realizes the error of her ways and rejects the fantasies ("En la hora de morir, Josefina recobró, como suele suceder, parte del seso que había perdido, y con el seso le revivió momentáneamente de ser pasado, reconociendo, cual Don Quijote moribundo, los disparates de la época de su viudez y abominando de ellos," p. 21). In this moment of apparent lucidity, Doña Josefina delivers her daughter to Don Lope.

The narrator seems to deliberately impose a pattern of idealism and a tendency to exalt the literary over the real not only on Doña Josefina but on Tristana as well. Within this system, one can rationalize Tristana's subsequent actions in terms of an inheritance of madness, absurd idealism, and a final awakening to reality. Like her mother, Tristana can be seen to escape the real by wishing for the impossible ideal, and she will be defeated in her irrational quest. Read ironically, on the other hand, the account of Doña Josefina can serve as an inverse analogue of Tristana's case. In the first instance, a woman who cannot face reality hides behind a literary facade, while in the second a woman fights for absolute values in a society given to relative and arbitrary values. Don Lope, the so-called protector of Tristana, sacrifices his collection of arms to pay Doña Josefina's debts (without, however, giving up his collection of portraits of beautiful women), and as repayment he dishonors Tristana within two months. The stage is set for Tristana's confrontation with society.

In the previous chapter, the narrator introduced what may be considered a false analogy between Tristana and her mother. In Chapter IV, he continues this convention with a startling simile, an omen of Tristana's fate. Speaking of Don Lope, he says that "al sentido moral del buen caballero le faltaba una pieza importante, cual órgano que ha sufrido una mutilación y sólo functiona con limitaciones o paradas deplorables" (p. 23). As in the case of Doña Josefina, the comparison may be seen to underscore the differences. There is no poetic justice in the denouement of *Tristana*, and the lack of differentiation in the narration makes the injustice more striking. The narrator, the figure responsible for linguistic choice, uses forms of *Tristana* and *Reluz* (primarily *triste, tristeza,* and *luz*) with reference to all of the major characters.[8]

In the same chapter, the narrator presents Tristana in the context of Don Lope's perverse ethical code ("sus perversas doctrinas," p. 24), verified in his rationalization of his treatment of her: "¿No me pidió Josefina que la amparase? Pues más amparo no cabe. Bien defendida la tengo de todo peligro; que ahora nadie se atreverá a tocarle el pelo de la ropa" (p. 25). At first, Tristana accepts the ideas of her guardian without realizing the gravity of his actions. She is open to the imaginative notions, seen as compatible with her readiness to idealize ("estimulaba la fácil disposición de la joven para idealizar las cosas, para verlo todo como no es, o como nos conviene o nos gusta que sea," p. 26). Shortly afterwards, however, Tristana recognizes the ludicrous position of Don Lope ("Bruscamente vio en Don Lope al viejo, y agrandaba con su fantasía la ridícula presunción del anciano que, contraviniendo la ley de la Naturaleza, hace papeles de galán," pp. 26-27), and at the same time she recognizes something in herself, an intrinsic self-worth, a "conciencia de no ser una persona vulgar" (p. 27). This consciousness on Tristana's part represents a rejection of societal values in favor of absolute values. After eight months with Don Lope, and metaphorically linked to a premature infant, Tristana undergoes a spiritual awakening that will mark her future. Her new moral sense could hardly have been learned from Don Lope. His lessons have taught her to reject the future and her aim now is to transcend the present. Certain of Tristana's ideas, such as a negative view of marriage, will conform to Don Lope's outlook, but the narrator has made clear in this chapter that a distinction must be made between the moral base of the two ideologies; the rationale is different, even when the ideas are the same.

The friendship between Tristana and the servant Saturna allows for a dialogue on the social restrictions of women. The conversation is not a debate because both women feel that while women should be both free and honorable, society makes the two categories mutually exclusive. Nevertheless, Saturna adopts a realistic position ("pintándole el mundo y los hombre con sincero realismo," pp. 28-29), while Tristana in her idealism dreams of changes ("armando castilletes de la vida futura," p. 29). Saturna discourses on the possibilities for women: "sólo tres carreras pueden seguir las que visten faldas: a casarse, que carrera es, o el teatro . . . , vamos, ser cómica, que es buen modo de vivir, o . . . no quiero nombrar lo otro. Figúreselo" (p. 29). Tristana is disturbed by the options because she has the inclination and the talent for none of them; what she would prefer is a so-called man's job: "Si nos hicieran médicas, abogadas, siquiera boticarias o escribanas, ya que no ministras y senadoras, podríamos . . . " (p. 30). Tristana here is not groping at windmills. Conscious of both the enemy and the difficulties implicit in the struggle, she feels a need for self-fulfillment and for exploration of her full potential ("ideas, lo que llamamos ideas, creo que no me faltan," p. 30). In this chapter, the narrator lets the characters speak for themselves; there is no burlesque tone to weaken the argument, and the result is a clearly established mutual sympathy between the women.

Chapter VI marks the culmination of a literary transformation: Don Lope changes from an antithetical Quijote figure to a Don Juan grown old ("el Don Juan caído," p. 33). Faced with poverty and old age, he loses self-confidence but not pride. He is given to fits of jealousy, and when the narrator speaks of "el viejo y la niña" (p. 36), another literary tradition comes into play. The old man's jealousy prepares the way for the introduction of the third member of the amorous triangle in the following chapter. The scene is set as well for an ironic reversal. The narrator stresses the ridiculous egotism of Don Lope before introducing a young lover who, if the traditional literary analogue is completed, will make a fool of the old man and carry off the young lady. This would be the world of poetic justice, not the world of *Tristana*.

Before the meeting with Horacio, the narrator reaffirms the moral superiority of Tristana ("la tranquilidad de su conciencia dábale valor contra el tirano," p. 37). Her profound sympathy for the blind children at the orphan asylum has self-referential and symbolic overtones:

> Tal compasión inspiraban a Tristana aquellos infelices, que casi casi le hacía daño mirarlos. ¡Cuidado que no ver! No acababan de

ser personas: faltábales la facultad de enterarse, y ¡qué trabajo tener que enterarse de todo pensándolo! (pp. 39-40).

Tristana seems to see herself in the incomplete world of the handicapped, as one whose mental processes surpass her options. Ironically, she notices Horacio as she is warning Saturno not to play with fire, and her love for the artist begins at that moment. From the beginning of their relationship, Tristana cannot bring herself to play conventional social roles, to subtly let herself be courted; she speaks sincerely and directly to Horacio. In a manner of speaking, she enters blindly into the affair with Horacio. She is guided primarily by the initial attraction—partly physical, partly idealized—and by her wish to abandon Don Lope. Because the narrator has consistently contrasted Tristana's honesty with Don Lope's hypocrisy, the reader may view the expression of Tristana's love as real and the progression of that love as credible.

Tristana's love for Horacio grows on two levels, based on her contact with him and her absence from him. In the first case, she becomes intrigued by the events of his life, which she sees as a type of martyrdom, and in the second, she glorifies Horacio in combined adulation and spiritualism ("un espiritualismo delirante," p. 45). Love is both immediate and atemporal ("Te estoy queriendo, te estoy buscando desde antes de nacer," p. 44), and the letters to Horacio offer Tristana a means of self-expression. Although in her exaltation of Horacio Tristana does not intuit the similarity of their backgrounds, the narrator makes clear the figurative slavery of each. The radical difference is that Horacio, once freed from the dominance of his tyrannical grandfather, is able to experience life, to make mistakes, and to continue to have society's approval of his actions, while Tristana will never be free of Don Lope. The narrator seems aware of the irony of Tristana's sympathy when he says that Horacio's story "casi parecía vida de un santo digna de un huequecito en el martirologio" (p. 51).[9] In a society that is beginning to accept and respect the concept of upward mobility, the new alternatives apply exclusively to men, and women are to remain the true martyrs of the will.

The idealism of Tristana is matched by that of Horacio, who views his present idyllic state as the poetically just conclusion of a long period of misery. He is as prone as Tristana to verbalize his feelings of ecstasy:

> Nuestro romanticismo, nuestra exaltación, no nos parecieron absurdos. Nos sorprendimos con hambre atrasada, el hambre espi-

ritual, noble y pura que mueve el mundo, y por la cual existimos, y existirán miles de generaciones después de nosotros. Te reconocí mía y me declaraste tuyo. Esto es vivir; lo demás, ¿qué es? (p. 54).

The narrator becomes part of this romanticized universe in his descriptions of the lovers' actions ("la separación, algunas noches tan dolorosa y patética como si Horacio se marchara para el fin del mundo y Tristana se despidiera para meterse monja," p. 56). This realm of mutual exaltation exists unencumbered by the presence of Don Lope, who does not appear in Chapters VII, VIII, and IX. When he returns in Chapter X, the narrator's recourse to courtly love imagery once again becomes ironic; Tristana, the captive of love, becomes once more the literal captive of Don Lope ("cautiva y tirano," p. 57). Yet at this point, Tristana sees herself as a true romantic heroine, willing to suffer for her love, and in an ironic passage she says,

> Créete que en vez de apurar la felicidad, nos vendría bien ahora algún contratiempo, una miajita de desgracia. El amor es sacrificio, y para la abnegación y el dolor debemos estar preparados siempre (p. 61).

Tristana is, thus, a symbolic prisoner of love, a real prisoner of Don Lope and of social mores, and, as a literary character, the victim of an ironist who makes literal her figurative speech. Even her thoughts reflect the linguistic influence of the narrator; when she contemplates pardoning Don Lope for her dishonor, she believes that his most serious flaw is "la perversidad monomaníaca de la persecución de mujeres" (p. 58), echoing the narrator's reference to a "perversa doctrina."

Correspondingly, after Tristana makes her confession to Horacio—quite possibly the sacrificial act she has imagined, but ironically only a minor indication of the suffering to come—she describes Don Lope in the same terms as the narrator, as a Don Juan Tenorio with a wide range of victims. The narrator himself vacillates in his allusions; he describes Horacio's "resolución de burlar al burlador" (p. 65), Don Lope's meal, "más de carnero que de vaca" (p. 66), and the tyrant, "el Don Juan en decadencia" (p. 67). The characters draw from the narrator, who in turn draws from literature to create a contemporary social analogue. Don Lope, conscious of the role imposed upon him by Doña Josefina, shows the outward signs of a gentleman whose only concern is Tristana's well-being ("Tu mamá te confió a mí para que te amparase, y te amparé, y decidido estoy a protegerte contra toda clase de asechanzas y a defender tu honor,"

p. 68). Tristana calls him a hypocrite and a liar, and the narrator mocks him, using a literary convention as his point of attack ("¡Lástima que no hablara en verso para ser perfecta imagen del *padre noble* de antigua comedia!," p. 70). The narrator sustains the literary points of reference in Don Lope's inversion of the *carpe diem* motif ("cogí flores en la edad en que no me correspondía tocar más que abrojos," p. 71).[10] Don Lope's role-playing makes Tristana more determined than ever to escape the repressive environment; if he is to emulate the vengeful father of Golden Age drama, she will justify his wrath by meeting with Horacio in his study ("Si este hombre me mata, máteme con razón," p. 74).

For the narrator, Tristana's decision marks a fusion of the real and the ideal:

> Pasearon . . . en el breve campo del estudio, desde el polo de lo ideal al de las realidades; recorrieron toda la esfera, desde lo humano a lo divino, sin poder determinar fácilmente la divisoria entre uno y otro, pues lo humano les parecía del cielo y lo divino revestíase a sus ojos de carne mortal (p. 75).

The experience opens Tristana's eyes, making her aware of the beauty of nature and art as well as of her own shortcomings. Her contact with Horacio allows her to note the results of a lack of encouragement in the past and of her inadequate education. The success of her early efforts at painting both emphasizes the wasted years and indicates that the opportunities available to Horacio, and to men in general, do not exist for women.[11]

The narrator takes care to provide a realistic rather than an idealistic backdrop for Tristana's paean to honorable freedom. The physical encounters with Horacio broaden her perspective and allow her to see that happiness is within her grasp. Present reality, to an extent, supports her idealism. As Tristana grows intellectually and as her goals increase, she profoundly affects both Horacio and Don Lope. With respect to Horacio,

> empezó a notar que la enamorada joven se iba creciendo a los ojos de él y le empequeñecía. En verdad que esto le causaba sorpresa, y casi casi empezaba a contrariarle, porque había soñado en Tristana la mujer subordinada al hombre en inteligencia y en voluntad, la esposa que vive de la savia moral e intelectual del esposo y que con los ojos y con el corazón de él ve y siente (p. 77).

The spiritual awakening is reciprocal, but although Horacio is profoundly moved by Tristana's ideas and recognizes the impact of these ideas upon his life, he seems surprisingly conventional when his apparently progressive attitude is put to the test. He wants a woman who will be an extension of himself, whose inferior status will accentuate his own superiority. He accepts Tristana's idealism up to the point at which it could materialize. In his way, he is as hypocritical as Don Lope. Blinded by love, Tristana mistakes Horacio's condescension for sincerity. Her faith in him, whether justified or not, gives her the strength necessary to defy Don Lope, and the old man dares not scold her, "adivinando que, al menor choque, la esclava sabría mostrar intenciones de no serlo" (p. 79). One can note a somewhat misleading triumph for Tristana. She seems to have won the love of a man willing to disregard the negative aspects of her past, and in doing so she has freed herself from dependence on Don Lope. The path has been cleared for her confrontation with society, reflected in her personal concept of freedom. Her trust in Horacio is misfounded, however; while outwardly supporting her, he thinks otherwise ("Esperaba que su constante cariño y la acción del tiempo rebajarían un poco la talla imaginativa y razonante de su ídolo, haciéndola más mujer, más doméstica, más corriente y útil," p. 82). If Tristana may be judged overly optimistic in her hopes for social change, Horacio seems to want to convert the "new woman" whom he loves into a conventional domestic servant. Tristana's idealism becomes ironic when, on defending the position of a mother regarding her child, she says, "la naturaleza me da más derechos que a ti" (p. 85). The reader will see that nature's rights will mean very little when superseded by those of society. Tristana is bound by absolute principles in a world that exalts relative values.

In Chapter XV, the narrator establishes a literary and at times symbolic base for the treatment of the social issue. The most obvious convention is the creation of a lovers' vocabulary, an intricate and intimate use of language by Tristana and Horacio.[12] Their expressions of love adopt literary forms; their primary models are Dante and Leopardi, and Horacio teaches Tristana Italian. The section is significant for a number of reasons. Tristana shows exceptional linguistic and histrionic skills ("Tristana dominó en breves días la pronunciación," "a las dos semanas recitaba con admirable entonación de actriz consumada," p. 89), just as earlier she had shown a talent for art, and she is a master at creating new language from old. The intellectual stimulus leads to introspection and to an awareness of her abilities. "Es que sirvo," she tells Horacio, "que podré servir para las cosas grandes; pero que decididamente no sirvo para las pequeñas" (p. 94). The passage may be seen as a type of consciousness of her historic role, amplified by the symbolic nature of the narrator's commentary. He states that Tristana "sabía ser dulce y amarga, blanda y fresca como el agua, ardiente como el fuego, vaga y rumorosa como el aire" (p. 88); seen symbolically, she is water, fire, and air, everything but earth and a figurative Earth Mother. She and Horacio read selections from the *Inferno* and the *Purgatorio*, associating themselves with tragic lovers and perhaps intuiting that Paradise will be denied them. Their lovers' vocabulary contains repetitions of the narrator's literary language; Horacio refers to Don Lope as "tu Tenorio arrumbado" and Tristana says that "ni por nada del mundo hace él el celoso de comedia" (p. 92).

The glorification of language and the glorification of ideals through language, as well as Tristana's thoughts of a higher order, contrast with Horacio's views of love. While Tristana synthesizes her romantic idealism with reality, Horacio moves from one realm to the other with no intention of combining the two. Tristana tends to see the figurative as an expression of the real, but for Horacio the dichotomy will always remain. The distinction is important, because Tristana takes her role seriously and Horacio considers it a lovers' game. On reentering reality, he is as conventional as before in expecting Tristana to conform to traditional domesticity:

> Entrégate a mí sin reserva. ¡Ser mi compañera de toda la vida; ayudarme y sostenerme con tu cariño! . . . ¿Te parece que hay un oficio mejor ni arte más hermoso? Hacer feliz a un hombre que te hará feliz, ¿qué más? (p. 93).

It is perhaps precisely this "¿qué más?" that forms the ideological foundation of *Tristana*.

The conceptual separation of Tristana and Horacio is mirrored in the following chapter by their physical separation, a separation that seems to affect Tristana more profoundly than Horacio ("respiraba con desahogo, como jornalero en sábado por la tarde, después de una semana de destajo," p. 98). Anticipating her subsequent devotion to the Church, Tristana hears mass and prays during Horacio's absence. The two lovers begin a correspondence that continues their recourse to a lovers' vocabulary. Even in his show of passion, Horacio sounds ironic in passages such as "la gloria de ser tu dueño" (p. 100) because the narrator has informed the reader of Horacio's attitude toward the separation.

Tristana's letters reflect a growing illusion over what strikes her as ideal love (expressed ironically as "Soy tan feliz, que a veces paréceme que vivo suspendida en el aire, que mis pies no tocan la tierra," p. 102), in addition to a more contemplative tone with respect to her freedom. Her condemnation of marriage and a male-oriented society inadvertently conflicts with Horacio's standpoint. Here, as in the passage on having children, Tristana apologizes for her audacity ("Estoy cargante, ¿verdad? No hagas caso de mí. ¡Qué locuras! No sé lo que pienso ni lo que escribo; mi cabeza es un nidal de disparates," p. 104), but there are no disparities in her remarks. Her anti-marital perspective has nothing to do with the libertinism of Don Lope, but is rather a rejection of obligatory devotion in favor of love built upon faith and a call to arms against a system that regards women as subservient to men. This is followed, again ironically, by Horacio's request that Tristana move to the country and marry him.

Tristana's constant focus on her idealism seems to indicate that she can distinguish between her aspirations (the impossible) and her status in society (the real). Her introspection continues:

> Oigo desde aquí las palomitas, y entiendo sus arrullos. Pregúntales por qué tengo yo esta ambición loca que no me deja vivir; por qué aspiro a lo imposible, y aspiraré siempre, hasta que el imposible mismo se me plante enfrente y me diga: "Pero ¿no me ve usted, so . . .?" Pregúntales por qué sueño despierta con mi propio ser transportado a otro mundo, en el cual me veo libre y honrada (pp. 107-08).

So do her efforts at self-improvement. Her study of English with Doña Malvina, a liberated woman who is free from the social structure that inhibits Tristana,[13] gives the latter the opportunity to broaden her knowledge and to augment her linguistic and acting skills. The lovers' vocabulary now includes Anglicisms and quotations from Shakespeare. Ironically, while Tristana jests about Doña Malvina, writing Horacio that "la creerías del género masculino o del neutro" (p. 108), she calls Lady Macbeth her friend and says that "*Unsex me here* . . . me hace estremecer y despierta no sé qué terribles emociones en lo más profundo de mi naturaleza" (p. 112). Tristana uses the Shakespearian passage to express her dissatisfaction with the lot of women. She does not want to become manly or sexless but rather clings to the notion of a change in role models: "Eso de que dos que se aman han de volverse iguales y han de pensar lo mismo, no me cabe a mí en la cabeza. . . . Sea cada cual como Dios le ha hecho, y siendo distintos, se amarán más" (p. 111). Tristana has become a standard for the women's cause, and the individual and the subjective are replaced by the universal; even Horacio loses his distinctive features ("se me ha borrado tu imagen," "te me vuelves espíritu puro," p. 114).

In Chapter XIX, Tristana makes her first allusion to the pain in her leg. In the preceding chapter, she speaks of Don Lope's temporary illness in terms of vengeance ("El reuma se está encargando de vengar el sinnúmero de maridillos que burló, y a las vírgenes honestas o esposas frágiles que inmoló en el ara nefanda de su liviandad," p. 108). In the ironic reversal of fortunes, Tristana must judge her own illness in terms of retribution. Chapter XIX contains three references to her illness as an act of God:

> (1) ¿No te parece cruel lo que hace Dios conmigo? ¡Que a ese perdulario le cargue de achaques en su vejez como castigo de una juventud de crímenes contra la moral, muy santo y muy bueno; pero que a mí, jovenzuela que empiezo a pecar, que apenas . . . , y esto con circunstancias atenuantes; que a mí me aflija, a las primeras de cambio, con tan fiero castigo . . . ! (p. 116);
> (2) ¿Qué crimen he cometido? ¿Quererte? ¡Vaya un crimen! Como tengo esta maldita costumbre de buscar siempre el *perché delle cose*, cavilo que Dios se ha equivocado con respecto a mí (p. 119);
> (3) ¿Me querrás cojita? No, si me curaré . . . ¡Pues no faltaba más! Si no, sería una injusticia muy grande, una barbaridad de la Providencia, del Altísimo, del . . . no sé qué decir (p. 120).

The irony here is especially complex, because Tristana at first is willing to rationalize the events in a framework of divine or poetic justice and then is forced to seek another explanation. The reader must note, however, that her logic is correct. Her illness can be explained as a divine order operating to punish her for her sins, but this system would call for a more severe punishment for Don Lope's moral offenses. Since this is not the case, Tristana resolves that either there is no absolute system of retribution or a mistake has been made. If one is to accept this position, the inescapable conclusion would be that poetic justice is not being served or perhaps that Tristana's sins are to be considered more serious because she is a woman.

After establishing a foundation of irony, the narrator to a degree stays in the background. While he is as manipulative as in the early part of the novel, the events themselves prove ironic without the need for clarification. Tristana's decision to become an actress, for example, to follow a path acceptable in society's eyes, comes at the moment of her debilitating illness, and there seems to be a type of unconscious insight in her wish to become an "actriz del género trágico" (p. 129). Even more ironic is the narrator's treatment of Don Lope. The reader has been both told and shown that Don

Lope is a hypocrite, the true culprit of the novel. In Chapter XX, the narrator offers a subtle criticism within praise:

> fuera de su absoluta ceguera moral en cosas de amor, el libertino inservible era hombre de buenos sentimientos y no podía ver padecer a las personas de su intimidad. Cierto que él había deshonrado a Tristana, matándola para la sociedad y el matrimonio, hollando su fresca juventud; pero lo cortés no quitaba lo valiente; la quería con entrañable afecto (p. 122).

If telling has been modified somewhat, showing remains the same. In this chapter, Don Lope dares to pardon Tristana for her sins ("Sé que has claudicado moralmente, antes de cojear con tu piernecita. . . . Te lo perdono . . . Absolución total," p. 125) and advises her to avoid marriage ("El matrimonio te zambulliría en la vulgaridad," p. 126). On reaching the concluding chapter of *Tristana*, the reader cannot ignore the irony and the veracity of this advice and of Don Lope's continued emphasis on "ridiculizar la vida boba, la unión eterna con un ser vulgar y las prosas de la intimidad matrimoñesca" (pp. 128-29).

The combination of suffering and the tendency toward idealization of her love leads Tristana to increased abstraction, which she accepts as part of her development. It is not the narrator but Tristana herself who first reveals her emphasis on the spiritual and the creation of a perfect lover modeled after but distinct from Horacio. The language of her letters reflects her faith in the ineffable and she no longer uses the lovers' vocabulary of the past. Once again, the dichotomy showing/telling comes into play. The narrator's statements in Chapter XXI center on Tristana's fantasies; Horacio, he informs the reader, has become a purely mental image: "De aquel bonito fantasma iba haciendo Tristana la verdad elemental de su existencia, pues sólo para él, sin caer en la cuenta de que tributaba culto a un Dios de su propia cosecha" (p. 132). Nevertheless, the narrator has shown that Tristana is conscious of this second Horacio, the logical product of the absence of the real Horacio and the severity of her pain. Tristana's letters demonstrate her belief in a higher spiritual realm in which love is unaffected by physical matters ("Tan espiritualmente amaré con una pierna, como con dos," p. 133). Rebuked by the physical world and deprived of Horacio's sympathy, Tristana depends more and more on an abstract world. The narrator may bring to light the danger of her retreat from reality, but he continues to make it clear that no alternative exists for her. She is the victim not only of an unkind fate, but of the failure of those who surround her to provide the love she merits. Tristana is not ranting thoughtlessly when she writes to Horacio, "Si tú no tuvieras brazos ni piernas, yo te querría lo mismo" (p. 143). She is at the mercy of her oppressor, Don Lope, who delights in his triumph:

> Triste es mi victoria, pero cierta. . . . Quiso alejarse de mí, quiso volar; pero no contaba con su destino, que no le permite revoloteos ni correrías; no contaba con Dios, que me tiene ley . . . , no sé por qué . . . , pues siempre se pone de mi parte en estas contiendas (pp. 143-44).

The events following the amputation of Tristana's leg lead to the consummately ironic denouement and center primarily on Don Lope and Horacio, simultaneously enemies and ideological brothers. Don Lope, conspicuous by his hypocritical presence, and Horacio, conspicuous by his absence and by the narrator's failure to include his letters after Chapter XVIII, both suggest the purchase of an organ for Tristana, clearly intended as a replacement for the lost limb. At their initial meeting, each man feels respect for his opponent; Don Lope considers Horacio "un hombre sesudo, que al fin y a la postre verá las cosas como las veo yo" (p. 162). Declaring that Tristana "es ya mujer inútil para siempre" (p. 160), Don Lope frees his rival of any obligation to her ("¿Cómo sostener su promesa ante una mujer que ha de andar con muletas? . . . La naturaleza se impone," p. 165) and speaks of the inevitable separation as a type of figurative divorce ("Incompatibilidad de caracteres . . . , incompatibilidad absoluta, diferencias irreducibles," p. 169). In the conversation with Horacio, the narrator allows Don Lope's words to betray him. With absolutely no conviction, Don Lope pretends to see Tristana's attitude as a vision of truth: "Quizá ve más que todos nosotros; quizá su mirada perspicua, o cierto instinto de adivinación concedido a las mujeres superiores, ve la sociedad futura que nosotros no vemos" (p. 168). Artfully manipulated by the narrator, the words of a hypocrite, intending to be deceptive, state the novel's major social theme.

After Tristana's operation, the narrator writes:

> empezó el despertar lento y triste de la señorita de Reluz, su nueva vida, después de aquel simulacro de muerte, su resurrección, dejándose un pie y dos tercios de la pierna en el seno de aquel sepulcro que a manzanas olía" (p. 147).

The arrival of the new organ, a gift of Horacio with music lessons courtesy of Don Lope, is also "como una resurrección súbita" (p. 173) for its owner. The organ is symbolic not only of the amputated leg but of Tristana's conversion, of her withdrawal into full spirituality. Once again separated from Horacio, this time permanently, Tristana replaces the man she has made into a god with God and the idyllic visions of love and a new society with religious fervor. Tristana at the novel's end is a consummate musician, an expert pastry cook, and the wife of Don Lope. She is no longer the Tristana of honorable freedom, of conceptual precocity, and of verbal wit.

An examination of Tristana's conversion is made difficult by the fact that she says very little in the novel after the operation. During Horacio's first visit, the narrator expresses Tristana's disappointment that the man she has worshipped treats her with pity rather than love ("De los labios del *señó Juan* no salieron más que las conmiseraciones que se dan a todo enfermo, . . . y en todo lo que dijo referente a la constancia de su amor veíase el artificio trabajosamente edificado por la compasión," p. 165). In their conversations, Tristana and Horacio stop speaking of the past, and her "marasmo espiritual" (p. 173) is broken only by the delivery of the organ. Even before the announcement of Horacio's marriage, Tristana has committed herself to self-imposed seclusion and concentration on music. "No tuvo la vejez de Don Lope toda la tristeza y soledad que él se merecía, como término de una vida disipada y viciosa," the narrator writes at the beginning of the final chapter (p. 180), as what may be considered an introductory statement on the concept of poetic justice. He seems to be warning the reader that justice is not at work, that what will follow may be disguised as a logical consequence of the events but is really an elaborate system of contradictions.

The narrator has demonstrated that Tristana, on awakening into maturity, has been able to synthesize Don Lope's anti-social ideology with her own observations to form her own view of society and specifically of women's role in it. Her standpoint, based on a foundation of equality and absolute values, is radical only in the sense that it clashes with the relative and oppressive ethical code of the society she lives in; that society insists on a rigid distinction between what is manly and what is womanly, while Tristana's ideal refuses to admit dichotomies of this type. Her rejection of domestic duties, traditional marriage, and conventional careers cannot be seen as a rejection of femininity but as an assertion of the potential of women, who should be free to emerge from the kitchen to enter the realm of ideas. Her own prodigiousness, attested to by Doña Malvina and the music teacher, indicates the validity of her position. She is not fighting for a libertinism for women as a counterpart to that of Don Lope, but instead insists that the new social freedom accorded to men should apply as well to women. Tristana's idealism is a necessary consequence of her undertaking, and the major element of her disillusionment is the realization that Horacio, the model of male superiority for her new society, is of the same cast as Don Lope, representative *par excellence* of the old society. The narrator clearly formulates a pattern of Don Lope's hypocrisy and defamation of women as well as a discrepancy between the progressive nature of what Horacio says and the conventional nature of his thoughts concerning social roles. In addition, the narrator gives an ironic twist to Don Lope's words and silences Horacio as a supporter of Tristana's cause.

The narrator thus goes to great lengths to promote reader sympathy for Tristana, an act that he seems to negate in the final conversion. Yet at that point the reader has been made privy to the ironic level of the narrative and should not be surprised by an ironic final reversal. The narrator says in the last sentence of the novel that one cannot be sure if Tristana and Don Lope are happy in their new roles.Perhaps, he tells the reader, Tristana has found final consolation in religion, a spiritual support to match the *muletas* that have become part of her. Perhaps Don Lope is content with his financial independence and his victory over a rebellious spirit. The relative happiness of the characters is less significant than the implications of the novel's open-endedness. Tristana's story, as the literary analogue of a social situation, may be seen as a battle that forms part of a war. The loss of one battle does not determine the ultimate loss of the war. Just as in the thesis novels, Galdós allows for the triumph of intolerance to underline the need for tolerance, and here he creates a narrator to convey his message in the indirect terms of art. In Chapter XXIII, Tristana writes to Horacio, "¿Te acuerdas de aquel grillo que tuvimos, y que cantaba más y mejor después de arrancarle una de las patitas?" (p. 143). Like this symbolic cricket, the resonance of Tristana's voice becomes stronger and more effective after the amputation, even though—ironically—she seems to have been silenced.

A key to the narrator's use of irony is the literariness of the work. In the early part of the novel, both the narrator and the characters depend upon literary allusions, while in the second part the literary figure has become a product of the narrator's self-referential posture and a character in its own right. Don Lope, for example, goes from an anachronistic Don Quijote, a sedentary knight, to an aged and ridiculous Don Juan, and finally surpasses the derivative identities to become a unique image of personified hypocrisy. His idiosyncrasies are brought to light in comparative terms, and the narrator's interest diminishes once the character has been defined. In the second part of the novel, then, the narrator can play with his own creation because he has shown the reader what to expect from the character. In other words, once the truth has been established, new forms of irony may be introduced. This technique allows the narrator to strengthen the novel's statement by exaggerating the moral distance between the characters while apparently increasing his own critical detachment.

The traditional criticism of *Tristana* relies very little on Galdos' ironic perspective. For Emilia Pardo Bazán, Galdós' contemporary, the crux of the dramatic events lies in Tristana's willingness to cast herself into an unequal battle to escape the indignities of her life with Don Lope. Pardo Bazán's essay stresses the feminist orientation of *Tristana*, and in recognizing the impossibility of victory it hints (probably unconsciously) at the novel's ironic potential.[14] A number of more recent studies discount both Galdós' feminism and the irony of the text. A case in point is an article by Leon Livingstone.[15] The great equalizing agent for Livingstone is the incontrovertible harmony of nature. Man errs when he attempts to contradict nature, yet it is always nature that ultimately triumphs: "the denaturalization process consists of the imposing of artificial constraints or unattainable goals on the individual by himself or by others."[16] The first example of one who carries an attitude to unreasonable extremes is Doña Josefina; the description of her two manias "establishes the author's basic position and sets the burlesque tone of the novel."[17] The second is the case of Don Lope, "who, the author takes pains to let us know, outside of his one obsession is an essentially decent and even exemplary character."[18] The idea of a burlesque tone is disregarded here, even though Don Lope's single flaw involves destroying women's lives by dishonoring them and their families, and Livingstone's analysis depends on a literal interpretation of Don Lope. The critic says that Don Lope is finally obliged to recognize the absurdity of his role as gallant, "contraviniendo la ley de la Naturaleza,"[19] but is this really true? Moreover, he believes that Don Lope is "so contrite in the presence of Tristana's misfortune that he is willing to make the greatest of all sacrifices and surrender her to his rival,"[20] but he makes this gesture only when he is positive that Tristana is tied to him forever.[21]

Basing his discussion of *Tristana* on the intricacies of the love triangle, made more complex by literary self-reference, Germán Gullón rejects the idea of an ironic ending, "pues los personajes con resignación muestran su conformidad con el destino, y parecen entender que 'los sueños sueños son.' "[22] Throughout the novel, however, resignation is seen as something less than consistent,[23] and the final resignation is more a recognition of a lack of possibilities than an awakening. What Gullón calls Tristana's conformity to her destiny comes only after man, society, and nature (illness) have destroyed her dreams, after all hope has been removed. The narrator terms the marriage plan an "absurdo proyecto" and emphasizes Tristana's indifference to the plan and to all earthly things: "No sentía el acto, lo aceptaba como un hecho impuesto por el mundo exterior, como el empadronamiento, como la contribución, como làs reglas de policía" (p. 182).

Tristana's spirit has been broken and Don Lope has fallen into the vulgarity of the conventionalism he abhors. This is ironic because the force of her struggle still remains and because the man whom destiny has favored is made to seem especially ridiculous and part of a dying breed. Tristana fades into the background in the final chapters of the novel not because she ceases to be important, but because she ceases to be important as a *person*. She is now a symbol of the need for equality and of the search for social and poetic justice. *She* is now the literary allusion, and her name (echoed in the numerous uses of the word *triste*, especially by Don Lope, in the concluding chapters) evokes the idea of a continued struggle. The final image of a contented Don Lope with his crippled and dominated pastry cook cries for revision in the same way that the social analogue cries for revision. The story has ended for Tristana the person but not for Tristana the symbol, and the open ending is fully appropriate. Dreams are dreams not—as Gullón would have it—because they are distinct from reality, but because they are the mainstay of reality.

Michael Nimetz speaks of the ending as a sign of the "irony of incongruity," in which the incongruous relationship between Tristana and Don Lope continues and is legalized. For Nimetz, the irony lies in the unexpected events rather than in the symbolic implications of these events. The two characters readjust, make compatible the incongruities, and so compromise themselves that they are

> seemingly unaware of their descent into vulgarity. The wonderful old rake and the unique girl cease to be interesting. When the reader perceives this, he confronts the culminating irony of the novel: Tristana and Don Lope are oblivious to their fate.[24]

Nimetz, in his discussion of the irony of *Tristana*, fails to consider the ironic voice of the narrator, who provides the reasons for Tristana's uniqueness and treats Don Lope as more than a "wonderful old rake." The narrator's voice gives meaning to the characters and to the events, so that the novel's actions are more than conditioning agents. If Tristana and Don Lope are oblivious to their fate, it is not because they are vulgar but because they are symbolic. Only symbolically does the final compromise make sense. Tristana is born predestined to fail because the society of her time would not permit "libertad honrada," but—and this is a crucial element of the novel's irony— Galdós has created a woman who could succeed.[25] It takes a stroke of fate to definitively frustrate the goals of a woman who singlehandedly defies society. Her failure is inevitable, but to an extent she is doomed not by the social system but by her creator, who shows that success is within her grasp. Within this perspective, it is thematically but not socially imperative that Tristana fail.

The irony of *Tristana* may be seen as the irony of contradiction. Literature competes with life and with itself. The narrator defines the characters, and although they remain consistent with his definitions, he begins to shift his position, but only to underscore the validity of the initial stance. The impossibility for Tristana, the reason for her struggle and for her defeat, is the intrinsic contradiction between a socially realistic attitude (expressed by Saturna) and true self-respect. Tristana's goal of honorable freedom is a chimera not because it contradicts absolute morality but because it contradicts the social conscience of her time; self-respect and social respectability operate on different and mutually exclusive planes. In *Tristana* not only is reconciliation (Tristana's entry into the world of spiritual seclusion) apparent at best, but the dichotomy between reality (the real Horacio) and illusion (the ideal Horacio) is overshadowed by Tristana's false perception of reality (her inaccurate social vision of Horacio), which negates the dichotomy. Galdós has, then, in his manipulation of novelistic recourses, accentuated the impossibility of synthesis by denying the dialectic, by fusing and confusing reality and illusion, and by silencing Tristana in the final chapters.

If in *Fortunata y Jacinta* Galdós chooses what John Sinnigen calls "redemption rather than revolution" for Fortunata,[26] the ambiguity of Tristana's retreat into a type of mysticism seems to strengthen the novel's subtle revolutionary spirit. The consciously absurd rendering of a union between Tristana and Don Lope, together with the unexplained illness, is—if anything—a parody of redemption, and Tristana's final convictions are not disclosed. The narrator creates a literary imbalance to equal a social imbalance, yet within this structure he becomes a proponent of Tristana's cause. Stephen Gilman says that the theme of all great novels since the *Quijote* is "the creation of significance out of insignificance, or, as Lukacs tells us, a search for values which in apparent failure nevertheless succeeds."[27] This is what makes *Tristana* artistic and what makes it ironic.

It is not the anachronistic gentleman described in Cervantine terms, but a woman fighting social windmills, who most resembles Don Quijote. It is not the victim of a tyrannical grandfather in his clean transition into bourgeois society, but a woman denied the benefits of her intellectual and artistic potential, who achieves the status of martyr. It is not nature, but society's dogmatic and male-oriented codes, which reduces women to subservience. It is not God, but man acting as God, who determines the limits and abuses of morality. And finally, it is not Tristana's redemption, but Galdós' refusal to redeem her, which points toward a new society. The reader is left, then, to intuit the novel's irony, to understand when the narrator is mocking his subject and when he is respecting it, and when an apparent *volte-face* is consistent with a previously established perspective.

The third of Wayne Booth's four steps of reconstruction of stable irony is that "a decision must . . . be made about the author's knowledge or beliefs," an undertaking which Booth admits brings the critic dangerously close to committing the "intentional fallacy."[28] To attribute to Galdós an unrelenting faith in tolerance and in a system of absolute values seems reasonable, and for him to favor Tristana's views over those of an intolerant society and its relative values would follow. To read *Tristana* literally is to accept or rationalize intolerance and an unjust and arbitrarily derived system of values. To read *Tristana* ironically is to decide both that Tristana must lose her struggle and that her defeat is a defeat for poetic justice. The defeat and the novel are ironic because they are stages of a victory and because Galdós is an eloquent spokesman for poetic justice.

ARIZONA STATE UNIVERSITY

Notes

[1]Wayne C. Booth, *A Rhetoric of Irony* (Chicago: The University of Chicago Press, 1974), pp. 10-11. See Booth's *The Rhetoric of Fiction* (Chicago: The University of Chicago Press, 1961), esp. pp. 71-77 and 211-21, for a discussion of the implied author. See also Wolfgang Iser, *The Act of Reading* (Baltimore: The Johns Hopkins Press, 1978).

[2]Booth's classification of ironies in *A Rhetoric of Irony*, esp. pp. 233-77, uses as a point of departure the categories of D. C. Muecke in *The Compass of Irony* (London: Methuen & Co., Ltd., 1969). Muecke speaks of three grades of irony: overt, covert, and private.

[3]David I. Grossvogel, "Buñuel's Obsessed Camera: Tristana Dismembered," *Diacritics*, 2 (Spring 1972), 53. The article compares Galdós' narrative technique with Luis Buñuel's film style in his *Tristana* (1970).

[4]Ibid., p. 57

[5]Ibid., p. 53.

[6]Benito Pérez Galdós, *Tristana* (Madrid: Alianza Editorial, 1969), p. 7. All subsequent quotations from the novel will refer to this edition, and page numbers will be indicated in parentheses.

[7]Note the antithetical allusions to Don Quijote. Don Lope, who has already been called an *hidalgo*, is "el ingenioso don Lope," and Galdós uses the word *desocupado*, the first word of Cervantes' prologue to Part I of the *Quijote*.

[8]The repetition of the forms of *triste* seems to point continually to the sadness of Tristana's situation, seen perhaps most clearly in Don Lope's "Triste es mi victoria" (p. 143). The narrator also depends heavily on forms of *feliz* and *infeliz*. The forms of *luz* function in a similar fashion; for example, Tristana cries, "Quiero luz, más luz, siempre más luz" (p. 119), and the narrator says of her, "ni salieron a relucir aquellas aspiraciones o antojos sublimes de su espíritu" (p. 149). Ruth A. Schmidt mentions the symbolic use of these terms in "*Tristana* and the Importance of Opportunity," *AG*, 9 (1974), 137.

[9]Note that the narrator has earlier referred to Horacio's story as "aquel fondo de tristeza y martirio" (p. 47), linguistically linking Tristana to the idea of martyrdom.

[10]There are allusions to art as well as to literature. Don Lope, for example, "parecía figura escapada del *Cuadro de las Lanzas*" (p. 63).

[11]Tristana says, "Ahora me parece a mí que si de niña me hubiesen enseñado el dibujo, hoy sabría yo pintar y podría ganarme la vida y ser independiente con mi honrado trabajo. Pero mi pobre mamá no pensó más que en darme la educación insustancial de las niñas que aprenden para llevar un buen yerno a casa, a saber: un poco de piano, el indispensable barniz de francés y qué sé yo . . . , tonterías" (p. 76). See Schmidt, p. 137, and Frank Durand, "Two Problems in Galdós' *Tormento*," *MLN*, 79 (1964), 514-15, for considerations of Galdós' representation of the education of women.

[12]See Gonzalo Sobejano, "Galdós y el vocabulario de los amantes," *AG*, 1 (1966), 85-100. According to Sobejano, "Los capítulos XIV a XXI de *Tristana* constituyen un ejercicio de penetración en la realidad del lenguaje amoroso no llevado hasta este límite por ningún novelista español del siglo XIX ni por Galdós mismo en otra de sus novelas" (p. 86).

[13]See Schmidt, p. 138: "The one career woman whom Tristana meets does not fit into the three careers outlined by Saturna. Doña Malvina, an English woman

who becomes Tristana's tutor in the English language, is described as a former *sacerdota protestanta* of the *capilla evangélica* who was forced to take up a second career when 'le cortaron los víveres.' It should be noted in passing that this one example in the book of a woman earning her own living is of a non-Spanish person whose two careers would generally be unavailable to a Spanish woman like Tristana—that of a Protestant minister and a teacher of English."

[14]Emilia Pardo Bazán, *"Tristana,"* in *Nuevo Teatro Crítico*, II, no. 17 (May 1892), 77-90. Rather than pursue the idea of the awakening of consciousness in a woman roused to rebellion via Galdós' trajectory, Pardo Bazán allows her preoccupation with what Galdós might have done to overshadow what he has done.

[15]Leon Livingstone, "The Law of Nature and Women's Liberation in *Tristana*," *AG*, 7 (1972), 93-100.

[16]Ibid., p. 93.

[17]Ibid., p. 94.

[18]Ibid., p. 94.

[19]Ibid., p. 95.

[20]Ibid., p. 97. Livingsone sees the ending in marriage as a restoration of natural harmony: "If their union was initially a violation of nature because of the disparity between them in age and experience, the maturing of Tristana and her physical suffering—which have aged her to the point that although only twenty-five she now looks forty—conveniently annul this imbalance" (p. 98). In this reading, the disparities as well as the irony of the marriage need to be ignored, and the partners must be seen as "comparable and compatible (but different) equals" in a union that "constitutes a positive force in the onward movement of society" (p. 99). Livingstone calls upon the reader to accept the supposition that one must adhere to society's criteria, here intimately connected with natural laws, as being higher than the individuals who create (and precede) them. The reader must accept as well the possibility that a woman may be dignified and subservient in this paradoxical separate-but-equal system. And, finally, the reader must accept—in an analysis based on the condemnation of excesses—that the most exemplary character is Don Lope.

[21]See also Sherman Eoff, *The Novels of Pérez Galdós: The Concept of Life as Dynamic Process* (St. Louis: Washington University Studies, 1954), esp. pp. 50-52. For Eoff, *Tristana* "exemplifies Galdós' interest in the 'inexorable law of adaptation'" (p. 50). In an earlier article, "The Treatment of Individual Personality in *Fortunata y Jacinta*" (*HR*, 17 [1949], 269-89), Eoff emphasizes that "in the author's opinion the basic requisite for morality is first of all to be true to oneself" (p. 283), a concept which he disregards in his discussion of *Tristana*. According to Joaquín Casalduero, *Tristana* demonstrates Galdós' belief in the submission of woman to man by nature, a belief based on his reading of anti-feminist material. Tristana's failure is nothing more than a discovery of this natural law (which strongly resembles social law, despite Casalduero's distinction). See *Vida y obra de Galdós*, 3a ed. ampliada (Madrid: Editorial Gredos, S. A., 1970), pp. 104-08. Carmen Bravo-Villasante, in *Galdós visto por sí mismo* (Madrid: Colección Novelas y Cuentos, 1970), pp. 118-23, sees 1985 and the premiere of *Voluntad* as the beginning of Galdós' sympathy for women. But can Galdós' world view and his system of values really be judged in terms of a pre-1895 set of concepts vs. a post-1895 set? And can an anti-feminist bias be seen in the works prior to 1895? In *"Tristana o la imposibilidad del ser,"* *CHA*, 250-52 (1970-71), 505-22, Emilio Miró attempts to show that woman must be submissive, faithful, and humble because if she were emancipated, independent, and free, the familial structure—and ultimately that of the State and society at large—would

be destroyed. To argue this point is to argue that suppression is valid when it is socially, politically, or economically favorable. Carlos Feal Deibe attributes Tristana's idealistic propensities to Ortega y Gasset's belief that the impossibility of fulfilling a desire leads to dependence on the ideal—that the glorious ideal supplants the adverse real. Though the direction is somewhat different, the conclusion— that the individual must always submit to higher forces—resembles those of Casalduero, Livingstone, and Miró. See "*Tristana* de Galdós: capítulo en la historia de la liberación femenina," *Sin Nombre*, 7, no. 3 (1976), 116-29. In "Resistance and Rebellion in *Tristana*" (*MLN*, 91 [1976], 277-91), John Sinnigen compares *Tristana* to other novels in which Galdós presents an "outsider-society duality" and concludes that Tristana's failure stems from an inadequate vision of the society against whose conventions she is rebelling. And yet one wonders what success Tristana could have achieved if she had had a more accurate vision of society and of her role as dissenter. Sinnigen considers Don Lope, Horacio, and Tristana to be social rebels. Perhaps Don Lope, in his desire for a return to a former hierarchy, should be seen instead as the antithesis of a rebel, a retrogressive force in society. His marriage to Tristana has nothing to do with social consciousness; he has merely found one more sacred institution to mock. Horacio, on the other hand, never justifies Tristana's faith in him. Intrigued by Tristana's ideology and her physical presence, he condescends to her principles while consistently betraying his conventionality. His reaction to a repressive adolescence differs from that of Tristana because his possibilities have not been destroyed as have hers. If Don Lope is a symbol of the past, Horacio is a symbol of the *status quo*. Tristana, looking toward the future, has no allies. Kay Engler, in "The Ghostly Lover: The Portrayal of the Animus in *Tristana*" (*AG*, 13 [1977], 95-109), uses Jungian psychology to explain Tristana's idealization of Horacio and its effect on her actions.

22Germán Gullón, "*Tristana*: Literaturización y estructura novelesca," *HR*, 45 (1977), 27.

23See, for example: "[Tristana] parecía resignada a ser petaca, y siempre petaca" (p. 17); "el buen caballero soportaba con resignación los gastos de aquella familia sin ventura" (p. 20); "[Horacio] resignábase a sufrir hasta lo indecible antes que poner a su tirano en el disparadero" (p. 48); "Nos resignamos porque no hay más remedio" (Don Lope, p. 72); "*Paquita de Rímini* espera confiada y se resigna con su *soled*" (p. 99); "¿Qué importa el dolor físico? Nada. Lo soportaré con resignación, siempre que tú . . . no me duelas" (Tristana to Horacio, p. 133).

24Michael Nimetz, *Humor in Galdós* (New Haven: Yale University Press, 1968), p. 91. Maryellen Bieder believes that "a parody of conventional matrimony is fundamental and forms the basis for the novel's humor, satiric in *Memorias de un solterón*, ironic in *Tristana*." See "Capitulation: Marriage, not Freedom, A Study of Emilia Pardo Bazán's *Memorias de un solterón* and Galdós' *Tristana*," *Symposium*, 30 (1976), 105; Bieder's model for irony is Nimetz.

25See Marina Mayoral, "Tristana: ¿una feminista galdosiana?," *Insula*, nos. 320-21 (July-August 1973), 28: "si Tristana no se pone enferma, si no llega a ser porque le cortan una pierna, Tristana se hubiera salido con la suya." Depending in part on an unpublished dissertation by Elizabeth T. Stout ("Women in the Novels of Benito Pérez Galdós," University of New Mexico, 1953, esp. pp. 7-8), Ruth Schmidt draws the same conclusion (p. 137).

26John H. Sinnigen, "Individual, Class, and Society in *Fortunata y Jacinta*," in *Galdós Studies II*, ed. Robert J. Weber (London: Tamesis Books Limited, 1974), 66.

[27]Stephen Gilman, "The Consciousness of Fortunata," *AG*, 5 (1970), 59.

[28]Booth, *A Rhetoric of Irony*, p. 11. For a study of the irony of repetition in Galdós' works, see Monroe Z. Hafter, "Ironic Reprise in Galdós' Novels," *PMLA*, 76 (1961), 233-39.

"LA LOCA, LA TONTA, LA LITERATA": WOMAN'S DESTINY IN CLARIN'S *LA REGENTA*

Sara E. Schyfter

The traditional reading of Clarín's *La Regenta* views Ana de Ozores as a conventional victim of a corrupt society that allows and even encourages her fall.[1] But this reading largely ignores how Ana's condition as woman determines her fate. For Ana's story is that of a woman's struggle with sexuality and creativity in a world where woman is offered only three possible ways of life: Virgin, Wife or Whore. Her life thus conforms to the classic female pattern of powerlessness, self-rejection, and failed attempts to escape her plight.

Indeed, Ana embodies the tragedy of the alienated female: psychologically mutilated by those who socialize her, she lives amid confusion and is an easy victim of those eager to use her. Phyllis Chesler's portrait in *Women and Madness*[2] of the condition of gifted women in patriarchal society almost perfectly describes Ana:

> For years they denied themselves—or were denied—the duties and privileges of talent and conscience. Like many women, they buried their own destinies in motherhood, and in approved female pleasure. However, their repressed energies eventually struggled free, demanding long overdue and therefore heavier prices: marital and material "disloyalty," social ostracism, imprisonment, and death (p. 5).

Though Ana does not commit physical suicide in the novel, her depressions, nervous crises, desperate acts of self-sacrifice, and her unique form of spiritual and physical prostitution at the hands of Fermín, the priest, and Alvaro, the local, aged Don Juan, must be viewed as suicidal acts directed against her own womanhood.

Ana's life as archetypal tragic female begins its unhappy course when she is four years old: her mother, the lower-class Italian wife of a free-thinking Spanish aristocrat, dies, depriving the child of much-needed maternal affection and female kinship. Throughout her life, Ana will search unsuccessfully for an acceptable mother substitute who can supply the physical and emotional support lost to her so early. This unmet need for maternal nurturing affects Ana's character with a lasting wound and an aching sense of childhood abandonment and anguish. Even consoling memories or fantasies of her mother are denied Ana by the repeated public insinuations that the former was originally not a respectable lower-class "modista" but was actually a "bailarina italiana," a scandalous figure of female sensuality and exhibitionism. And when Ana seeks satisfaction in active and creative pursuits outside of the accepted female roles, her actions are judged a consequence of her perverse maternal heritage.

In the place of her mother's love, Ana must submit to the instruction of the harsh, hypocritical, English-trained Doña Camila, who knows nothing of warmth and affection. Doña Camila further reinforces Ana's sense of isolation, helplessness, and hopelessness by punishing her with "encierros y ayunos." This punishment symbolizes, foreshadows, and shapes Ana's role as a woman in society, for it is a punishment by imprisonment in the house. Boys are traditionally spanked, an active, short-term discipline that allows the boy-child to return to life quickly. Imprisonment, however, is a vague, passive form of castigation to which primarily young girls are subjected.[3] And because it cuts the child off from all outside experience for an indefinite period, it is the more damaging to the ego. Ana's imprisonments lock her both in her room and out of the world, while the "ayunos" that accompany the "encierros" are a vivid illustration of the deprivations she suffers.

Ana responds to her imprisonments by imagining herself miraculously saved and free, able to roam like the butterflies; though a captive, her spirit soars through a vast expanse: "iba volando por el azul que veía allá arriba" (p. 68). She also creates a fantasy of her own strength and pride, rejecting all thoughts of forgiveness and acceptance: "Nuna pedía perdón; no lo necesitaba. Salía del encierro pensativa, altanera, callada; seguía soñando; la dieta le daba nueva fuerza para ello" (p. 68). Ana's imagination thus provides a means of escape and a semblance of power, the only power allowed a female whose sphere of action is continuously limited: the power of fantasy.

At the age of six, Ana begins what she calls the poem of her life:

> ... Ana Ozores hubiera podido contar aquel poema desde el principio al fin, y eso que en cada edad le había añadido una parte. En la primera había una paloma encantada con un alfiler negro clavado en la cabeza: era la reina mora; su madre, la madre de Ana que no parecía. Todas las palomas con manchas negras en la cabeza podían ser una madre, según la poética de Anita (p. 68).[4]

Motherhood, "las palomas con manchas negras," is hereby perceived by the resentful girl as a black stain on the mind and the spirit, an inner flaw in the longed-for Good Mother who never comes to save the female child.[5]

As a very young girl, Ana discovers a new avenue of escape and transcendence—reading. In her creative mind, the lessons of geography become poetic accounts of nature, while the Bible provides the basis for an epic vision of reality; what is more, Ana's youthful imagination is intrepid—or naive—enabling her, for instance, to welcome male strength and sexuality without fear and to praise the "pierna desnuda, musculosa y velluda" of idealized warriors as consonant with a "rostro curtido, triste y bondadoso" (p. 69).

The vitality of Ana's imagination also appears in her childhood games with Germán, a frequent companion, with whom she fantasizes risky trips to convert the infidel in remote countries "que él ni el nombre conocía" (p. 69). These games suggest Ana's affinity with Santa Teresa, who also dreamed as a child of Christianizing the infidel, which later would give rise to a keen identification, although Ana could not successfully emulate the saint. Like Santa Teresa, Ana "quería ir a tierra de moros de verdad," but while she and Germán steep themselves in these fantasies of spiritual heroism, Ana's real purpose is to escape totally from Loreto and Doña Camila. And unfortunately the only time Ana is able to convince the more timid Germán to act out one of her adventures, the game ends in disaster. Deciding on an "escapatoria nocturna para ver juntos la luna desde la barca y contarse cuentos" (p. 69), the two plan a little ride on the boat. But unable to dislodge the boat from the shore they fall asleep, to be awakened in shame by moralistic adults.

Doña Camila's interpretation of this misadventure as a sexual scandal ("dijo un refrán desvergonzado en que se insultaba a su madre y a ella" [p. 54]) and its humiliating consequences bring to a close the slight freedom and companionship experienced by Ana as a child. From this time—her tenth year—onwards, she is no longer allowed out alone, a punishment ludicrous in its severity, especially given the sexual promiscuity of Doña Camila with her lover.

The child has been cast into the role of Whore. The entire village now views her as sexually promiscuous and she arouses the curiosity of all, particularly that of the men who hungrily await her physical development. One of them says that she already looks like "una mujercita," and "se la devoraban con los ojos; se deseaba un milagroso crecimiento instantánea de aquellos encantos que no estaban en la niña, sino en la imaginación de los socios del casino" (p. 70). Indeed, Doña Camila's lover beleaguers the child with requests for kisses whenever he finds her alone. In this manner Ana discovers her potential sexuality and learns to associate it with her emotions of anger, fear, and self-blame. Her first experiences of female sexuality are thus defined by the leering desires of those who long to consume her in lust.

As a consequence of this initiation into adult sexual mores, Ana turns toward the familiar female device of dissociating her bodily experiences from the edifying idealizations born of reading and thinking. The conflict between sexual attractiveness and pleasure on one side and guilt and anxiety on the other forces her to withdraw and to avoid close relationships:

> . . . como de abandonarse a sus instintos, a sus ensueños y quimeras se había originado la nebulosa aventura de la barca de Trébol, que la avergonzaba todavía, miraba con desconfianza y hasta repugnancia moral cuanto hablaba de relaciones entre hombres y mujeres, si de ellas nacía algún placer, por ideal que fuese (p. 73).

Not surprisingly, when her father returns from exile to live with her in Madrid, he is disappointed to find a submissive and quiet adolescent excessively reserved for her young years. Indeed, Ana has begrudgingly accepted the dictates of her society on female sexuality and freedom. After the incident in the boat "se declaró vencida, siguió la conducta moral que se le impuso, sin discutirla, ciegamente, sin fe en ella, pero sin hacer traición nunca" (p. 71).

In real life, Ana feels extreme repugnance towards sex: she has been separated from men "como se aparta del fuego una materia inflamable" (p. 73). Her own father treats her "como si no tuviera sexo,"[6] and his supposed enlightened attitude towards women, which "pedía a grito pelado la emancipación de la mujer" (p. 74), is false and hypocritical: "en el fondo de su conciencia tenía a la hembra por un ser inferior, como un buen animal doméstico" (p. 74). Ana is, therefore, subjected to a continual series of contradictions: on the one hand her father proclaims the equality of women while on the other he sees his daughter as chattel.

He nevertheless encourages Ana to read in his extensive library.

There she discovers the religious writings of St. Augustine and Chateaubriand; she learns from the mystic poets how to sublimate sexuality into religious ecstasy, with the result that she develops an intense affection for the Virgin. Her love for the Virgin is awakened especially by the poetry of Fray Luis de León and the Song of Songs. Growing into a "locura de amor religioso" (p. 78), she is even inspired to write prayers and verses to the Virgin, to whom she speaks in "Versos a lo San Juan . . . que . . . le salían a borbotones" (p. 78).

Ana's passionate identification with the Virgin Mary betrays at least two significant attributes of the young girl. For one, it represents Ana's longing for a nurturing and loving mother, a female role model and an exemplar of emotional expressiveness. But it also marks Ana's acceptance of the Mariolatry of Spanish Catholicism, which places the worship of the Virgin at the heart of Christianity. The Ave-Eve dichotomy that took hold in the High Middle Ages made of the Virgin the ideal image of the female. Supportive, loving, motherly, chaste, she serves as a mediator between the sinner and the male Trinity above. At the same time, however, from a different perspective the Virgin represents an image of woman as separate from male dominance. As Mary Daly suggests in *Beyond God the Father:* "The woman who is defined as virgin is not defined exclusively by her relationships with men . . . 'Virgin Mother' can be heard to say something about female autonomy within the context of sexual and parental relationships."[7] The Mary symbol has given Catholic women (as opposed to Protestant women who have denied Mary's divinity) the possibility of a spiritual identity independent of patriarchal rule. The sanctification of the Virgin thus mitigates the power of the myth of feminine evil and frees woman of the need to be saved by the male. The Virgin at the same time rescues the feminine from the profane and gives it a place in the realm of the sacred.

Although Clarín vividly conveys Ana's lively imagination and spirituality, he repeatedly regards them as the fruit of a nervous, excited disposition—a common description of talented and dissatisfied women who, like Ana, are made to feel that their creative urge, their need for self-assertion, and their desire to transcend sexual identity issue from "nerves" or sexual frustration. Such women are punished by society[8] and by the authors[9] who describe them as being on the verge of insanity whenver they confront their multiple conflicts. Indeed, Clarín continually tells of La Regenta's fear of madness, of her sense that her entire being will be annihilated in inner chaos:

> . . . el extremo de la tortura era el desprecio de la lógica, la duda de las leyes del pensamiento y de la palabra, y por último el desvanecimiento de la conciencia de su unidad; creía la Regenta que sus facultades morales se separaban, que dentro de ella ya no había nadie que fuese ella . . . la horrorizaba la idea de su locura y el miedo del dolor desconocido, extraña, del cerebro descompuesto (p. 571).

Ana's potential for madness produces in her creator the classic ambivalence toward the gifted heroine.[10] At times Clarín presents her poetic, religious longings in sympathetic, even admiring terms. But often he condescends to her as a feeble female. When, for example, after a mental crisis she turns to creativity to assuage her estrangement, he remarks ironically: "las primeras fuerzas que tuvo las gastó el cerebro imaginando poemas, novelas, dramas y poesías sueltas" (p. 88). And he says she did this not only for self-entertainment but because "este componer constante . . . halagaba su vanidad" (p. 88). Frequently Clarín minimizes Ana's alienation and restlessness and labels her unhappiness egoism and self-pity. When her father dies and she is left feeling totally alone, she experiences not true loss but what Clarín calls "un egoísmo horrible, lleno de remordimientos" (p. 82).[11] Likewise, when Ana's religious fervor wanes as she discovers that the terror of abandonment is not cured by prayers to the Virgin, the narrator belittles the disappointment as a cheap lapse of faith.

It is symbolic that Ana's menarche occurs at the time of her father's death, creating in the young girl a terrifying awareness of her isolated femininity and precipitating a nervous breakdown. The physical changes seem to confirm her lowly position as a woman, while her body, just as after the episode in the boat, once more becomes a source of public embarrassment and shame, for everyone knows that her illness is due to menstruation.[12] In *The Second Sex*, Simone de Beauvoir speaks of the emotional crisis the adolescent girl experiences at this time:

> The mistrust that as a small child she felt in regard to her "insides" helps to give the menstrual crisis the dubious character that renders it odious to her. It is because of the psychic state induced by her menstrual slavery that it constitutes a heavy handicap. . . . The horror this inspires has repercussions throughout her organic structure and intensifies its disturbed and painful condition. . . . The disorders of puberty are made worse by the upsetting effect their discovery has upon the young girl. Because her body seems

suspect to her, and because she views it with alarm, it seems to her to be sick . . . [13]

The father's death, the menstrual crisis, her poverty and loneliness combine to convince Ana that she cannot confront life alone. In desperation, she resigns herself to living with her maiden aunts in Vetusta, where her female role as sexual object, outsider, and socioeconomic inferior will be hereafter confirmed.

In Vetusta, Ana's physical development astonishes everyone as she recuperates, gains weight, and becomes the most beautiful woman in the city. She is the communal sexual object exhibited to outside visitors along with the cathedral and the elegant Paseo de Verano. Accepted into her aunts' upper-class society, she honors that society as a "caballo de sangre y de piel de seda honra la caballeriza y hasta la casa de un potentado" (p. 91).

While her beauty grants Ana social acceptance and guarantees public esteem, she nevertheless continues to manifest her psychological discontent in poetry penned secretly. These poetic strivings, embraced as a form of escape, serve to further undermine Ana's allegiance to the social order. And eventually even this escape is closed. When one of her aunts finds Ana's hidden notebook full of poems, "manifestó igual asombro que si hubiera visto un revólver, una baraja o una botella de aguardiente. Aquello era una cosa hombruna" (p. 95). Although the poems are praised by Ripamilón, a priest ("Son imitaciones de Lamartine en estilo seudoclásico; no me gustan, aunque demuestran gran habilidad an Anita. Además las mujeres deben ocuparse en más dulces tareas, las musas no escriben, inspiran" [p. 96]), the Marquesa de Vegallana condemns them for being "mojigatos." Recalling her own unsatisfied desire to write a novel, and convinced that she could have been a great writer if able to live "en otra atmósfera" (p. 96), the Marquesa determines, out of resentment, to stifle Ana's belief in her own talent. Ana thus becomes a victim of both men and women with the result that "ella misma se creyó en ridículo y engañada por la vanidad" (p. 96).

Thereafter, the young woman swears never to write again, never to aspire to be that abnormal creature—a woman writer—and "tuvo que renunciar en absoluto a la pluma; se juró a sí misma no ser 'la literata', aquel ente híbrido y abominable de que se hablaba en Vetusta como de los monstruos asquerosos y horribles" (p. 96). This new humiliation proves to be as consequential as the one she suffered after the boat incident, when she learned to despise her own sexuality. Discovering that a woman who writes not only gains self-importance and confidence of expression but also exposes her heart and threatens the hegemony of patriarchal authority, she knows she must now renounce her cherished powers of imagination. She inaugurates this renunciation by belittling her abilities and dismissing her literary yearnings as "algún crimen suyo que se hubiera descubierto" (p. 96). The message is clear: female creativity outside of the female capacity to create life in the womb is inappropriate and borders on scandal.

Restricted spiritually, socially, and economically—"ella no podía ganarse la vida trabajando; antes la hubieran asesinado los Ozores" (p. 95)—Ana resorts to exploiting her beauty to gain some control over her destiny. Clarín, however, unmasks the myth that beauty in women is power. For a time Ana believes that her body will bring her both money and position and she enjoys the flattery of men's attentions. But beautiful as she is, the moneyed aristocrats of Vetusta will not marry her. Her aunts recognize this but still hold hopes of profiting from her marriage. They see their niece as meat to be marketed: "Para Doña Agueda la belleza de Ana era uno de los mejores embutidos; estaba orgullosa de aquella cara como pudiera estarlo de una morcilla" (p. 94). Ana is thus fated to be an object, to exist *outside* instead of in herself. She becomes resigned to a mediocre married life amid the general stupidity of the people of Betusta. With an obdurate pessimism, the young woman concludes that in spite of her spiritual and moral strivings, "estaba debajo, era la vencida" (p. 95).

Though Ana once thinks of escaping her fate by entering a convent, she is dissuaded from this too. The same men who yawn during the religious rituals of the Church tell her that she has no true vocation. Her confessor urges her to marry and Ana finally acquiesces. Yet even her marriage to the aged Don Víctor bears signs of defiance, since it is disapproved by both the aristocracy and her venal aunts, who had chosen for her a rich *indiano* bent on possessing her along with the best house and the best carriages in Vetusta. But typical of female defiance in oppressive circumstances, this marriage is more an act of helpless resignation and self-sacrifice than an affirmation of self: "Todo había concluido . . . sin haber empezado" (p. 105) are Ana's words as she leaves Vetusta with Don Víctor.

Ana's last hope for fulfillment after her marriage is through motherhood. She has allowed herself to be confined and immobilized in a marriage that infantilizes and sexually frustrates her, and since her marriage is sterile, she is unable to live out the specific function of her sex. The father-child relationship that develops between Don Víctor and Ana as a result is clearly stated and understood by the heroine herself:

> Don Víctor no era pesado, eso era verdad, se había cansado pronto de hacer el galán, y paulatinamente había pasado al papel de barba, que le sentaba mejor. ¡Oh, y lo que es como un padre se había hecho querer, eso sí; no podía ella acostarse sin un beso de su marido en la frente (p. 190).

Because Ana has been denied all forms of creativity except the biological by her society, the closing of this last opportunity leaves her feeling completely empty and emotionally destitute: "Un hijo, un hijo hubiera puesto fin a tanta angustia, en todas aquellas luchas de su espíritu ocioso, que buscaba *fuera del centro natural de la vida*, fuera del hogar, pábulo para el afán de amor, objeto para la sed de sacrificios . . . " (p. 50, my italics). The novelist's view of the female's need for maternity as both a biological and a psychological imperative echoes the traditional patriarchal judgment on female destiny, given theoretical expression by Erik Erikson in *Identity, Youth, and Crisis*. Erikson believes that women have a positive somatic identity based on their possession of "an inner productive space," the womb.[14] Such an orientation creates in the infertile woman of traditional society a sense of total hollowness:

> . . . the inner productive space exposes women to a sense of specific loneliness, to a fear of being left empty or deprived of treasures, of remaining unfulfilled and of drying up. . . . clinical observation suggests that in female experience an "inner space" is at the center of despair even as it is the very center of potential fulfillment. Emptiness is the female form of perdition, known at times to men of the inner life . . . but standard experience for all women.[15]

It is this supposed emptiness and lack of biological fulfillment, therefore, that makes Ana's "perdition" at the hands of Fermín and Alvaro inevitable. Within the context of the novel, Clarín's view of female destiny is as limited as Erikson's, even if his artist's eye allows him to repeatedly unmask the myth at the foundation of patriarchal order.

Yet the dynamics of Ana's fall and her double prostitution as Virgin and Whore are best explained from the perspective of game theory. Johan Huizinga in *Homo Ludens* suggests that play is one of the main bases of civilization. The game represents the desire to create order out of chaos, an intellectual formulation in which time, space, tension, and resolution are used as a means of testing "the player's prowess: his courage, tenacity, resources and, last but not least, his spiritual powers." Furthermore, the one who refuses to play "reveals the relativity and fragility of the play world ... he must be cast out for he threatens the existence of the play-community."[16] It is clear that Clarín's heroine becomes a reluctant player in a game where she is the hunted and Fermín and Alvaro are the hunters. The two men engage in a contest of pursuit predicated on Ana's unhappiness, on her rejection of life in Vetusta, and on the limited possibilities that her marriage, her social circle, and her childless state allow her. Fermín offers her

> la salvación, la promesa de una vida virtuosa sin aburrimiento, llena de ocupaciones nobles, poéticas, que exigían esfuerzos, sacrificios, pero que por lo mismo daban dignidad y grandeza a la existencia muerta, animal, insoportable que Vetusta le ofrecía hasta el dia (p. 266).

Alvaro, on the other hand, seduces her with the dream of romantic love and the forbidden pleasures of the flesh.

La Regenta's virtue, however, and her struggle against both Fermín and Alvaro place her in the role of the "spoil sport," the one who refuses to play the game or to play according to accepted rules. In Vetusta the "game" is the lust for power and/or sexual pleasure, while the "rules" are that all is permitted as long as appearances are preserved. The heroine knows the game, for her aunts had explained it clearly: "lo perdonaban todo, menos las apariencias" (p. 86). Ana nevertheless refuses to play at first, continually spurning the social and moral deceptions practiced by others. And even when she enters the game she plays improperly, mistaking for reality what are only the illusions of serious play.

As the "spoil-sport," Ana becomes the prize of a hunting game played not only by Alvaro and Fermín but by their respective allies—the Casino and Visitación on one side, the Church and Doña Petronila on the other. The Casino requires Ana's fall in order to sustain the exploitation of women as sexual objects, while Visitación, who prepares the terrain for Alvaro's advances, is open in her desire to see "aquél armiño en el lodo ... procurar que Ana fuese al fin y al cabo como todas" (p. 157). At the same time, the Church desires Ana's defeat because she wishes to experience religion intensively and subjectively. Doña Petronila, "el Gran Constantino" who is totally subservient to Fermín and provides her house for his secret encounter with Ana, wants to see another woman under her master's power, as do all the women in her circle: "Las beatas que servían de cuestores de palacio en el del Gran Constantino, las del *cónclave* . . . esperaban con ansiedad mística y con una curiosidad maligna a la nueva compañera" (p. 377).

These *beatas* who have yielded their own lives to Vetusta's patriarchal society and to its staunchest supporter, the Church, cannot allow another woman to escape their fate. Thus they form a compact to ensure Ana's ruin. Ana's entrapment and defeat are thereby assured by both men and women in a game of power that aligns all the forces of corruption against a single innocent.

Ana's first entrapment comes at the hands of Fermín. Hoping to protect herself from Alvaro's advances, and wishing to show her public support for Fermín, she walks in the Holy Week procession barefoot and "vestida de Nazareno" (p. 554). But during the procession, La Regenta suddenly realizes that: "Ella era una loca que había caído en una especie de prostitución singular . . . Allí iba la tonta, la literata, la Jorge Sandio, la mística, la fatua, la loca, la loca sin vergüenza" (p. 558).

This illumination frees Ana from Fermín, but it allows the second hunt and entrapment to begin at the hands of Alvaro. Escape through the spirit having once more been denied her, she now assumes a purely sexual identity, seeking in eroticism the liberation and fulfillment denied her elsewhere. But this too proves to be a cruel "desengaño."

An adulteress, Ana de Ozores becomes more isolated and powerless than ever. For she has committed the elemental crime against patriarchal society: violating the male-determined sacrament of marriage that underpins the established social order. Now she is deemed a threat to the entire community, representing instinctual forces that traditional male-dominated society must repress, especially in its women. Hence she is blamed for unleashing the unconscious, natural evil associated with her sexuality. Men have become assassins under her spell—not only Alvaro, who has killed her husband, but even Fermín, who takes "un paso asesino" (p. 676) toward her in the church. In addition, her body awakens in Celedonio, "el acólito afeminado," a new perverted lust: "Celedonio sintió un deseo miserable, una perversión de la perversión de su lascivia" (p. 676).

Under Ana's influence, the rule of order has given way to primal chaos, and she must therefore undergo the social ostracism, torture, and symbolic death of the evildoer, the adulteress, the embodiment of sin: "Y se le castigó rompiendo con ella toda clase de relaciones . . . Es necesario aislarla. . . . Nada, nada de trato con la *hija de la bailarina italiana*" (p. 669). Passively Ana accepts society's judgment and, unlike the young girl who never asked forgiveness, she seeks a final redemption through the male. In an act of self-abasement, a search for atonement from the very power that corrupted her, Ana returns to Fermín. But Fermín now sees in her the proof of his defeat in the game with Alvaro. La Regenta had been the "prize" that went first to the victor; the loser's consolation is now to reject this prize obtained second hand. Ana is no longer of any value: controlling her carries no prestige. The game is over, the males are victorious, the prize is tossed aside, order has returned to Vetusta.

STATE UNIVERSITY OF NEW YORK AT ALBANY

Notes

[1]Noteworthy in the extensive bibliography on *La Regenta* are the following: Frank Durand, "Structural Unity in Leopoldo Alas' *La Regenta*," *Hispanic Review*, XXXI (1963), 324-35, and also his "Characterization in *La Regenta*: Point of View and Theme," *Bulletin of Hispanic Studies*, XLI (1964), 86-100; Sherman H. Eoff, *The Modern Spanish Novel* (New York: NYU Press, 1961), pp. 71-84; Michael Nimetz, "*Eros* and *Ecclesia* in Clarín's Vetusta," *Modern Language Notes*, LXXXVI (1971), 242-44; Frances Wyers Weber, "The Dynamics of Motif in Leopoldo Alas' *La Regenta*," *Romanic Review*, LVII (1966), 188-99, and "Ideology and Religious Parody in the Novels of Leopoldo Alas," *Bulletin of Hispanic Studies*, XLII (1966), 197-208.

[2](Garden City, NY: Doubleday, 1972).

[3]For a discussion on differences of child training in relation to sex see Robert R. Sears, Eleanor E. Maccoby and Harry Levin, *Patterns of Child Rearing* (Evanston: Row, Peterson, 1957), pp. 396-407.

[4]All quotations for *La Regenta* are from the Alianza Editorial edition (Madrid: 1969) and are given as page citations in the text. A new edition with an excellent introduction by Gonzalo Sobejano has recently appeared (Madrid: Noguer, 1977).

[5]See Phyllis Chesler, op. cit., pp. 17-25, for a discussion of women as motherless children in modern Judeo-Christian societies.

[6]See Michael Nimetz, op. cit., for an extended analysis of the general "neutralization of sex" in *La Regenta*.

[7](Boston: Beacon Press, 1973), pp. 24-25.

[8]On the double standard of what constitutes mental health see the findings of Inge K. Broverman et al., quoted by Phyllis Chesler, op. cit., pp. 67-69.

[9]For parallels between Ana Ozores and Flaubert's Emma Bovary see Sherman H. Eoff, op. cit., chapter entitled "In Quest of a God of Love: Gustave Flaubert - Leopoldo Alas," pp. 51-84, and Juan V. Agudiez, "Emma Bovary - Ana Ozores o El símbolo del amor," *Romanic Review*, LIV (1963), pp. 20-29. On Ana Ozores

and Maggie Tulliver in George Eliot's *The Mill on the Floss*, see B. W. Ife, "Idealism and Materialism in Clarín's *La Regenta*: Two Comparative Studies," *Revue de Litérature Comparée*, XLIV (1970), pp. 273-95, who states: "A general impression of the personalities of both Maggie and Ana is that they are intensely unstable to a degree much greater than mere indecision . . ." (p. 276).

[10]The novelist's ambivalence in the presentation of Ana has led, not surprisingly, to contradictory interpretations of Clarín's view of his heroine. Clifford R. Thompson, in "Egoism and Alienation in the Works of Leopoldo Alas," *Romanische Forschungen*, LXXXI (1969), pp. 192-203, states that "it is her own egoism which is primarily responsible for Ana's downfall" (p. 200), while Ricardo Gullón, in "Aspectos de Clarín," *Archivum*, II (1952), writes that Ana falls "por la falta de densidad moral" (p. 166). An alternate, more sympathetic view of Ana is found in Frances Wyers Weber's "Ideology and Religious Parody." She finds that Clarín "contrasts the young woman's religious and emotional sensitivity to the egotism, cynicism, and sexual libertinism of the Vetustans" (p. 198). Also, Frank Durand, in "Characterization in *La Regenta*," observes that unlike other of the novel's characters, Ana is never ridiculed by Clarín and that the novelist focuses not on her "weaknesses and failings, which could have been so treated as to seem foolish, but on the ironic tragedy of her situation" (p. 99).

[11]A similar attitude on the part of the novelist is apparent when Ana contrasts her sexless life to that of her maid and the workers who fill the streets after a day's work: "Ana participó un momento de aquella voluptuosidad andrajosa. Pensó en sí misma, en su vida consagrada al sacrificio, a una prohibición absoluta del placer, y se tuvo esa lástima profunda del egoísmo excitado ante las propias desdichas" (p. 173).

[12]"Era una fiebre nerviosa; una crisis terrible, había dicho el médico; la enfermedad había coincidido con ciertas transformaciones propias de la edad; propias sí, pero delante de señoritas no debían explicarse con la claridad y los pormenores que empleaba el doctor" (p. 81).

[13](New York: Modern Library, 1968), p. 332.

[14]For an analysis of Erikson's ideas on female identity, see Patricia Martin Doyle, "Women and Religion: Psychological and Cultural Implications," in *Religion and Sexism*, ed. Rosemary Radford Ruether (New York: Simon & Schuster, 1974), pp. 15-39. For an attack on Erikson, see Kate Millet, *Sexual Politics* (New York: Doubleday, 1970), pp. 210-20. Also see Adrienne Rich, *Of Woman Born* (New York: Norton, 1976), pp. 84-109, for a redefinition of female creativity and its concomitant power.

[15]Erikson, *Identity, Youth, and Crisis* (New York: Norton, 1968), p. 278. See also Erikson's article, "Inner and Outer Space: Reflections on Womanhood," *Daedalus*, XCIII (1964), pp. 582-606.

[16]Johan Huizinga, *Homo Ludens* (Boston: Beacaon Press, 1955), p. 11.

WOMEN AS MORAL AND POLITICAL ALTERNATIVES IN CONRAD'S EARLY NOVELS

Ruth Nadelhaft

As recently as 1973, critics of Joseph Conrad were still writing such misguided lines as "Conrad could no more have conceived of a woman hero than could Dickens." Carolyn G. Heilbrun, author of this rather typical misstatement, went on to write that Conrad was a creator "of artistic worlds in which women have no part, or no continually essential part."[1] In fact, Heilbrun is just one in a long parade of critics who have not understood that women are, and always were, central to Conrad's vision as a political and moral novelist.[2] For Conrad's novels and tales are about political morality, particularly the morality of imperialism and colonialism, a theme at least partially recognized by Jonah Raskin, who wrote of Conrad, in a study of imperialism in the works of late nineteenth-century authors, that he "fought against his society. He is most representative of his time because he stands in the sharpest opposition to it."[3]

In his earliest novels, *Almayer's Folly* (1895) and *An Outcast of the Islands* (1896),[4] Conrad embodies his already-formed ambivalent and searching criticism of the colonialism that makes up much of the books' real subject matter. Women, frequently half-breeds, represent the clearest means of challenging and revealing Western male insularity and domination. These first two novels, like the women who embody many of their insights, are frequently overlooked by critics, who prefer to concentrate on the more central revelations of the acknowledged great middle novels of Conrad's career. Conrad's questioning and pessimistic analysis of the colonial relationship finds expression through the complex dependency of character revealed in character doubling, a technique usually understood to function between men in the middle and late novels. In fact, in the early novels European society is projected through white men and half-caste women on whom such men are halfway dependent. The continuum ranges from the bluff (and destructive) confidence of Tom Lingard, through the hesitating and torn Almayer or Willems, to the half-caste Nina (also represented by Mrs. Willems and Mrs. Almayer with their strikingly similar stories), and ends in Aissa, a brilliantly militant woman and an outspoken hater of whites. Women are shown to be especially vulnerable to white colonialism; unable to force white men to take them seriously (the goal of women everywhere), they resort to cunning and subversion to destroy the identity of the very men who enslave them. In these two books, the complex relationship between men and women, designed to confirm the identity of men, results instead in limiting the effect of white power, in revealing the liberating potential of native vitality, and in projecting the doom of male European colonialism.

From the outset of both these early novels, whose plots concern the early rise and subsequent disintegration of white European men, it is the protagonist's good opinion of himself that hangs in the balance; for Conrad a man's vision of himself is ordinarily the ironic stillpoint upon which the action turns. In these books, as in others to follow, that vision is largely determined by the piercing evaluation of women. These women, protagonists in their own right, have been largely ignored by their own society and by literary critics, most of whom have been male. The observant women provide a sort of gallery—whistling, catcalling, weeping—to comment on the action and to insist that action goes on offstage as well. Nina in *Almayer's Folly* and Aissa in *An Outcast of the Islands* are tautly imagined and described, full-fledged characterizations complete with all the ambiguity of Conrad's traditionally ambiguous men. Further, they possess character doubles as well, traditionally a measure of the complexity of the male central character. Character doubles, usually physically similar to the psychologically divided central characters, serve to personify in their own lives the possible alternatives imperfectly understood by the protagonists. In these early novels, it is significant that the women are projected through their doubles (for Nina, the slave-girl Taminah, as an example); in such classic works as *Lord Jim* and "The Secret Sharer," character doubles project and embody crucial moral dilemmas and complex personalities for central male characters. A remarkable use of character doubling in these two novels is the projection of alternatives for the men through the women they fear and misuse. So doubling is central in at least two respects: the complexity of the women is presented through the use of paired female characters, and the central women (Nina in *Almayer's Folly*, Aissa in *An Outcast of the Islands*) embody the personal, moral, and political possibilities of the male protagonist.

Kaspar Almayer's good opinion of himself, so central to the opening chapters of *Almayer's Folly*, rests in fact on the approbation first of his wife (whom he misunderstands) and then of his daughter, Nina (of whom his apprehension is totally incorrect). White culture exists in the persons of Almayer, Lingard, and the white officers (themselves differing in temperament and response to Nina); the natives in both *Almayer's Folly* and *An Outcast of the Islands* are a complex presentation as well. Nina chooses between the culture of her father and that of the natives, who range from her lover, Dain, to the cunning and opportunistic Babalatchi; the subtlety and range of characterizations ensure that the choice for Nina is a real one. Ideally, such a central character opts for fusion, reconciliation. In fact, as the closing chapters of *Almayer's Folly* make clear, there has been too much history; Almayer is the end of colonialism and Nina its inevitable product.

Through the characterization of Nina's mother, Almayer's wife, and using the image of kidnapping (for Mrs. Almayer was a pirate's daughter snatched from her culture by Almayer's mentor, Captain Lingard), Conrad succeeds in dramatizing the imposition of imperial history upon private sensibility. As much as Almayer, his wife is the creation of Lingard, the embodiment of bluff, well-intentioned English imperialism. (It was, after all, George Orwell who said that of all colonialism he would choose the British variety.) Lingard's capture of the young fighting girl and his placement of her in a cool, repressive convent are the symbolic core of women's experience in this book. Lingard has captured Almayer as well and placed him in as confined an existence as that of the wild and savage woman who is to become his wife. Blindly, meaning the best, he has forced together white and native. The future that results is called Nina.

Conrad, in juxtaposing white and Malay cultures, uses the flawed characters of Almayer and his wife to plead their cases before Nina, a scrupulous and sorrowful judge. At the end of the book, in their lengthy conversation on the beach, Almayer and Nina at last touch with language the real struggle between his culture and what is to be hers. "Did you not see me struggling before your eyes,"

Nina asks him. "I have listened to your voice and to her voice. Then I saw that you could not understand me; for was I not part of that woman? Of her who was the regret and shame of your life. I had to choose—I hesitated" (p. 191). In this speech, and throughout the long dialogue with her father that surrounds it, Nina shows clearly that she understands the imposition of the past upon the present, understands her parents' inability to think and feel beyond their historical context. "What is there to forgive," Nina asks, "as if arguing with herself" (p. 190). Her father's rigid ambitions for her are paralleled by the limits of her mother's insight; Nina must create a complete future of her own duality. For what her mother offers, what Conrad drily describes as "the lost possibilities of murder and mischief," cannot satisfy the more humane and complex nature of the daughter. Neither can the pathetic and subservient love of Taminah, the slave-girl, express the future adequately for Nina. Taminah, physically almost identical to Nina, possesses no self-knowledge, no self-consciousness; paradoxically, though self-consciousness may paralyze Europeans, it is also their great advantage over the least civilized native when properly fused with resolution.

In both these novels, which are dramas of choice expressed through male-female relationships, the native Babalatchi may represent the human ideal; a superb go-between, Babalatchi is a perfectly rational animal who expresses physically his instinctive and reasonable adaptation to his surroundings. To Mrs. Almayer's ravings, her taunts about his age and lack of courage, Babalatchi answers in terms of survival: "A man knows when to fight and when to tell peaceful lies. You would know that if you were not a woman" (p. 155). The issue is here joined, fittingly enough between two Malays; it is never entirely to be resolved, but it is always clear. The women, taken seriously by neither white men nor natives, must find subtle, often misunderstood means to live beyond history, to alter culture. Even her mother's parting advice to Nina makes such a commitment clear. "When I hear of white men driven from the islands, then I shall know that you are alive, and that you remember my words" (p. 152). Indirection, subtlety, the use of love to achieve power, are the message of Nina's mother; having failed through direct conflict, she perceives that history must be imposed on individual lives. "Do not let him look too long in your eyes, nor lay his head on your knees without reminding him that men should fight before they rest" (p. 152). The use of the past to change the future lies with women; it is to Nina's self-awareness, coupled with her instinctive passion, that both her parents appeal. In turn, Nina offers to them the chance to escape their own cultural prisons. "No woman is worth a man's life," says Babalatchi, the cynical go-between, speaking from his own historical limitation (p. 183). In fact, through Nina, Conrad portrays an equality between men and women that denies Babalatchi's cynicism as well as her mother's subtle violence. The sentimental information, after the conclusion of the story, that Nina's male child has been safely born may encourage speculation at the end of *Almayer's Folly*. However, even though the child is male, it is clear that through the complex introspective figure of the half-caste woman Conrad has explored the process and future of colonialism. Almayer's exhaustion contrasts with the self-conscious and articulate portrait of Nina, who shows understanding both of the man and of the historical process that shaped and then abandoned him. Her awareness, in fact, is far greater than his.

Thus, the creation of a subtle, self-conscious, and developing woman was possible for Conrad very early in his career. Nevertheless, it is the character of Aissa in his second book, *An Outcast of the Islands*, which shows even better the role of women in expressing, altering, and creating historical individuality. Just as Nina represents aspects of Almayer, as he clearly perceives in his moment of choice, so Aissa in *An Outcast of the Islands* is the central representation of the inner Willems. The two early novels, having the same location and many of the same characters, share as well the theme of colonialism and the distintegration of the men who exemplify it. The pitting of one sex against the other, which in these novels serves also to pit race against race, serves only to destroy; ordinarily, as character doubling functions, it splits rather than reconciles aspects of characters. In fact, as *Almayer's Folly* is the first to show, only through a reconciliation and identification between man and woman can wholeness of character, of civilization, even be attempted.

From the beginning of *An Outcast of the Islands*, the self-deluded Willems looks only to men for models; he relegates his wife to abject posturing and approval of his fantasies. (Like Almayer he does not perceive his wife as fully human.) The significance of the native Aissa, as a character and as a projection of the possibilities open to Willems as her lover, lies in her being a woman who consciously rejects the tradition from which Willems comes and to which he blindly determines to return. Native culture (which he equates with savagery) as a deliberate alternative to European culture always terrifies Willems. But as in *Almayer's Folly*, it is usually the natives who act with caution, with reason, and with adherence to understandable rules and traditions. The real savagery, as Conrad shows in both these books, comes from the thoughtless and impetuous imposition of the powerful personalities of white men. Almayer and Willems act out the colonial fantasies of their superiors, Hudig and Lingard. Native women are orphaned, their identity stripped from them, and then married to white men to carry out the paternalism of their real or adoptive fathers. The revenge of such women is slow and vicious; their competition and concern for their half-caste children are obsessive and immediately understandable. As Mrs. Almayer shows most clearly, the child is used to reject and destroy the culture with which the men mistakenly claim their identification. Only through an acceptance of native culture, paradoxically, can the white man forge a real identity, but such acceptance is literally out of the question for him; in Willems' life, it drives him mad.

The native woman Aissa, who captivates and terrifies Willems, represents in *An Outcast of the Islands* not only a love affair but also a personification of native culture in all its wildness and its passionate self-consciousness. Fleeing failure, Willems confronts in Aissa both himself and his history. As a character, Aissa suffers from overwriting and from some fairly hysterical prose cadences. But her grandeur (greater than Nina's) ultimately emerges, particularly toward the end of the book, in her confrontation on the island with the appalling and horrified Captain Lingard. Her estimate of herself and of the men around her strikingly parallels the understanding reached earlier by Mrs. Almayer. The deviousness of white men holds no appeal for such women. Both are nostalgic for direct and courageous action, and both remember their own secret success in battle in the roles of men. The challenge such women offer, even in their own cultures, is often resented. To the white man, Lingard, Aissa is frightening.

This encounter between Aissa and Captain Lingard, while the exhausted and terrified Willems sleeps, is the crucial point of *An Outcast of the Islands*. Conrad has traditionally been judged incapable of creating viable women characters; "overwriting and rhetorical excess"[5] according to one critic are the major limitations of Conrad's attempts in *Almayer's Folly*. For his psychoanalytical biographer, Bernard C. Meyer, the only explanation for any success in depicting the love relationship between Aissa and Willems rests on its parallel to Conrad's own developing relationship with Jessie George.[6] The power, the self-consciousness that distinguish and illuminate Aissa have been ignored, except when they have been studiously judged as "overwrought," by critics and Captain Lingard alike. Her rejection reflects more upon the culture and expectations of our critics than upon Captain Lingard; the accusation Aissa levels at him is one that affronts us all. "That was my life. What has been yours?" (p. 246).

For the apprehension—the fear—that Aissa creates in Lingard and in Willems (who repeatedly imagines his soul vanishing under her steady gaze, in the classic double experience) is not merely fear of herself; it is rather that anxiety before a powerful, integrated personality, a thoroughly alive woman who silences captains and critics alike. From the earliest moments of their relationship, Willems perceives himself as facing annihilation. Half asleep, he often has fleeting dreams of his figure vanishing. "He had a notion of being lost among shapeless things that were dangerous and ghastly" (p. 80). A moment before, he was fearful for his civilization; thus his ego and his whiteness are inextricably entwined. Paradoxically, of course, it is always the woman who surrenders, and that very willingness to lose herself constitutes a threat so grave that he clutches at himself and rejects the very concept of surrender. Only a character certain of his own role, his own manhood, and his own identity can risk surrender to a relationship that will result in two new people, a new dual identity. Ironically, Dain in *Almayer's Folly* possesses that kind of inner security, coming as he does from a royal family to which he will certainly return. Both Almayer and Willems have only Captain Lingard to look to for security; having failed in the white world, they have been adopted as his surrogate sons. Lingard's certainty is often described by Conrad in terms of the deceptive surface of the river, "that river whose entrances only himself knew" (*Almayer's Folly*, p. 8). Baffled by depths, inevitably Lingard is wrecked by the passionate river he has pretended to master and which he has claimed to own. He is bluff, hearty, and has a captivating stupidity, and he is all Almayer and Willems have before them as a model male. Thus, his terrified response to Aissa's direct challenge is a revelation of what she threatens to less secure men such as Willems.

Clearly, what Conrad describes is the defensiveness common to all the male characters in *An Outcast of the Islands*, but the lucid understanding of Lingard's involuntary response takes us a good deal further. For in his involuntary shudder, Tom Lingard is one of us. Generations of readers and critics have responded to Aissa as did Lingard, and for precisely the same reason.[7] Leo Gurko is just one of those who equate Aissa with savagery, with a retreat from the blessings of civilization; in this novel, he says, "Willems' journey

. . . is from man to animal." It is "a steep psychological descent."[8] Willems' fear of what is not himself, of the other, contrasts starkly with Aissa's desire to know, her consuming need to understand others. Looking at Lingard,

> she gave him the look that was like a stab, not of anger but of desire; of the intense, overpowering desire to see in, to see through, to understand everything: every thought, emotion, purpose; every impulse, every hesitation inside that man . . . (*An Outcast of the Islands*, p. 247).

This desire to know, the conscious cultivation of probing sensitivity, is not only characteristic of Aissa. It is true of all the women in these first two books and, in general, it remains true of Conrad's women up to Winnie Verloc's reasoned defensiveness in *The Secret Agent*, her stolid awareness that things do not bear too much looking into.

Early Conradian white men are distinguished by their lack of knowing, their determined ignorance. Almayer, Willems, and Lingard are all men of the surface, all self-deluded. In fact, the self-deluded protagonist is a recognizable constant in Conrad's work. The crisis of identity comes as it does only to a protagonist wrapped in delusion. In sharp contrast, these women of the early books are distinguished by their passionate apprehension of knowledge— about themselves and about the white men who use them. The natives have to be passionately intelligent to survive the white men. Not sex but intelligent sex is what frightens Willems; the grace and beauty of the natives are only appalling when they are seen to cover the intelligent mystery.

It is interesting that strong emotion brings consciousness to the women of these early novels; even Taminah, the slave girl in *Almayer's Folly*, comes to a crushing sense of the reality of her slave's life through the desire for Dain that abruptly enters her awareness. None of the women fears this consciousness; none resists it. Consciousness comes as a threat to the white men and they reject it. Almayer's great desire is forgetfulness, even at the cost of losing both his daughter and himself. Both Almayer and Willems, who are remarkably similar in their preoccupation with status, with whiteness, with the figures they cut, instinctively reject the kind of self-knowledge that passionate apprehension of a woman involves. They attribute it to savagery and sharply contrast this savagery with what they call Europeanism. Willems says frantically, "I did not know there was something in me she could get hold of. She, a savage. I, a civilized European, and clever. She that knew no more than a wild animal! Well, she found out something in me" (*An Outcast of the Islands*, p. 269).

When one compares Willems' assessment of Aissa with Conrad's account of her consuming desire to know, to understand, the discrepancy between Willems' rationalization and the reality of her humanity is startling. Even in a letter to his early mentor, Edward Garnett, Conrad wrote evenly of the two: "they both long to have a significance in the order of nature or of society."[9] In the books, the white men's consistent explanation of the women's incomprehensible behavior has to do with their savagery, with their instinctive acts that must not derive from any mutually intelligible source. In fact, the women (as well as their native male counterparts) act out of deliberate and skeptical assessments of white men; they observe, they wonder, they calculate. All the white men act impetuously and irrationally, blaming the predictable consequences on the natives in general and the women in particular. It is a familiar pattern. What has not been so clear before is the way in which sex and sexual doubling function in these books to show a departure route from the pattern. Nina and Dain, somewhat sentimentally, represent a future to *Almayer's Folly*. More graphically, more realistically, and more unhappily, Aissa offers such a departure to Willems in *An Outcast of the Islands*.

It is usual in these early books for Conrad to create a rounded character or action out of the combination of two or three less completely drawn fragments. Thus, Taminah and Mrs. Almayer round out the portrait of the half-caste of which the central figure is Nina. Both Mrs. Almayer and Taminah illustrate the bitter resolution possible to the kind of submissive relationship traditionally experienced by native and white women. Conrad's awareness of the unhappy and shattering possibilities finds expression through Mrs. Almayer's bitterness and Taminah's vulnerability and eventual death. Against these two tentative doubles, Nina emerges more clearly and without sentimentality. Her physical resemblance to Taminah is so extraordinary that the description of one stands perfectly for the other. "In that supple figure straight as an arrow, so graceful and free in its walk, behind those soft eyes that spoke of nothing but of unconscious resignation, there slept all fears, the curse of life and the consolation of death" (*Almayer's Folly*, p. 112). This description of Taminah parallels the accounts of Nina, whose inner division and anxiety are quite invisible to her father and eventually to her lover as well. Taminah "shrank from Nina as she would have shrunk from the sharp blade of a knife cutting into her flesh, but she kept on visit-

ing the brig to feed her dumb ignorant soul on her own despair"
(p. 116). These traditional character doublings serve several purposes: not only do they delineate the potential of each character but
they intensify what ultimately happens to each. They provide, as
well, an opening toward the more complex doubling which, juxtaposing as it does a man and a woman, provides the most telling
means of simultaneously defining and showing the limits of consciousness of the male identity.

Almayer, Dain, Lingard, and Willems all resist and are threatened by the full identification of self through a woman. Only Dain
has the security of his tribal hierarchy behind him that allows his
complete identification with Nina. He is the only male in these early
books who is not terrified by the implications of a woman's submission. Nina, acting out her mother's advice, perceives in Dain's
moment of triumph his real submission. The account of their crucial
meeting and of their final commitment to one another is strikingly
similar to the initial description of Aissa's surrender to Willems.
What is remarkable is the difference between the reactions of the
men. Of Nina, Conrad writes:

> She drew back her head and fastened her eyes on his in one of those
> long looks that are a woman's most terrible weapons, a look that
> is more stirring than the closest touch, and more dangerous than
> the thrust of a dagger, because it also whips the soul out of the body,
> but leaves the body alive and helpless, to be swayed here and there
> by the capricious tempests of passion and desire; a look that enwraps
> the whole body, and that penetrates into the innermost recesses
> of the being, bringing terrible defeat in the delirious uplifting of
> accomplished conquest. It has the same meaning for the man of the
> forests and the sea as for the man threading the paths of the more
> dangerous wilderness of houses and streets (p. 171).

Significantly, at this moment Dain responds with a shout of joy;
falling at her feet, he experiences his triumph. The contrast with
Willems, who reacts with terror to Aissa's surrender, could not be
more clear.

> And . . . look at her . . . she took me as if I did not belong to myself.
> She did. I did not know there was something in me she could get
> hold of. She, a savage. I, a civilized European, and clever! She that
> knew no more than a wild animal! Well, she found out something
> in me. She found it out, and I was lost. I knew it. She tormented
> me. I was ready to do anything. I resisted—but I was ready (*An
> Outcast of the Islands*, p. 269).

Dain's sense that with Nina he has the strength to accomplish everything has its tortured counterpart in Willems' terror that Aissa will,

in her surrender, bring out his latent powers for what he calls savage action. What the women possess, what they offer, is the same. The key lies rather in the response found within the men who represent the varieties of colonial experience. And, in the remarkable difference between the responses of whites and Malays, there is visible the corrupting effect of the colonial relationship. Like Charles Gould, who responds inadequately to Emilia in *Nostromo*, the white men have been in some sense reduced, lessened as men, through their dependence upon European civilization and materialism.

The ambiguity inherent in a complex relationship is not ignored by Conrad even in the romanticism of Nina and Dain's relationship. Aware of the triumph inherent in surrender, Conrad describes with great ambiguity the smile hovering about Nina's mouth. "Who can tell in the fitful light of a camp fire? It might have been a smile of triumph, or of conscious power, or of tender pity, or, perhaps, of love" (*Almayer's Folly*, p. 172). These relationships offer an expansion of self, a redefining of self. The men are defined not only through their similarities and identification with other men, as is usual, but through their ability to identify themselves with these "savage" or half-caste women. And because these men represent the colonial empires both literally, as their agents, and figuratively, as their products, their inability to achieve identification with the native women is a serious reflection upon the nature and future of their colonial civilization.

Many of these elements of Conrad's early work have been separately considered and understood. But there has been a tendency, easily understandable in light of the society we represent, to view aspects of Conrad's work in fragments. Character doubling has been considered as a device, as a psychological mechanism for exploring character, occasionally as a revelation of Conrad's psychic inadequacies. In these early works it seems clear that it is far more than any of these fragmentary means. It is instead the full-fledged expression of the juxtaposition of men and women, culture and culture, through which lies the only possibility for resolution of difference and active creation of a new life. Consistently, the men identify themselves, just as do Almayer, Willems, and Lingard, with Western imperialism (in the guise of "civilization") and against savagery. And, just as consistently, it remains for the women to offer in their characterization the humanity that goes beyond Western civilization.

In these early novels, customarily judged to be interesting but naturally inferior to the later, more accomplished creations, it is clear that Conrad has already mastered the complex art of making each element of the novel serve simultaneously on several levels, The love relationship, which successive waves of criticism have judged badly wrought, actually works convincingly in these early novels, not only personally but historically as well. Further, it is important to consider Conrad's entire novelistic production as a unified entity, one in which elements juxtaposed with one another provide in some sense new meanings and new insights which, considered singly, are not readily apparent. These early works, especially as they use characters jointly, need to be considered together. And, particularly, the parallel relationship between Nina and Dain, Aissa and Willems, is a revelation when seen in this dual light.

These early women are neither inarticulate nor unaware of the critical value of their lives and their perceptions set against white men and white society. Their comments are lucid and important. Nina's awareness of submission as potential triumph emerges clearly in her thoughts as she contemplates Dain's figure huddled at her feet. "As she glanced down at his kneeling form she felt a great pitying tenderness for that man she was used to calling—even in her thoughts—the master of life" (*Almayer's Folly*, p. 172). Aissa is more lucid than Nina, more despairing in the face of Willems' determination to return to Europe despite her. "She was appalled, surprised and angry with the anger of unexpected humiliation; and her eyes looked fixedly, sombre and steady, at that man born in the land of violence and evil wherefrom nothing but misfortune comes to those who are not white." A moment later she arrives at her conscious and deliberate resolution to keep him with her, "a slave and a master" (*An Outcast*, p. 153). Unlike Nina, Aissa cannot turn to positive use the dual slave-master relationship that they both so accurately assess. The nature of colonialism, its spreading contamination, demands of each human being a choice; in the end, Willems chooses to be white and Aissa kills him for that.

The dual relationship of master and slave offers the threat of destruction only to the insecure white colonialist. Native men, even those who distrust the strength of Aissa, take for granted the subtle shifts and interchanges marking the total exchange of affection between man and woman. Babalatchi's respect for Aissa sharply contrasts with Lingard's distaste and revulsion from her intense questions. And yet, even in her ferocious desire for knowledge and her sense of her own value, she instinctively falls at Lingard's feet and leaves him appalled by her willingness to abase herself. The ability to express contradictions, to admit opposites within one nature, baffles and revolts a single-minded white man. The challenge that Aissa hurls at Lingard is the one these women hurl at us all. "Get out of my path," Lingard tells Aissa. "You ought to know that when men meet in daylight women must be silent and abide their fate."

> "Women!" she retorted, with subdued vehemence. "Yes, I am a woman! Your eyes see that, O Rajah Laut, but can you see my life? I have also heard—O man of many fights—I have also heard the voice of firearms; I also have felt the rain of young twigs and of leaves cut up by bullets fall down about my head; I also know how to look in silence at angry faces and at strong hands raised high grasping sharp steel. I also saw men fall dead around me without a cry of fear and of mourning; and I have watched the sleep of weary fugitives, and looked at night shadows full of menace and death with eyes that knew nothing but watchfulness. And," she went on with a mournful drop in her voice, "I have faced the heartless sea, held on my lap the heads of those who died raving from thirst, and from their cold hands took the paddle and worked so that those with me did not know that one man more was dead. I did all this. What more have you done? That was my life. What has been yours?" (p. 245-6).

Even Lingard is stunned into silence. But even more telling than this superlative tirade is the line that follows, a line that is the essence of what these women represent as potential identities for these shells of men. "And I have knelt at your feet! And I am afraid!" (p. 256). Lingard can only reject her in his self-satisfied role as Rajah Laut.

That confrontation, the dramatic high point of *An Outcast of the Islands*, epitomizes the success of Conrad's treatment of women in these two novels. They function on so many levels simultaneously that they testify to the maturity of the author even at this early stage in his career. The native and half-caste women do not blur into one another. Rather, they are sharply drawn facets of a complex portrayal of strong and self-conscious women. They speak clearly of a historical awareness, a sense of lost time and rapidly vanishing possibilities for redemption. Through the personal relationship, in which identities merge and reform, they offer the possibility of transcending history. Sadly, only their own doomed kind are capable of accepting this gift of identity with its master-slave ambiguity. The white men, those who might have gained most humanity from such a doubling, have not the humanity to accept it.

BANGOR COMMUNITY COLLEGE,
UNIVERSITY OF MAINE AT ORONO

Notes

[1] *Toward a Recognition of Androgyny* (New York: Knopf, 1973), p. 94.

[2] Such important critics of the psychological aspects of Conrad's work as Jocelyn Baines (*Joseph Conrad*, London: Weidenfeld and Nicolson, 1959), Frederick R. Karl (*A Reader's Guide to Joseph Conrad*, New York: Noonday Press, 1960), and Morton D. Zabel ("Chance and Recognition," in R. W. Stallman, ed., *The Art of Joseph Conrad: A Critical Symposium*, East Lansing: Michigan State University Press, 1960; also his introductions to the Anchor paperback editions of Conrad's works) have not taken women seriously at all. The only psychologically oriented critic who has, Bernard C. Meyer (*Joseph Conrad: A Psychoanalytic Biography*, Princeton: Princeton University Press, 1967), sees women as destructive and fearful monsters. No critic, to my knowledge, has made connections between the treatment of women and Conrad's political statements.

[3] *The Mythology of Imperialism* (New York: Random House, 1971), p. 36.

[4] Page references in this article are to the following editions: *Almayer's Folly* (New York: Doubleday, Page & Co., 1923); *An Outcast of the Islands* (New York: Doubleday, Page & Co., 1925).

[5] John H. Hicks, "*Almayer's Folly:* Structure, Theme, and Critics," *Nineteenth-Century Fiction*, XIX (1964), 19.

[6] Meyer, *Joseph Conrad*, pp. 216-17.

[7] Throughout *Women and Madness* (New York: Doubleday, 1972), the first full-length study to treat together the psychology and literature of women, Dr. Phyllis Chesler makes the point that "help seeking" women, that is those aware of their problems and the connections between their problems and their men, are "not particularly valued or understood in our culture. Helpseekers are pitied, mistrusted, tranquilized, physically beaten, given shock therapy, lied to, yelled at, and ultimately neglected" (p. XXIII). All these treatments, at one time or another, are Aissa's; perhaps the most appalling is the pity that reduces her rage to the tantrum of an over-tired child.

[8] *Joseph Conrad: Giant in Exile* (New York: Macmillan, 1962), pp. 59-60.

[9] Sept. 24, 1895, in Gerard Jean-Aubry, *Joseph Conrad: Life and Letters* (3 vols., New York: Doubleday, Page & Co., 1927), I, 181.

VIPERS, VICTIMS, AND VIRGINS: WOMEN AND THEIR RELATIONSHIPS WITH MEN IN THE POETRY OF NICANOR PARRA

Karen S. Van Hooft

One aspect of the work of the Chilean poet Nicanor Parra that has been insufficiently studied is the role played by women and the related themes of love and sex. This is surprising, for even a superficial examination of Parra's works from *Poemas y antipoemas* (1954) to the controversial *Artefactos* (1972) reveals a considerable preoccupation with women and with men's relationships to them.

The typical analysis of this theme in Parra's poetry has focused on his misogynic portrayal of women and his negative attitude toward love and sex. Indeed, there is considerable textual basis for such an analysis. However, a closer and more balanced reading of the poet's works, one which relates his treatment of women to other central themes in his poetry, gives a somewhat different picture. In this reading, women are seen *in their relationships* with men, and one is obliged to conclude that the latter are not portrayed in a particularly more sympathetic light. Parra's men are seen to be as hindered in the quest for fulfillment by sexual stereotypes and role playing as the women they relate to and as incapable of finding a satisfactory solution to the resulting war between the sexes.

The problem thus becomes one of understanding Parra's critical attitude toward innumerable facets of contemporary life, from sexual stereotyping and role playing to the over-reliance on Freudian psychology, and so on. I shall attempt to show that Parra's treatment of women is part of a larger assault on our most cherished institutions and mental habits; it is basically the attack of an anarchistic poetic *persona* who delights in the evidence of decay around him but who offers no real solutions. To single out the poet's misogynic treatment of women without considering these other factors is to distort his basic intent.

The principal poems I will analyze are from *Poemas y anti-poemas*,[1] although some reference will be made to poems from other works. There are two reasons for this selectivity: (1) the poems in the first volume adequately reveal the attitudes found in the entire body of Parra's poetry, and (2) while the subject of women and love is continuously present, a considerable change in stylistic treatment occurs in the course of Parra's poetic development. In *Poemas y anti-poemas* the subject is dealt with extensively in poems of a confession-al nature such as "La víbora"; in later works (*La camisa de fuerza, Otros poemas*, the new poems of *Emergency Poems*, and especially the *Artefactos*) the subject is treated much more fragmentarily. This change in treatment corresponds to the variations observable in Parra's poetic *personae*. In his first volume the *persona* is most often a passive, suffering voice who narrates his erotic (mis)adventures with bitter irony, whereas in the later works the narrative aspect is almost completely lost and the attitudes are usually expressed as psychic outbursts of a different type of poetic protagonist, the *energúmeno*.[2] And finally, in the *Artefactos* this latter tendency is developed to the extreme, and the *persona* becomes something akin to the anonymous writer of graffiti.[3]

The obvious place to begin an analysis of the subject of women, love, and sex in Parra's work is with the poem "La víbora" (*Poemas y antipoemas*), for this is the most complete expression of the atti-tudes I will be discussing.

> Durante largos años estuve condenado a adorar a una mujer
> despreciable
> Sacrificarme por ella, sufrir humillaciones y burlas sin cuento,
> Trabajar día y noche para alimentarla y vestirla,
> Llevar a cabo algunos delitos, cometer algunas faltas,
> A la luz de la luna realizar pequeños robos,
> Falsificaciones de documentos comprometedores,
> So pena de caer en descrédito ante sus ojos fascinantes (p. 42).

In the title and introduction we are presented with the essential facts: the speaker of the poem informs us that the woman in question is "a viper" and "una mujer despreciable." Furthermore, he states that he was "condemned" to "adore" her, an interesting combination of the vocabulary of love with a word suggesting imprisonment, and finally he reveals that this imprisonment, with its serious consequences of suffering, sacrifice, and crime, was involuntary, for he was trapped by the viper's "fascinating eyes." One of Parra's critics has noted that this last element may refer to the traditional belief that snakes can hypnotize their victims.[4] While this is certainly one level of meaning present here, there are several other levels, both more simple and more complex, which contribute to the total impact. For example, the idea of a man being trapped by a woman's captivating eyes is an everyday commonplace, and the expression "ojos fascinantes" can be simply related to the banal vocabulary of advertisements for eye makeup and the like. The use of colloquial language related to common experience is a striking feature of Parra's poetry and has been amply studied elsewhere.[5] If one wishes to continue the search for additional levels of meaning, one can also refer to the Biblical story of the Fall, in which the serpent, closely identified with the female, Eve, seduces Adam and causes the expulsion from the Garden and the condemnation of humanity to work, suffering, and sacrifice.

Parra's use of irony as an important element of his poetic technique, which has also been extensively studied,[6] is visible in the opening section of the poem. It is in fact supremely ironic for the poetic protagonist to state that he was trapped in a life of personal suffering, humiliation, and petty crime by something so apparently trivial as a pair of captivating eyes. Of course, the reader sees beyond this lame excuse and begins to suspect some deeper cause of the speaker's suffering.

In the next section of the poem the *persona* refers to the "horas de comprensión" (p. 43) between himself and the viper when they would have their picture taken together in the park or would go to a club, "Donde nos entregábamos a un baile desenfrenado / Que se prolongaba hasta altas horas de la madrugada" (p. 43). The first of these activities suggests the falsity of their "understanding," for what the reader sees is not any real togetherness or communication but rather a posture that substitutes for it (posing for a picture). It is as if the lovers are trying to capture their togetherness by creating some proof that it exists. This idea, the lack of true contact and communication between human beings and the futility of attempts to achieve it, is an important motive in Parra's poetry. The second activity, the "baile desenfrenado," introduces the motive of the erotic dance and the idea, suggested by "desenfrenado," of uncontrolled, orgiastic activity associated with sex.

The protagonist continues:

> Largos años viví prisionero del encanto de aquella mujer
> Que solía presentarse a mi oficina completamente desnuda
> Ejecutando las contorsiones más difíciles de imaginar
> Con el propósito de incorporar mi pobre alma a su órbita
> Y, sobre todo, para extorsionarme hasta el último centavo.
> Me prohibía estrictamente que me relacionase con mi familia,
> Mis amigos eran separados de mí mediante libelos infamantes
> Que la víbora hacía publicar en un diario de su propiedad (p. 43).

In the first line of this section the imprisonment motive is repeated, this time in association with the word "encanto," giving a similar ironic contrast to that seen previously. Of course, "encanto" has several levels of meaning; on one level is the commonplace idea of being trapped by a woman's "charms" and on another that of being the victim of an evil hypnotic spell. This second level is strengthened by the reader's previous understanding that the viper is a contemptible woman. The following lines emphasize this point, for the woman's intent is apparently to control the man's soul and extort his last cent. She intends to possess him so completely that he is separated from his family and friends by her manipulations.

At the same time another motive is developed, that of the woman's aggressive and exaggerated sexuality and her exploitation of the man.

> Apasionada hasta el delirio no me daba un instante de tregua,
> Exigiéndome perentoriamente que besara su boca
> Y que contestase sin dilación sus necias preguntas
> Varias de ellas referentes a la eternidad y a la vida futura
> Temas que producían en mí un lamentable estado de ánimo,
> Zumbidos de oídos, entrecortadas náuseas, desvanecimientos
>   prematuros
> Que ella sabía aprovechar con ese espíritu práctico que la carac-
>   terizaba
> Para vestirse rápidamente sin pérdida de tiempo
> Y abandonar mi departamento dejándome con un palmo de
>   narices (p. 43).

At this point the reader begins to associate the previous labeling of the woman as a viper with the obvious symbolic possibilities present. For example, the viper can be seen as a phallic symbol, thereby suggesting that her aggressive sexuality is "masculine." And this idea can then be related to the myth of the Fall, for in one interpretation the serpent symbolizes sexuality and what it offers Eve is sexual knowledge, which she in turn uses to seduce Adam.[7]

After describing the viper's attempts to seduce him, the poetic protagonist refers to her "necias preguntas" of a metaphysical nature and his resulting "lamentable estado de ánimo" and physical malaise. The close association of her sexual advances with these metaphysical questions (note the apparent reversal of roles) serves to suggest that his symptoms of illness are not entirely caused by the questions. In fact, the speaker indicates that the final result is really impotence and frustration on all levels, physical and mental, which the woman compounds by her calculated flight.

In the next section of the poem we are informed that the affair with the viper went on for more than five years, a seemingly incredible amount of time to endure such suffering. During some of this time they lived together, "... en una pieza redonda / Que pagábamos a medias en un barrio de lujo cerca del cementerio" (p. 43). Here the prison, disguised as a love nest, takes the form of a round room—a female symbol in Freudian terms. It is, significantly, near a cemetery, thereby associating their relationship with death, another important motive in Parra. In a typical use of irony, this living arrangement is called a "honeymoon" and then the image is immediately deflated by describing their battle with "las ratas que se colaban por la ventana" (p. 43).

Next we are informed of other details relating to the viper's exploitative nature, particularly her intent to take economic advantage of her victim. She accuses her lover of ruining her youth, and with "flashing eyes" (another commonplace but suggestive description) she threatens to take him to court to collect the money he owes her. One begins to wonder who is exploiting whom! We remember that early in the poem the speaker claims to work night and day to feed and clothe the viper, but later he states that they share the rent in the round room, and now he is apparently borrowing money from her. Obviously he means to indicate that she is causing his ruin, for next he must live on charity and is reduced to sleeping on park benches.

> Felizmente aquel estado de cosas no pasó más adelante,
> Porque cierta vez en que yo me encontraba en una plaza también
> Posando frente a una cámara fotográfica
> Unas deliciosas manos femeninas me vendaron de pronto la vista
> Mientras una voz amada para mí me preguntaba quién soy yo.
> Tú eres mi amor, respondí con serenidad.
> ¡Angel mío, dijo ella nerviosamente,
> Permite que me siente en tus rodillas una vez más!
> Entonces pude percatarme de que ella se presentaba ahora pro-
> vista de un pequeño taparrabos (p. 44).

The scene of the viper's reappearance is full of "notas discordantes": the protagonist posing for a picture while living on charity; the woman showing up dressed in a loincloth, playing a child's game with her former victim and asking to sit on his lap;[8] and the male reacting with the hackneyed phrases "deliciosas manos femeninas," "voz amada," and "tú eres mi amor." The juxtaposition of this banal love vocabulary with the "discordant" description of the viper's appearance again provides an ironic contrast that underscores the true nature of the relationship.

The speaker next discovers that the viper has new plans for them:

Me he comprado una parcela, no lejos del matadero, exclamó,
Allí pienso construir una especie de pirámide
En la que podamos pasar los últimos días de nuestra vida.
Ya he terminado mis estudios, me he recibido de abogado,
Dispongo de un buen capital;
Dediquémonos a un negocio productivo, los dos, amor mío, agregó,
Lejos del mundo construyamos nuestro nido (p. 44).

Significantly, the plot of land is near the slaughterhouse and the new love nest will be a pyramid, both things again suggesting that their love is akin to death. Furthermore, the plan is to structure their new relationship as a business deal, emphasizing the viper's materialistic nature and the baseness of their love. But the protagonist rejects her plans and finally begins to demand something real and necessary from her: that she give him water and food, if she is to give him anything. He flatly states that the affair is over: "No puedo trabajar más para ti, / Todo ha terminado entre nosotros" (p. 45). He is at last unwilling to go on allowing her to imprison him. However, it is clear that this affirmative decision is not all that hopeful for him, for he is old and "profundamente agotado."[9]

In summary, the attitudes present in this poem toward love, women, and sex are decidedly negative. Love here is an exploitative relationship in which the woman imprisons the man, causing physical and mental suffering and his eventual perdition. Furthermore, it is seen as a death-trap which must ultimately be rejected. The sexual component of love participates quite virulently in these characteristics; sex is seen as being little more than an uncontrolled, orgiastic, and finally futile and frustrating activity. The failure in sex, then, is indicative of the more general failure to establish a satisfying and communicating relationship.

The woman in the poem, the viper, does not correspond to the conventional female stereotype of the passive "homebody," for she appears both sexually and intellectually aggressive. However, the description the poetic voice gives us in fact contains a number of contradictions. In spite of the viper's supposed ability to support herself (we are told that she owns a daily newspaper), she still demands at the beginning that the man provide for her or at least collaborate in her maintenance. Her aggressive sexuality, which the reader sees in an obviously exaggerated form, threatens the protagonist's established masculine role and renders him impotent. Still, the viper makes rather traditional demands for affection. Finally, her metaphysical questionings of him suggest an underlying intellectual passivity stereotypically associated with women. The reader notes that she asks questions, seemingly looking to the male for guidance, rather than expressing or asserting her own ideas. In other words, the viper partially usurps the traditional masculine role, but not completely. But for the male this is sufficient to make her deadly; she is able to entrap and manipulate him, ostensibly against his will. She ultimately contributes to his impotence on all levels.

The protagonist himself is shown to be powerless and easily duped. Trapped by this aggressive woman who definitely represents a threat to his well-being and whom he is unable to handle, he has neither the will nor the ability to escape until the end, when it may be too late. While she is presented as being truly malevolent, he is not any better a person, for he is not only incapable of communicating with the woman, whom he views in purely sexual terms, but he · is also deluded as to the true cause of his suffering—his own inability to take the action necessary to free himself from her clutches.

The poem following "La víbora" in *Poemas y antipoemas*, "La trampa," presents a complementary view of the themes elaborated above. Whereas in the first poem the most visible motive is that of frustration and ruin due to female malevolence and exploitation, here it is that of intellectual and sexual failure caused by the inability to communicate successfully. The imprisonment motive is also important, as is indicated by the title. The viper's trap was presented as being a hypnotic spell cast by her enchanting eyes; here the trap is objectively represented by a telephone.

The first part of the poem is a description of the poetic protagonist's mental imprisonment. He is unable to cope with "las escenas demasiado misteriosas" and his "pensamientos atrabiliarios" (p. 45), so he flees social contact, preferring to remain at home. Although he states that "En la soledad poseía un dominio absoluto sobre mí mismo, / Iba de un lado a otro con plena conciencia de mis actos" (p. 45), the reader is soon aware that this is not true, for one proceeds to observe the protagonist's aimless pursuits: ". . . dilucidando algunas cuestiones / Referentes a la reproducción de las arañas"; "O también en mangas de camisa, en actitud desafiante, / Solía lanzar iracundas miradas a la luna"; "O me tendía entre las tablas de la bodega / A soñar, a idear mecanismos . . ." (p. 45). The speaker of the poem next admits that these attempts at avoidance are futile. He cannot escape his desire to establish communication with someone. But he fails in his attempt.

> Comenzaba a deslizarme automáticamente por una especie de
>   plano inclinado,
> Como un globo que se desinfla mi alma perdía altura,
> El instinto de conservación dejaba de funcionar
> Y privado de mis prejuicios más esenciales
> Caía fatalmente en la trampa del teléfono
> Que como un abismo atrae a los objetos que lo rodean
> Y con manos trémulas marcaba ese número maldito
> Que aún suelo repetir automáticamente mientras duermo.
> De incertidumbre y de miseria eran aquellos segundos
> En que yo, como un esqueleto de pie delante de esa mesa del
>   infierno
> Cubierta de una cretona amarilla,
> Esperaba una respuesta desde el otro extremo del mundo,
> La otra mitad de mi ser prisionera en un hoyo (p. 46).

This part of the poem is introduced with the images of sliding and falling, and Edith Grossman's analysis of it summarizes the main points:

> . . . the second half of the poem, dealing with the protagonist's tortured eroticism as he slips into the chasm of frustrated sexuality is, significantly, conceived of as the fall. In the intellectual abyss, the protagonist avoids contact through withdrawal; in the sexual abyss, he avoids profound sexual contact through the removed communication of the telephone, through false and unsatisfied stimulation, through meetings in public places.[10]

We see here the now familiar association of sexuality with imprisonment and with the Fall, and again there is the suggestion of death in the use of the words "esqueleto" and "infierno." The reader also notes that the subject suffers symptoms of physical malaise as did the protagonist of "La víbora": "manos trémulas," "incertidumbre y miseria," "comenzaba a transpirar y tartamudear" (p. 46), "Me producía malestares difusos / Perturbaciones locales de angustia . . ." (p. 47). And finally these symptoms become directly sexual in the form of "incipientes erecciones y . . . una sensación de fracaso" (p. 47). The theme of frustrated communication is also found in the lines following the section quoted above, as is another reference to death:

> Mi lengua parecida a un beefsteak de ternera
> Se interponía entre mi ser y mi interlocutora
> Como esas cortinas negras que nos separan de los muertos (p. 46).

The woman whom the subject is speaking to is hardly described at all, but when she *is* referred to it is in terms of her attempts to be overly intimate (she calls him by his first name, "En ese tono de familiaridad forzada") and her sexuality (the protagonist refers to her excited state as "efervescencia pseudoerótico"). Again the reader receives the impression of a clinging, overly erotic female whose reactions are identified by the subject as a cause of his "feeling of failure."

Finally, the speaker admits that he is left in a state of mental prostration ("aquellas catástrofes tan deprimentes para mi espíritu"). This prostration is so closely connected with his statements of purely physical symptoms as to make the sexual failure inseparable from it. At the end of the poem no solution is in sight, for the "stupid idyll" will continue: the man has arranged to see the woman the next day at a soda fountain or the door of a church, both public places that will again frustrate the desire for intimate communication. Of note is that the protagonist in this poem is somewhat more aware that his own weakness is a cause of his suffering: "Yo no deseaba sostener esas conversaciones demasiado íntimas / Que, sin embargo, yo mismo provocaba en forma torpe" (p. 46).

A third important poem in *Poemas y antipoemas* is "Recuerdos de juventud." It begins with a statement by the speaker that, unlike the *persona* of "La trampa," he has no illusions of being in control of himself:

> Lo cierto es que yo iba de un lado a otro,
> A veces chocaba con los árboles,
> Chocaba con los mendigos,
> Me abría paso a través de un bosque de sillas y mesas (p. 39).

But his attempts to find his way through this "forest of chairs and tables" are futile: "Cada vez me hundía más y más en una especie de jalea" (p. 39). The image of sinking recalls the sliding and falling of "La trampa," and the jelly has a possible sexual connotation. The poetic voice continues:

> La gente se reía de mis arrebatos,
> ....
> Y las mujeres me dirigían miradas de odio

Haciéndome subir, haciéndome bajar,
Haciéndome llorar y reír en contra de mi voluntad (p. 39).

The word "arrebatos," which closely follows upon the image of sinking into the jelly, recalls the "desenfreno"—the uncontrolled, orgiastic activity—in "La víbora" and strengthens the possible sexual connotation. And the next three lines cited are a direct statement of the protagonist's victimization by women, who manipulate him both emotionally (the references to laughing and crying) and sexually (the suggestive use of "subir" and "bajar") against his will.

"De todo esto resultó un sentimiento de asco," states the *persona*. Since this line follows the section on women, the reader suspects that a large part of the repulsion is sexual, although the character at first states that it manifested itself as ". . . una tempestad de frases incoherentes, / Amenazas, insultos, juramentos . . ." (p. 39). However, the next section confirms the original suspicion:

Resultaron unos movimientos agotadores de caderas,
Aquellos bailes fúnebres
Que me dejaban sin respiración
Y que me impedían levantar cabeza durante días,
Durante noches (p. 39).

The sexual reference could not be clearer. Sex is seen as a dance, recalling the erotic dance in "La víbora," and is associated again with physical prostration and death ("fúnebre"). Therefore sexual activity is presented here as both a causal factor in the protagonist's situation and as a desperate attempt to resolve it, one which only leads to further repulsion and alienation.

The protagonist's next attempts to escape are intellectual rather than sexual: "Con una hoja de papel y un lápiz yo entraba en los cementerios / Dispuesto a no dejarme engañar" (p. 39). We note that this effort involves writing as a form of communication (a possible biographical reference) and that it takes place in cemeteries, relating it to the death motive. Following this is a description of other intellectual endeavors and attempts to communicate in classrooms, literary circles and private houses, but all efforts fail:

Con el filo de la lengua traté de comunicarme con los espectadores:
Ellos leían el periódico
O desaparecían detrás de un taxi (p. 40).

The last two lines of the poem reflect the protagonist's complete despair: "Yo pensaba en un trozo de cebolla visto durante la cena / Y en el abismo que nos separa de los otros abismos" (p. 40). The startling first line signals the continuation of his disconcerted mental state and the second his awareness of the futility of his attempts to communicate with others, who are as trapped in the abyss as he is.

Other poems from *Poemas y antipoemas* that belong to the same thematic unit, in that they express the same attitudes, are "El túnel," "El peregrino," and "Notas de viaje." In "El túnel" there is another version of the imprisonment theme, this time presenting a protagonist who is considerably younger. Interestingly, the figures who trap and manipulate him are his aunts, "tres ancianas histéricas," "temibles damas"; they oblige him to work for them and deceive him cruelly by feigning helplessness in the form of illness and paralysis. The imprisonment here is referred to in terms of the tunnel of the title, the "interior de una botella de mesa" (p. 41), a "malla impenetrable," and a "campana de vidrio." The first two of these, especially, in association with the figures of the aunts and the imprisonment motive, can be seen as symbolically representing female malevolence (comparable to the round room in "La víbora").

The young protagonist in "El túnel" has essentially the same problems as the previous *personae*. At the hands of his aunts he suffers a constant martyrdom, revulsion, anguish, and finally ruin and misery, which he attempts to escape by another type of flight, that of playing a role to please them: ". . . angustia que yo trataba de disimular al máximo / Con el objeto de no despertar curiosidad en torno a mi persona" (p. 41). He experiences the same failures of understanding and communication seen previously, for he has a distorted perception of reality ("Yo lo veía todo a través de un prisma") and he is isolated from others:

> Un joven de escasos recursos no se da cuenta de las cosas.
> El vive en una campana de vidrio que se llama Arte
> Que se llama Lujuria, que se llama Ciencia
> Tratando de establecer contacto con un mundo de relaciones
> Que sólo existen para él y para un pequeño grupo de amigos (p. 41).

"El peregrino" again refers to the sexual and intellectual abyss in which the protagonist lives and his abortive attempts to communicate with other people:

> Un alma que ha estado embotellada durante años
> En una especie de abismo sexual e intelectual
> Alimentándose escasamente por la nariz
> Desea hacerse escuchar por ustedes.
> Deseo que se me informe sobre algunas materias,
> Necesito un poco de luz . . . (p. 36).

Finally, in "Notas de viaje" the *persona* tries to flee the abyss by abandoning his job and travelling. In spite of his flight, however, he still attempts to communicate superficially with others by "exchanging impressions." The dance motive is present again and is related to thoughts of "cosas absurdas" and "cosas fantásticas relacionadas con mi familia" (p. 34), which bring to mind the "desenfreno" seen previously in reference to the dance. And the image of the boat entering the river ". . . a través de un banco de medusas" (p. 34) has suggested to one critic a concretely sexual picture.[11] This vision affects the protagonist's spirit, obliging him to resort to a self-imposed imprisonment.

The remaining poems examined in this paper offer somewhat different stylistic treatments of the subject of women, love, and sex. Nevertheless, most of these poems express attitudes that are the same or complementary to those already discussed, while only a few appear to offer contradictory views.

The poem "Canción" presents a different type of woman from that seen previously.

> Quién eres tú repentina
> Doncella que te desplomas
> Como la araña que pende
> Del pétalo de una rosa.
>
> Tu cuerpo relampaguea
> Entre las maduras pomas
> Que el aire arranca
> Del árbol de la centolla.
>
> Caes con el sol, esclava
> Dorada de la amapola
> Y lloras entre los brazos
> Del hombre que te deshoja (p. 27).

This is not the sexually domineering and manipulating woman of "La víbora" and other poems. Instead she is virginal, receptive, and submissive. The term "esclava" refers to the fact that she is bound both to her nascent, uncontrolled passions and, to a lesser degree, to the man who deflowers her.

> Herida en lo más profundo
> Del cáliz, te desenrollas,
> Gimes de placer, te estiras,
> Te rompes como una copa.
>
> Mujer parecida al mar,
> —Violada entre ola y ola—
> Eres más ardiente aún
> Que un cielo de nubes rojas.

La mesa está puesta, muerde
La uva que te trastorna
Y besa con ira el duro
Cristal que te vuelve loca (pp. 27-28).

In contrast with previous poems, it is the woman who is here associated with imagery of physical and emotional distress and pain related to sex ("te desplomas," "herida," "Te rompes," "violada"; "lloras," "gimes," "ira"). Similar to the "unhinged" male protagonists seen earlier, she has lost control ("La uva que te trastorna," "Cristal que te vuelve loca"); this contrasts with the consciously manipulative sexual extravagances of "La víbora." Therefore in this poem the roles are reversed. Whereas previously woman has been the manipulator and sexual aggressor, now she is manipulated (and thus a potential victim); where previously she caused suffering, now she suffers, albeit for the "higher" purpose of sexual initiation. Both types of women are presented in the poems in such a way as to be ultimately negative: the one because she controls and effectively castrates the male, and the other because she is at the mercy of unbridled instincts that do her physical violence and cast her in the unenviable and limited role of submissive receptacle of the phallus.

A poem that deals with the theme of male victimization of woman is "Las tablas." This poem has many different levels of meaning, and the following brief analysis is only one possible reading.

Soñé que me encontraba en un desierto y que hastiado de mí mismo
Comenzaba a golpear a una mujer.
Hacía un frío de los demonios; era necesario hacer algo,
Hacer fuego, hacer un poco de ejercicio;
Pero a mí me dolía la cabeza, me sentía fatigado
Sólo quería dormir, quería morir (p. 51).

The poem begins with the familiar idea of the protagonist not being able to stand himself or cope with the world; this time he seeks an escape through action in the form of sexual violence. We next discover that he is, in fact, beating his mother: " 'Por qué maltratas a tu madre' me preguntaba entonces una piedra" (p. 51). The poetic *persona* is plagued by accusatory voices and visions ("Y veía la imagen de ese ídolo / Mi dios que me miraba hacer estas cosas") and he reacts by trembling, biting his nails, and attempting to divert his thoughts.

All of this is useless, for the voices return in other forms: the "tablets of the law" and the birds that will record his crimes. He soon becomes bored with listening to the voices, and failing to be rid of them:

> Entonces y me volví de nuevo a mi dama
> Y le empecé a dar más firme que antes.
> Para mantenerse despierto había que hacer algo
> Estaba en la obligación de actuar (p. 53).

Finally he makes one last effort ("Y decidí quemar el busto del dios"), only to discover that in ridding himself of his guilt he has also lost the one thing he may successfully take out his frustration on: "Mi madre me había abandonado" (p. 52). Because of his actions he is cut off from any human contact, with further action of any kind frustrated ("Ya no podía más"). He has destroyed the "tablets of the law," the norms of social behavior, and is therefore excluded from society.

"Las tablas" complements the negative view of sexuality seen elsewhere, and the inclusion of the mother figure adds a new dimension. The poem may be understood on one level as an expression of sexual loathing, the type of expression that often takes its strongest form in dreams such as this. The mother figure's humiliation suggests the whole question of familial relations and their effect on male and female sexual behavior (e.g., sadistic and masochistic behavior, respectively).

It should be noted that there are generally few negative references to the family in Parra's poetry, and these usually relate to the wife rather than to mother, sisters, or daughters. For example, in "Lo que el difunto dijo de sí mismo" (*Versos de salón*), the *persona* reacts violently to a question regarding his abandonment of his wife: "Respondí con un golpe en el pupitre / 'Esa mujer se abandonó a sí misma' " (p. 103). In "Vida de perros" (*Versos de salón*) we see the following: "El hogar es un campo de batalla. / La mujer se defiende con las piernas" (p. 98).

In other poems extremely positive attitudes toward female family members are present. "Catalina Parra" (*Poemas y antipoemas*) is a nostalgic and affectionate poem about the poet's daughter. "Defensa de Violeta Parra" (*Otros poemas*) is a poem of praise, admiration, and respect for the poet's sister, the most positively drawn female in any of Parra's poems.

Two poems from *Poemas y antipoemas* provide a strange contrast with the others analyzed to this point. These are "Es olvido" and "Cartas a una desconocida." Their strangeness results from their unusually nostalgic, melancholic, and even somewhat romantic tone, a rarity in Parra's work, though it does appear elsewhere (See "Aromos" and other poems in *Canciones rusas*).

"Es olvido" is a lament on the death of a young girl whom the poet belatedly discovers was in love with him. She is presented in what is almost the classic vocabulary of romantic love poems: she is described as "una joven pálida y sombría" (p. 19), recalling the pale and sad princesses of Darío and others; she is also "una joven triste y pensativa" (p. 20), "múltiple rosa inmaculada," "una lámpara legítima," "una paloma fugitiva" (p. 21). Furthermore, the protagonist's relationship with her is partially expressed in similar tones: "Mas moriré llamándola María" (p. 19), "Y una que otra mención de golondrinas" (p. 20); her death causes ". . . tal desengaño / Que derramé una lágrima al oírla" (p. 19). All of this is not to say that the irony so typical of Parra is not present; the last line cited is followed by "Una lágrima, sí, ¡quién lo creyera! / Y eso que soy persona de energía" (p. 19). The poem is really a mixture of romantic and ironic elements.

Significantly, the protagonist affirms that for him this relationship meant little or nothing, for he cannot even remember the girl's real name. He indeed insists on this point:

> Debo creer, sin vacilar un punto,
> Que murió con mi nombre en las pupilas,
> Hecho que me sorprende, porque nunca
> Fue para mi otra cosa que una amiga
> . . . .
> . . . jamás vi en ella otro destino
> Que el de una joven triste y pensativa.
> . . . .
> Puede ser que una vez la haya besado
> ¡Quién es el que no besa a sus amigas!
> Pero tened presente que lo hice
> Sin darme cuenta bien de lo que hacía.
> No negaré, eso sí, que me gustaba
> Su inmaterial y vaga compañía
> . . . .
> Mas, a pesar de todo, es necesario
> Que comprendan que yo no la quería (pp. 19-20).

Aside from noting that her importance to him, and indeed his vision of her as a person, is rather limited, we may conclude that this is basically another example of a failure of communication. The girl offers him love and happiness, but he does not see it until it is too late.[12] The protagonist actually admits this frustrated communication in the line "Nada más que palabras y palabras" (p. 20). The fact that he has forgotten her, "Como todas las cosas de la vida" (p. 21) is a sad reflection of the transitory nature of human experience. Another melancholic and semi-romantic poem is the short "Cartas a una desconocida."

> Cuando pasen los años, cuando pasen
> Los años y el aire haya cavado un foso
> Entre tu alma y la mía; cuando pasen los años
> Y yo sólo sea un hombre que amó, un ser que se detuvo
> Un instante frente a tus labios,
> Un pobre hombre cansado de andar por los jardines,
> ¿Dónde estarás tú? ¡Dónde
> Estarás, oh hija de mis besos! (p. 33).

The title is important, for the woman is "una desconocida." The speaker's contact with her was brief, he does not really know her, and he sees that time and distance will destroy even his memory of her. The use of the word "foso" recalls the abyss of poems such as "Recuerdos de juventud"; the combined effect of the presentation of the unknown woman and the abyss again suggests isolation and non-communication. And the activity of "walking through gardens" reminds the reader of the aimless pursuits of the various protagonists elsewhere. Finally, the reader notes that in spite of the tone of the poem, the language is generally commonplace rather than elevated, contrasting with the usual language of love poetry. Therefore Parra here complements the view seen previously by emphasizing the mediocrity of human communication and feeling and the hopelessness of aspiring to the ideal of a lasting love relationship.

To expand the discussion of our subject, reference could be made to many other poems from Parra's later works. However, most of these poems deal with the same attitudes already discussed, although the particular treatment may vary the stress. One poem that should be examined is "Mujeres" *(Versos de salón).* This poem exemplifies the tendency to define women according to a limited or narrow framework; here they are categorized on the basis of their sexual attitudes or sexual behavior, or simply on the basis of appearance.

> La mujer imposible,
> La mujer de dos metros de estatura,
> La señora de mármol de Carrara
> Que no fuma ni bebe,
> La mujer que no quiere desnudarse
> Por temor a quedar embarazada,
> La vestal intocable
> Que no quiere ser madre de familia

> . . . .
> La que sólo se entrega por amor
> La doncella que mira con un ojo,
> La que sólo se deja poseer
> En el diván, al borde del abismo,
> La que odia los órganos sexuales,
> La que se une sólo con su perro,
> La mujer que se hace la dormida (pp. 83-84).

While there is considerable variation in the types presented, this is of course a limited and limiting view of women as people.[13]

A related motive in Parra's poetry is that of the search for some type of "ideal" woman, a search which is inevitably frustrated. (In the poem "Vida de perros" in *Versos de salón*, the poet cries "¡Dónde encontrar a la mujer precisa!"). It is never really clear what this ideal might be; it is certainly neither the aggressive, manipulating woman nor the submissive virgin. At the end of "Mujeres" the poet indicates his frustration and his ultimate inability to deal with any of the women he has described in such limiting and stereotypical terms.

> Todas estas walkirias[14]
> Todas estas matronas respetables
> Con sus labios mayores y menores
> Terminarán sacándome de quicio (p. 84).

The dislike—or even fear—of the sexually aggressive woman and the resultant impotence of the male are also present in "Mujeres,"[15] where the poet rejects

> La mujer que camina
> Virgen hacia la cámara nupcial
> Pero que reacciona como hombre (p. 83).

This idea is also very clear in "Conversación galante" *(Versos de salón)*, where the woman is the aggressor and the man is incapable of responding: "—Pero entonces, ¿por qué no reaccionas? / Tócalos, aproveca la ocasión. / —No me gusta tocarlos a la fuerza" (p. 85). And finally, "Cartas del poeta que duerme en una silla" *(Otros poemas)* presents a disguised statement of this attitude in the form of a dream. (Note the references to death, physical and mental suffering, war, and insanity.)

> Toda la noche sueño con mujeres
> Unas se ríen ostensiblemente de mí
> Otras me dan el golpe del conejo.
> No me dejan en paz.
> Están en guerra permanente conmigo.
>
> Me levanto con cara de trueno.

De lo que se deduce que estoy loco
O por lo menos que estoy muerto de susto (p. 178).

Other important poems are (1) "Se me ocurren ideas luminosas" (*Versos de salón*, pp. 89-90), where the emphasis is on role playing and the failure of verbal and sexual communication; (2) "La doncella y la muerte" (*Versos de salón*, pp. 82-83), which pictures woman as *femme fatale* or temptress and associates sexuality with death; and (3) "Como les iba diciendo" (*Emergency Poems*, p. 4), in which the protagonist brags of his sexual prowess.

It is hardly necessary to state that this is a generally dreadful picture of love and sex and women. In the world of Parra's poetry, love is impossible, sex is frustrating, and the women presented are certainly not people one would want to have relationships with. A superficial reader might dismiss these attitudes as misogynic, sick, perverted, or whatever; it is also possible, of course, that the reader might identify with these attitudes. Their dismissal is not so easy when they are taken in the total context of Parra's poetry. In fact, an understanding of these attitudes as an integral part of the poet's larger vision does much to clarify exactly what this vision is.

Parra's poetry presents a profoundly critical attack on the decaying world we live in and the poverty of the values we live by. Humanity in general is seen as being imprisoned by its cherished attitudes and mental habits, by its faulty perception of reality, and by its inability to communicate its despair or take positive action to remedy the situation. As José M. Ibáñez-Langlois aptly states:

> Los poemas de Nicanor Parra, en su caótico flujo, subvierten inveterados hábitos mentales de nuestra herencia filosófica, cultural, política. Toda una visión convencional del mundo, toda una estructura lógica del pensamiento, todo un edificio verbal que sustenta el orden establecido, todo un conjunto de seguridades tácitas que defienden el "paraíso del pequeño burgués", es revelado en su vacuidad y corroído desde su interior por el impacto de las descargas antipoéticas.[16]

As this quotation indicates, Parra employs a varied arsenal of weapons in his attack. Perhaps the most powerful of these are his use of irony and occasionally parody and the use of colloquial, anti-metaphorical language rather than traditionally "poetic" language.[17] Both of these techniques serve to demythologize or deflate the importance of traditional habits of thought, patterns of behavior, and values.

To accomplish this poetic deflation Parra first signals his targets. This paper has analyzed one such target: the attitudes toward women, sex, and love. This and other targets are catalogued in the poem "Los vicios del mundo moderno" *(Poemas y antipoemas)*:

> Los vicios del mundo moderno:
> El automóvil y el cine sonoro,
> Las discriminaciones raciales,
> El exterminio de los pieles rojas,
> Los trucos de la alta banca,
> La catástrofe de los ancianos,
> . . . .
> El auto-erotismo y la crueldad sexual
> . . . .
> El endiosamiento del falo,
> . . . .
> La destrucción de los ídolos,
> . . . .
> Las gotas de sangre que suelen encontrarse entre las sábanas de los recién desposados (pp. 48-49).

In sum, Parra's vision takes on all our cherished myths, our political and financial institutions, our social behavior, and even the gadgets, conveniences, and diversions of our daily life.

Parra's treatment of the subject of love and women has been seen to present, or at least allude to, the myth of the Fall, the impossibility of experiencing romantic love, and the stereotyping of both the male and the female along traditional lines. The use of the myth of the Fall is particularly revealing. In this myth and related ones such as that of Pandora's box, the female is assigned the unenviable role of being the cause of human suffering, knowledge, and sin. It is still an important foundation of our sexual attitudes, as is witnessed by the popular conception of the *femme fatale*, the sexual temptress.[18] These attitudes are clearly present in poems such as "La víbora." Nevertheless, Parra deflates the validity of this myth by revealing his protagonists to be at least partially responsible for their own suffering. In other words, the evil female is no more to blame for the situation than the man.

The myth of romantic love is also destroyed by its negative presentation. The use of irony, of hackneyed colloquial language, and the stress on the motives of failed communication, distance, and sexual frustration demonstrate the emptiness of traditional love as a form of human communion. This point is related to the stereotyping of male and female behavior. The playing of traditional sexual roles, roles that are defined by the stereotypes, is shown to be ultimately negative, for such roles are clearly very limiting. For example, if woman conforms to the ideal of physical and intellectual passivity, thereby casting the male in the role of the aggressor, her destiny is to be raped and the male becomes a rapist. If the reverse occurs, and woman becomes the aggressor, the male is left impotent. Neither of these is satisfactory, of course, and there is the strong suggestion that sexual role playing is closely linked to disastrous male-female relationships.

Most importantly, Parra's critical vision even attacks our ways of thinking about the world and analyzing our experience. Our "inveterados hábitos mentales" and our "estructura lógica del pensamiento" referred to by Ibáñez-Langlois are systematically undermined in poems such as "Siegmund Freud" *(Otros poemas)*. The particular point of this poem is to challenge the tendency in our culture to view the world in psychoanalytic terms, e.g., our exaggerated ability to see phallic symbols and the like everywhere. After a masterful parody in which the poet lists the numerous phallic possibilities, he concludes the poem with a section referring to himself visiting a factory in China and relating all he sees to sex organs. The use of the words "delirar" and "locura" (p. 162) indicates the distortion of reality resulting from reliance on this or any limited mode of thought. The end of the poem openly asserts that it is futile to try to understand human experience in such terms and that the system will eventually bring on its own destruction:

El laberinto no tiene salida.

El Occidente es una gran pirámide
Que termina y empieza en una psiquiatra:
La pirámide está por derrumbarse (p. 163).

The realization that even one's way of thinking is being challenged has a disconcerting effect on the reader of Parra's poems. We realize that we too are caught in the trap of conventional thinking. This problem certainly affects the analysis presented here, for it has been difficult to avoid speaking in terms of "themes" and "motives" and other traditional literary jargon. The references to sexual symbolism (for example, the female symbolism of the tunnel) were consciously made with tongue in cheek, for one wonders if the poet has not intentionally laid a trap for the reader by using such symbols.

A final question to examine is whether or not the poet presents any solution. The world is in a shambles, humanity is trapped by its conventions, and we are on the verge of self-destruction. Is there any hope? It might be claimed that the mere perception of the human situation, the acceptance of it, and the insight into the reasons for it, represent a type of hope: in other words, that knowledge and

understanding are the first step in a cure. But we have seen that for
the poet our supposed "knowledge" and "understanding" are actually part of the trap, so the answer must basically be negative.

Ibáñez-Langlois presents a convincing argument for viewing
the religious questioning of Parra's poems as a possible element of
hope.[19] But, as this critic also notes, in poems such as "La cruz"
(La camisa de fuerza), religious revelation is a future possibility,
not a present hope for the solution of humanity's dilemma.

One poem that seems to offer an immediate solution is "Los
vicios del mundo moderno":

> Tratemos de ser felices, recomiendo yo, chupando la miserable
>   costilla humana.
> Extraigamos de ella el líquido renovador,
> Cada cual de acuerdo con sus inclinaciones personales.
> ¡Aferrémonos a esta piltrafa divina!
> Jadeantes y tremebundos
> Chupemos estos labios que nos enloquecen;
> La suerte está echada.
> Aspiremos este perfume enervador y destructor
> Y vivamos un día más la vida de los elegidos:
> De sus axilas extrae el hombre la cera necesaria para forjar el
>   rostro de sus ídolos.
> Y del sexo de la mujer la paja y el barro de sus templos (pp. 50-51).

Edith Grossman has suggested that this is a somewhat sardonic
description of women (i.e., sex) as the salvation of humanity.[20] It is
certainly sardonic, but it is difficult to see that "salvation" is the
goal, especially for the female half of humanity. Rather, this would
seem to be simply a desperate recipe for male survival, for, after all,
"la suerte está echada."

This section of the poem has also been seen to suggest that
humanity simply try to maintain the illusion of happiness by clinging to what it has, impoverished and rotten as it is, and by continu-
ing to "suck" and "extract" from life all that it has to offer. Implicit
in this extraction is the continuation of the exploitation of others.[21]

However, the sexual references are too clear to ignore (or perhaps, again, too clear to take seriously!). The "costilla humana" can
be seen to refer to woman by association with the Biblical story of
the creation of Eve from Adam's rib. The subsequent references to
sucking on "maddening lips" and to breathing the "enervating and
destructive perfume" also appear to be female references. And finally, the statement that man extracts the straw and mud for his temples
from woman's sex is the clearest reference to the exploitation of
women, and suggests to this reader the often observed common-

place that men, not women, create our official culture; woman is seen as being creative only through the product of her sexuality. Therefore this solution to the dilemma is also a false one, at least as long as humanity clings to its condition so tenaciously. Perhaps, then, the only true hope for Parra is in the destruction of this condition, in the "crumbling of the pyramid." But no, for we are told in "Soliloquio del individuo" (*Poemas y antipoemas*) that this is a vain wish:

> Mejor es tal vez que vuelva a ese valle,
> A esa roca que me sirvió de hogar,
> Y empiece a grabar de nuevo,
> De atrás para adelante grabar
> El mundo al revés.
> Pero no: la vida no tiene sentido (p. 56).

In the end, then, the only hope for Parra would seem to be the acceptance of the situation ("la vida no tiene sentido") and the ability to laugh, or at least smile, at the insanity of it all.

> Por todo lo cual
> Cultivo un piojo en mi corbata
> Y sonrío a los imbéciles que bajan de los árboles.
> "Los vicios del mundo moderno," p. 51.

EASTERN MICHIGAN UNIVERSITY

Notes

[1]In this paper, quotations in Spanish from Parra's works are taken from *Obra gruesa* (Santiago de Chile: Editorial Universitaria, S.A., 1969). Page references refer to this edition. Where brief phrases have been cited in English, I have used *Poems and Antipoems*, ed. Miller Williams (New York: New Directions, 1967) and *Emergency Poems*, trans. Miller Williams (New York: New Directions, 1972).

[2]José M. Ibáñez-Langlois, "Prólogo," *Antipoemas* (Barcelona: Editorial Seix Barral, S.A., 1972), p. 46.

[3]In discussing the attitudes toward women, love, and sex in Parra's works, I have intentionally avoided speaking of the "poet's" attitudes; I maintain that they are not *necessarily* Parra's attitudes but rather those of the *personae* who people his poetic world and specifically those who "speak" the individual poems. Elsewhere I have shown that Parra speaks to us wearing a variety of masks, and therefore it is extremely risky to make any biographical affirmations, though it is sometimes possible and revealing. Therefore, it is the varying and occasionally contradictory attitudes of these *personae* that will be analyzed in this paper. For a discussion

of this question see my article "The *Artefactos* of Nicanor Parra: The Explosion of the Antipoem," *The Bilingual Review*, I, 1 (Jan.-Apr. 1974), pp. 76-80.

[4]Leonidas Morales T., *La poesía de Nicanor Parra* (Santiago de Chile: Coedición de la Univ. Austral de Chile y Ed. Andrés Bello, 1972), p. 76.

[5]Among the studies that deal with Parra's use of colloquial language are: Edith Grossman, *The Antipoetry of Nicanor Parra* (New York: New York Univ. Press, 1975), passim; Marlene Gottlieb, *No se termina nunca de nacer: La poesía de Nicanor Parra* (Madrid: Playor, Col. Nova Scholar, 1977), pp. 118-26; and Federico Schopf, "Prólogo," *Poemas y antipoemas* (Santiago de Chile: Editorial Nascimento, 1971), pp. 30-33.

[6]For Parra's use of irony, see Ibáñez-Langlois, "Prólogo," pp. 16-25, and Grossman, *Antipoetry*, passim.

[7]Kate Millet, *Sexual Politics* (New York: Avon Books, 1971), p. 53.

[8]Edith Grossman, "The Technique of Antipoetry," *Review* (Center for Inter-American Relations), Winter 1971-Spring 1972, p. 82.

[9]Ibid.

[10]Ibid., p. 78.

[11]Ibid.

[12]Schopf, "Prólogo," pp. 21-22.

[13]Erica Jong, in her poetry collection entitled *Half-Lives* (New York: Holt Rinehart & Winston, 1973), p. 38, has penned a response to Parra's poem "Mujeres" which through its humorous and exaggeratedly stereotypical portrait of men points out even more forcefully the limitations of such a view of women:

Men
(after a poem called "Women" by Nicanor Parra)

The impossible man
The man with the ebony penis ten feet tall
The man of pentelikon marble
The man with the veined bronze figleaf which comes unhinged
The man who's afraid to get pregnant
The man who screws in his socks

. . . .

The man who gets married a virgin
The man who marries a virgin
The man who wilts out of guilt

. . . .

All these Adonises
All these respectable gents
Those descended
& those undescended
will drive me out of my skull sooner or later.

[14]"Walkirias" refers to the mythic maidens who choose the heroes to be slain in battle and then conduct them to Valhalla: another association of women and death.

[15]Gottlieb, *La poesía de Nicanor Parra*, p. 110.

[16]Ibáñez-Langlois, "Prólogo," p. 20.

[17]Ibid., pp. 17, 22.

[18]Millet, *Sexual Politics*, p. 52.

[19]Ibáñez-Langlois, "Prólogo," pp. 35-43.

[20]Grossman, *Antipoetry*, p. 128.

[21]Schopf, "Prólogo," p. 35.

HACIA UN ANALISIS FEMINISTA DE
TRES TRISTES TIGRES

Eliana Rivero

Preámbulo necesario

Gran parte de la atención que hoy día se presta a la perspectiva feminista en las artes se centra en el rescate de la obra "oculta" de la mujer, artista y autora literaria que ha sido innumerables veces excluida de historias, antologías y colecciones. Los textos existentes son en muchas ocasiones culpables de pecados de omisión, porque su recopilación y esbozo dejan fuera a toda una serie de autoras cuya producción—de menor o mayor magnitud— ayuda a componer lo que son la sensibilidad y la posibilidad literarias y culturales del período histórico en cuestión.

Por otra parte, la obra artística se juzga de acuerdo a una visión masculina del mundo y de la sociedad, y así muchas escritoras son soslayadas por representar "lo femenino", en oposición a la reconocida transcendencia de la preocupación "humana" (léase "preconizada por autores del sexo masculino"). Quién lo negaría: al definir su mundo y su propio ser, la mujer artista debe enfrentarse a una conciencia masculina que ha sido históricamente igualada a la conciencia *humana*.[1] De ahí que la crítica feminista, en su proyección teórica, necesite abordar un proyecto contestatario: un arte y una observación crítica que expongan lo esencial de la condición humana, y que no continúen la propagación de falsas ideologías, i.e., la imperante en un sistema organizado sobre valores exclusivamente masculinos.[2]

Precisamente en ello consiste el a veces no bien definido *feminismo* de esta nueva crítica: en ir más allá de la diferente temática, perspectiva y aspectos formales de la escritura, y considerar el texto literario tal y como éste revela las relaciones hombre-mujer en un contexto socioeconómico, esa red de expectativas en que las mujeres se encuentran situadas con respecto al papel que deben desempeñar en la sociedad. Con este fin, el feminismo no puede ser simplemente otro aspecto de la crítica burguesa "vestido de mujer"; debe ser crítica ideológica y moral, revolucionaria.[3] La metodología feminista debe enfocar la cultura de manera radical, siempre en conciencia de que ésta es y siempre ha sido el privilegiado reino de las visiones masculinas. Claro que, como se puede apreciar en un acertado análisis ideológico, la exclusión y la distorsión de las mujeres en la literatura y en las artes son compartidas por los hombres que no pertenecen a la burguesía de la llamada "raza blanca"; de manera que la perspectiva proyectada por la ideología dominante resulta ser una estrecha visión sexista y racista de la realidad, hasta ahora admitida como "natural" en sus implicaciones opresivas, y que soslaya la labor cultural de significativos sectores de la sociedad humana.

El otro aspecto importante de un enfoque integral es corolario al rescate de las mujeres creadoras. Pero aun más que éste, se centra en el análisis de modelos distorsionados; vale decir, en el examen del personaje femenino creado a base de una ideología exclusivamente masculina, y en la visión de la realidad que tal creación conlleva—las relaciones sociojerárquicas y personales entre el hombre y la mujer. En la ficción del texto narrativo tradicional, la mujer se ha visto primero como *femenina*, y en segundo plano como *humana*; pero esta definición de "lo femenino" depende de la idealización o tergiversación masculinas del ser humano de otro sexo, y la heroína novelesca es más frecuentemente juzgada en cuanto logro o traición de aquella visión idealista. En realidad, este punto sólo puede ser plenamente discutido a la luz de la cuestión humanista, que considera la realización total del ser; pero hasta ahora, en el canon tradicional, dicha consideración ha sido reservada solamente al héroe o personaje masculino. A nuestro modo de ver, una creación que presuponga la aceptación incuestionable del *status quo*, y aun lo exalte descriptivamente en un ambiente degradado, se opone a la esencia misma de lo humano—sea éste masculino o femenino:

> Women and men alike, real or fictional, must be judged not by their fulfillment of preconceived and sex-based models, but by the degree of their humanity, by the extent to which they betray or fulfill the self. Only then may the scholar truly become the humanist.[4]

La razón de la sinrazón

La crítica tradicional tacha no pocas veces de sinsentido, o valora negativamente, un estudio como el que aquí se sugiere. Arguye que la buena caracterización, la creación creíble y completa de un ente imaginario no tiene nada que ver con la masculinidad o la feminidad. Sin embargo, el análisis serio de hoy día se obliga cada vez más a la redefinición conceptual y metodológica del problema.[5]

Sería una solemne perogrullada decir que *los* novelistas logran crear buenos personajes femeninos; siglos de narrativa han demostrado esa posibilidad hasta el exceso. Pero lo que aquí se plantea es realmente otro problema: si la calificación de *bueno*, o bien logrado, personaje (que obviamente conlleva un juicio valorativo fundado en patrones estéticos tradicionales) obedece a normas ideológicas que transmiten una visión incompleta de la mujer o del hombre como ser pensante y realizable. Las mujeres personajes de Norman Mailer, por ejemplo, serían ilustración concreta de esa "buena" y distorsionada caracterización; distorsión que, desde luego, perpetúa dentro de la visión básica de la obra un conglomerado de actitudes estereotipadas sobre la mujer. Lo mismo podría afirmarse, con respecto a la narrativa hispanoamericana de las últimas décadas, sobre los personajes femeninos de un Vargas Llosa, de un Onetti o de un Sábato. Dichas actitudes típicamente masculinas han sido internalizadas por el escritor, en su condición de ser inmerso en una cultura patentemente sexista, y después han sido expresadas por el discurso artístico, acto comunicativo que de alguna forma transmite y utiliza—ya "literarizadas"—las experiencias del autor.[6]

Por otra parte, y ya esto es menos aceptable para algunos, se impone cuestionarse si de veras esas "buenas" caracterizaciones lo son. Para decidir este álgido punto, habría que aplicar criterios divergentes: uno que definiría al personaje dentro del conjunto de relaciones internas a la obra, otorgándole relevancia en el interior del universo ficticio, y sólo en él; y otro criterio que lo asociaría en parte al sustrato sociocultural que, desde fuera y por analogía, da base referencial y coherente a ese mundo creado por la ficción. En tanto que el personaje se proyecta engarzado en un esquema de valores innegablemente vivos en nuestra cultura, y en cuanto esa caracterización insufla vida a esos modelos dentro de la obra literaria, la llamaríamos "buena" en el sentido tradicional. Pero en la medida en que las caracterizaciones sólo utilizan rasgos que parcialmente definen a un ser humano, que lo dibujan en perspectiva caricaturesca o resaltadora de líneas clásicamente estereotipadas, hay que

señalar dentro del análisis crítico la perpetuación de mitos que—
como las estadísticas—encierran una corta expresión de verdad en
sus generalizaciones y una considerable dosis de falsedad en los
casos particulares. O sea: que si el concepto de personaje bien logrado depende de su proceso de desarrollo dentro de la acción narrativa, de cómo se da al lector en potencialidad múltiple, de cuán eficaz
es para expresar la ambigüedad y conflictos de su mundo, pero a la
vez depende *también* de su capacidad de ser algo más que figura
unidimensional en relación a categorías complejamente humanas,
entonces el crítico se verá obligado a reformular su concepto de
caracterización. Que el escritor adapte los patrones culturales do-
minantes al construir un objeto artístico, y que los entregue como
parte integral de la visión del texto, no es sorprendente; pero aun
cuando ocurra la mejor captación estética por parte del autor, sus
figuras no son necesariamente creaciones de verdadero valor huma-
nístico. Es decir: que no otorgan la misma gama de posibilidades
vitales al personaje femenino que al masculino.

¿Es el rutinario desarrollo del personaje mujer, con limitación
de opciones, una *visión dinámica del infinito potencial humano*,
condición *sine qua non* a la obra literaria de significación universal?
Si la clásica amplitud de carácter del héroe narrativo es una composición de expectativas históricas, a la vez que un patrón de posibilidades del ser de volición y pensamiento, ¿qué representa la estrechez
evolutiva de la heroína en tanto que cifra de realización personal?[7]
La respuesta a estos interrogantes queda parcialmente en suspenso,
porque el arte todavía se encuentra distanciado de un logro que de-
fienda la integridad del ser humano contra toda degradación y toda
distorsión. Pero la crítica, si bien de primeriza intención cabal en
estas páginas, puede (y debe) comenzar a dar cuenta de una plasma-
ción literaria que cumpla a medias con la verdad más legítima del
hombre—y de la mujer.

Las mujeres del juego

Estos párrafos de breve alcance se proponen dar un resumen
de cómo la visión de ese secreto mundo nocturno, en cuyo espacio
se mueven los tristes tigres de Cabrera Infante, ofrece una distorsionada realización de personajes en general, y de cómo los femeninos, si bien centro vital en los diálogos de personajes-narradores
masculinos y presentes a todo lo largo de la obra, no son figuras de
acción y ni siquiera—en la mayoría de los casos—de habla propia
determinante. Desde la perspectiva de las figuras femeninas, in-

mersas en situaciones sociales definidas por su sexualidad, no se percibe sino una multitud de relaciones fragmentarias y aun caóticas.

Pero lo que hace que estas caracterizaciones sean notablemente unilaterales no es en sí el hecho de que constituyan tipos sexuales y sociales; lo que sucede es que la visión global de la realidad creada en *Tres tristes tigres* nos deja con un cuadro lúdico en cuyo marco sólo parecen caber la nostalgia y el vago deseo de perpetuar—en el recuerdo—esa ciudad de noche con sus excesos, sus vicios, sus locuras, sus normas de conducta. Es en ese panorama último de apreciación, en esa visión definitiva percibida en la totalidad del discurso, donde el lector no encuentra ningún elemento que haga entender como indeseable el sistema de valores puesto en escena (y en práctica) por los personajes eje de la acción y complementado por las figuras femeninas.

En las 451 páginas de la novela aparecen diecinueve figuras y/o voces de mujer, cuya relevancia al desarrollo del discurso narrativo es de diversa índole (no consideramos sino incidentales a las dieciocho que solamente aparecen nombradas, vagamente descritas, por otros personajes y narradores).[8] La principal es Laura Díaz,[9] quien amada por dos de los "tigres" no figura sino fantasmagóricamente en los relatos en primera persona de Silvestre y de Arsenio Cué. Es ésta la mujer psicoanalizada, sin nombre,[10] cuyos once diálogos unilaterales con su psiquiatra van atando hilos claves al proceso interior de los personajes masculinos y su búsqueda errabunda. En dichos once fragmentos se va revelando sutilmente el trauma causado por la violación de Laura cuando niña, hecho perpetrado por su padrastro, y se da una indicación de conclusiones futuras por medio de continuas referencias al marido escritor (recordemos que los diálogos entre Arsenio Cué y Silvestre terminan con la confesión del último de que se va a casar con Laura). Otras tres figuras de mujer tienen importancia en el mundo nocturno de los tigres: Estrella Rodríguez, la Ballena negra, monumental gorda cocinera que llega a la fama cantando boleros con "feeling"; Cuba Venegas (Gloria Pérez), "la Puta Nacional", vedette, cantante y modelo de anuncios de cerveza; y Vivian Smith-Corona, la "niña de sociedad" que entrega su virginidad a un jovencito confuso para ayudarle con sus problemas de inseguridad. Las tres comparten dosis fluctuantes de sexualidad, sea reprimida o sin freno, y constituyen focos de atracción para el escritor, el músico y el actor—los tres tigres. Otras nueve figuras femeninas hacen espóradicos actos de presencia en el relato de los narradores masculinos: ocho son mujeres de la noche, coristas, modelos, "puntos fáciles", de tendencias bisexuales o francamente lesbianas (Irenita, Raquelita-Manolito el Toro, Sibila, Livia, Mirtila, Ingrid Bérgamo, Helena la hebrea, Pepe). La novena es la madre de Aurelita, niña que hace "cositas" con una narradora infantil. Las voces esporádicas, desde cuyo punto de vista se estructura un fragmento de texto (sea escrito o monologado), son tres: Delia Doce, mujer campesina, semianalfabeta, cuya carta informa a la madre de Cuba Venegas sobre la vida desordenada de la hija; Mrs. Campbell, la mujer del norteamericano cuyo bastón origina un cuento relatado seis veces con variaciones, y la cual disfruta los espectáculos "porno" de La Habana nocturna; y la vieja loca del epílogo, que con fuerte vocabulario escatológico expresa sus obsesiones y manías sexo-religiosas. Hay otras tres voces femeninas que aparecen una sola vez, hablando desde el interior de las figuras, pero éstas son después incorporadas como menciones en el discurso de algún narrador: la niña (sin nombre), amiga de Aurelita; Magdalena Cruz (Magalena Crús), "punto fácil", bisexual, concubina de un anunciador radial; y Beba Longoria, la vulgar esposa de un general de patio.

Como se observa, no existe una sola figura femenina que no se halle, directa o indirectamente, perfilada en relación a su interés o conducta sexual, sea como actor o como espectador-*voyeur*. Aun las niñas, excitadas por el espectáculo de unos novios indiscretos, "hacen cositas" debajo de un camión. Las tres madres de la trama (las de Cuba Venegas, Petra Cabrera y la narradora-niña) sólo hablan a sus hijas, o sobre ellas, en relación a patrones de conducta sexual; la tercera, divertida por los chismes que su hija cuenta acerca de Petra Cabrera y el novio, hace gala ante el pueblo entero de los relatos subidos de color que tan bien detalla la muchachita. Por otra parte, los personajes masculinos principales, a pesar de que hacen del sexo y el erotismo un importante renglón de su rejuego, se realizan en discursos que los proyectan como poseedores de una vasta cultura "pop" y literaria, de una capacidad lingüística que les permite ampliar su horizonte. Sus oficios u ocupaciones tienen relación directa con las artes; y esto les otorga, nominalmente al menos, categoría válida (aunque, por supuesto, el conjunto de los tigres y su limitada "cultura del ocio" proyecta asimismo una perspectiva distorsionada de la realidad humana en un país de graves problemas sociales). Por contraste, en toda la novela se hacen solamente dos vagas menciones a figuras femeninas con ocupación profesional de alguna seriedad: la recitadora Minerva Eros y una maestra de historia, Virginia Ubría o Hubris o Ubres. Además de la broma sarcástica de sus nombres, la primera atrae al público por "su decir suave y acariciador" y su "figura escultural",[11] mientras que la segunda ha dejado su puesto para dedicarse a la prostitución. Los hombres son conocedores de literatura, música, cinematografía y arte (Silvestre, Arsenio Cué, Eribó y Códac son escritor, actor, músico y fotógrafo, respectivamente), mientras las mujeres son tontas de inseguridad ignorante:

> . . . *es seguro uno de los amigos intelectuales de Arsen ¿no?* Sí digo yo *él es Silvestre Isla, el autor de Por quién doblan las esquinas.* La amiga de Livia es entrometida, para su desgracia: *Ay* dice *¿no es Las campanas?* Sí digo yo *también escribió ésa que es la primera parte.* Dice la amiga *¿De verdá?* hablando más bien con Silvestre. *De verdá* dice Silvestre con su cara de palo (p. 141).

En la trayectoria de juerga y *tour de force* lingüístico que recorren los "tigres", las mujeres quedan—sin excepción—fuera de las actividades paraintelectuales,[12] incluso sin entender nada del idioma de los apartes: "to esa habladera en inglé y sin titulito" (p. 374). En la extensa sección titulada "Bachata", donde Arsenio Cué y Silvestre recogen en su automóvil a Beba y Magalena y las asustan con un exhibicionismo de ingenio y de lenguaje que sustituye al sexo, se las declara incapaces de los estimulantes pasatiempos de los hombres:

> El juego terminó, pero nada más que para nosotros. Para ellas nunca comenzó y solamente lo jugamos Arsenio Cué y yo. Las ninfas miraban con ojos ciegos a la noche dentro de la noche del bar. Women! dijo Arsenio. De no existir habría sido preciso inventar a Dios para que las creara (p. 391).

Sin embargo, cuando en caso raro una mujer escribe o habla de forma menos común, literaria o retóricamente, se la ridiculiza a ella y al género femenino en su totalidad:

> . . . entonces y el telegrama del estribo de Amapola del Campo, Dios mío qué seudónimo, el telegrama un día azul y ahora amarillo que todavía dice en un español aprendido por radio: el tiempo y la distancia me hacen comprender que te he perdido: escribir eso, señores del jurado, y dárselo al hombre del telégrafo en Bayamo ¿no demuestra que las mujeres o están todas locas o tienen más cojones que Maceo y su caballo heroico? (p. 223).

Tales comentarios generalizadores y ultrasexistas, que atribuyen a la mujer nada de cerebro y, si se muestran decididas, la dotan de órganos masculinos, hallan eco en numerosas instancias del discurso de los narradores. Por ejemplo, al referirse a la confesión de Vivian Smith-Corona sobre su desfloración, le comenta Cué a Silvestre:

> . . . Las mujeres dicen siempre mentiras. Todas . . . diciendo una verdad que necesita su templo, que en la mujer han estado escon-

didos durante mucho tiempo un esclavo y un tirano, que en el mejor de los casos es una vaca. Eksakto. Vacas, chivas, animales sin alma. Una especie inferior (p. 432).

Otra vez en "Bachata", al divisar por la calle a Beba y a Magdalena, el siguiente diálogo y monólogo interior ocurren mezclados:

—¿De veras la conoces?
—Sí viejo sí. Códac me la presentó.
—Esas mujeres no se presentan, se regalan.
Iban por la esquina. Era bien ella, ¿cómo se llamaba? Seguro con una amiga. Le amiche. The tits of lovelyness. Bixfocales. Se dice tetralogía, trilogía y hasta pentalogía si alguien se atreve a llegar a cinco. ¿Se dirá sexología para las seis obras? ¿Biología? Dice Freud que a las mujeres primitivas como a los niños se les puede inducir a cualquier experiencia sexual. No dijo subdesarrolladas. No las conocía . . . (p. 364).

Y en una instancia de narrador femenino, la voz de Mrs. Campbell habla de lo que su marido opina que es el prototipo de la mujer común: "un ser inválido, con el IQ de un morón y la oportunidad de un acreedor a la cabecera de un moribundo" (p. 182). Aseveraciones como éstas, esparcidas a través de todo el libro, no sólo dan por sentado como aceptable el humor grotesco de la misoginia cultural, sino que entronizan la representación del personaje femenino como dependiente, atado a su sexualidad, incapaz de actividad alguna que no esté relacionada a una afirmación de identidad por medio del sexo.[13]

Desde otro ángulo, si consideramos a los personajes narrativos en relación al acontecer del texto, las figuras de mujer son todas secundarias o incidentales en *Tres tristes tigres*, ya que—sin desempeñar un papel decisivo importante en el desarrollo de la acción—proporcionan un mayor grado de coherencia y consistencia al relato o cumplen una función catalítica que entraba y relaciona, ampliándolo, tal desarrollo. Por otra parte, si pensamos en el desenvolvimiento de dicho acontecer, las figuras femeninas son planas, dadas por un solo rasgo dominante, un solo atributo, una sola faceta del existir. Así, muchas de las pseudofiguras que se nombran en el relato de los tigres (las dieciocho mencionadas) son personajes tipo, estáticos y caricaturescos, descritos de un solo plumazo: Nena la Chiquita, "vieja encogida y sin dientes y sucia, y con un insaciable apetito sexual" (p. 39); Lesbia Dumois, una "generosa puta de quince años" (p. 36); y doña Lala, "la dadivosa y vieja y casi venerada mantenida del triple héroe: aviador, coronel, político" (p. 36).

Aunque mucha de la crítica rechaza los enfoques valorativos

que en estas páginas se proponen, por considerar la literatura como espacio sagrado donde no se debe entrar con otro propósito que el estético *sensu stricto*,[14] nos arriesgamos aquí a romper unos cuantos linderos de mitificación. Se ha dicho hasta la saciedad que *Tres tristes tigres* es una novela del lenguaje;[15] pero queremos recordar que todo lenguaje, como sistema modelador del universo que contempla, lleva implícita una ordenación de prioridades y de "verdades" aceptadas como tales, plasmadas en la metáfora del modismo y la frase hecha en su caso más ejemplar. De ahí que todo discurso, como instancia de habla, implique un sistema de valores que se da por válido, un orden moral y social jerarquizante que se toma como natural. La voluntad organizadora de la obra, en la subjetividad de la composición y estructuración de las voces y figuras del texto, acepta (o rechaza, si llega a tomar conciencia de su antihumanismo) los patrones del modelo sociocultural y entrega su perspectiva pasiva o crítica, percibida por el lector a través de la visión básica que es la que otorga su verdadera significación a la obra.[16] El mundo creado en *Tres tristes tigres*, representación de una metrópolis visitada por el ocio, los vicios y una cultura imbuida de valores humanamente distorsionados, tiene una gran fuerza impactante en su logro lingüístico, en la ingeniosa trama de los códigos culturales y literarios que entretejen su texto. Pero su visión básica, porque no abre otra vía que la del recuerdo nostálgico y el juego verbal, deja también puerta libre a la crítica del estereotipo y la caracterización grotescamente parcializada de sus personajes femeninos, que a la luz de los criterios aquí expuestos sólo contribuyen a perpetuar y a afianzar los mitos alimentados por una mentalidad retrógrada. La mujer resulta así un específico "objeto de cama y mesa",[17] capaz de esa única función doble que le adscribe la cultura del macho:

> ... y muestra los grandes medios senos redondos que son como las tapas de unas ollas maravillosas que cocinan el único alimento que hace a los hombres dioses, la ambrosía del sexo . . . (p. 278).

Bajo estos términos, gran parte del público lector no podrá cumplir los deseos del novelista, a quien le hubiera gustado "que el libro se tomara como una gran broma escrita".[18] A nosotros, como a muchos otros, nos parece que esa larga broma cae incontables veces en la insensibilidad, si no en un repetido mal gusto que reiteradamente intensifica todas las variedades de la opresión, tanto sexual como clasista. El autor, en su intencionada dedicación a la masculinidad, ha escrito—por admisión propia—"un libro más para hombres que para mujeres".[19] De eso no hay duda: porque tanto el escritor como el crítico masculinos se apropian del mundo, creen absolutamente—como señalaba Beauvoir—que la realidad pertenece al varón. Mientras las mujeres de *Tres tristes tigres* se mueven dentro de un ambiente desordenado en el que medran o son destruidas en función de su "ser hembras", la crítica admite como normal que esa novela sea una aproximación a los "éxtasis" de que se compone la vida: "tomar una taza de café, beberse un *mojito*, reírse a mandíbula batiente con una frase determinada irrepetible, contemplar deslumbrado una 'pierna canela' ". . .[20] actividades que según se aprecia patentemente, corresponden a un ser despreocupado, ocioso, bohemio—y sobre todo, masculino.

Todo lo cual no es óbice, sino más bien acicate, para que otra crítica verdaderamente humanista apunte los fundamentos reales de esa visión, ensimismada en su ensoñadora apología de una cultura "bastarda".[21] El juicio ético se hace en este caso inseparable del juicio estético; la estrecha perspectiva nocturna de la ciudad en eterna fiesta, convertida en júbilo sexual y en "choteo" antillano, se amplía en una integradora revisión de las premisas ideológicas del discurso que la plasma. Y dicha valoración alcanza mucho más que señalar el antihumanismo de las obras consagradas por el canon tradicional. La aplicación de un análisis como el que aquí se propone aclara lo que realmente significa el seguir diciendo: "ese es un libro sexista, pero es *buena* literatura". *Tres tristes tigres* podrá constituir un experimento lúdico para su creador y una visión "normal" de las relaciones humanas para cierto sector de la crítica; pero también habrá entonces que aceptar un descubrimiento objetivo de las reglas (y armas) de ese juego.

UNIVERSITY OF ARIZONA

Notas

[1]"In redefining herself and her world, the woman poet's chief confrontation is with a masculine consciousness which has become synonymous with the human consciousness." Prólogo a Barbara Segnitz and Carol Rainey, eds., *Psyche: The Feminine Poetic Consciousness* (New York: Dell Publishing, 1973), p. 18. Para una discusión más amplia del problema cultural de identidad femenina, véase el capítulo 8, "(Male) Culture", del libro de Shulamith Firestone, *The Dialectic of Sex* (New York: William Morrow, 1970), pp. 156-69, donde apropiadamente se glosa la frase de Simone de Beauvoir: "Representation of the world, like the world

itself, is the work of men; they describe it from their own point of view, which they confuse with absolute truth."

²"Feminist critics, by recognizing ourselves as women, are in the process of balancing that kind of lopsided view of humanity and reality. We are questioning and analyzing the depictions of women and the treatment of women's lives in literature. We are searching for a truly revolutionary art. The content of a given piece need not be feminist, of course, for that piece to be humanist, and therefore revolutionary. Revolutionary art is that which roots out the essentials about the human condition rather than perpetuating false ideologies." Así se expresa Marcia Holly en su ensayo "Consciousness and Authenticity: Toward a Feminist Aesthetic", en Josephine Donovan, ed., *Feminist Literary Criticism. Explorations in Theory* (Lexington: The University of Kentucky Press, 1975), p. 42.

³"To be effective, feminist criticism cannot become simply bourgeois criticism in drag. It must be ideological and moral criticism; it must be revolutionary", según Lillian S. Robinson, "Dwelling in Decencies: Radical Criticism and the Feminist Perspective", *College English*, vol. 32, no. 8 (May 1971), pp. 879 y sigs. Para una discusión más amplia del tema, son útiles los estudios de Annis Pratt, "The New Feminist Criticism", y de Judith H. Montgomery, "The American Galatea", en el mismo tomo de *College English* (pp. 872-78 y 890-99, respectivamente); y el de Annette Kolodny, "Some Notes on Defining a 'Feminist Literary Criticism' ", en *Critical Inquiry*, vol. 2, no. 1 (Autumn 1975), pp. 75-92.

⁴Montgomery, "The American Galatea", p. 899.

⁵Entre los más recientes estudios sobre los problemas literarios anexos a la dicotomía sexual de la cultura, sobresale la excelente discusión de Lucía Guerra-Cunningham en "La mujer latinoamericana ante las letras (algunas reflexiones teóricas sobre la literatura femenina)", *La Semana de Bellas Artes* (México, D.F.), no. 97 (10 de octubre de 1979), pp. 2-5. Este artículo propone una revisión histórico-ideológica de la "visión masculina del mundo" predominante en las artes y en la crítica, y señala pautas para una integral valoración de las letras hispanas a partir de esquemas reconocedores y correctores de dicha visión.

⁶De la copiosa bibliografía al respecto, se destaca la ya clásica "política sexual" examinada por Kate Millet en su devastador análisis de las obras de Norman Mailer, D. H. Lawrence y Henry Miller (*Sexual Politics*, Garden City, N. Y.: Doubleday, 1970). Una ficha relacionada, que interesaría nombrar aquí por su audaz interpretación del problema, es la colección de ensayos titulada "*Sexual Politics, A Marxist Appreciation*", en Linda Jennes, ed., *Feminism and Socialism* (New York: Pathfinder Press, 1972), part III ("The Literary Storm"), pp. 103-28.

⁷Cierto sector de la crítica feminista arguye que el desarrollo "trunco" del personaje femenino es un punto débil de la obra literaria y representa la aceptación de normas culturales masculinas; véase Linda Goul Levine, "María Luisa Bombal from a Feminist Perspective", *Revista/Review Interamericana*, vol. IV, no. 2 ("The Latin American Woman: Image and Reality"), Summer 1974, pp. 148-61.

⁸Son éstas Aurelita, Edith Cabell, Minerva Eros, Virginia Ubría o Hubris, Amapola del Campo, Petra Cabrera, Ciana Cabrera, Elena Burke, las dos Capellas, Balbina, Lesbia Dumois, doña Lala, Olivia la rumbera, Mademoiselle Martín Carol, Yossie Martínez, Nena la Chiquita y Estelvina.

⁹Aunque hay críticos que aseveran que el personaje principal es La Estrella, "who represents spontaneous creativity" (Raymond D. Souza, *Major Cuban Novelists: Innovation and Tradition*, Columbia: University of Missouri Press, 1976, p. 86). En realidad no existe contradicción cuando se piensa que Laura Díaz es

una voz-figura, que funciona *in absentia* de la acción principal con la excepción de dos breves apariciones indirectas en la narración.

[10]El misterio sobre la identidad de este "personaje" queda aclarado por el mismo Cabrera Infante en carta a Emir Rodríguez Monegal del 11 de septiembre de 1968, aclaración que el crítico publica como apéndice a su artículo "Estructura y significaciones de *Tres tristes tigres*", en Julio Ortega et al., *Guillermo Cabrera Infante* (Caracas: Editorial Fundamentos, 1974), pp. 125-26.

[11]Guillermo Cabrera Infante, *Tres tristes tigres* (Barcelona: Seix Barral, 1965), p. 18. Todas las referencias subsiguientes a la obra, dadas entre paréntesis después de las citas, remiten a la misma edición.

[12]Visiones hay todavía, sin embargo, que en base a ciertas metodologías críticas consideran a las mujeres en *Tres tristes tigres* como poseedoras de un papel "cósmico", según el cual llevan a cabo las funciones junguianas del ánima; y que ven a los personajes femeninos en "an expanded role for women in which they themselves become the portents of cataclysmic changes to come", como la Estrella, "cometa" que anuncia el fin de una era. Véase William Siemens, "Women as Cosmic Phenomena in *Tres tristes tigres*", *Journal of Spanish Studies: Twentieth Century*, vol. 3, no. 3 (winter 1975), pp. 199-209.

[13]Por cierto, que el problema de identidad—evidenciado en el continuo cambio onomástico y en la vaguedad del nombrar, y asociado a la falsedad del ambiente— aflige tanto a los personajes masculinos como a los femeninos. Véase el estudio de Reynaldo L. Jiménez, *Guillermo Cabrera Infante y Tres tristes tigres* (Miami: Ediciones Universal, 1977), pp. 76 y sigs. Además, en la fluidez ambigua del texto, los "tristes tigres"—como los tres mosqueteros de Dumas—son en realidad cuatro: Cué, Silvestre, Eribó y Códac (¿o cinco, con la sempiterna presencia lingüística de Bustrófedon?).

[14]La crítica establecida advierte contra el "juicio ético" sobre *Tres tristes tigres*, "forma practicada por los puritanos, cualquiera que sea la ideología bajo la que se disfracen" (Rodríguez Monegal, op. cit., p. 91).

[15]Entre varios estudios que enfocan la obra desde este ángulo, se encuentran el citado de Rodríguez Monegal (notas 10 y 14, supra); el de Suzanne Jill Levine, "Writing as Translation: *Three Trapped Tigers* and a *Cobra*", *Modern Language Notes*, vol. 90, no. 2 (March 1975), pp. 265-77; y el de David P. Gallagher, "Guillermo Cabrera Infante (Cuba, 1929-)", en Julio Ortega et al., pp. 47-79.

[16]Alguna de la más reciente e informada crítica, con vista a la comprensión del discurso como muestra ideológica, elabora el concepto de la norma lingüística dominante como estructuradora de la "conciencia espontánea y natural" de su usuario, y lo hace en relación al estudio de otras obras narrativas consideradas como "novelas de lenguaje" (si bien aquéllas que cuestionan el orden social en que surgen): "puede decirse que el lenguaje no es un instrumento neutro, natural e indiferente, sino que porta en sí caracteres que le permiten no sólo apuntar a la realidad sino que en cierto modo contribuyen a establecer ciertos modos de percepción de la misma. Y que en una norma lingüística se tienden a fijar los rasgos en función de la concepción del mundo dominante en la sociedad correspondiente. Por todo esto es que el lenguaje, que sirve para *des-cubrir* el mundo como realidad para el hombre, suele comenzar también a servir para *en-cubrirlo*." Nelson Osorio T., "Lenguaje narrativo y estructura significativa de *El señor Presidente* de Asturias", *Escritura*, nos. 5-6 (enero-diciembre de 1978), p. 106.

[17]Según el análisis que de la cultura popular hace Heloneida Studart en su libro *Mulher: objeto de cama e mesa* (Petrópolis: Editora Vozes, 1974).

[18]Así declara en su entrevista con Rita Guibert, publicada en inglés como parte del libro *Seven Voices* (New York: Alfred A. Knopf, 1972), y reproducida en español en Julio Ortega et al., pp. 19-46. Referencias específicas a la "literatura como juego" y a "la gran broma" se encuentran en las pp. 20 y 29, respectivamente.

[19]Guibert, p. 27. Una interpretación freudiana de la obra llega a la misma conclusión: "The naive female reader (or passive reader) leaves 'the room' created by the text, allowing Cabrera Infante and his *macho* readers to engage in mutual and auto-eroticism, a strange new form of vicarious masturbation through time and space." Véase Claudia Cairo Resnick, "The Use of Jokes in Cabrera Infante's *Tres tristes tigres*", *Latin American Literary Review*, vol. IV, no. 9 (fall-winter 1976), pp. 14-21.

[20]Así lo percibe David P. Gallagher en su artículo (nota 14, supra), p. 69.

[21]". . . in 1959—the bastard culture of an island dependent on North Americans", según la idea de Jean Franco en *A Literary History of Spain* (New York: Barnes and Noble, 1973), p. 272, y concepto que desarrolla Bonnie K. Frederick en "*Tres tristes tigres*: The Lost City", *Mester*, vol. VII, nos. 1-2 (May 1978), pp. 21-31.